POWER IN ACTION

POWER IN ACTION

Democracy, Citizenship and Social Justice

STEVEN FRIEDMAN

WITS UNIVERSITY PRESS

Published in South Africa by:
Wits University Press
1 Jan Smuts Avenue
Johannesburg 2001

www.witspress.co.za

First published 2018

http://dx.doi.org.10.18772/12018113023

978-1-77614-302-3 (Paperback)
978-1-77614-303-0 (Web PDF)
978-1-77614-304-7 (EPUB)
978-1-77614-305-4 (Mobi)

Project manager: Elna Harmse
Copyeditor: Margaret Labuschagne
Proofreader: Lisa Compton
Indexer: Marlene Burger
Cover design: Hybrid Creative
Typesetter: Newgen
Typeset in 10 point MinionPro-Regular

CONTENTS

INTRODUCTION

Is democracy good for Africans in general and South Africans in particular? Does it really belong to us or is it a Western idea imposed to enslave us? If democracy is both ours and good for us, how do we know a democracy when we see one? And, if we do see one, how do we know whether and how it will survive? How do we do what we can to make it flourish and grow?

A few years ago, it seemed absurd to question democracy's value or its survival. Formal democracy, in the shape of regular multi-party elections and at least some of the liberties and rights which are meant to accompany them, was no longer a rarity, practised mostly by rich countries. It had become the norm in Africa and Latin America and had taken root in parts of Asia (which also houses the world's largest democracy, India). Much of humanity lived in democracies, many of which, only a decade or two ago, were not democratic. Democracy had also become almost hegemonic in the sense that it was considered the normal, common-sense way of arranging politics: with some isolated exceptions, governments which wanted respectability insisted that they were democratic, whatever reality might suggest. In South Africa, formal democracy ended decades of white minority rule and was widely embraced by most citizens. This mirrored the international trend – modern people were confirmed democrats and the system's only opponents were small groups of hold-outs on the right and left.

This brief period of democratic triumph is now under threat. In contrast to earlier periods of democratic breakdown – the collapse of democracies in Europe in the 1930s[1] and in Latin America in the 1970s[2] – democracies have not been replaced by other forms of government. But champions of the liberal democracy which spread across the globe from 1974, when a coup in Portugal triggered a series of transitions from authoritarian rule, have moved from unbridled optimism to deep anxiety.[3] American scholar Francis Fukuyama's 1992 claim that history had ended because liberal democracy was the only credible political and value system[4] now seems ridiculous – 'a quaint artefact of a vanished unipolar moment'.[5] The idea that democracy is in trouble is now almost as universal in mainstream scholarship as were claims that it had triumphed forever: 'Today, it would be easier to assemble those who *did not* think something fundamental was amiss than those who did'.[6]

The anxiety is based less on a sense that democracy may be dying, although some claim that it is losing ground, particularly in Africa.[7] Instead, from the United States of America (USA) of Donald Trump and the Russia of Vladimir Putin, through the Philippines of Rodrigo Duterte to the Zimbabwe of Emmerson Mnangagwa, there are deep fears that authoritarians are able not only to win elections and operate within ostensibly democratic constitutions, but also to govern in deeply undemocratic ways. And, if this is the problem which worries mainstream scholars and commentators, other important voices warn that, even in those democracies which continue to operate in seemingly democratic ways, 'neoliberal rationality'[8] preserves democratic form but denies citizens the control over their lives which democracy is meant to offer. The 'neoliberal rationality' they warn against can be understood not only as an economic framework which allows markets rather than elected representatives to govern, but also as a reliance on decisions taken by 'experts' rather than citizens.

Some of the pessimists remain firm democrats, distressed that the system of government which they support may be under pressure. But not all are: some insist that the problem may be democracy itself. Current writings on democracy suggest that the problems the system faces can be addressed only by 'abandoning the Fukuyaman narrative and instead adopting a position that better appreciates the limits and flaws of this form of rule'[9] – by accepting that democracy, in its current form at least, is not the perfect system which late-twentieth-century triumphalism held it to be. Most of the new doubters would not go as far as the scholar John Dunn, who, after years of writing about democracy, now warns the rich countries of the West that they should see the system as a 'happy accident' rather than a 'magic formula'.[10] Still, the uncritical tone of a decade ago has been replaced by reflection on democracy's faults as well as its fragility.

South Africa is not immune from doubts about democracy's survival or its merits. On the contrary, so widespread are these sentiments that South Africans often seem to believe that their democracy is the only one on the planet whose citizens fear for democracy's future or doubt its merits. Anxiety that democracy is doomed is a constant feature of public debate.[11] And, while few mainstream voices reject democracy in principle, critiques of 'Western democracy', or of the constraints which constitutional democracy places on a majority government,[12] are features of a public debate in which many voices charge that the bargain of 1994 which established democracy has failed to address racial inequality. These concerns often underpin discussions, in the seminar room or at the kitchen table, and occupy the thoughts of citizens experiencing for the first time the uncharted territory of democratic self-government.

However, whatever democracy's fate, the tide of democratic discontent is overstated. First, democracy's decline is less pronounced than in previous eras of retreat – and off a much higher base. For much of the twentieth century (and most of human history), democracy has been restricted to a few countries, some of which saw no contradiction between extending democratic rights to their citizens while denying them to the Africans and Asians they colonised. Before the current wave of democratisation in Africa began, only two countries, Botswana and Mauritius, maintained working democracies over decades. Despite retreats from democracy in some countries, democracy is far more widespread than at any previous period – in Africa and in the rest of the world. And, as serious as the backsliding is, the fact that most countries retain democratic form and insist that they are democratic creates opportunities for citizens to express themselves and hold power to account which are not available in despotic systems. The claim, made 15 years ago, that '[t]he democratic idea is close to non-negotiable in today's world'[13] is under stress. But it may not be as dated as it seems, given the continued need of governments which do not value democracy to continue operating within its form, and claiming allegiance to its values.

As for the idea that democracy is a Western imposition, perhaps the strongest argument against it is evidence that citizens outside the West want the rights and freedoms which democracy offers. We will return to this evidence, but, for now, we need only note that persistent majorities of African citizens opt for democracy if given the choice. Democracy's critics 'disregard the sustained demand of African peoples – amply demonstrated in one Afrobarometer survey after another – for democratic polities that promise to help citizens hold those in power accountable'.[14] The survey evidence is given added credibility by the fact that African citizens have, in several countries, mobilised to oppose abuses of power by their governments – attempts by heads of government to extend their term of office, for example.[15] In South Africa, despite disillusion with the bargain of 1994, the voices urging that democracy be rescued from political power-holders far exceed those that want rights and freedoms curbed.

So democracy may be staggering, but it is not about to fall. It may well not only weather its current trials, but emerge from them stronger. Understanding where democracy comes from, what nurtures it and what threatens it remains essential if we wish to chart South Africa's future. Nor, despite the necessary end of Fukuyama's triumphalism, is democracy discredited as a system of government capable of realising human freedom. One of apartheid's few useful legacies is the determination of the vast majority of citizens to ensure that the country never returns to it, which ensures that democracy is more attractive than it might be to citizens to whom the alternative was being treated as a lesser type of being.

Rejection of democracy in South Africa remains a marginal position because it flies in the face of lived reality. Anyone who has been fortunate enough to live through the transition from apartheid – and who does not harbour a longing for white supremacy – is now able to speak and act in ways which were not possible then. People who were once crushed under foot by power are now free to develop as thinking and acting individuals able to command the respect they were denied. Politics, that process in which citizens engage in open co-operation, contest and conversation, is now possible in ways which were then precluded. South African democracy, like that of all other countries, is limited and flawed. But it has opened possibilities which were obstructed in the past. And, while the bargain of 1994 did not steer the economy onto a new path which would eliminate the divide between insiders and outsiders,[16] it has changed material lives too: there is no better illustration than the reality that millions of South Africans living with HIV and AIDS are alive today simply because democratic politics made it possible for them to gain access to life-giving medication.[17]

South Africa's democracy may have been built on a bargain which left the social and economic patterns of the past intact. It may hear only the better off and the better connected. But, as this book will try to show, it is not a Western imposition designed to smother African voices and demands for social and economic change. Preserving democracy and strengthening it is therefore essential to attempts to build a society which will move beyond the exclusion and domination of the past. And so, we need to understand democracy, what might threaten it and what it needs to survive. We need also to examine the factors that strengthen or weaken the democracy which decades of resistance to minority rule produced.

This book is an attempt to address these questions. Its chief concern is to examine, from a South African perspective, what makes democracies survive and grow. But that question begs others. If we see democracy purely as a system in which (almost) all adults vote for competing candidates and parties, trying to understand its survival prospects is a relatively limited exercise – we need analyse only the factors likely to ensure or block the holding of regular competitive elections. But, while some theorists once fell prey to the 'electoralist fallacy' which holds that democracy can be reduced to the holding of elections,[18] both scholars and citizens now expect more of democracy than only the right to choose leaders – even if that 'more' consists merely of the right to speak freely. And so, to examine whether democracy will survive, we need to ask what it is and how we know whether we have more or less of it. This work will examine these questions too.

Because democracy in South Africa is little more than two decades old and most democracies on the African continent are not much older,[19] this book is primarily concerned with the fate of new democracies: South Africa's in particular, Africa's in general and, even more generally, those of Latin America, Southern and Eastern Europe and Asia. This focus does not endorse the assumption, common in some literature on democracy, that it is only new democracies which face challenges – one of its pivotal arguments is that all democracies are always flawed because no democracy can ever be a 'finished product'. But we are all creatures of our environment: what worries or excites us is shaped by where we live. And so, my intention is to shed light primarily on problems which confront new democracies in general and South Africa's in particular. However, because it is not possible to talk about how we recognise South African or African democracy – or that in the global South – without discussing democracy in general, this book hopes to shed light not only on how we in new democracies should see ourselves, but also on how we ought to see the older democracies too. It is, therefore, rooted in the African and South African experience but concerned to contribute to our understanding of democracy's nature, challenges and prospects everywhere.

This book was initially the result of a period of study and engagement made possible by a generous grant from the Ford Foundation. This is the second time that I have written a book with the support of the Foundation: my gratitude is even greater this time because the grant was awarded at a difficult time in my professional life. It was Ford's generosity which made it possible to continue my work as a student and theorist of politics – and, of course, to dedicate a sustained period of time to writing this book. I hope that this book goes some way to justifying Ford's faith in my work.

The grant which enabled me to research and write required me to base myself at an organisation. Fortunately, a second rescuer was available – the Institute for Democracy in South Africa (Idasa), which took over the administration of the Ford grant and contracted me to write the book. This was no small contribution since Idasa was not an academic institution – it largely devoted itself to concrete democracy-promotion projects – and so hosting an author seeking to write a book engaging academic debates on democracy entailed a risk. My association with Idasa on this project was deeply rewarding, and I owe an immense debt to the many people at Idasa whose support, warmth and integrity made me feel at home and able to write in a welcoming environment. Sadly, Idasa ceased to exist in 2013.

Hopefully this book will help to contribute to the democratic commitment which underpinned its work.

Thirdly, the Department of Political and International Studies at Rhodes University, with which I was associated throughout the writing of this book as a Visiting Professor, provided me with several opportunities to engage with colleagues on the ideas which shaped the book. To everyone who attended the seminars at which I was able to present them, my thanks for your contribution to honing my ideas. I hope that these colleagues too will find something of value in the work they helped to make possible.

The book project was placed in abeyance for some years after I became director of the Centre for the Study of Democracy established by Rhodes and the University of Johannesburg: for a time it seemed as though Centre duties would prevent me from completing the book and revising the analysis in the light of later trends. Fortunately, the Centre's board agreed to grant me the time to work on the draft and to ensure that the book's analysis was as contemporary as possible. I am, of course, grateful to the board for allowing this book's completion. The Centre too has ceased to exist and the book was completed as part of my work as a Research Professor in the Humanities Faculty at the University of Johannesburg.

Thanks are also due to colleagues who had to listen repeatedly to promises of a book which always seemed imminent but beyond grasp, and to those among them who were willing not only to listen to my ideas, but to read chapters and respond. I hope that its completion, very long after it was meant to be submitted to a publisher, offers you all the relief of knowing that you will not have to hear me talk about the process of writing it any longer.

1

The Journey Lasts Forever: Beyond 'Democratic Consolidation'

How do we know that a society has become a democracy – or will remain one?

This question is frequently asked in new democracies in general, and South Africa's in particular.[1] Comparing the country to others, particularly in North America and Western Europe, is a national pastime. Whether the country is a 'real' democracy is a theme in the public debate. It has also been asked, repeatedly, by Western scholars of democracy anxious to discover whether the democratic systems which have spread to Africa, Asia, Latin America and Eastern Europe are likely to last and are 'the real thing', not a cheap 'Third World' imitation. They ask the question through a framework, the 'consolidation' paradigm, which has influenced the thinking of most South African scholars of democracy[2] as well as many elsewhere in Africa. It also, almost unnoticed, has shaped the way non-academic participants in the public debate think of democracy and its challenges. Since the paradigm shapes South African and African attitudes to democracy, what is it and how useful is it as a tool?

For a while, as many more societies adopted democratic rule, the test of whether a country was 'really' democratic seemed, to some mainstream scholars and practitioners, simple. Countries were democratic if they held regular elections in which political parties freely established by citizens were allowed to compete. Later, the writings of more than a few scholars – and the concrete experiences of citizens – began to recognise that societies are not democratic simply because they hold multi-party elections. The 'fallacy of electoralism' noted in the intro- duction – the idea that a country has 'become democratic' simply because it holds competitive elections – has been largely discredited in the academic literature which sought to understand and explain the spread of formal democracy across the globe.[3] The limits of an 'electoral democracy' which offers the vote but not the freedoms and the right to choose which must accompany it[4] are now widely acknowledged, particularly since elections propelled leaders with little regard for democratic rules to power in the United States and Eastern Europe as well as parts of the global South.

But, if we are unable to rely on the neat division between societies which hold multi-party elections and those which do not, how do we tell the difference between election-holding countries which realise the democratic rights of their citizens and honour their choices and those which do not? How do we tell whether a country has 'become democratic' in substance rather than merely in form?

The dominant approach through which scholars have tried to answer this question is the 'consolidation' paradigm, which claims to tell us how and whether democracies 'consolidate'. It is a successor to the 'transition' literature of the 1980s, which studied how authoritarian regimes in Latin America, Southern and then Eastern Europe became 'uncertain' democracies.[5] Having studied how formal democracy emerged out of authoritarianism, it was perhaps predictable that scholars would try to understand whether the democratic promise of the transitions would be realised and sustained. This raised two questions: whether and under what circumstances the new formally democratic orders would remain formal democracies, and whether and how they would become 'real' democracies. In one scholar's view, interest in consolidation originally arose 'to describe the challenge of making new democracies secure'[6] – understanding what was needed to ensure that they remained formal democracies. Later, some scholars came to equate democratic consolidation 'with completing democracy, with supplying its missing features'.[7] In two ways, then, 'consolidation' is meant to tell us whether 'uncertain' new democracies can become 'certain' – by determining both whether they are sure to survive and whether they have become 'full' democracies.

But, the 'consolidation' approach does not enable us to tell a 'certain' from an 'uncertain' democracy. It cannot provide sure guides to democracies' survival prospects, while its attempt to sort out the finished product from the aspirant democracy is unhelpful to new democracies because it is vague, teleological and ethnocentric. It is concerned less with trying to understand new democracies than with testing whether they are progressing towards an idealised image of the democracies of North America and Western Europe, which are always assumed to be consolidated and are, therefore, the benchmark to which new democracies are meant to aspire.

'CONSOLIDATION' AND ITS LIMITS

Literature on 'consolidation' is far better at using the term than at explaining what it means or examining it critically. This failure to specify the term's meaning has been noticed not only by sceptics, but also by those who believe that it helps us to understand democratic prospects. In 1998, Andreas Schedler observed of 'consolidation':

> At this point, with people using the concept any way they like, nobody can be sure what it means to others, but all maintain the illusion of speaking to one another in some comprehensible way. While 'democratic consolidation' may have been a nebulous concept since its very inception, the conceptual fog that veils the term has only become thicker and thicker the more it has spread through the academic as well as the political world.[8]

Schedler goes on to warn that, if scientific advance depends on participants sharing a common understanding of key terms, 'the study of democratic consolidation, at its current state of conceptual confusion, is condemned to stagnation'.[9] The warning has remained largely unheeded, for no greater conceptual clarity has been attached to 'consolidation'. And yet it became the dominant prism through which the prospects of new democracies are viewed.

Growing pessimism on democracy's health and prospects in the countries which are considered the role models to which new democracies should aspire has prompted some doubts on whether the finished product is as finished as it seemed. Besides concerns at the rise of parties and governments in the North which are hostile to democratic values, citizens of 'consolidated' democracies are disenchanted with the operation of their political system and the parties which have traditionally dominated it. While an influential academic view is unruffled, claiming that it shows that voters are becoming better able to think for themselves and less willing to tolerate elites,[10] some voices worry that democracy in the North may be 'deconsolidating'.[11] They make the 'heretical' point that democratic values seem more firmly rooted among young people in China, India and sub-Saharan Africa than in Western Europe and North America.[12]

These scholars have received some support from Philippe Schmitter, a doyen of 'transition to democracy' scholarship who, in a recent article, warned of the 'tumultuous' and 'uncertain' future of 'Real-Existing Democracy' (RED).[13] In a response to Fukuyama, he suggests that the democracy which was meant to end history (and is also the 'finished product' of the 'consolidation' paradigm) 'is not what it used to be or seemed to be'.[14] REDs, he believes, enjoyed an 'exceptional period of stability' in the four decades after the Second World War because two factors coincided: the threat of revolution and 'the resources provided by a continuously expanding Capitalism'. The former gave ruling elites reason to compromise and the latter gave them the resources to afford it. The result was a 'symbiosis' between democracy and capitalism which masked the fact that they are based 'on fundamentally different operative principles' because 'democracy promises and promotes equality; capitalism depends on and rewards inequality'.[15]

Those days, Schmitter believes, are now over: 'The incentives for reform are not there; neither are the resources to pay for them', while democracy 'may still depend on capitalism, but capitalism does not depend on democracy'.[16] In this new period, democracy might increasingly obstruct capitalism's performance. These changes mean that democracy's future will 'not be as tranquil and assured as he [Fukuyama] assumed'[17] because they have created a crisis in which political rights and entitlements have diminished and more people have become marginalised. Citizens are thus increasingly unhappy with this model of democracy.

Crucially for the 'consolidation' paradigm, Schmitter argues that this has created 'the political paradox of our times': precisely at the moment when many new democracies 'emerged with the declared intention of imitating pre-existing ones', older democracies were 'entering into the compounded crisis we have described above'.[18] Their citizens have been questioning 'the "normal" institutions and practices that new democratizers have been trying so hard to imitate and have found them...defective'.[19] Schmitter believes democracy will survive the crisis because, following the democratic theorist Robert Dahl, he argues that it has always been able to adapt. But his key point, that the 'consolidation' paradigm assumes that new democracies must aspire to ways of ordering politics which citizens of older democracies now reject, pulls the rug from under the key assumption which underpins it.

In the mainstream, anxiety about the state of democracy in the North has not challenged the 'consolidation' paradigm and its key assumption – that new democracies must be measured by the degree to which they become carbon copies of their democratic elders and betters (or at least of how older democracies see themselves). Nor has it prompted scholars who are wedded to the 'consolidation' idea to provide a coherent definition of how we would tell a 'consolidated' democracy from one which is not.

A Question of Attitude?

Perhaps the most-used definition of democratic consolidation is Juan Linz and Alfred Stepan's claim that it occurs when democracy becomes the 'only game in town', when 'none of the major political actors consider that there is any alternative to democratic processes to gain power … '. [20] Similarly, Adam Przeworski sees it as a condition in which 'no one can imagine acting outside democratic institutions'.[21]

Both views stress the attitudes of political actors as the test for 'consolidation'. Other approaches see the degree of 'institutionalisation' of formal democracies as the measure of their progress towards 'consolidation'.[22] This seems to move beyond the feelings of political actors by focussing on the degree to which organisations such as opposition parties or institutions such as the courts have become entrenched. But it also ends up relying on sentiments: institutions can be said to be 'institutionalised' only when the rules which underpin them are 'widely shared and deeply rooted'.[23]

The common thread between these views is that democratic consolidation is a recognition within society that there is no alternative to democracy. This seems sensible, but is less useful than it seems. It is not clear who is meant to regard democracy as 'the only game in town' – political elites, citizens or both? References to 'major political actors' imply that it is the elites who need to accept that there is no alternative to democratic rules. But the message is often ambiguous. Some studies within the 'consolidation' framework measure not elite attitudes but those of citizens – they imply that democracy's fate depends, at least to a degree, on citizens' openness to anti-democratic appeals or their willingness to defend democratic rules.[24] The pessimistic view of the state of Northern democracies is based to some degree on readings of the attitudes of voters, not elites. This implies that, unless democracy is rooted in the hearts and minds of citizens, it cannot be 'consolidated', even if the elites have concluded that they have no other options.

The answer to the question who is meant to view democracy as the only alternative would tell us much about how the 'consolidation' approach understands democracy – whether it sees it as a system which relies on citizens or on elites. If the future of democracy depends on elites, citizens are largely reduced to bystanders, able to choose between competing leadership groups if democracy endures, but unable to shape either its ability to survive or whether it moves from 'partial' to 'complete' democracy. This would make the 'consolidation' approach a variety of 'democratic elitism', which sees democracy as a system which allows citizens to choose between competing elites but not to take part in public debate and decision-making.[25] It may also require a less demanding test of whether a democracy is 'consolidated' than those which insist also on citizen support for democratic norms and values. If only elite attitudes matter, formal democracy may survive even if most citizens doubt its worth, particularly if the doubters are not strong enough to act on their misgivings. By contrast, an understanding of democracy's prospects which insists on citizens recognising that it is irreplaceable would make 'consolidation' the product of a lengthier and far more complex process than an acceptance by elites that they have no other options. Who is meant to see democracy as 'the only game in town' is, therefore, a fundamental question. But the 'consolidation' literature does not tell us.

And how do we know when those who are meant to recognise that there is no alternative to democracy have done so? It is fairly easy to establish when democracy is *not* 'the only game in town': its opponents are often vocal and visible. Where there are large anti-system parties – as in Weimar Germany – or military officers challenge democracy's merits – as in Indonesia or Spain during their early democratisation – democracy is clearly not 'consolidated'. But, today, these signs are more the exception than the rule. As the introduction pointed out, even those who have severe doubts about democracy feel obliged to endorse it, including authoritarians who operate within at least a semblance of democratic rule. In most formal democracies, it may be difficult to find elites who admit to believing that there are alternatives to democracy, even if the way they govern shows that they doubt democracy's merits. The 'consolidation' approach is often surprisingly vague on how we might distinguish the attitudes of those who really believe that democracy is the only 'game in town' from those who find it convenient to pretend that they do.

Przeworski's approach uses game theory to test whether political actors have accepted democratic rules. His approach focusses less on expressions of democratic goodwill than on the hard strategic calculations of political actors – the degree to which parties have settled on democracy not necessarily because they want it but because it is the best strategic option available. This may be a useful way of describing how some 'late democratisers' – in Africa and elsewhere – settle for the system. The argument is not new; it was discussed in a celebrated 1970 article by Dankwart Rustow.[26] He argued that democracy was the outcome of protracted conflict between adversaries who settled on democratic rules not because this was their first choice, but because they preferred competition within agreed rules to continued fighting. (Although Rustow believed that strategic calculation was not the only motive for settling on democracy, it was central to his analysis.) But the resort to game theory is meant to tell us not only when parties resign themselves to democracy, but when they assume that it is the only feasible way of conducting politics in future. It purports to tell us not only why democracy was achieved, but whether it will survive.

But how do we know whether those whose strategic calculations tell them to opt for democracy now will continue to settle for it if circumstances change, as they always do? Are there no circumstances in which a Putin, Duterte or Trump might decide that there are games in town other than democracy which better achieve their goals? If we accept game theory's (disputed) assumption that parties are motivated purely by strategic calculations, its analysis could tell us the circumstances under which parties in a new democracy with the power to derail the system might want to do so. This would offer an important insight into democracy's prospects. But Przeworski's definition is not meant to tell us how to work out when democracies might survive or collapse. Like the 'consolidation' approach, it claims to tell us how to determine when democracy's future is secure – when it will not collapse whatever happens.

To do this, it must be able to explain more than the strategic calculations which led parties to choose democracy and to stick with it for the time being. It would also need to show that there are no conceivable future circumstances in which their calculations might shift enough for them to abandon democracy's rules. But a strategic conclusion reached under one set of circumstances cannot be assumed to apply to *all* future possible sets of circumstances. If there are *any* future circumstances which might persuade key parties to abandon democracy, it has not become a permanent fixture. It is hard to imagine how it might be possible to claim that there are no conceivable future circumstances in which key parties would abandon democracy, and so it is impossible to insist that parties will always choose democratic rules. Przeworski's game theory may describe what exists, but it cannot tell us what will happen in future. There is no political system of which we can say that democratic rules will always remain the strategic choice of all actors who can threaten democracy, and there never will be. If enduring strategic support for democracy is the test of 'consolidation', no democracy can ever be 'consolidated'. Just as elite or citizen attitudes cannot tell us whether a democracy is 'consolidated', neither can the strategic analysis offered by game theory.

Some scholars of 'consolidation' do suggest criteria other than politicians' or citizens' attitudes. A detailed attempt to describe the 'tests' of whether a democracy is 'consolidated' is offered by the authors of a study of Southern European 'late democratisers'. They declare that a 'consolidated' democracy has these features: alternation in power between former rivals; continued stability in times of economic hardship; 'successful defeat and punishment of a handful of strategically placed rebels'; stability in the face of a 'radical restructuring of the party system'; and the absence of politically significant anti-system parties or social movements.[27]

The last criterion mentioned shares the same flaw as Linz, Stepan and Przeworski's precondition: how do we know that significant anti-democratic parties will not emerge later? The other criteria may be useful summaries of the pressures which once faced new Southern European democracies, but they are of no use beyond that. On its own, alternation of power, whether and how often governments change at the ballot box, is not, despite its popularity among 'consolidation' theorists, a necessary test. If it were, post-Second World War Japan and Italy or India for some 30 years after independence would not qualify; neither would Sweden for decades after the 1930s.[28] Since virtually all the new democracies which have emerged in the past three decades continue to survive at least in form, stability in the face of economic hardship would qualify virtually all as 'consolidated'. Defeat of 'strategically placed' rebels would mean that no democracy is 'consolidated' if it is (un)fortunate enough to lack the required rebels. Similarly, if a 'radical restructuring' of party systems means introducing free multi-party competition, all new democracies qualify by definition. If it means something else, it is unclear why democracies which have neglected to alter their party systems should be considered any less 'consolidated'. Nor are we shown why achieving the listed tasks now will enable these democracies to survive in future.

These criteria describe difficulties which faced a few new democracies in one part of the globe. Since the authors fail to say why their criteria are essential to 'consolidation' of democracies everywhere – or anywhere – they do not show why they should help to identify the challenges which face others elsewhere. Nor do they tell us whether those democracies which they study will survive. At most, it describes the conditions under which they had done so then. This study is discussed only because it is one of the rare examples of an attempt to say what 'consolidation' means. Its failure to do so confirms that this approach is influential despite failing to offer a credible definition of 'consolidation'.

The 'consolidation' literature cannot tell us whether democracies will survive because it provides no coherent way of determining the circumstances under which reversals might occur. While, since the Second World War, no established Northern democracy has collapsed (although, as noted earlier, some are in serious trouble), it is trite to point out that democratic progress can be reversed. It was reversed before the Second World War when several European democracies collapsed in the face of authoritarian pressures,[29] and more recently in the global South. Pinochet's rule in Chile followed a long period of democratic government, while India's 50-year democratic experience was interrupted, albeit briefly, by Indira Gandhi's state of emergency. We have already noted democratic erosion in the North. The 'consolidation' approach cannot explain any of this because it assumes that, once a democracy is 'consolidated', reverses are impossible.

The 'consolidation' literature is aware of this reality, for, even before the current wave of democratic anxiety, warnings that 'consolidated' democracies can break down were sounded by scholars working in this paradigm. The literature includes analyses of 'deconsolidation' – Venezuela's democracy became a favourite example long before its current crisis.[30] (Needless to say, detention without trial in the United States did not make it a candidate for 'deconsolidation'.) But, if 'consolidated' democracies can be 'deconsolidated', 'consolidation' literature tells us nothing about any democracy's survival prospects – surely 'consolidated' democracies are called that because they are meant to last forever? Scholars working within this framework are forced to acknowledge that we cannot know whether democracies will last. This problem is not a design flaw which could be remedied by finding better ways of determining which democracies are certain to endure. The task to which the 'consolidation' literature committed itself is an impossibility. It is not possible to establish which democracies are sure to last because none are: 'democracy ... is an always fragile conquest that needs to be defended as well as deepened. There is no threshold of democracy that once reached will guarantee its continued existence'.[31] And so, there is no way in which democracies can be divided into those which are sure to survive and those whose futures remain uncertain.

FALSE CERTAINTIES: THE QUEST FOR COMPLETION

If the 'consolidation' literature cannot tell us when democracies are 'safe', can it not at least tell us whether formally democratic countries have become 'real' democracies?

For one celebrated scholar of 'consolidation', Samuel Huntington, electoral alternation, the change of government after an election, is the key to whether a democracy is 'consolidated'. 'Consolidation' literature cites approvingly his 'two turnover' test, which proposes that a democracy is 'consolidated' only when two ruling parties have lost power after a defeat at the polls: 'if the party or group that takes power in the initial election at the time of transition loses a subsequent election and turns over power to those election winners, and if those election winners then peacefully turn over power to winners of a later election'.[32]

This assumes, but does not show, that circulation of elites – rather than the vigour of citizen participation or opportunities for public debate or any other democratic criterion we might propose – determines whether a democracy has become a 'finished' product. In this view, a democracy in which elites replace each other after elections is more 'complete' than one which has not experienced the required turnover but in which government decisions are likely to reflect citizens' wishes – or whose institutions enjoy legitimacy among citizens. Japan and Italy would have been 'unconsolidated' for decades after their transitions in the 1940s, while Weimar Germany, with its frequent elections and unstable governments, would have been consolidated – despite the fact that political competition was often expressed in violent street clashes and that democracy was constantly under threat and was ultimately defeated.

This 'test' may apply to new democracies standards it would not use to measure older ones. Sweden – old enough a democracy to have been the subject of Rustow's study of the system's modern origins – would not have passed the 'two turnover' test for decades as elections routinely returned the same coalition to power. But no literature of which this author is aware has suggested applying the 'two turnover' test to Sweden. Huntington's supporters would point out that he is interested only in new democracies – hence his reference to a 'transition'. But why would a society which had not experienced a turnover in four or five decades be more democratic than a new democracy which had not experienced one in one or two? It is hard to understand why a test based on criteria which have not been justified and which expects some democracies to submit to standards from which others are exempt should provide a reliable guide to democracy's prospects or to whether countries 'really are' democratic.

The 'two turnover test' is as near as 'consolidation' literature comes to telling us how we are to tell a 'completed' from an uncompleted democracy. Given its flaws, this means that the paradigm does not tell us what a 'real' democracy looks like. Guillermo O'Donnell points out that this does not prevent consolidation writing from assuming that all democracies are meant to become like the role models which it never defines:

> Furthermore, this mode of reasoning carries a strong teleological flavor. Cases that have not 'arrived' at full institutionalization, or that do not seem to be moving in this direction, are seen as stunted, frozen, protractedly unconsolidated, and the like. Such a view presupposes that there are, or should be, factors working in favor of increased consolidation or institutionalization, but that countervailing 'obstacles' stymie a process of change that otherwise would operate unfettered.[33]

A particular end-point is assumed, without argument, to be normal and natural, and failure to achieve it is considered pathological. That it may be possible for different democracies to reach different end-points and remain democratic is not considered.

The 'consolidation' paradigm does not assume that progress towards democracy is inevitable – if it was, there would be no setbacks to analyse. Thus Schedler, while agreeing that the 'consolidation' approach is distinctly teleological, rejects the assumption that progress is normal and natural. He notes that teleology does not need to assume 'some kind of automatic or "natural" progression' towards a goal; it can refer rather to 'some normative goal or practical task'.[34] It would then describe where democracies ought to be heading, without insisting that they are bound to arrive if they want to be considered 'real'. This raises questions about who decides where democracies ought to head and on what grounds. But these questions do not arise since, in this teleology, 'consolidation' is not just a desired goal but a 'natural' end-point which democracies reach unless they are in some way aberrant.

Rather than seeing democracy as a hard-won goal, the result of a difficult, continued attempt to hold power-holders to account, the 'consolidation' approach sees it as a 'normal' state of political being to which all formal democracies ought to be evolving (but which the vast majority, which are outside the North, have been unable to achieve). By implication, some democracies (which are not subjects of 'consolidation' scholarship) are the norm, while others are deviant unless they can be shown to be on their way to becoming the norm. This explains why the 'tests' which rely on achieving consensus in support of democracy offer no coherent theory of how it may be maintained. The consensus is considered 'normal' and its absence an aberration, despite copious evidence that consensus on democratic norms is everywhere difficult to achieve and preserve.

This, O'Donnell and others note, leads to some perverse conclusions, one of which is that stable democracies can be portrayed as unstable if the country in question does not conform to the democratic standards of 'consolidation' scholars. Similarly, Schmitter and Terry Karl point out that some countries are said to be in a state of 'protracted unconsolidation' for two decades![35] The possibility that they may have reached an equilibrium, but one not to the liking of consolidation scholars, is not considered. So, even if a democracy operates without challenge for decades, it will not be considered 'consolidated' unless it reaches the state favoured by the 'consolidation' paradigm. While the 'consolidation' literature does not specify this, it is clear what it has in mind.

One consequence of claiming that new democracies are defective unless they meet an idealised standard is to impose on them unrealistic expectations which ensure that democratic gains are seen as setbacks. This is particularly evident in South Africa, where a section of society's identification with Europe and North America ensures that any threat to democracy, no matter how minor, is seen as evidence that democracy is both on the verge of collapse and not 'real'. To illustrate: a threat by security agencies to bring a legal action against a journalist who published an exposé on the president is taken as evidence that democratic institutions no longer operate, despite the fact that no successful action has been taken in the courts and the sole effect of the threat was to boost sales of the journalist's book.[36] It is assumed that in 'real democracies' public office holders would never dream of threatening journalists who write exposés, despite the fact that this happens in 'established' democracies too.[37]

There is nothing normal or natural about the democratic idea that political office holders should accept limitations on their power imposed by the electorate or the courts or the media. This becomes rooted in society, if at all, only after tests in which power-holders face restraints on what they may do, resist them but then accept them, often after bitter battles. Nor does this happen only in new democracies – US President Roosevelt's 1937 threat to appoint new judges to the Supreme Court to preclude the court from frustrating his New Deal legislation is but one example of attempts in older democracies to change the rules if they prevent governments from doing what they wish to do.[38] Assuming that the perfect functioning of democratic institutions is a natural state, and that societies which have not yet achieved it are inferior, sets standards for democracies which they cannot meet. It also fails to understand how democracies progress through tests of strength that set the boundaries which decide what power-holders cannot do. Conflicts in which power-holders resist being held to account but then grudgingly submit could be (mis)understood as a crisis, rather than as progress.

But what if the 'consolidation' teleology was merely proposing a goal which democracy ought to try to reach, rather than imposing a 'normality' which is highly abnormal? This is Schedler's view and it is hard to fault in principle: 'consolidation' scholars are as entitled as anyone else to hold opinions on the goals which democracies ought to meet. However, these views can contribute to the debate only if they are proposed not as unchallengeable truths but as opinions which must be subjected to criticism. This means their supporters must say where they think new democracies ought to be heading and be willing to debate their view. But we have noted that the 'consolidation' literature is reluctant to spell out how we would recognise a 'consolidated' democracy if we saw one – it mostly lacks a clear definition of democracy supported by argument. (Schedler himself does take this further in principle by specifying 'liberal democracy' as his end goal and identifying some of its characteristics. But he does not discuss this in detail nor offer a defence of his position.) We are not, therefore, told where new democracies ought to be headed and why. This closes off any debate on goals by imposing, without justification, a view of what democracy should do and how it should look. The effect is not to focus on agreed goals, but to avoid a much-needed debate on the criteria to which democracies should aspire.

Making 'Them' into 'Us'

'Consolidation tests' – two turnovers in office or agreement on 'the only game in town' – make implicit claims about the nature of 'consolidated' democracies. Huntington's test says that democracy is meant to be a system in which the elites who hold office change regularly, while Linz and Stepan see agreement among (unspecified) social actors on political rules as the key. What the literature does not tell is why these – or any other – criteria should determine whether an 'uncertain' democracy has become 'certain'. It assumes, rather than argues, what democracy is and, therefore, what new democracies should be.

Why would an influential body of literature which has shaped the way democracy is viewed by most analyses, and is the work of scholars used to defining their terms and defending their positions, not bother to spell out the essential features of a 'completed' democracy? The reason lies, surely, in the third weakness of the 'consolidation' literature: its ethnocentric bias. Liberal democracy as practised in the North – or, more accurately, an idealised version of it[39] – is simply assumed to be the best form of democratic politics and, therefore, the goal towards which all democracies should evolve. It is no accident that the democracies of the North are very rarely subjected to the 'consolidation' test: they are assumed, without any supporting evidence, to be 'consolidated' because the word is a synonym for 'becoming a Northern democracy' (or, more accurately, some scholars' notion of a Northern democracy). 'Consolidation' literature assumes that there are some democracies whose democratic status is irreversible – because, whatever trials democracies may have to endure elsewhere, those in the North are assumed to be invincible. The teleology's 'normal' democracy is an understanding of Northern democracies which ignores the many flaws and challenges that beset them.

Even if we were to accept that democracy has reached some sort of perfected state in the North, a view which is no longer held even by its most emphatic advocate, Fukuyama,[40] how would new democracies know which model to follow? Is corporatism[41] – structured and often legally enforced policy bargaining between economic interests – undemocratic because it bypasses elected legislatures or 'real' democracy because it includes important social interests in decisions? Is a formal role for traditional leadership – a feature of centuries of British democracy – a retreat from democracy because it allows the unelected to veto laws or does it express democratic respect for tradition? And, given the importance of ethnic difference in Africa, does the consociationalism so enthusiastically advocated by Arend Lijphart[42] on the strength of the Dutch and (troubled) Belgian experience – in which identity groups are afforded a guaranteed role in politics – move away from or towards democracy? Are federal democracies superior because they allow for decentralised decisions or inferior because they allow regional elites to escape the will of national electorates? There are many more examples which illustrate that a range of democratic form is found in the North and that there is no prototype to which democracies seeking 'consolidation' can aspire. Our view depends on our understandings of democracy – an issue the 'consolidation' literature sees no need to address in any more than a cursory manner.

The most reasonable explanation for this omission is that most 'consolidation' writers do not believe any definition of a consolidated democracy is needed since all know that it is an 'ideal type' of Northern liberal democracy. Schmitter notes that scholarship on new democracies – whether these use 'consolidation' or 'democratic quality' to describe the desired end-point – generates a host of terms describing their deficiencies in contrast to the assumed virtues of the older ones: 'Usually without specifying the grounds for such a negative judgment, it is just taken for granted that these democracies are inferior to existing Western democracies and that they have a long way to go before they can possibly catch up to such exalted "models" of political behavior.'[43]

To slightly distort a famous opinion on pornography by former US Supreme Court Justice Potter Stewart, the 'consolidation' specialists do not need to define democracy since they (and, by implication, we) know it when they see it.[44] And they see it in North America and Western Europe. This assumption that an idealised and undefined version of democracy in the North is the goal towards which Southern democracies should gravitate is shared by many Southern scholars, and for understandable reasons: during authoritarian periods, the teleology was less an expression of cultural self-hatred than a passionate desire to escape tyranny. O'Donnell suggests that it might even have been useful as a critique of the present and an instrument to mobilise a more workable future. Hence his reflections on the climate in which Southern intellectuals and activists waged their struggle for democracy:

Democracy even if – or, perhaps precisely because – it had so many different meanings attached to it, was the central mobilizing demand that had to be achieved and preserved forever. Somehow, it was felt, this democracy would soon come to resemble the sort...found in admired countries of the

Northwest – admired for their long-enduring regimes and for their wealth, and because both things seemed to go together ... the Northwest was seen as the endpoint of a trajectory that would largely be traversed by getting rid of authoritarian rulers. This illusion was extremely useful during the hard and uncertain times of the transition ... (its) analytical cogency is another matter.[45]

A useful illusion does not make a workable theory. 'Consolidation' literature does not tell us how to establish whether a democracy is 'consolidated'. Instead, it assumes a democratic norm against which new democracies should be measured without defining it or showing why it should be seen as appropriate, and it assumes, rather than demonstrates, that the *telos* is an undefined variant of Northern democracy. It is not unfair to boil much of 'consolidology' down to a desire to establish (in the North) when and how 'they' will become 'us' or (in the South) how 'we' will become 'them'.

But is 'consolidation' writing not, as O'Donnell suggests, 'pragmatically valid' because many, if not most, new democracies need a standard to inspire them to improve? He mentions one symptom, common in Latin American new democracies, which might require this remedy. Although regular and free elections have been entrenched, power-holders continue to blur or ignore 'the ... distinction between a public and a private sphere'.[46] Power achieved – or, more accurately, confirmed – by election becomes a route to public resources which are used for private purposes. Pre-democratic power relations remain and citizenship is a right exercised only at election time. While the rules of politics may be universal and democratic, the gap between rules and behaviour is wide. This malaise affects more than a few new democracies – including South Africa. But this is surely less an argument for the 'consolidation' paradigm as for the opposite – refusing to close off continued debate on the nature of democracy by settling on an agreed standard for the 'finished product' or, worse still, silencing the debate by assuming that everyone knows how to recognise that end-point when they see it. Debate on democracy's nature is far more likely to bring these realities into focus than imposing a never-explained democratic standard.

By dividing democracies into those which are 'consolidated' and those which are not, the paradigm also ignores the extent to which, in varying degrees, this gap between the rules and reality, between full citizenship and its limitation or denial in practice, remains a feature of democracy in many Northern societies too. A famous academic example is post-Second World War Italy. The gulf between democracy's promise and its practice in the Italian South prompted Robert Putnam's celebrated study of the value of 'social capital'.[47] Until relatively recently, machine politics also existed alongside democratic institutions in the US; in the United Kingdom (UK), long periods of single-party rule in local government[48] in some regions entrenched patterns of corruption which eroded the value of universal citizenship. Since the gap between promise and reality exists in all democracies, setting a standard to which we expect all to aspire would be defensible only if it was stressed that no democracies had yet achieved them. But that would collapse the 'consolidation' framework because there would then be no consolidated democracies.

If popular participation in democratic politics is a feature of 'consolidated' democracies, the US is 'unconsolidated'. Nor do the imperfections of democracy in the US end there. Would an African democracy whose president's election hinged on a dispute over faulty voting machines in a state of which his brother was the governor qualify as 'consolidated'? We can safely assume that, if the state was Burundi or Nigeria, it would not. And yet that is how the 2000 US presidential election was decided. This is by no means the only example of the US's recent failure to meet liberal democratic norms. It practises detention without trial following the tragedy of 11 September 2001: inmates have been held without charge for almost two decades,[49] longer than anyone was held without trial by apartheid South Africa. That most basic of democratic rights, the vote, is not guaranteed to all adults in the US since some states impose voter registration criteria which place unreasonable obstacles in the way of people seeking to vote, in particular racial minorities and the poor: 'voter suppression' was a point of controversy before the 2012[50] and 2016[51] presidential elections.

And, after the 2016 election, it is legitimate to ask whether the US meets the most basic test, that its leaders are elected by the majority of citizens. For not the first time, the candidate who received most votes did not win the election; instead, minority support was enough to give the president's party control over both houses of the legislature and over the Supreme Court, which sets the political rules. It is safe to assume that, if this happened in Africa or Asia, it would spawn a cottage industry of learned articles complaining about the low quality of democracy. Nor is the US the only manifestly imperfect Northern democracy. If an unelected legislative chamber is a disqualification, Britain's House of Lords disqualifies it from the ranks of 'consolidated' democracies. And Britain, too, of course, has introduced detention without trial for up to 28 days.[52] New democracies like South Africa's have no reason for an inferiority complex when their democratic practice is compared to this record.

There is no consensus in Northern democracies that they are the 'finished product'– appropriately so, since the free speech which democracy confers also entails the right to question the democratic credentials of democracies. Critiques by Northern theorists, written within the democratic paradigm, may not reflect mainstream thinking but do confirm that it is by no means automatic to assume that the current Northern form is an unquestioned realisation of the democratic ideal.[53] As we have already seen, doubts about the health of Northern democracies have spread to mainstream scholars such as Fukuyama. Pippa Norris, whose view that discontent with democracy shows the system's health, mentioned earlier, partly justifies her view by noting that there is an unavoidable gap between existing democracies and the democratic ideal, which means that democracies must always monitor and assess their own progress and introduce the changes needed to inch closer to what they are meant to be.[54] Given these realities, dividing democracies into the 'consolidated' and 'unconsolidated' resembles more a prejudice than an analysis. Far from offering us a goal, enabling a critique of the gap between democratic form and substance in the South, the assumption that some democracies represent an end-point prevents citizens of new democracies from examining what they aspire to when they seek an enduring democratic future.

It could be argued that the 'consolidation' literature's implied standards remove a frequent complaint of African democratisers – that influential Northern opinion is content with 'second grade' standards for African democracies. But measuring African or any other democracies against an abstract ideal and perpetually pronouncing them 'unconsolidated' is counterproductive since it obstructs analysis of and debate on the democratic progress which is achievable in current conditions. To insist that Africa – or anywhere else – should not be content with 'second best' is useful only if it begins a debate on what is best. Proposing criteria which are realised only in the self-image of some authors' favourite Northern democracy – and are challenged by some within that democracy – ensures that the debate proceeds in wilful disregard of concrete conditions in new democracies, and of the possibility that democracy can look very different in its diverse homes but nevertheless offer citizens freedom and self-government.

The 'consolidation' approach's inability to provide an agreed criterion for measuring democratic progress does not mean that this is impossible or inappropriate. It is obviously possible – and highly appropriate – to propose criteria which might help us better understand what might threaten or derail any democracy and to show that some have greater survival prospects than others. It is also essential to examine whether democracies are achieving greater democratic substance. But that task cannot be accommodated within an approach that must distinguish between democracies which have 'made it' and those which have not – and must inevitably prompt unwarranted complacency among the 'consolidated' and unnecessary despair among those who have failed to achieve this exalted status.

In reality, no democracy is completed – a point which was not lost on Robert Dahl, celebrated American theorist of democracy, who called his study of formal democracy 'polyarchy' because he believed democracy to be a goal to which all 'established' democracies aspire but which none achieves.[55] Schedler tries to rescue the 'consolidation' approach from this problem by inviting us to understand 'consolidation' not as a means of distinguishing between complete and incomplete democracies but as a measure of 'democratic deepening, a task which is never completed', coming to the logical conclusion that '[i']n this sense, no democracy will ever be "fully consolidated"'.[56] It is hard to see how the 'consolidation' approach could adopt Schedler's suggestion and still serve its purpose, since it exists to decide whether democracies have reached a spurious completion – safety from authoritarian regress or graduation to 'finished product'. His approach would fundamentally break with this. The paradigm can be rescued in the way he proposes only by changing it so much that it would become unrecognisable.

Another credible attempt to preserve 'consolidation' as a usable concept, but without the assumption that there are 'certain' and 'uncertain' democracies, is Schmitter's view that 'consolidation' 'involves getting people to compete and cooperate according to mutually acceptable rules…'.[57] This is Linz and Stepan's 'only game in town' again, but Schmitter insists that both citizens and elites must endorse the rules. It is also more modest: agreement is needed not on an entire system but only on the rules which govern political competition. It does not insist that a set of rules be 'the only ones in town' but simply that they are accepted as the best way of regulating politics. It is of particular interest to new African democracies in which election results are often disputed by losers.

Schmitter aims to tell us the minimum required if democracy has taken root enough to continue functioning. Whether it achieves that goal is open to question – Mozambique still operates as a democracy despite the fact that the largest opposition party, Renamo, rejected the result of an election and boycotted the National Election Commission.[58] And does acceptance of the rules mean endorsing the way they are phrased in the law and constitution or agreement that in practice they are implemented fairly? If the former, there are few if any democracies, including those in which election results are not accepted by losers, in which the formal rules are rejected. If the latter, disaffection in the US about electoral outcomes (scepticism about the 2000 presidential election or the fairness of electoral districts)[59] would question its consolidation. Schmitter's view is, therefore, a useful reminder of one challenge facing new democracies – but not a test of whether democracies have crossed a necessary threshold.

There is no possibility of achieving consensus on the features of a 'completed' democracy: even if agreement could be reached, all democracies would fall short of the ideal. So the distinction between 'finished products' and 'democracies in the making' is untenable. Instead of dividing democracies into those which have 'made it' and those which have not, we need to see all democracies as incomplete.

THE DEMOCRATIC JOURNEY

Democracies cannot be divided into 'consolidated' and 'unconsolidated' variants because there are always gaps between democracy's promise and its concrete reality – and always will be. We are more likely to best understand societies' attempts to deepen democracy and to make it more sustainable if we place them on a continuum on which all are moving further towards – or away from – an always unattainable democratic ideal. Democracy is, in this view, never completed, and the search for it is a journey which democrats and democratic societies undertake in the knowledge that the journey has no reachable destination. Democracy, a scholar of Indian democratisation notes, 'is a *continuous* variable (expressed as "more" or "less"), not a *dichotomous* variable (expressed as "yes" or "no")'.[60] Some democracies are more or less democratic than others (and themselves at various historical moments), but this does not mean that some are 'really' democratic and others are not.

Even this oversimplifies, for it implies that it is always possible to declare democracies further from or closer to the democratic ideal. But democracies which have made progress on some key democratic indicators may lag behind on others. South Africa may trail other democracies on some measures but is ahead of all or most on voter participation or gender equality in public office. This further unsettles the idea of a 'consolidated' democracy since seemingly 'complete' democracies can retain some very 'incomplete' features. Precisely because all democracies are engaged in an ever-incomplete journey, all will be found wanting in at least some areas of democratic performance. For Northern democracies, this warns against complacency. For those in the South, it suggests a need to aspire to higher democratic standards – but not those set by an often romanticised image of Northern democracy. This opens the way for more innovative approaches to the details of democracy: a search for institutions and conventions which match concrete local realities within the context of democratic values, rather than an attempt to imitate those of the North.

This may be particularly important in South Africa, where, as indicated earlier, concerns that the country is not a 'real' democracy are common. South Africa is as real – and as flawed – as any other democracy. It could become less flawed if its commentators and middle-class citizens worried less about how it can one day resemble an idealised version of Toronto or London and more about how to ensure that it gets better at doing what democracies need to do. This approach begs an obvious question: what are democracies meant to do? If the 'consolidation' literature fails to tell us how to recognise progress towards or retreat from the democratic ideal when we see it, what criteria tell us whether political systems – or some of their particular features – are becoming more or less democratic? This question is the focus of the next chapter.

2

Deeper and Broader: What Makes Democracies More or Less Democratic?

If democracy is a (never completed) journey, how do we know whether we are moving towards its always elusive goal?

Democracies are misled when they assume that they can one day become 'completed'. But that does not mean that they should not aspire to become more democratic. On the contrary – if we shed the belief that democracies should be judged by whether they are becoming more like those of the North, it becomes even more essential to offer clear criteria for democratic advance or retreat. On what must our judgment of democratic progress rest? An answer requires us to answer another question – what is democracy's defining feature, which sets it off against other political systems?

THE ELUSIVE DESTINATION: DEMOCRACY AS POPULAR SOVEREIGNTY

As a popular text points out, 'Democracy comes from the Greek words *demos* meaning people and *kratos* meaning authority or power'.[1] This basic definition clearly separates democracy from other forms of rule – in particular, monarchy (rule by an individual), oligarchy (rule by a few) or meritocracy (in which power is wielded by an elite considered inherently better able to govern). David Estlund, following Plato's *Republic*, has called this last strain 'epistocracy' or 'rule of the knowers'.[2] Democracy is distinguished from all these alternatives because it is, by definition, a system in which 'the people' – all adult members of a political community – are meant to exercise power. If this sounds straightforward and obvious, it is anything but that.

First, how do we decide who belongs to the political community whose members are to govern themselves? Most South Africans would agree wholeheartedly that every citizen should enjoy equal rights, but what about people who have lived in the country for a long period yet are not citizens? And how do we decide who is an adult? Is the present criterion, that people may vote when they turn 18, too high a barrier – or not high enough? These two examples illustrate that deciding who is included and who is not can become complicated.

Most political thinkers have ignored this problem – Dahl, however, did not. Almost half a century ago, he drew attention to the 'boundary problem', the way in which people are included in or excluded from the community entitled to decide, and pointed out that democrats simply assume that a 'people' already exists.[3] But 'the people' who are allowed to decide is created – and usually not in a democratic fashion. Who constitutes 'the people', Dahl pointed out, is likely to have been a product of 'political action and conflict', often accompanied by violence and coercion, not of 'reasoned inferences from democratic principles and practices'.[4] As another author put it: 'The people cannot decide until somebody decides who are the people.'[5] Dahl recognised that there is no democratic solution to the problem. While constitutions can try to solve the problem by allowing people who wish to secede from a country to do so – the Ethiopian constitution offers this most explicitly[6] – the groups which are allowed to secede are themselves created by history, not democratic choice. As long as human beings are divided into different political communities, there is no 'objective' test which can determine how to draw the boundaries between them. And there is no democratic test either since, as Dahl points out, only the people can decide, and so, if there is no agreement on who constitutes the people, there is no agreement on who can decide.[7]

But that does not mean that the boundary problem should be ignored: few issues can be decided by an agreed standard. It means that the problem can and must be open to democratic debate. Disputes over who should and should not be included in a democratic community are topical, in South Africa and elsewhere. And many of the criteria which are used to exclude and are usually seen as 'common sense' rules are less obviously justified than they seem. Many political communities place restrictions on the exercise of the vote by criminals and the insane. This is implicitly or explicitly justified on the grounds that people whose actions have placed them outside the community or whose mental state prevents them from exercising a considered choice do not enjoy the right to decide. But it is hardly self-evident that conviction for a crime should automatically exclude anyone from this right:

citizenship is arguably a right, like that to health and life, which does not lapse when a person commits a crime. Nor are distinctions between the sane and insane always clear-cut. These limits on the exercise of citizenship are, therefore, contested[8] – although usually at the edges of public debate. As suggested earlier, where to set the voting age is debatable. For some, lowering the age at which people can vote deepens democracy; for others, it places power in the hands of people too young to know how to use it.[9]

Second, and more topically, the exclusion of non-citizens from the right to vote (and from many other rights too) is also often seen as self-evident. But that people should be denied the vote in the country in which they live because they are not citizens is not beyond debate: not all countries see the vote as a natural expression of citizenship which should be withheld from resident outsiders. In the USA, '[n]oncitizens voted from 1776 until 1926 in forty states and federal territories in local, state and even federal elections. Noncitizens also held public office'.[10] In Chile, Malawi, New Zealand and Uruguay, non-citizens can vote in national elections,[11] while in some European cities, they may vote in local elections. Some countries also grant legal resident aliens the right to access basic public services, creating at least an in-principle recognition of a right to a say in policy decisions.[12] Some thinkers question the view that we can belong to a political community only if we enjoy formal citizenship.[13] These debates affect the rights of the millions across the globe who live in democracies but, rightly or wrongly, cannot participate in them. The point is mentioned here because it reinforces one of our themes, the impossibility of neatly dividing between complete and incomplete democracies.

As long as the most basic democratic question – who is entitled to be considered part of the *demos*, the people who are entitled to rule – is contested, and it always will be, those who feel that exclusions are unjustified will insist that established democracies have not met even the most formal of qualifications for democratic completeness. The debate over the boundaries of democratic communities illustrates, therefore, the degree to which the 'completeness' of the more 'complete' democracies remains open to challenge. Equally importantly, from its inception, the notion of rule by the *demos* has been highly exclusionary. In ancient Greece, it did not preclude slavery (although a study suggests that this caused the Greeks more unease than we have been told).[14] During the 'classic' period of liberal theory, democracy referred to the rights of property-owning men only.[15] It took almost two millennia from the birth of democracy for women to be granted the vote, and so political systems found it perfectly normal to describe themselves as democracies even as they excluded at least half the adult population from the right to a say. We could see democracy's history partly as a contest over who should be considered part of the community considered worthy of deciding – which continues in even the oldest democracies. The reality that not even the formal composition of the community which ought to govern itself is the subject of consensus reminds us to see democracy as an always unfinished and open-ended project.

But whatever criterion is used to define membership of the political community, democracy, at its core, distinguishes itself from monarchy, oligarchy and meritocracy as a system in which communities are governed not by those whose birth or breeding is said to have raised them above others, nor by those whose technical expertise or exceptional wisdom is believed to give them a superior right to decide, but by all their members. While other forms of government have no difficulty with the notion that we can be members of a community but barred from the decisions which govern it, democracy insists, in principle, that membership automatically means a right to decide.

Democracy rests on the assumption that, just as the arbitrariness of birth does not give anyone stronger claims to a right to decide, neither do purported skills or abilities, since the claim to know more than another may be as arbitrary as that to higher birth. Technical qualifications do not give anyone a greater right to decide public policy questions because there is no indisputably 'right' or 'wrong' answer to them. Highly qualified specialists do not agree on how to achieve even measurable goals such as higher economic growth – policy questions are products of opinion as well as training. Our response to many of these issues depends on our values. The view of the labourer on what is good or bad is as valid as that of a Nobel Prize-winning scholar – education or qualifications do not enable us to judge better whether the state should kill murderers or whether we should reward personal initiative. Since no one's opinion is 'better' than anyone else's, the only fair arrangement is to allow everyone's view the same weight. The core democratic idea is thus that every adult human being should enjoy an equal right to a say in all decisions which affect them.[16]

Democracy is, therefore, in essence a system of popular sovereignty,[17] in which the political community governs itself through the exercise of the equal decision-making rights and powers of each of its members: 'The very legitimacy of liberal democracy is based on the idea of popular sovereignty...',[18] while 'the idea that the people are the sole legitimate source of power has come to be taken for granted'.[19] The primary expression of sovereignty – without which the people can never govern – is the election or referendum, in which citizens choose who will rule or pronounce on a question deemed to affect them all. Between elections, although self-government is exercised through elected representatives, rather than directly, the principle of popular sovereignty requires that those who hold office do what they believe the people want them to do: 'Representation entails the idea of accountability: somehow the representative is held responsible for the ways in which he [sic] acts in the name of those for whom he claims to be entitled to speak'.[20]

Popular sovereignty is not exercised only at elections and does not cease between them: self-government by all is a permanent and defining feature of democracy. A decision to endorse a candidate or party at the ballot box is a mandate to a particular person or group to govern – it is not necessarily an endorsement of every policy position advanced by the representative or party. Rarely, if ever, does a vote entail endorsement of every position advanced by the candidate. Voters, rather, choose the candidate or party whose positions come closest to their own.[21] A vote for a governing party cannot, therefore, mean support for any particular policy position, and citizen support for a government initiative cannot be assumed simply because most adults voted for the governing party (since it could be seeking to implement one of those policies which most of its voters happen to reject). Governments may also face new circumstances which did not exist at the previous election, which means, of course, that a vote for a party or person could not possibly have been an endorsement of any particular response to the new reality.

Popular sovereignty thus means, in principle, the continuous right of citizens to a role in decision-making between elections – an equal say, at any time, for any voter who seeks it: 'Elections occur intermittently and only allow citizens to choose between the highly aggregated alternatives offered by political parties, which can ... proliferate in a bewildering variety. During the intervals between elections, citizens can seek to influence public policy through a wide variety of other intermediaries ...'.[22] In principle, all decisions in a democracy are meant to reflect the popular will and are legitimate only to the extent to which they can be shown to reflect the wishes of most citizens.

Since all citizens are entitled to a share in the process of deciding, the democratic content of each public decision must be assessed by the degree to which all members of the political community enjoyed a real opportunity to participate in discussing and deciding. The right to decide is meaningless unless it is accompanied by a right to persuade others, and unless the person deciding enjoys access to the information required to make a choice. This means that not only the degree to which everyone affected was asked their opinion, but also whether all enjoyed access to enough information to choose and were afforded an opportunity to debate alternatives, are important tests of the degree to which the people really are sovereign.[23] This does not mean an obligation to participate, but it does mean that the opportunity to do so and the information enabling participation must be available to all.

A further condition for popular sovereignty is whether democratic governments can turn what citizens want into reality – government capacity and authority are also crucial ingredients of popular sovereignty.[24] Since many new democracies are said to be unable to generate authoritative government, either because of the distribution of power in the international system or because they lack the administrative or political capacity to ensure that democratic decisions are implemented, the quest for popular sovereignty must address not only the capacity of citizens to influence government, but also government's ability to act in response to their mandate.[25] This clearly applies in those cases in which democratic states are too weak to defend citizens' rights. O'Donnell writes of 'brown areas' in new democracies: geographical or social spaces in which there is low presence or an entire absence of the state understood as 'a set of reasonably effective bureaucracies and of the effectiveness of properly sanctioned legality',[26] and in which citizens remain at the mercy of unaccountable power even while they enjoy formal democratic rights. But it also holds where citizens do enjoy a share in decisions but governments cannot implement law and policy. Popular sovereignty requires not only freedom, but also legitimate order.

While it is common for citizens of new democracies – South Africa's in particular – to complain about the quality of government, the problem is rarely that governments are powerless to defend everyone's rights. As O'Donnell shows, it is rather that they protect some and not others: affluent and connected Latin Americans do not live in 'brown areas'. This is a very South African reality. While residents of the affluent suburbs in the major cities are far more likely to complain about government capacity, the evidence shows that, despite the end of racial minority rule, post-1994 government is a great deal better at protecting their rights than those of people in shack settlements or townships. This ensures a differential form of citizenship – some have full democratic rights (which they often use to complain about the post-apartheid order which protects them), while others find that the constitution is no protection against unaccountable power and official indifference.[27]

This understanding of democracy enables us to begin to answer a question posed in the previous chapter: how to determine whether particular practices (such as corporatism or recognising traditional leadership) are democratic. It also offers a prism on a key debate in Asia and Africa on the degree to which institutions in formal democracies should be tailored to local conditions, and not simply modelled on those found in the North. An insistence on particular practices simply because they are said to reflect Northern norms can prevent new democracies from developing in a manner suited to their circumstances. Both of Africa's longest-lasting democracies, Mauritius and Botswana, have adopted institutions designed for indigenous circumstances, voting systems which ensure ethnic representativeness in the one case and a significant role for traditional leadership in the other. These innovations may well have helped them to remain democratic. But authoritarians often insist that their regime – or some of its key features – is a form of 'democracy' tailored to local beliefs and conditions. We will return to this problem. But the approach proposed here argues that political practices and systems are democratic to the extent that they contribute to popular sovereignty – the people's power to govern themselves.

'GOOD GOVERNANCE' OR DEMOCRACY?

This last claim challenges one of the paradigms through which government in South Africa and other countries of the global South is often currently viewed – that of 'good governance', which is often advanced as the required goal of new democracies (as well as non-democracies). Given South African concerns about the quality of government, it is no surprise that 'good governance' is often proposed as a key goal.[28] Like 'consolidation', it has become a widely used term – almost so widely used that its usefulness as a measure of progress is often assumed to be self-evident.

Since 'good' is among the most value-laden of terms, it comes as no surprise that there is a plethora of definitions of 'good governance'. In the view of a United Nations (UN) agency: 'Governance is the process whereby public institutions conduct public affairs, manage public resources and guarantee the realization of human rights. Good governance accomplishes this in a manner essentially free of abuse and corruption, and with due regard for the rule of law'.[29] While this agency goes on to list features of 'good governance' which are heavily centred on the protection of rights, the International Monetary Fund (IMF), unsurprisingly, associates it far more with economic management consistent with its preference for business-led growth. Among other goals, it stresses 'supporting the development and maintenance of a transparent and stable economic and regulatory environment conducive to efficient private sector activities'.[30] This obviously highlights an immediate problem. After which version of 'good governance' are states which wish to embrace this goal meant to strive?

To urge 'good governance' on new democracies is to beg an obvious question. Since the definition of the good is always subjective, whose definition of 'good' should prevail? The democratic answer, premised on the principle of popular sovereignty, is that 'good' governance is that which is considered so by most of the governed after free debate between all contending visions – if it preserves the right of all to continue to participate in decisions. The goal of democracies is to move as far as they can towards ensuring that all can participate in determining which forms of governance are good. The prime purpose of democratic governance cannot be the promotion of human rights or a particular view of economic efficiency. It is, rather, the maximum possible participation by citizens and the preconditions needed to achieve this.

While some formulations of 'good governance' do contain democratic features – the UN lists 'accountability', 'participation' and 'responsiveness to the needs of the people'[31] – proposing particular governance features or policy goals, rather than deeper democracy, as the purpose of new democracies weakens the democratic project by subjecting popular sovereignty to a vision of what is desirable generated by technical 'experts'. It allows some to decide on behalf of others, presumably because they are assumed to know better what is in the interests of societies than their citizens do. And so it can and does become a vehicle for imposing on people in the South the values of people in the North.

If the aim of governance is to achieve some goal other than determining and implementing the wishes of most members of the political community, there is no guarantee that democracy is best suited to the task: its defining feature is its promise of a share in decisions for all, not its ability to achieve other goals. It is not automatic that all rights are best protected by democracy – the right to property may be threatened by democratic decision-making. It is even less plausible to argue that democracy always reduces poverty.[32] There may, therefore, be tensions or contradictions between popular sovereignty and 'good governance' – if the latter is a priority, democracy is expendable, and with it the right of people to decide what is best for them. The moment a goal other than popular sovereignty – no matter how self-evidently 'good' – is proposed, the progress of political systems towards deeper democracy is threatened.

Similarly, to set any goal for democracy other than deepening popular sovereignty is to close down options, to direct the popular will in particular directions. That this threatens the democratic ideal is partly expressed by some understandings of democracy. Przeworski's view that it is a system in which contending interests (and, presumably, values) contend under conditions of 'institutionalised uncertainty'[33] does suggest that all outcomes should always be open to debate aimed at distilling the majority's will. So too, from a very different tradition, does the concern of post-modernist and post-Marxist theorists to insist on the perpetual open-endedness of democracy. Claude Lefort asserts that democracy made possible 'the dissolution of the markers of certainty'[34] and is 'the theatre of an uncontrollable adventure'.[35]

Chantal Mouffe decries the 'illusion that we can finally dispense with the notion of antagonism'.[36] She opposes any model of democracy which denies 'the dimension of undecidability and the ineradicability of antagonism which are constitutive of the political'.[37] In her view, '[m]odern democracy's specificity lies in the recognition and legitimation of conflict and the refusal to suppress it ...'.[38] And the South African political philosopher Peter Hudson notes that democracy is threatened if 'in my identification with and support for some determinate political object or project I "forget" that ... [in democracy] ... the "place" of social and political power is constitutively empty and cannot be identified a priori with any determinate political project'.[39] These views all warn against any attempt to shut down the contest of ideas and the right to decide, which are the defining features of democracy understood as a system of popular sovereignty. The right of a political community to decide is not merely a feature of democracy among others – it defines it: any attempt to subject democracy to other goals jeopardises its survival and progress.

But why insist on democracy, if it cannot guarantee desirable goals such as economic growth or the rights of citizens? As a cliché much used by South Africans has it, 'you can't eat democracy'.[40] The answer lies in the core democratic principle that opinions on what is desirable are subjective and that each is equal to all others. Economic growth might be desired by many, but some would argue that growth which depletes resources will destroy us. Among those who wish for growth, opinions on how to achieve it differ markedly. No 'science' can break the deadlock, and so the argument can be settled only by the preferences of the majority of those affected. Rights can often be just as controversial. Arguments over whether the right to life requires a ban on capital punishment because the state may put no one to death or mandates the death penalty because only it can protect the lives of innocents, or debate about whether free speech also means the right to express views hurtful to people of a particular race, gender or sexual orientation, generate great heat and passion in very old democracies.

To insist, therefore, that 'good governance' entails a particular route to growth or even protection of a parcel of rights is to deny a hearing to views whose claim to be heard is as valid as that of any others. Even well-intentioned attempts to help new democracies towards 'good governance', rather than deeper democracy, threaten popular sovereignty. While some defenders of the 'good governance' paradigm insist it is meant to promote democracy, but is forced to hide this so as to wean undemocratic regimes away from authoritarianism in a way which does not threaten them, its effect is to undermine democratic progress by urging new democracies to place other goals ahead of the quest to ensure the right to an equal say in decisions for all.

POPULAR BUT NOT (SIMPLY) MAJORITARIAN

Placing popular sovereignty at the core of democracy does not mean that the 'true' democracy is one in which the majority does as it pleases and the minority is forced to live with this.

Because members of a political community inevitably differ in their interests, values and opinions, popular sovereignty is exercised in practice by majority vote. But unrestrained majority rule is not popular sovereignty – if the majority could do whatever it wished, it might suppress the minority, denying to some members of the political community their share in sovereignty.[41] Because popular sovereignty means that everyone is entitled to an equal say in all decisions which affect them, members of a political community do not lose the right to participate because their view is in the minority. Measures which limit majority power by ensuring that it does not deny the minority its right to a say are, therefore, as essential to democracy as popular sovereignty. The minority does not decide which laws and policies are adopted, but it retains the right to take part in decisions and all the freedoms which make that possible.

Theorists point out that if this point is ignored, popular sovereignty risks becoming another form of tyranny because it allows some to silence others by insisting that they alone speak for the people. It does this because it can be used to deny difference: 'the people' are assumed to share a single mind and will. Those who differ are, therefore, not really part of the people – this is, of course, a strong theme in current right-wing populist politics. Populist interpretations of Jean-Jacques Rousseau's notion of the 'general will'[42] assume that it is possible to determine the 'will of the people' and then to translate it into law and policy. The historian of democracy Pierre Rosanvallon notes that this view 'behave(s) as though the majority were the same as the whole'.[43] The notion of 'the people' is always marked by difference of value and of interest, and so 'the will of the people' is always that of most people, not all people. Those who are not part of the momentary majority remain free citizens with a right to participate in decisions despite this. Lefort, whose concern was chiefly to argue against totalitarian understandings of democracy which he believed had influenced the French left,[44] argued that democracy relied on representatives not simply because it was inconvenient for people to meet daily to take decisions, but because representation recognised difference; this, he believed, was essential to guard against the 'temptation to restore unity in society'.[45] To recognise difference is to acknowledge the rights of the minority as well as the prerogatives of the majority.

The notion of popular sovereignty proposed here recognises that members of a political community are always divided by differing opinions and interests, and that a contest of ideas is intrinsic to a free society.[46] It insists, therefore, that central to popular sovereignty is the notion that everyone's will must be assured free expression, regardless of the degree of support for their view. Popular sovereignty is expressed not in the imposition of one will but in a contest between many wills – it cannot function without respect for difference. The 'people' govern in this view through a continuing contest between ideas and interests in which, in principle, no question – besides the right of each member of the community to participate in decisions – is ever closed. This is because to declare a debate settled is to silence discussion and so to deny citizens a right to decide freely in the future. The majority rules, but the minority retains the right to keep open and perpetually revisit the debate, while regular elections hold open to it the permanent prospect of becoming a majority.

In South Africa, racial minority rule and its legacy have distorted this point – 'minority rights' were very often advanced during the constitutional negotiation period[47] (and still are) as a means of protecting white privilege from majority rule. Minority rights were seen in racial terms: as the right of a minority race to escape the reality that the racial 'other' is in the majority. Given this, it is no surprise that black South Africans might see minority rights as a means to protect the privileges of the privileged. But minority rights in the sense that they are used here have nothing to do with race – the term refers only to the rights of people whose chosen view does not govern and whose preferred policies have not been adopted. A supporter of black consciousness is in the South African minority and is thus entitled to a full set of political rights despite that. Given the country's demographics, minority rights protect far more black citizens than their white counterparts.

This understanding of democracy is consistent with most liberal democratic understandings. But it does differ from influential current formulations in its reason for justifying limits on majority rule. Mouffe, following the German critic of liberal democracy Carl Schmitt, argues that the 'democratic paradox' is that '[w]hat cannot be contestable in a liberal democracy is the idea that it is legitimate to establish limits to popular sovereignty in the name of liberty'.[48] But this is an uncomfortable dilemma only if we understand popular sovereignty and liberty as competing values – which is what some defences of civil liberties do. They assume that individuals can never be free if they are subjected to the will of the majority, so their chief purpose is to protect individuals from a popular will which might deprive them of their freedom. This view of rights, the political philosopher CB MacPherson showed, assumes that individuals have what they have as a product of their own efforts only: society has played no role in producing what they enjoy and so has no claim over them.[49] In this view, rights entail no responsibilities – to the poor, to the weak or, as an important critique points out, to the environment.[50] Democracy understood as popular sovereignty is, in this view, a threat to the individual – rights are meant to reduce or eliminate this threat.

The view proposed here sees rights not as protection against popular sovereignty but as its precondition. Jürgen Habermas notes that these rights are 'necessary conditions of popular sovereignty';[51] 'popular sovereignty and human rights', he adds, 'go hand in hand'.[52] Rights are essential to popular sovereignty because, without them, members of the political community cannot participate in decisions. Since no member of the community can enjoy a say without the right to think, speak and act freely within agreed norms designed to preserve the rights of others, minority rights and civil liberties are essential features of popular sovereignty, not limits on its reach.

Mouffe argues that the paradox does not disappear because, even if we understand rights as preconditions for popular sovereignty, they do constrain majority decisions. And, like all important questions in a democracy, which rights are essential to popular sovereignty and how one is balanced against another are always contested. Libertarians insist that only basic civil liberties are necessary. Some social democrats argue that the right to decide cannot be fully exercised without sufficient capacity; people cannot decide unless they enjoy access to enough food, water and other goods to be able to act as autonomous citizens – the social citizenship of which TH Marshall spoke.[53] These rights are thus at least as important as basic freedoms. There is no agreed definition of which rights are essential to popular sovereignty because few if any debates are ever settled in a democracy. Arguing that rights must enable popular sovereignty, not limit it, does not end the debate on which rights are needed, nor is it meant to do this. But the distinction remains important because the way in which we protect and extend rights differs markedly if they are seen as means of enabling rather than curbing popular sovereignty. Courts which assume that rights are meant to enable people and groups to exercise citizenship would rule differently from those which assume that they are meant to protect them from what the majority wants.

This view is hinted at or expressly proposed in some influential discussions of democracy's core features. For Claude Ake, 'the principles of democracy include widespread participation, consent of the governed, and public accountability of those in power – principles that permeated traditional African political systems'.[54] Benjamin Barber defines 'strong democracy' as 'the participation of all of the people in at least some aspects of self-government at least some of the time'.[55] Karl and Schmitter define 'modern democracy' as 'a system of governance in which rulers are held accountable for their actions in the public realm by citizens acting indirectly through the competition and co-operation of their elected representatives'.[56] Dahl sees democracy as a system whose features include effective participation, enlightened understanding, and inclusion of all adult members in collective decisions.[57] Despite their differences, these definitions share the notion that democratic government is always accountable to citizens because, in principle, it exists to do their will. They all imply, in different ways, that all democracies should be judged by the degree to which they offer every citizen a say in the decisions which affect them.

To insist that democracy is popular sovereignty may seem self-evident. It is not, for it challenges current understandings, in South Africa and elsewhere. Thus Leonardo Avritzer argues that 'the hegemonic theory of the postwar period' is not democracy understood as popular sovereignty, but 'democratic elitism' which 'assumes a contradiction between political participation and democratic government'.[58] Democracy as popular sovereignty has, he argues, been constantly weakened by democratic elitism which, by the first half of the twentieth century, had developed three main lines of criticism of democracy as a system in which citizens decide. First, it argued that 'complex administration required the substitution of popular sovereignty by the rule of those embodying technical knowledge'. That is, government was too complicated for citizens: only those with the necessary knowledge could decide. Second, it 'pointed out the problems caused by the penetration of particular interests into arenas designed for rational argument and the generalization of interests'. If left to the people, democracy became a free-for-all for special interests which claimed to speak for everyone but served the interests of a few. Third, 'mass society' would 'bypass the institutions in charge of the formation of the general will' – democracy would allow elected authoritarians to ignore the rules and so to bypass democracy. And so 'the preservation of the values of democracy was entrusted to the insulation of elites from the political pressure of the masses'.[59] Rule by the people allowed leaders to manipulate citizens to claim power for themselves, as today's illiberal elected presidents are accused of doing. So popular sovereignty threatens democracy because it allows those without technical knowledge to take decisions, compromises rational decision-making by opening the way to special interests, and may subject democratic institutions to the pressure of mob rule.

To claim that government decisions require technical expertise which is beyond the citizenry; that democratic politics drowns out reasoned argument by substituting the grubby competition of sectional interests for deliberation by those concerned with society's greater good; and that grassroots citizens cannot use democratic institutions in the way their designers intended is hardly the preserve of a few elitist philosophers. On the contrary, these assumptions often dominate public debate; they are the bedrock of a conventional wisdom which sees democracy as useful, provided it is kept within strict limits. It takes many forms – in South African debate, it often expresses itself in a demand for 'leadership'[60] or in insisting that technical ability, not the capacity to respond to what citizens want, is what is needed from people in government.[61] The stress on leaders relegates the citizen to at best a supporting cast member rather than the star: it is often less a concrete proposal than a cry for help because it assumes that, when societies face difficult problems, they cannot solve them unless a leader does this for them. And the stress on technical ability places 'enlightened' technicians, not democratic citizens, at the centre of public decision-making.

That this is elitist hardly needs explaining. What is odd is that it also considers itself democratic. The claims which underpin 'democratic elitism' do not argue for another view of democracy – they propose less democracy. It is rule by the *demos* which sets democracy apart from other systems. To insist that the people are fit to govern only within strict limits is to insist that democracy must be limited or caged. At best, it argues that some democracy may be needed but not in quantities which would interfere with the elite's scope to decide. It insists not on a more complete version of democracy, but on its partial replacement. Elitism is not democratic because it attaches that label to itself, and so arguments – often heard in South Africa and elsewhere – which favour decision-making by the few at the expense of the many want to curb democracy, not to make it work better. While some of the arguments raised by democratic elitists identify real problems, the solution to each lies not in less democracy but in more – elected authoritarians, for example, can be curbed only if citizens have more power to curb them. The more mainstream thinking judges new democracies by criteria other than whether they offer popular sovereignty and the freedoms which make it possible, the more it seeks, wittingly or unwittingly, to curb democratic progress.

This argument is of great importance to assessing whether democracy is deepening. If popular sovereignty – with the limits on majoritarianism which ensure that all citizens retain the right to decide – is intrinsic to democracy, it provides the standard against which democratic progress or retreat is measured. It is the power of the people which decides how democratic a country is, not the criteria elitists seek to impose on citizens.

Stating the Not-at-All Obvious

It is not only democratic elitists who do not want to place popular sovereignty at democracy's heart. Many other voices, in the academy and the political arena, insist that democracy is important but do not accept unreservedly that it is essentially a system in which political communities exercise sovereignty.

Fukuyama, whose enthusiasm for democracy prompted him to declare the end of history, harbours no similar affection for popular sovereignty. In his discussion of the current poor performance of democracies, he offers a set of definitions in which the people's right to govern itself gets no mention. The nearest he comes is his definition of 'democratic accountability', which 'seeks to ensure that government acts in the interests of the whole community, rather than simply in the self-interest of the rulers'.[62] This does not necessarily mean that the people decide anything – governments could meet his definition without asking for citizens' views. For the rest, he is far more interested in whether the state is functioning efficiently and the rule of law is maintained than in whether people are governing themselves.

Even among scholars who share a commitment to popular self-government, definitions of democracy often skirt around this question. Thus Ian Shapiro describes democracy as 'a means to manage power relations so as to minimize domination'.[63] Democracy is meant not to reduce domination but to end it by ensuring an equal share in sovereignty for every member of the political community. Shapiro's definition suggests that this is a Utopian goal; in a sense it is, because democracy will never be fully achieved. But the reality that democracy's promise can never be fully realised does not change the nature of that promise – world peace may be an elusive goal, but peace is not a minimisation of violence, it is its cessation. There is a vast difference between seeing democracy as a system of popular sovereignty which will never be entirely realised and insisting that reality dictates that it is a system of, at most, partial sovereignty. The difference affects what we look for when we assess the democratisation of any society.

Similarly, Charles Tilly, after a discussion of a wide range of definitions of democracy, none of which unambiguously asserts the principle of popular sovereignty, arrives at the claim that 'a regime is democratic to the degree that political relations between the state and its citizens feature broad, equal, protected and mutually binding consultation'.[64] This comes nearer to the notion of popular sovereignty because it concentrates on decision-making. But what is 'broad' consultation? What proportion of the political community's members would need to be included for consultation to be sufficiently broad? More important, how can a political community in which only some members share in decisions be sovereign? And what does 'mutually binding consultation' between the state and its citizens mean? Assuming that 'state' is here used as a synonym for government, to see citizens and government as separate actors each with a claim on the other is to deny the democratic ideal of the government as an expression of the will of its citizens. By elevating state or government to an autonomous actor with equal rights in relation to the people, this definition seems to leave considerable leeway for restricting popular sovereignty in the name of the state or government's right to a share in decisions. The state no longer serves the people, it bargains with them.

Finally, mutual consultation, however binding, seems a far weaker understanding of citizens' rights in a democracy than popular sovereignty. While the latter insists clearly that the citizenry is meant to decide and the state to implement its decisions – provided they do not deny some members of the community their right to decide – Tilly's definition leaves open the degree to which governments must implement the will of the governed and allows popular sovereignty to be diluted. His definition may describe actual practice in existing democracies. But the purpose of defining democracy is not to describe what exists – it is to signal that to which it should aspire.

These are only three of many definitions of democracy. But they, with the other definitions discussed by Tilly[65] and many others currently available, skirt the core issue. They do not acknowledge without qualification that democracy distinguishes itself from other systems, in its goal if not always in its practice, by its insistence on the equal right to decide of all members of a political community, and on its assumption that this right outweighs all other considerations, precisely because the definition of what is good is always subjective and that what is good for political communities can be decided only by those communities.

Inevitably, understandings which assume that democracy is about something other than political communities' right to decide for themselves influence political practice. It is one rationale behind the tendency of Western powers to impose preferences on the South in the name of democracy. During the Cold War, the West felt compelled to intervene from time to time to overturn free electoral choices in the South if they were seen to advance Soviet interests – however tenuous that link may have been. In Guatemala, the non-communist Bosch government was overthrown because it wanted to expropriate land owned by the United Fruit Company – it was willing to pay compensation, but on the land values declared by the company in its tax returns, not at the amount United Fruit really believed the land to be worth.[66] The intervention was defended on the grounds that Western democracy was being saved from totalitarian communism. Currently, electoral choices are denied if they are considered to advance the cause of Islamic fundamentalism. Perhaps the most poignant example of this is the rejection by North America and Western Europe of a 2006 Palestinian election deemed free and fair by observers because the winning party, Hamas, was considered hostile to Western interests.[67] Instead of recognising the elected government, Western powers proceeded to starve it of resources. Since the rationale for ignoring electoral choices in both cases is the purported desire to protect the societies whose choice is rejected, Western governments are acting – or claiming to act – from a conviction that there are more important aspects of democracy than the right of political communities to choose their own governments.

This approach is explicitly justified by Samantha Power, who denounced 'the reification of elections' and urged the need to avoid 'electocracy' – to refuse to accept election results which do not confirm a particular moral vision. She invoked in her support a 'long tradition' in the United States of 'promoting elections up to the point that you get an outcome you don't like. Look at Latin America in the Cold War'.[68] Power's view is significant not only because her academic writings consistently advocate the aggressive use of force in pursuit of 'humanitarian' objectives, but also because she is a former US ambassador to the UN. Clearly, the view that popular sovereignty depends on approval by American 'humanitarians' with access to the means of force is not a fringe view. Since many of the interventions which this perspective justifies are said by the governments who engage in them to protect democracy, the theoretical rationale for these aggressive rejections of popular sovereignty is, presumably, the claim that democracy is about something other than the right of political communities to choose.

Governments do not impose themselves in this way because they are influenced by academic debates on democracy. They are driven by strategic considerations, fear of communism or Islamic fundamentalism. But ideas remain important because, directly or indirectly, immediately or over time, they play an important role in shaping whether political actions are seen as defensible. And so it is of some importance that the assumption that democracy is about something other than the electoral choices of some political communities seems to be strongly held among many mainstream scholars. The rejection of the expressed preference of Palestinians, one of the few Middle Eastern electorates then allowed a free choice, attracted no disapproval from these scholars. One of the doyens of academic democracy promotion in the US addressed the issue directly in a manner which suggests that popular sovereignty is not the defining characteristic of democracy. In an interview with the *Brown Journal of World Affairs*, Larry Diamond of Stanford University said of Hamas's victory:

> Hamas must somehow govern, but there is no guarantee that they will govern democratically. It is important that the international community

hold them to basic norms of democratic governance and to the binding commitments the Palestinian authority has made to recognize the right of Israel to exist ...[69]

Diamond's view is quoted here because it is much more respectful of popular sovereignty than many other perspectives – he acknowledges the winner's right to govern, albeit with the qualification 'somehow'. But he does go on to suggest that this right should be conditional: the 'international community' must not only hold the winning government to democratic norms, but must also impose on it a policy choice, 'the right of Israel to exist'. This is a highly contested term whose endorsement may not be consistent with liberal democratic values: for many, it is shorthand for 'right to exist as a Jewish state', as a state for one ethnic group in an area where others also lay claim to a share of the state. In principle, it is rejected not only by the election winners, Hamas, but also by the West's then negotiating partner, Palestinian Authority president Mahmoud Abbas.[70] Whether any elected Palestinian government does what Diamond wants it to do is a strategy or policy choice, not a matter of democratic principle. By insisting that the 'international community' hold an elected government to a particular choice, he is insisting that this electorate is not sovereign. Democracy is here not essentially popular sovereignty because the choice of governments and their electorates is subordinated to other values.

Nor is this the only occasion on which Northern powers' commitment to 'democratise' other societies has prompted them to reject popular sovereignty. In Bosnia, the Northern democracies, under the guise of democratising the society, ensured that institutions created by the Dayton Accords 'tended to restrict democratic accountability rather than develop mechanisms which would allow a transition away from international administration towards self-government'.[71] This was, it appears, no accident since it was assumed, despite evidence to the contrary, that tensions in Bosnia had been caused by an excess of popular sovereignty which had inflamed inter-communal tensions. Among Northern scholars and policy-makers, '[h]ighlighting the issue of identity has led to the questioning of liberal democracy in the region'.[72] Strategy for 'democratising' Bosnia was, paradoxically, therefore premised on 'the assumption ... that some cultures are not rational or civil enough to govern themselves'.[73] Whatever form of democracy the major powers were seeking to build in Bosnia, it was not one which rested on popular sovereignty. On the contrary, democratisation strategy seemed to be based on imposing, just as the consolidation paradigm does, a particular vision of what is needed and declaring that it is democracy: a society is democratic not if its people decide, but if it conforms to the preferences of Northern scholars and governments.

THE BARE MINIMUM: DEMOCRACY'S MINIMUM REQUIREMENTS

Using the approach proposed here, how do we know when a democracy has achieved full popular sovereignty? The short answer, suggested in the previous chapter, is that we don't: no democracy has ever achieved full popular sovereignty and none ever will.

This is a claim of principle, not of fact: 'To imagine that pluralist democracy could ever be perfectly instantiated is to transform it into a self-refuting ideal, since the condition of possibility of a pluralist democracy is at the same time the condition of impossibility of its perfect implementation'.[74] To insist that a democracy had been perfected would be to claim that the debate over democratic form and practice in that society was over. Discussing whether the democracy was functioning as it should would be no longer possible – this is an obvious restriction on popular sovereignty. Since a democracy is always a society in which rational adults will disagree on the extent to which popular sovereignty is being realised, and in which democratic principle requires continuing debate on this question, a democracy which claimed to be 'perfected' would be highly imperfect. This makes a 'completed' democracy a logical impossibility.

We cannot, therefore, use the attainment of full popular sovereignty as a measure of whether a political system can be considered a democracy – if we did, none would qualify. Popular sovereignty is not an achievable goal but an aspiration. If we understand teleology in the way Schedler proposes we do – as a goal – full popular sovereignty is the end-point to which all democracies aspire, but one which is never achieved. It cannot be used to determine when democracies have 'made it', but only to assess their often uneven progress towards a never-to-be-fully-achieved goal.

But if there are no 'completed' democracies, how do we know whether a political system is an incomplete democracy? Since virtually all states insist that they are democratic, how do we decide whether they really are? The question is anything but academic – it has very direct implications for political action by governments and citizens. Since democrats presumably support the principle that each person should enjoy an equal say over the decisions which affect them, they also presumably are morally obliged to support the right of citizens everywhere to decide. That means placing pressure on governments which are not democratic to concede decision-making powers to citizens – and defending those societies in which citizens do enjoy a say in decisions from attempts to impose the will of others on them. The former principle is used to justify American intervention in other countries (or was until the Trump administration), the latter was used repeatedly by the

South African government in support of its refusal to pressure Zimbabwe. If Iraq or Afghanistan or Zimbabwe are democracies, they should be left alone – if they are not, democrats are presumably duty-bound to press them to become democratic. But how do we know? In theory, the framework suggested here means that two considerations would shape the answer. First, to be labelled a democracy a political system would need to allow some form of popular choice. Second, the definition would need to be as 'minimalist' as possible because the more it adds to the definition, the more it would be repeating the 'consolidation' approach's division of democracies into 'full' and 'partial'. Both criteria are arguably met by Leonardo Morlino, who has proposed as a minimum standard for a democracy 'universal adult suffrage, recurring free, fair and competitive elections, more than one political party and more than one source of information'.[75]

The criterion is extremely 'minimalist'– far more so than Dahl's minimal conditions: that control over government decisions be vested in elected officials, chosen in frequent and fairly conducted elections in which 'practically all adults' have the right to vote and run for office; that coercion is 'comparatively uncommon'; and that citizens have a right to express themselves on political matters, to seek out alternative sources of information which exist and are protected by law, and to form 'relatively independent' associations or organizations, including independent political parties and interest groups.[76] These conditions contain several features, such as the right to expression and the comparative absence of coercion, which describe stages on the journey, not its point of departure. It is not clear how to decide whether coercion is 'comparatively uncommon' (or associations are 'relatively independent'). All democratic systems impose some coercion – states always coerce citizens to some degree. One element, effective control over bureaucrats by elected officials, might be regarded as an aspiration which no modern democracy has ever achieved.

An advantage of Morlino's definition is that most of its elements are not subjective and so can be easily verified. Whether elections are 'free' and 'fair' is not always straightforward. But, since there is no objective test of whether an election is free and fair, the only workable test is whether the losers accept the results (the winners, for obvious reasons, always accept them) – which can be verified. The flaw is that this creates an easy escape route for election losers – if they contest the result, they can deny legitimacy to the election. Even this minimalist and very basic criterion may, therefore, be largely a matter of opinion. It could also be argued that Morlino's criteria are far too minimalist – a country in which the only sources of information were a media source controlled by the government and another controlled by a single corporation sympathetic to it would qualify.

This shows that even a minimal definition of whether countries are democratic is likely to be contested and open to unending debate, as every aspect of democracy is. Whether a country is democratic, and thus in need of support, or undemocratic, and so in need of pressure to ensure that its people do govern, will always be settled by politics rather than 'science'. But effective democracy support – backing for democracies or pressure on non-democracies – is, fortunately, never the work of technicians. It is the work of citizens and the governments they elect. Given this, the debate over what criteria to apply to determine whether a political system is democratic is not as important as it seems. If the understanding of democracy proposed here is followed, a society has met the minimum standards of democracy if its citizens take some decisions over some of the issues which affect their lives. Whether this is the reality in any particular society is always debatable – and always should be. It is obviously inconsistent to argue that all issues should be open to contest in a democracy, but that whether particular political systems are democratic is beyond debate.

ASSESSING PROGRESS: THE SEARCH FOR DEMOCRATIC DEPTH

The core test of whether societies are more or less democratic is whether more and more citizens are enabled to decide on more and more issues which affect them. We cannot determine this unless we also examine the degree to which people enjoy the freedoms which enable them to do that, and whether political institutions are capable of responding to those decisions. But how can we do this?

Evaluating democracy is a constant concern of scholars and activists working within the 'consolidation' paradigm.[77] While there has been an attempt to assess the quality of established democracies,[78] most attention is focussed on whether new democracies are progressing to their satisfaction.[79] The most frequently used measure of democratic quality simply repeats the prejudices of the paradigm in a new form. Despite this, it dominates the work of Northern scholars checking on the progress of new democracies.

More Than Just a Number

The most celebrated attempt to measure progress towards democracy is the annual Freedom House assessment of 'Freedom in the World'.[80] Along with less widely used measures such as Polity[81] and (to a much lesser extent) V-Dem,[82] these assessments are used frequently in academic studies of democracy across the globe.

In the Freedom House rankings, countries are rated by analysts on a range of criteria and are awarded a score of between 1 and 7. They are ranked as 'Free' (a score of 1 to 2.5), 'Partly Free' (3 to 5) and 'Not Free' (5.5 to 7).[83] While Freedom House insists it is assessing 'freedom', not democracy (Polity and V-Dem acknowledge that they are measuring democracy), in much academic work 'freedom' is used as a synonym for democracy, for scholars regularly use Freedom House scores to assess the state of democracy across the globe. Because Freedom House assigns a numerical weight to its judgment, scholars can feed its rankings into regression analysis and claim to measure trends in democracies across the globe.[84] But measuring progress towards popular sovereignty in this way obscures more than it clarifies – if democratisation is too complicated to be encapsulated in a 'pass' or 'needs further work' grade, so too is it unlikely to be understood by reducing it to a series of scores on a chart.

Freedom House's method subjects information gathered by its research team to 'a multi-layered process of analysis and evaluation by a team of regional experts and scholars'.[85] While Freedom House insists that its ratings process 'emphasizes intellectual rigor and balanced and unbiased judgments', it acknowledges, appropriately, that 'there is an element of subjectivity inherent in the survey findings'.[86] This should not be a damaging admission: all assessments of democratic progress rely on subjective judgment. Intrinsic to the argument proposed here is that democracy is a system in which everything except the political community's right to decide is open to debate and contest – whether particular countries are making progress towards popular sovereignty is a question on which continuous debate is required. If Freedom House's survey is seen purely as an analytical judgment expressed by a team of scholars, as one of many perspectives on the topic, it can contribute to debate.

But, if this exercise is presented as a 'scientific' measure of democratic progress which, without thorough analysis of the evidence and criteria used by the specialist team to reach its conclusions, can be used to understand democratic progress and the factors which strengthen or obstruct it, it blocks understanding. There is little difference between insisting that we can recognise a 'certain' democracy and assuming that a group of scholars can judge whether a society is 'free', 'partially free' or 'not free' in so precise a way that it can be fed into a computer and used to make claims about the progress of democracy.

Freedom House rankings, despite presenting themselves as a 'scientific measure', display the same ethnocentric biases as the 'consolidation' paradigm. No Northern democracy has even been rated less than entirely 'free'. Given the flaws in American democracy discussed earlier, it is surely worth asking what would need to happen in that country for Freedom House to declare it less than free. If minority rule, the denial of the vote to people fitting particular racial profiles, and detention without trial are not sufficient, what is? The rankings also seem immune to the concerns among mainstream scholars about Western democracy which were discussed earlier – despite the fact that Freedom House is not only aware of them, but seems to agree with them: its article discussing its 2015 report mentions 'security measures' which 'threaten the core values of an open society' in Western democracies.[87] But this is treated as a minor blemish to be mentioned in passing, not a reason for concluding that the 'free world' is not as free as it thinks. Freedom House rankings are most accurately described as a measure which assumes, regardless of evidence, that Northern democracies are the finished product and then measures whether the others have managed to attain their exalted status – as an attempt to translate the 'consolidation' paradigm into numbers.

Even a democracy measure which avoided these biases would be inadequate if it tried to reduce the health of democracy to numbers, as Freedom House's rival Polity also does. Understanding whether each democracy and particular practices and institutions within each are progressing towards or retreating from popular sovereignty cannot be reduced to a numerical rating exercise by scholars using criteria and judgments which are, inevitably, open to challenge, but are never stated. The task requires far greater respect for the rich texture of detail in each society and far greater openness to the need to debate judgments. If the consequence is that fewer scholars conduct fewer exercises in which the particularity of the quest for democracy in each society is flattened out, drained of much of its meaning and reduced to a number, understanding democracy's trials and triumphs will be enhanced. The regressions and other calculations based on these methods do not provide us with an adequate understanding because the methods they employ cannot yield one.

A more satisfactory way of examining democratic progress is the judgment of citizens themselves. If democracy is understood as a system of popular sovereignty, the key test is whether the level of self-government which the political community enjoys satisfies the citizens who are meant to govern. Some scholars argue that this also tells us much about democracy's survival prospects: 'whether citizens are satisfied, whether they have trust in institutions, and whether they perceive their democracies as … responsive and accountable ultimately matters more for the future of democracy than any objective evaluation of these dimensions'.[88] Assessing citizen satisfaction with democracy has attracted great interest from scholars: regional attitude surveys are used to determine citizen satisfaction with democracy throughout the world.[89]

Analysing citizens' perceptions promises a more accurate understanding of democratic progress than a numerical index which measures specialist opinion.

But caution is needed. The value of attitude surveys depends on what questions are asked, how they are asked and who is asked. An obvious objection to measuring the depth of democracy by citizens' responses to surveys is that people whose right to speak or choose is restricted may be unable to speak their mind. It is hardly straightforward to determine whether satisfaction is freely expressed or a tacit expression of fear. In theory, we might expect the highest levels of satisfaction in societies in which democracy is most shallow: higher levels of dissatisfaction might indicate democratic deepening because citizens are more inclined to express themselves. It might also show, as Norris and Ronald Inglehart argue, another potential source of democratic deepening: citizens who expect more and who will hold those who exercise authority to higher standards. These realities caution against using attitude research alone to determine whether citizens believe their countries are democratic.

In the democracies in which these surveys are currently conducted, it is unlikely that the entire citizenry is living in a fear which prevents it from speaking its mind – the high levels of expressed dissatisfaction recorded in surveys testifies to this. But the capacity, confidence and context which enables people to speak freely is not distributed evenly. Some may feel more confident to speak than others, and this may ensure survey results which overstate satisfaction with democracy – and prevent us from identifying democratic deficits because those whom they deprive of voice do not speak freely (or at all). In any democracy, the ability to exercise sovereignty is certain to be unevenly distributed among citizens: some are better placed than others to exercise the voice which democracy offers. We would expect those who have voice to experience less constraint to expression than those who do not – even if surveys are able physically to reach those who lack voice.

The depth of democracy also cannot be determined purely by majority opinion. While popular sovereignty requires that government decisions reflect the majority view, it rests also on the sovereignty of each citizen, and so the right to seek to shape public decisions cannot be the preserve of majorities alone. Since the citizenry is sovereign in principle only if each citizen can take part in decisions, denying the effective right to speak and act to one individual would indicate a democratic deficit. If, therefore, majorities believe that democracies are working for them and minorities do not, this does not in principle make the task of democratic deepening any less urgent. Since a majority response could hide the degree to which democracy is not working for those minorities who need it most, citizen responses may be meaningful only if they are analysed with sensitivity to the relationship between opinions and the place in society of those who express them.

Surveys could be offering a voice to those able to speak while failing to hear those who cannot. Where this is so, they would not only be failing to discern the health of democracy, but may also be perpetuating the problem they seek to research – deficits which make some unwilling or unable to speak – and so ensuring that 'the voice of the people' is that of the better resourced and connected. The measure of democracy's depth could then become one symptom of its shallowness.

The Uncertain Way Forward

The approach discussed here does not promise an easy mathematical measure which can tell us whether democracy is becoming stronger or weaker, deeper or shallower. Nor does it offer certainty – a clear and indisputable means of assessing democratic progress. But it does offer new (and older) democracies a more appropriate way of measuring their progress. Instead of an unrealisable goal, it offers achievable targets. Instead of a perpetual inferiority complex, born of an always doomed attempt to imitate an idealised portrait of other democracies, it offers a potential source of pride in progress even as it urges an aspiration to achieve more. Instead of an uncritical devotion to the democratic form of the North, it invites an exploration of those forms which might best enable democratic ideals to be pursued in the circumstances of each society.

It does this by being both specific and open-ended. On the one hand, it seeks to move beyond the vague or unstated criteria by which democratic progress and quality are currently assessed by returning to democracy's roots and insisting that it is fundamentally about people's right to decide on the issues which affect them. On the other, it does not claim to 'scientifically' decide issues which will always be hotly debated. It seeks to bring clarity to the quest for deeper and more enduring democracy by defining its (never-to-be-achieved) goal, and also to keep open debate about democracy's progress by rejecting the idea that any democracy can be perfected.

But this begs a vital question: what enables democracies to grow nearer to or shrink further from the democratic ideal? What do they need to develop if they are to progress towards greater popular sovereignty? The following chapters address this issue.

3

Democracy in Deed: The Centrality of Collective Action

What do democracies need if they are to remain democratic – and to become deeper and broader?

The previous chapter examined how we might recognise a democracy when we see one, and how we would know whether it was making progress towards fuller democratisation. But this says nothing about the ingredients which make it more likely that a democracy will be born – and, when it is, how it will deepen or broaden. And so it tells new democracies, and those who seek to understand them, nothing about what is required if they are to move closer to the goal of popular sovereignty.

A celebrated article by the American scholar Seymour Martin Lipset suggests that we can identify the elements which democracies require to be born and to survive by distinguishing between the system's maintenance and support. Lipset noted that democracies need internal mechanisms to sustain themselves, such as 'the specific rules of the political game', but they are also, he thought, supported by factors which make democracy more likely.[1] Maintenance factors are those internal features which keep it going, while support factors are the elements in the environment it requires to operate at all. This chapter will argue that democracy's key maintenance factor is also its key support factor: the capacity of citizens to act collectively to hold governments to account and ensure that they respond to voters.

Analyses which stress the support factors claim that democracy cannot emerge or grow unless preconditions are met. They are common in the academic literature and can broadly be divided into the material and the historical. The former insists that democracy cannot be sustained in societies which have not reached particular stages of economic development or levels of wealth. The latter points to historical legacies which ensure that societies are more or less likely to become democracies: these may be cultural or the product of past patterns, such as how contending interests resolved their conflicts. Neither set is comforting to new democracies, particularly those in Africa, since both suggest that democracies can survive and deepen only if conditions exist which were produced by processes that developed over centuries and are usually said to be absent in Africa. The implication is either that democracy will remain elusive for a very long time or that it will have to wait until the economy develops to the required level – development must presumably be given priority over democratisation since democracy is impossible without it. And both, whatever the intention of their authors, imply very strongly that many countries and peoples are 'not ready for democracy'.

The claim that some people are not yet ready to become political adults by governing themselves violates the democratic principle that everyone has a right to an equal say. It is particularly disturbing to people who have lived under colonial rule or who, like South Africans not that long ago, have been dominated by racial oligarchies because the coloniser and the apartheid apologist relied partly on the claim that the people who were dominated had not yet reached (and in some claims never could reach) a level of development which could sustain democracy. It will equally offend people living under authoritarian rule, which is often justified by the rulers on the grounds that the populace is not ready to assume the responsibility of self-government. Claims that preconditions must be met before societies can sustain democracy are, therefore, open to the same objection as all authoritarianism – that they assume, falsely, a hierarchy among human beings in which only some have the qualities needed for self-government.

That it is offensive does not, however, necessarily make it untrue. It may be conveying an unpalatable truth which democrats would prefer not to hear – that, alas, there are many people for whom the rights and responsibilities of decision and choice are not possible, either for now or forever. How strong, then, are these arguments that democracy must remain elusive unless certain conditions are present?

DOOMED NOT YET TO DECIDE? THE PRESUMED PRECONDITIONS FOR DEMOCRACY

The most influential argument that particular levels of economic development are required for democracy was made by Lipset in the late 1950s. In the article mentioned above, he examined a hypothesis which he traced back to Aristotle: 'that only in a wealthy society in which relatively few citizens lived in real poverty could a situation exist in which the mass of the population could intelligently participate in politics and could develop the self-restraint necessary to avoid succumbing to the appeals of irresponsible demagogues'.[2] To test this, Lipset sought to measure levels of wealth, industrialisation, urbanisation and education and their relationship to democracy. He claimed to have found a positive correlation and concluded that 'a more systematic and up to date version of Aristotle's hypothesis ... is valid'.[3] And so Max Weber, Lipset suggests, may have been right to insist that 'modern democracy in its clearest forms can only occur under the unique conditions of capitalist industrialisation'.[4]

A key element of Lipset's analysis is the claim that economic development aided democracy because it reduced polarisation, ensuring that less was at stake in political contests. While he acknowledged the role of working people in fighting for democracy, he believed the system was threatened by 'working class authoritarianism', the tendency of people in poorer economic circumstances to be less committed to democratic values. In contrast to Karl Marx's belief that workers were the bearers of a new freedom, he feared that people deprived of education and wealth were likely to be intolerant and rigid. His claim that economically deprived people were more hostile to democracy implies that greater prosperity will produce fewer authoritarians and so is more favourable for democracy.[5] Lipset argued that democracy could be sustained only by 'political cosmopolitanism'– a state of mind in which political actors did not isolate themselves from others and were more tolerant of difference. This needed 'the growth of urbanization, education, communications media and increased wealth'.[6] The poorer people were, the less likely they were to harbour the needed attitudes. Democracy for Lipset is for rich societies and well-off people.

A multi-country study by Przeworski and colleagues in the mid-1990s claims to support a theory similar to Lipset's. It rejects some of the cruder claims about 'readiness for democracy'. It finds no evidence for the claim that countries need a particular level of economic development to become democracies. The authors define democracies as 'regimes that hold elections in which the opposition has some chance of winning and taking office'.[7] This not only requires very subjective judgments about likely election results but would, at times, disqualify some 'model' Western democracies.) The data, the authors insist, refute the claim, often made at the time their study was conducted, that societies need a period of economic growth inspired by a dictatorship before they can become democratic. There was, they reported, no evidence that dictatorship was more likely to ensure growth than democracy, therefore none that societies needed to pass through a period of economic growth under authoritarianism before they could become democracies.

But, if wealth is not needed to become democratic, they do insist that economic development decides whether countries stay democratic. They found that poor democracies had a much weaker chance of surviving than rich ones. Indeed, they claim that once per capita income exceeds $6 000 a year, 'democracies are impregnable and can be expected to live forever: no democratic system has ever fallen in a country where per-capita income exceeds $6,055'.[8] By contrast, a democracy with per capita income below $1 000 can be expected to last on average only eight and a half years, and those with between $1 000 and $2 000 for only 16 years.

These averages do not enable us to predict the fate of particular democracies – if they did, Indian democracy would have collapsed in 1956.[9] Przeworski and his team would reply that they are only interested in showing what is probable, not what is inevitable. They also qualify their findings in another way: poor democracies can survive, they report, if they experience rapid economic growth with moderate inflation: 'When the economy grows rapidly with a moderate rate of inflation, democracy is much more likely to last even in the poorest lands'.[10] They also find that parliamentary democracies have greater survival prospects than presidential systems. Besides its strong claim that no democracy can collapse once per capita income exceeds $6 055, this theory does not insist that poorer countries can never remain democratic for long. It claims only to identify circumstances in which democracies are more likely to survive or collapse – and to identify action which might be taken to defend democracy (since democracies can give priority to economic growth and anti-inflation measures and can make collapse less likely by adopting parliamentary systems). So it does not declare some societies necessarily unready for democracy. That said, the study is open to objections.

The first is that it is unclear how statistical analysis can determine a level at which democracy cannot end: the fact that no democracy above a particular income level has ever collapsed does not necessarily mean that none ever will. The second is that the patterns revealed by statistical analysis do not necessarily uncover causal links. The fact that democracy ends more quickly in poorer countries does not necessarily mean that their poverty is the cause of democratic collapse – there may be other reasons. (A celebrated economist illustrates the problem of claiming that statistics show causes by reporting, tongue in cheek, that statistical analysis shows that countries are more likely to escape civil conflict the more mountains and rivers they have.)[11] The real causes might be unrelated to those shown by statistical correlation: poverty may have implications – such as weak capacity to engage in collective action – which may explain the collapse of democracy. If so, ability to act collectively would be the key variable, not poverty. Third, the authors' insistence that they are identifying what is probable, not what is certain, means that the study cannot, as the Indian example shows, necessarily tell us anything about the prospects of any particular society. This may not be a criticism – the authors are not claiming to make hard predictions – but it is a warning against relying on the study to explain developments in South Africa or any other democracy. These criticisms apply more generally to claims that democracy is possible only at particular levels of wealth. We cannot simply 'read off' democratic prospects from levels of economic development; we must examine other factors. Finally, Przeworski and his colleagues are concerned only with whether formal democracy survives, not whether it broadens or deepens. And so their study does not tell us whether rich countries can retreat from democracy while remaining formally democratic, nor whether poorer countries may experience democratic gains. While its data may help to identify the preconditions of formal democracy and democratisation, the study does not tell us whether democracies will survive, let alone whether they will broaden and deepen.

Cultural Conditions

Lipset does not link democracy's prospects to levels of economic growth alone. His argument is reinforced by cultural explanations and assumptions – although culture is, in his view, significantly shaped by economic development.

He assumes that certain non-Western cultures are at first hostile to democracy but can change through economic development. The motor of economic growth turns the 'pre-modern pre-democrats' of the Orient (and, by implication, Africa) into Western moderns ready for democracy, although perhaps with some habits not shared by the original bearers of democratic culture. Having cited sources claiming to show that hostility to democracy is inherent in Muslim and Asian culture, he declared in 1993: 'The situation, of course, has changed in recent years in response to rapid economic growth, reflecting the ways in which economic changes can impact on the political system undermining autocracy'.[12] More generally, 'belief systems change; and the rise of capitalism, a large middle class, an organised working class, increased wealth, and education are associated with secularism and the institutions of civil society which help create autonomy for the state and facilitate other preconditions for democracy'.[13] Like the 'consolidation' literature, Lipset sees democratic progress as a process in which non-Western societies come to resemble the West – in which 'they' become 'us'.

The most obvious problem with this teleology is that there are democracies in which many of Lipset's preconditions are very weak – India might not meet some, while Botswana qualifies on even fewer. Lipset knew this and took out intellectual insurance. He insisted that the existence of 'deviant cases' which do not support the theory 'cannot be the sole basis for rejecting the hypothesis'. On the contrary:

> A deviant case, considered within a context which marshals the evidence in all relevant cases, often may actually strengthen the basic hypothesis of an intensive study if it reveals the special conditions which prevented the usual relationship from appearing.[14]

It is not clear how the failure of a claimed causal relationship to work in all cases can be said to strengthen it. The exceptions might show that it is valid except in unusual circumstances – but would still weaken it by showing that cause and effect are not as clear as the hypothesis claimed. Would the exceptions in this case support or refute Lipset's view? That would depend on whether the 'deviant' case (or cases) can be shown to be exceptions born of highly unusual circumstances. But a source as sympathetic to Lipset's view as the Economist Intelligence Unit has listed as democracies at least three dozen African, Asian, Latin American and Eastern European countries which do not meet his criteria: indeed, the 'deviant' cases outnumber the less than two dozen rich countries which do make the democratic grade.[15] We can safely agree that a theory which is wrong more times than it is right has not been strengthened – that it has, rather, been shown to explain nothing.

In a much later revision of his work on democratic preconditions, Lipset did appear to concede that the link between economic development, culture and democracy is not as clear-cut as he supposed. He noted that India, Botswana, Papua New Guinea and Sri Lanka all contradicted the hypothesis: 'The diffusion of democracy to some poor Less Developed Countries in recent years also undermines the correlation, although this happened in large part due to the end of a bi-polar world – Third-World dictators can no longer take advantage of the tension between the Soviet Union and the West ...'.[16] This is a weak rescue attempt. What was supposed to be an inevitable result of a lack of economic growth is now an accidental product of a particular historical moment. Lipset knows this and is forced into retreat, admitting that his 'socioeconomic correlations' do not necessarily show whether democracy is possible and that 'other variables' may also matter. This is, of course, an admission that the link between development and democracy is not automatic. Lipset admits as much. His explanation, he insists, does not declare some societies to be unready for democracy: he does not want to discourage political action by claiming that the correlation is so clear-cut 'that men [sic] cannot feel that they can change the direction of affairs by their actions'.[17] So he was not saying that anything is inevitable – merely warning democrats in societies which did not meet his criteria of the obstacles they faced.

Despite these admissions, Lipset did not give up on his dogged attempt to hold the fate of new democracies hostage to economic growth. Responding to Karl and Schmitter's argument that pacts between power-holders and challengers make democracy possible, he argues that pacts are impossible unless his economic preconditions operate.[18] This seems little more than a nostalgic attachment to a position whose foundations have collapsed: if 'other variables' matter, why can pacts not be one of them? He retreats further when he claims that his economic preconditions do not show whether countries can become democratic, but whether they can stay that way. This seems to contradict his earlier claims but does not help him since India has been a democracy for 70 years, Botswana for more than 50. The retreats seem to be a desperate attempt to explain away the gulf between the hypothesis, which was proposed when democracy was largely the preserve of rich countries, and later developments in new democracies, which make the theory seem far more a cultural prejudice than an explanation. This makes it all the more peculiar that Lipset concludes his analysis by returning to his intellectual roots and claiming that economic development is the key to resolving the political problems of new democracies – even as he recognises that the strains caused by growth may undermine democracy's stability.[19] Given his acknowledgement of the weaknesses of his hypothesis, his continued embrace of economic development as a precondition for democracy seems based more on faith than on reason.

Why does Lipset want to have his cake and eat it too by insisting both that only the rich(er) can enjoy democracy and that poorer countries enjoy the power to be democratic too? On the one hand, he does not want to be seen to be discouraging aspirant democrats in the South. On the other, he seems to want to signal that they will have to become like Westerners if they want to be democratic – he still claims that 'the prognosis for the perpetuation of political democracy in Asia and Africa is bleak', and that exceptions were likely to be those societies which 'tend to resemble Europe in one or more major factors'.[20] So democrats in poor countries should try their best to achieve democracy, even though the odds are against them. And they can succeed only if they become Western, if only in part. The billions who are unfortunate enough not to be Western may hope for self-government only if they cease to be themselves.

Lipset's explicit claims to cultural superiority say what the 'consolidation' paradigm assumes: that democracy is a status which some have achieved and to which others can only aspire – and that those who want it can get it only by becoming like those who have it. Democracy is not here self-government, in which societies shape their own paths through their choices; it is conformity to the choices of others. As long as democracy is seen as a submission to the cultures of others, not the right to choose freely, it will be seen in much of the South more as humiliation than as liberation. And so it is only by asserting democracy as a right to choose *not* to be European that we can free it from the cultural baggage which presents it as a Northern imposition, not a path to freedom.

Eligible by Association?

Lipset's claim that industrial development creates a culture favourable to democracy is not the only attempt to show that democracy requires conditions which may not be present in Africa.

Some argue simply that particular attitudes and values are necessary if democracy is to survive. And, while some share Lipset's affirmation of Western Europe and North America as the repository of democratic values, not all do. Perhaps the most celebrated study of cultural preconditions – which makes no claims about Northern cultural superiority since both its democratic model and its example of thwarted democracy are Western European – is Robert Putnam's *Making Democracy Work*, which argues that associational life in Northern Italy built, over centuries, a store of 'social capital' which was favourable to democracy, but was not found in that country's South.[21] Even if the associations in which people participated were not designed to give them a say in decisions – choral societies or sports clubs, for example – they equipped people for democracy by imparting 'social capital'. This explained why Northern Italy was in good democratic health and the South was not. The implication for new democracies was not reassuring: if they lacked the civic traditions Putnam and his colleagues said were necessary for sustainable democracy – which they invariably did – they appeared to face a wait of several centuries (during which they would need to form many clubs and societies) before lasting democracy became possible.

Putnam's work does not help to tell us whether countries remain formal democracies. The Southern Italy whose lack of civic traditions is said to have explained why political bosses handed out patronage, not democratic accountability, is part of a democracy which has survived for six decades – despite its lack of 'social capital' and civic traditions. Rather, Putnam wants to make a point about the circumstances under which democracy broadens and deepens; he argues that democratisation will be limited by weak civic traditions and a lack of social capital, not that it cannot survive without them. The new democracies of the South might, then, remain formally democratic for generations without the required civic traditions and 'social capital', but their citizens will still find progress towards popular sovereignty more elusive than in societies which have the necessary civic traditions. Putnam does not insist that some societies are not ready for democracy: he suggests, rather, that some are not ready for democratisation.

But how useful is this analysis? It is crucial to distinguish between two aspects of Putnam's argument; one is helpful in understanding what democratisation needs, the other is not. Citizens cannot exercise popular sovereignty unless they combine freely with others to hold elected governments to account. Popular sovereignty is a product of the exercise of a right which each of us possesses by virtue of our humanity but is exercised collectively, since individuals must combine with others if the majority's will is to prevail. The opportunity and capacity to associate in a manner which amplifies citizen voice is, therefore, essential to popular sovereignty. Given this, we should expect, as Putnam maintains, that participation in associations which give voice to citizens helps to make popular sovereignty more possible.[22]

Far more dubious is Putnam's claim that long histories of associating in organisations not designed to give citizens a voice in decisions aid democracy because such association instils a sense of 'civicness'. First, the theory lacks evidence outside his Italian study: no body of data suggests that it applies elsewhere. Second, democratisation has made progress where there is no tradition of civicness of the sort Putnam describes. Mauritius is widely acknowledged to be one of Africa's more vigorous democracies, as well as one of its most enduring, but there is no evidence of the civic traditions which, in Putnam's view, are essential to democracy.[23] Third, the theory can be interpreted in ways which ignore the crucial role of power in determining opportunities for and obstacles to participation and, therefore, popular sovereignty. It is not association which deepens democracy but collective action to hold power to account. By proposing that all forms of association make democratisation possible, rather than only those which allow citizens to act in concert to redistribute power in the political system and society, Putnam fails to identify those forms of association which make democratisation possible.

Schools of Democracy or Sources of Power?

The idea that participation in horizontally organised associations (those in which there is formal equality between members) is an important training ground for democracy can be traced to the French observer of American democracy, Alexis de

Tocqueville, who saw associations as 'large free schools': 'it is by the enjoyment of a dangerous freedom [to associate] that the Americans learn the art of rendering the dangers of freedom less formidable'.[24] Americans, he believed, daily acquired 'a general taste for association ... They afterwards transfer to civil life the notions they have thus acquired ...'.[25] He was convinced that combining independently with others was crucial to the maintenance of democracy – and, indeed, civilisation: 'In democratic countries the science of association is the mother of science; the progress of all the rest depends upon the progress it has made'.[26]

This is open to two broad interpretations. The first is that, by associating in a democratic way rather than in obedience to unaccountable power-holders, citizens learn the art of democracy and can apply it in politics. This implies that democratic participation – and, therefore, popular sovereignty – is a learned art, a product of acquiring those 'habits of the heart' (in De Tocqueville's famous phrase) which Putnam calls 'civicness': tolerance for others and support for rules which respect others' rights. Any association, whether or not it seeks to give citizens a voice which will enable them to challenge power, can inculcate those values and behaviours, and so, the longer citizens have been participating in associations, the more likely they are to exercise democratic sovereignty. Societies which lack the needed 'civic traditions' are, therefore, indeed 'not ready for democracy', for their citizens have not yet acquired, through participation in associations, the habits which can sustain it as a vehicle for participation within rules which respect the rights of all.

A second view would also see association as important, but for very different reasons. Here, the barrier to participation is that citizens lack not habits but power. The problem is not that the citizenry has not yet learned the art of democracy, but that it has been denied the power to exercise voice, which is at the heart of popular sovereignty. The voice of all is not heard and participation is therefore limited, not because citizens do not know how to be democrats but because they are denied the power to speak or act. In this view, association is not enough: everything depends on its nature. If citizens combine in associations which give them a voice in public affairs, democratisation is possible. If these associations are to act as channels for citizen voice, and thus for deeper and broader popular sovereignty, they must be democratically organised, for, if they are not, the voice exercised will not be that of their members, but of those who presume to lead them. But it is essential too that they offer citizens a voice in public policy.[27] To make democratisation possible, associations must offer their members a voice – and act effectively enough to ensure that it is heard by power-holders.

De Tocqueville falls between seeing associations as training grounds and as vehicles for holding the state to account. Associations, he believed, offered citizens power which enabled them to curb that of the state. They protected people from tyranny, and are thus a form of what would later be called 'countervailing power':

> If each citizen did not learn, in proportion as he [*sic*] individually becomes feebler and consequently more incapable of preserving his freedom single-handed, to combine with his fellow citizens for the purpose of defending it, it is clear that tyranny would unavoidably increase together with equality.[28]

Voluntary associations, he believed, also curtailed the power of governments by limiting the tasks they needed to perform. The more citizens acted in associations to meet their social needs, the less they would rely on governments to do it for them and the less power governments would accumulate:

> Governments, therefore, should not be the only active powers; associations ought, in democratic nations, to stand in lieu of those powerful private individuals whom the equality of conditions has swept away.[29]

It is not clear whether De Tocqueville's problem here is how citizens are to make themselves heard or how they are to prevent the state from intruding in their lives. The latter concern is far more compatible with those of people seeking to hold on to what they have than with those who hope to place their concerns on the public agenda because they do not yet have what they need. But, crucially, he does see association as a means of holding power in check, not as a 'school of citizenship' entirely divorced from the problem of power.

The view proposed here sees association as the means by which citizens combine to hold the state to account and force it to respond. Democratic deficits occur when citizens lack the power to speak or believe that they do. If we see democratisation – or setbacks to it – as a consequence of changes in power relations which allow or block action by citizens to hold power to account, we can answer a question begged by Putnam's argument: why did access to civic traditions not protect Northern Italians from fascism, which 'developed in those regions where civil society was more robust, the same regions included in Putnam's Most Civic Regions'?[30] Since the civic traditions were presumably not suspended for 20 years, the plausible theory is that citizens were unable to withstand the power of the fascists. Participating in associations does not deepen democracy unless it enables citizens to exercise voice. Only if they alter the power relations between citizens and government (and between groups of citizens) – by providing those who lack power with a lever to make their voice heard to those who hold it – can they extend popular sovereignty and democratise their societies.

This crucially changes the question. At issue is no longer whether societies' traditions enable their citizens to behave in the manner required by democracy. It is, rather, whether enough citizens are able to combine in ways which broaden voice and so allow a challenge to power relations which deny a voice to many. It might be helpful if tradition encourages people to band together in organisations, but there is no reason in principle why people who lack a tradition of using association to pursue common claims on political power-holders should not acquire this ability. It is not a particular 'civic culture' which is democracy's precondition, but the capacity to organise and associate in ways which hold power – private as well as public – to account.

In principle, a 'complete' democracy would exist only if everyone had entirely equal capacity to act collectively. Universal access to collective action plays the same role here as the ability of all to participate equally in public debate plays in theories of deliberative democracy, in whose ideal society all questions are settled by deliberation.[31] These ideal states have never been and will never be achieved. But moving as close as possible to them is a key goal of democratisation: the more people can act and speak about more issues, the more a society is democratic. No society will ever achieve a free and equal power to act for all. But all societies must be judged by how closely they move towards it.

An influential strain of analysis takes the opposing view, insisting that too much collective action by mass publics is a dire threat to democracy. Mass power in the streets, presumably a product of the 'working class authoritarianism' Lipset feared, is blamed, in this view, for the collapse of democratic regimes during the twentieth century.[32] But an important study by Nancy Bermeo[33] refutes this claim. In a wide-ranging examination of democratic breakdowns, beginning with democracy's collapse in Europe between the world wars and proceeding to authoritarian reversions in the global South later in the century, she shows that democracy was almost always defeated by elite disaffection, not mass rebellion. In some cases, collective action by people outside the elite did play a role, but largely as a support to elites' anti-democratic activity: it was never the prime cause of democracy's collapse. It was not the 'masses' who were unready for democracy but the elites.

Bermeo's evidence is crucial since it refutes the 'democratic elitist' claim that independently organised collective action outside the elite is a threat to democracy because mass publics are not refined enough to appreciate the system's merits and may rebel against it when it does not deliver outcomes to their liking. Far from showing that too much collective action is a threat to democracy, Bermeo's evidence suggests that the problem is not enough access to collective action, since a public better equipped and positioned to defend popular sovereignty may have been able to rescue democracy from those in its national elites who found popular sovereignty an obstacle to their interests.

Evidence that formal democracy does not need to be protected from citizens is found in the Afrobarometer data mentioned earlier. These data show both that most citizens across the continent value democracy and equally important, that they want more democratic government than they are getting. Data released in late 2016 show that 67 per cent of respondents across the continent prefer democracy to any other system – 78 per cent reject dictatorship and one-party rule. Demand for democracy among citizens declined for the first time in a decade, but is still higher than it was ten years ago. Afrobarometer also finds that 'popular demand for democracy still exceeds citizen perceptions of the available supply of democracy in most African countries (26 out of 36 in 2015)' – in other words, in most countries, citizens want more democracy than they are getting.[34]

This finding is consistent with global trends reported in surveys. The most recent World Values Survey (2010–2014) found 80 per cent support for democracy across the world;[35] a 2017 Pew Research Centre multi-country study found 78 per cent support for representative democracy and 66 per cent support for 'direct democracy'.[36] The support for direct democracy suggests a desire for more, not less, democracy, which is consistent with responses in older surveys of all five continents in which only 30 per cent agreed that their country is 'governed by the will of the people'. Only 37 per cent in North America and 31 per cent in Western Europe believed their countries were governed by the people's will.[37] Opinion surveys are, as suggested earlier, not always the best method of uncovering the subtleties of people's attitudes to politics. But the only available information on citizens' attitudes suggests that people do endorse democracy in substantial numbers and do want more of it. It erodes when citizens lack the power needed to prevent elites from depriving them of their freedoms, not when the people cannot appreciate the benefits of taking decisions.

Not all forms of collective action democratise power. All political events are in some way the product of collective action – even an *autogolpe*, a seizure of authoritarian power by an elected leader, needs the collective action of armed forces in support of the ruler. Since collective action by some interests is a constant and necessary feature of all societies, its mere presence does not guarantee or strengthen democracy. But it is only through collective action that citizens acquire the power to hold those who decide their fate to account – and it is only when they act together that democracy can endure and deepen. Democracy is born and democratisation occurs when the ability to act passes to social groups who have been excluded from decisions, when they use it to force their way into decision-making and when they do this in a way which extends the formal right to decide to all.

SUPPORTING AND MAINTAINING DEMOCRACY

Because democratic broadening and deepening depend on the degree to which ever-greater numbers of citizens can act increasingly effectively in concert to hold power-holders to account, collective action is essential to the maintenance of democracy. It broadens and deepens the system by ensuring that citizens can translate their right to sovereignty into an actual expression of citizenship. The more the capacity to act collectively within rules which respect others' right to do the same is diffused throughout a democracy, the more it broadens and deepens.

But collective action not only broadens and deepens democracy, it is also a support factor because it enables societies to become formal democracies. In one sense, this is obvious. Democracy does not emerge from a vacuum – people have to create it, even if they are a small elite, and they do so collectively. But more is claimed here. Democracy emerges in response to the collective action of social groups which are denied a share in decisions and who combine to claim a say in what is decided: 'For a society to become democratic, the power balance in civil society has to shift… Since the major power resource of the many is collective organization, their chance to organize in associations, unions and parties gains crucial significance.'[38] Democracy emerges when it is seen as the only system of government able to allow a share in decisions for social groups who believe themselves excluded from the exercise of sovereignty and are capable of acting in concert to change power relations.

The manner in which older democracies emerged supports this claim. Action by the labour movement, harking back at least to resistance to the anti-combination laws of early-nineteenth-century England, was the motor of democratic reform in Western Europe from the 1830s: 'This period of transition to democracy in Europe was also marked by the arrival of the organised working class.'[39] In the US, independence was achieved by the collective action of property- (and slave-) owning settlers who rebelled against English rule; democratic advances which extended and deepened the franchise were a consequence of collective action by excluded groups. Action by organised labour was often crucial in later movements which sought democracy. John Stephens notes: 'Capitalist development is associated with the rise of democracy in part because it is associated with a transformation of the class structure strengthening the working class'.[40] Combination in mass production factories, with the growth in bargaining power associated with the withdrawal of labour, provided a powerful spur to organisation and collective action which shaped Western European politics for much of the twentieth century.[41] Democratisation in Africa was often initiated by citizen protests against authoritarianism: 'Africa's regime transitions in the early 1990s usually began with popular protests'.[42]

This does not mean that the collective action which establishes democracy always takes the form of mobilisation by the people, although it often does. As a later chapter will argue, collective action is not public mobilisation alone – it includes the routine ways in which citizens engage with political authorities. It is also not essential that everyone, or even most people, who are denied the right to speak must act if democracy is to emerge – only some excluded groups with the capacity to act need to see extending the right to participate as essential to their exercise of voice.

Democracy was often initiated by emerging social and economic elites who felt excluded from the political order – business and professional classes, for example. Lipset notes that a middle class 'that can stand up against the state and provide the resources of independent groups' sustains democracy.[43] It seems fair to assume that it can also play a vital role in ensuring that it emerges. This is one of the arguments of a celebrated account of transition to democracy which is often seen as highly deterministic – that of Barrington Moore Jr – but which relies on the collective action of groups other than the popular classes to explain democracy's emergence: 'a vigorous class of town dwellers has been an indispensable element in the growth of parliamentary democracy'.[44] For Moore, modernisation entails a revolution from either above or below: this decides whether societies become democratic or authoritarian. A key trigger to democracy was a 'bourgeois revolution' in which trading and manufacturing classes in the cities developed an interest in inclusion and, often in alliance with other classes, swept away or recruited to their cause the obstacles to democratic progress.[45] But earlier, where it developed enough power to check the monarch, 'an independent nobility' became 'an essential ingredient in the growth of democracy'.[46] The common thread is that the class is excluded but has the capacity to act collectively to change that.

Moore could be seen to restate Lipset and Przeworski's stress on economic growth as a precondition – democracy, he believed, was impossible without a bourgeoisie which emerges when the economy develops. He also fails to explain realities in societies where democratic pressures are led by actors other than the bourgeois class, such as organised labour (which played a crucial role in achieving democracy in South Africa).[47] But he does draw attention to the role of collective action in democracy's emergence and growth. His work does not assume that a particular level of wealth is required for democracy – still less does it insist on cultural prerequisites. It asserts, rather, that democracy requires the emergence of a class of people with an interest in broadening and deepening the range of citizens included in decisions and the access to collective action and organisation which ensures that their voices are heard.

If democracy is to deepen and broaden, the ability to be heard must become more widely distributed. This will not happen unless groups who believe themselves excluded act to gain access to decisions. Whether their collective action produces greater democracy will depend on whether they believe its emergence and deepening offers them the best route to inclusion – this is not inevitable and economic elites sometimes force themselves into a political order which continues to exclude most of their fellow citizens. But, if collective action by excluded groups is not enough to ensure democracy, it is necessary if it is to emerge. Democracy cannot be born and continue to exist unless people acting collectively press for a voice in a way which requires that rights to participate are extended – that 'a share for the underlying population in the making of rules' is achieved.[48]

It was noted earlier that all political interventions are a consequence of collective action. So are all political systems, even monarchies. It requires collective action *of a particular sort* to create democracy, as Moore suggests – that of those who have, or believe they have, an interest in ending oligarchy. Where this exists, democracy will emerge, regardless of the level of economic growth.

The centrality of collective action in establishing and maintaining democracy is recognised implicitly by some mainstream theorists, although not in the form suggested here. Lipset acknowledged the role of conflict between organised interests engaged in collective action: 'Democratic rights have developed in societies largely through the struggles of various groups ... against one another and against the group which controls the state. Each interest group may desire to carry out its own will, but if no one group is strong enough to gain complete power, the result is the development of tolerance'.[49] Similarly, '[i]nstead of struggling to attain elite political power, various groups ... compete with one another and the state for popular attention, for the power to carry out their own agendas ... such opposition groups must legitimise themselves by encouraging the rights of other groups to oppose them, thus providing a basis for democracy'.[50] He recognised too the importance of pressures from below: 'To legitimise themselves, governmental parties, even though they did not like it, ultimately had to recognise the right of oppositions to exist and compete freely'.[51] While cultural bias prompted him to see these realities only in the North, at a particular level of industrial development, he does acknowledge collective action as a precondition both for democracy's emergence and for democratisation.

This stress on collective action, and hence on human agency, seeks to challenge the determinism which has – since Aristotle – coloured much discussion of the preconditions for democracy. It shares this view with the literature on democratic transitions which preceded the 'consolidation' literature.[52] By stressing the degree to which democracy's transitions from authoritarianism could grow from human agency in unlikely circumstances, the transition studies saw democratic prospects as open-ended and, therefore, a source of hope. Democracy, they suggested, could, in principle, emerge anywhere. The democratic wave which followed the Portuguese coup of 1974 excited the imagination because it seemed to challenge the assumption that democracy was available only to the few who lived in 'modern' societies – just as it offered fresh possibilities to societies such as South Africa, where it was widely assumed that there was no alternative to repression or revolution. The stress on collective action makes a similar claim: that human agency creates democracy and enables it to broaden and deepen.

To insist that collective action is the key motor of democracy's support and maintenance is not to ignore the role of social structures in shaping what human beings can and cannot do. Collective action is not purely a product of the will – conditions must exist which enable people to act to extend participation. Structural realities, including access to economic resources, may inhibit or even prevent collective action by much of the citizenry, leaving the field open to unaccountable and unresponsive power. Where formal democracies emerge in structural conditions which do not favour collective action at the grassroots, it will be very difficult for many or most to act collectively to claim, and retain, a share in decisions. While democracy might survive, its depth and reach may be restricted to a relative elite which can act together to defend its interests.

Identifying capacity to organise and act collectively as the element which determines whether democracy will emerge, and whether democracies offer their citizens what democratic theory promises, shifts the enquiry. Rather than viewing structural elements as inevitable obstacles, it sees them as constraints to or supports for the organised human agency which is essential if democracy's promise is to be brought to life. In apartheid South Africa, for example, a scarcity of trained labour forced the government to allow employers to hire black workers in skilled positions.[53] This increased worker bargaining power because it was more difficult to fire strikers – and made possible the labour action which did much to end apartheid. The constraints identified by those who insist on democratic preconditions matter, but only if they inhibit collective action. And where they do matter, they shape the terrain within which collective action is attempted. The future is not inevitable, but those who want to act are reminded of the constraints which they face.

Organised human agency may also play a role in shaping another key ingredient of democratic deepening: the growth of states strong and broad enough to protect the rights of citizens and ensure a framework for political participation. State-building is also not purely an act of political will. If active citizens – or key organised interests – demand functioning democratic institutions, it is not inevitable that power-holders will be forced to concede them. But, where formal democratic rights have been won by citizenries, the capacity to act may play a significant role in deciding whether state institutions capable of translating the will of most citizens into concrete outcomes emerge in reaction to the demand for accountability and responsiveness.

It is crucial to stress human agency in shaping democracy. But excitement at possibilities may have led scholars and activists to ignore the structural factors which enhance or impede action. Both agency and structure matter: there are preconditions to democracy's emergence and growth. But they are rooted not in levels of economic development or the inheritance of cultures, but in the degree to which citizens who need a say in decisions can act collectively to win, keep and strengthen democracy.

A FAIR SHARE? DEMOCRACY, COLLECTIVE ACTION AND INEQUALITY[54]

The centrality of collective action in maintaining and deepening democracy also enables us to address a key challenge to democracy's global resurgence: the apparent inability of democracies to translate the preferences of the poor and weak into concrete economic and social change. South Africa is hardly the only country in which democracy's critics blame it for not changing the lives of the poor.[55]

The democratic wave which began in 1974 has not enabled citizens to wield great influence over their material conditions. Decades ago, the prospect of democracy inspired revolutionaries and horrified elites, since both saw votes for all as a threat to social inequality. During the nineteenth century, thinkers assumed that democracy and social inequality could not co-exist: Marx expected that universal suffrage would mean the victory of working-class power, while conservatives rejected universal adult franchise for precisely this reason.[56] Once the right to decide was claimed by most citizens, those at the bottom of the pile would, it was assumed, use their power to secure more of society's resources.

But extending the vote to all did not end economic inequality. One reason is that Marx's claim that the working class formed 'the great majority of the population'[57] proved inaccurate: as Przeworski has shown,[58] nowhere was the proletariat defined by Marxist theory a majority. But another reason, as Marshall suggested, was that market economies made adjustments to accommodate the enfranchisement of workers: 'citizenship and the class system have been at war (and) the former has imposed modifications on the latter'.[59] As the vote was broadened, those who gained it used it to elect governments which reduced inequalities. As Schmitter's analysis of democracy's current crisis, discussed in chapter 1, points out, economic elites offered material concessions to ensure that workers were incorporated into the market economy and so did not favour revolution. The welfare state, underpinned by the notion that democratic governments owed their citizens social and economic entitlements as well as the protection of their persons and rights, was largely a product of the extension of the vote to all.

This apparent property of representative democracy was described, analysed – and advocated – in Marshall's *Citizenship and Social Class,*[60] which argued that political citizenship would inevitably become a vehicle for its social equivalent. The tension between granting citizenship to all but restricting economic benefits to a few could not endure, and the recognition that all should enjoy political rights would lead inevitably to less inequality as the poor used their franchise to erode it. A theoretical account of how this happens is offered by Przeworski's analysis of the way in which the growth of labour parties in democracies produced bargains which did not threaten the market economy's survival, but ensured rising living standards for the working class. The process which he analyses seems to confirm collective action's ability to ensure that governments respond to the will of the majority and so realise democracy's promise.[61]

Yet, while this may describe the emergence of the welfare state in the liberal democracies of Western Europe, it does not fit the wave of democratisation in the global South. The liberal democracy Marshall expected to confer 'social citizenship' is more evident than ever but has rarely if ever reduced inequality – widening or stable inequality is the norm.[62] Either citizens choose inequality or democracies have lost that ability, which Marshall observed, to translate public preferences into social policy. Evidence that most citizens do not endorse inequality is the election of redistributive governments in Latin America – or, in the years after democracy's establishment, Eastern European electorates' support for parties which promised economic change. The unwillingness or inability of many Eastern European governments to introduce policies which do redress inequality[63] suggests that the failure to change economic policy does not stem from citizen consent, but from new democracies' incapacity to respond to citizens' expressed wishes. Is popular sovereignty not, then, an illusion – either because formal democracy always was a fig leaf masking the domination of the economically powerful or because the global economy rendered it so?

If democracy's capacity to ensure popular sovereignty depends on the distribution of collective action in society, we should not be surprised to see democracy failing to translate aspirations for greater equality into policy since formal democracy has not been accompanied by greater access by the poor to collective action. What people want does not automatically translate into policy, law or action. It does this only if it is expressed in organised collective action; and, because no group with a common interest constitutes a majority, preference becomes policy only when action produces coalitions able to shape the agenda. The difference between the democracy described by Marshall and Przeworski and that which we observe today lies not in the triumph of a particular economic recipe or mysterious changes in democracy's properties, but in highly unequal access to collective action. Marshall's 'social citizenship' was the outcome less of an inevitable democratic logic than of a moment in history when those with an interest in change – workers – could also engage in organised collective action. Democracies co-exist with inequality now not only because of the factors Schmitter mentions, but also because those with an interest in greater equality lack the capacity for effective collective action.

Democratic politics which tackled inequality was historically the product of an alliance between organised labour and other interests – a coalition which labour, by virtue of its numbers and organisation, led. In most new democracies, organised labour is too small or weak or both to lead a coalition for change. In South Africa, trends towards casual, dispersed and informal work have eroded labour's bargaining power, ensuring that worker organisation cannot achieve redistribution.[64] Organisational weaknesses have also prevented unions from engaging in the collective action which might produce change.[65] Similar trends are apparent in, for example, Argentina.[66] This means that most of those with an interest in redistribution do not enjoy the potential for organisation which would enable them to get what they want.

This emphasis on access to collective action offers a more plausible account of new democracies' inability to translate aspirations to greater equality into law and policy than the most frequently cited explanation, the power of the global economy.

Globalisation: The Opiate of the Intellectuals?

Across the political spectrum, all are agreed that 'globalisation', the power of the global market, exists and has sharply narrowed the options of states. It is often offered as an explanation for why new democracies (and, increasingly, older democracies too) cannot achieve the economic change which would enable them to address poverty.

But what is globalisation and does it really prevent states from doing what their citizens want? Changes in communications technology mean that information and culture travel across national boundaries far more easily than before. This has inevitable political and economic effects. But globalisation's power in people's minds (and, therefore, in policy-making) may be more real than its impact on the world. Schmitter observes: 'Politicians and scholars, active citizens and passive spectators … all invoke its omnipresence and omnipotence when trying to make sense of the multitude of uncertainties which surround them'.[67] This makes 'globalisation' powerful whether or not it actually exists: 'globalisation may not even exist in any material sense, but if enough people (and, especially, enough highly placed and resourceful people) believe that it is present and potent, then it will produce a significant effect by anticipated reaction'.[68] There is little doubt that the perception of globalisation shapes economic and political responses across the planet. But if it does not 'exist in any material sense', or if its effect is far less important than we are told, the obstacles it is said to pose to popular sovereignty might disappear if people who take decisions recognise that they are not blocked from pursuing options which seem best for their societies.

What reasons are there for suggesting that 'globalisation' does not prevent states from doing what their voters want? While technological change has opened unprecedented possibilities for the movement of information and capital across national borders, it has had no similar effect on the movement of goods, since the volume of international trade in the 1990s was no greater than at the turn of the previous century.[69] Nor, in purely numerical terms, has it generated cross-border movements of people greater than those at the beginning of the twentieth century.[70] To deny that capital flows across borders hold implications for governments would be foolish since they give investors more accessible exit options than in the past, limiting the scope for state intervention which investors dislike. But the limits may be far more limited than they seem.

First, the size of capital flows, while substantial in the context of small Southern economies, is often grossly exaggerated: in 1993, the peak year of 'emerging market' investment, only about three per cent of Northern investment was diverted from domestic use – the entire post-1990 'boom' in this investment diverted only about 0.5 per cent of the North's capital to the South.[71]

Second, states survive and retain much of their power despite movements of capital: however dysfunctional states may be, their elites or citizens or both seem to cling to them tenaciously. In Africa, where the weakness of the state is most pronounced, and in which current state boundaries are merely colonial administrative creations, the vast majority of states face no attempts by rebels to opt out. Citizens still expect the state to respond to their needs: Dahl suggested that 'people in democratic countries may want more governmental action, not less, simply in order to counter the adverse effects of international markets'.[72] A growing body of opinion suggests that traditional social democratic parties have been deserted by voters in many countries[73] not because they favour excessive meddling in the global marketplace but because they are too willing to accept the power of the market.

Third, inequities in capital accumulation between states preceded cross-border capital flows and are not caused by them. Common sense suggests that, before countries can become vulnerable to capital exports, they need private businesses with significant capital to move abroad. The oft-lamented 'marginalisation' of sections of the globe –Africa primary among them – is, therefore, a consequence not of excessive penetration by global capital, but of its opposite, the tendency for capital to avoid these regions, and of a lack of a domestic capital base sufficient to spur growth. Poor countries do, therefore, retain the option of seeking to build their domestic capital stocks, and, if 'globalisation' has any economic effect at all, it lies in a denial of opportunity, not of sovereignty. In some cases, the ability to move capital across boundaries can be a plus for Southern countries, enabling them to benefit from money sent home by expatriates living in the North. Even in a 'globalised' world – and across great distances – the call of kin and country continues to influence economic behaviour.

Fourth, while middle-income countries such as Brazil and Korea are vulnerable to capital exports by domestic investors during times of economic stress, this capital tends to return once domestic prospects improve. In South Africa in the years immediately after democracy was achieved, domestic capital which left tended not to return.[74] The difference stems from differing relations between domestic business classes and the state: while in Brazil and Korea, the owners of capital are fairly 'rooted' in their domestic states, those in South Africa are not. So, while domestic investors' capacity to export capital may give owners more options, whether and to what extent they do this depends on politics in individual states.

Fifth, direct foreign investment is not a cause but a consequence of growth in late economic developers.[75] Countries' growth prospects do not depend at the crucial initial stages on their ability to attract foreign investment, but on its domestic equivalent. This explains the disappointment of African and Eastern European states which faithfully applied the proposed recipe for attracting foreign investment but found that the promised bounty failed to appear. Investors are influenced by opportunities for profit, and these are available only if domestic investment, which depends crucially on politics, fuels growth. Contrary to an orthodoxy which restricts the role of the state, particularly in the South, to creating an environment friendly to global capital, countries which chart growth paths do so by stimulating domestic investors, ensuring growth rates which may attract their foreign counterparts.

While international economic inequalities are part of the reality with which new democracies in the South must contend, they do not prevent domestic policy from tackling poverty and inequality. Global developments have not deprived states of their power to address inequities, and the reason why formal democracy has failed to turn citizen preferences into policy lies at home.

Isolating the Poor

New democracies have not addressed inequality because its defenders are much better able to act in their interests than are its opponents. But popular mainstream development approaches to poverty make the prospect that the poor will be heard much less likely by isolating those who lack access to the collective action which would enable them to be heard from those who have it in abundance.

The approach which separates the poor from any hope of political influence is 'targeted social policy' which claims to ensure that anti-poverty programmes reach only the 'poorest of the poor' – an attractive goal until we examine its political effect. Its most influential promoter was initially the World Bank, which, until a shift in policy in 2004, effectively depoliticised poverty and inequality. In its concern to ensure that support reached only the poor,[76] it set a poverty level of $1 per person a day (now $2) and defined all those below it as the 'poor' and all above it as the 'non-poor'. It then claimed a conflict of interest between the two, insisting that measures which reach the 'non-poor' deprived the poor of resources. Its aim was to frame policies perfectly targeted to bypass the 'non-poor' as they reach the 'poor'. This approach remains influential in thinking about social policy today[77] – it also retains an influence on thinking in South Africa.[78]

The standard was arbitrary – those who earn just above $1 a day, and are classed as 'non-poor', may be in dire need. This approach also made democratic action against poverty almost impossible, prompting the Bank to convene, in 1999, a meeting of scholars to advise it on why governments were not 'pro-poor'. An examination of literature on the politics of social policy would have saved it the trouble. In his study of the creation of welfare state systems in Western Europe and the US,

Abram de Swaan argues that a crucial element in elites' willingness to address poverty and inequality was the development among them of a 'social consciousness' whose elements are an awareness of the interdependence of all social groups, a realisation that elites bear some responsibility for the sufferings of the poor, and a belief that efficacious means of assisting the poor exist or might be created.[79] This begs the question of how elites might come to hold these attitudes. The Bank's approach was almost sure to ensure that they would not since it separated those at the bottom of the ladder from the rest of society, and ruled out alliances between those who lacked the muscle to be heard and those who had it.

Because the poor are rarely able to organise themselves, social policy which aims to reduce poverty and inequality tends to win elite political support in two circumstances. The first is where changes are accepted because they are based on norms which cross class and interest barriers: the need to cater for Civil War veterans ensured a generous social policy regime in the US, despite American resistance to social spending, because it tapped into widespread support for soldiers who had defended the Union.[80] The second occurs where policy is supported by a significant interest group – historically, organised labour – which is able to forge alliances with other interests who also stand to benefit from action against inequality. Labour has always needed the support of other interests to achieve policy change,[81] but in South Africa (and elsewhere) organised labour led the pressure for redistribution: it was unions who initiated the post-1994 government's Reconstruction and Development Programme (RDP). It is hard to see how a successful attempt to create a more inclusive economy could ignore the unions, despite their current weakness, even though they would probably not play as central a role as in the past.[82] Without collective action and alliances, redistribution is unlikely.

Given these realities, separating the poor from the rest of the society – and insisting that their interests are in conflict with those of other groups – is certain to relegate their concerns to the peripheries, rendering democracies unable to address poverty or inequality. By creating an antagonism between the poor and other strata, the possibility of social consensus is excluded. It also eliminates the prospect of alliances between the poor and more organised and influential groups. The only mystery about the tendency of governments not to be 'pro-poor' in these circumstances is that anyone should see it as a mystery. Since the poor are usually the least influential group in society, the approach excludes them from policy influence. The hostility towards welfare recipients in the US,[83] who are distinguished from the social mainstream by race and (often) gender as well as social class, provides a useful illustration– so do constant complaints in South Africa that social grants create 'dependence'. If a contest for resources is created between the 'non-poor' and the 'poor', the former will use its influence on public opinion to deny the claims of the latter.

'Targeted' social policy separates the poor from those interests with access to collective action, ensuring that those who command the means to actualise popular sovereignty will not use it to champion the poor. While in South Africa and elsewhere it is usually justified by the claim that it is giving priority to the 'poorest of the poor', its effect is to marginalise the poor, not to place them at the centre of the discussion. By creating a wall between the 'poor' and 'non-poor', 'targeted' policy removes the incentive for better-organised interests to encourage collective action among the poor, ensuring that their concerns will remain unheard.

This section is not meant to offer a full discussion of the limits and possibilities of strategies to fight poverty and inequality in democratic societies. It aims, rather, to address the claim that democracy – and collective action – are now incapable of challenging poverty and inequality. It has tried to show that it is neither the workings of the global economic system nor formal democracy's properties which have ensured that the extension of formal democratic rights has usually not produced the capacity to address social inequality. The history of Western European labour movements discussed by Przeworski shows that, where the poor enjoy access to the means of collective action, they use it to force policy changes which redistribute resources. It is not democracy which obstructs greater social equity but highly unequal access to collective action. Democracy offers the poor and the weak the means to win material gains through the exercise of popular sovereignty – but only if they enjoy sufficient access to the means of collective action and the share in popular sovereignty which it produces to turn democracy's potential into reality.

4

Colonisation of a Sympathetic Type?
The Culture of Democracy

Does democracy mean the same to everyone? Or does our culture determine what sort of democracy we want or whether we want democracy at all? Are Africans who declare democracy – or the type of democracy currently practised on the continent – a Western imposition expressing a truth or missing the point?

The earlier discussion mentioned the constant refrain of authoritarian governments and Northern cultural supremacists that Africans, Asians, Eastern Europeans, Muslims or some Latin Americans are 'not ready for democracy'.[1] But similar arguments are made by scholars and commentators whose concern is precisely the opposite – to insist on the right of other cultures to avoid Western imposition. They seek not to show that Southern cultures are not yet ready for democracy, but that Northern imposition on the South of particular understandings of democracy, or democracy itself, is a form of cultural imperialism which ignores the understandings of governance held by the cultures of the South.

Whether this view has any merit depends in part on how democracy is understood. The view supported here is that democracy is the right of human beings to choose. If we view democracy as popular sovereignty, it does not seek to impose values but to ensure that values are freely determined by all, not imposed by elites. If this imposes on people, there must be societies in which people freely decide that they do not want to take decisions which affect them – they choose not to choose.

The idea that the right to choose is a Western cultural imposition seems odd when we consider that Western powers have been chiefly concerned to deny people in the South that right. The record of major powers in limiting Southern choices during the Cold War is well known. In Africa, it dates from the first months of independence, with the overthrow of Patrice Lumumba's elected Congolese government.[2] Chapter 2 has noted the use of Northern power to erode or deny popular sovereignty in the South where it was seen to threaten the North's strategic interests during the Cold War or, latterly, to aid Islamic fundamentalism. In these and other cases, the West has sought not to force other countries to choose, but to deny them choice when it clashes with Western interests. To claim that colonisers impose freedom of choice is to ignore colonisation's chief role: to deny popular sovereignty to the colonised. Popular sovereignty challenges colonisation; it does not endorse it.

Of course, critics of democracy as a cultural imposition are not saying that Western powers should decide for people in the South – they insist that people in Africa or Asia must decide for themselves. The debate hinges on which African or Asian people should decide. If we recall that democracy is a system in which every person has an equal right to decide, it can be a form of cultural imperialism only if there is something in the culture of (some) Africans or Asians which prompts many people to want others to decide for them. To support this claim, it is not enough to show that those who dominate – elites or men or members of the dominant ethnic group – believe they should decide for others, a claim which they make repeatedly: it is common for African or Asian anti-democrats who wield power to insist that they represent the 'true' indigenous culture which African or Asian democrats have rejected.[3] After all, the anti-democrats are not losing the right to decide, so they do not lose their share of sovereignty if democracy is denied. If democracy is foreign to indigenous culture, then people who are not allowed a say must be happy to be led by others because their belief system says that this is just.

Scholars who seek to defend Africa from Northern imposition by showing that citizens in the South reject popular sovereignty understand this. They want to show not that Africans reject particular ways of governing themselves, but that they want to be governed by others. And so the protest against imperialism is forced to join Lipset and others in arguing that popular sovereignty is foreign to Southern culture because people in Africa or Asia want elites to dominate them. While Lipset assumes that Africans are not good enough for democracy, this view suggests that democracy is not good enough for Africans.

DIFFERENT STROKES FOR DIFFERENT FOLKS: CULTURAL RELATIVISM AS POPULAR DISEMPOWERMENT

Consider the study of Botswana by the celebrated anthropologists John and Jean Comaroff published two decades ago.[4] The authors challenged the Northern tendency to 'ascribe the recent push for democracy in many parts of the world to the … "triumph" of the free market over communism' and the 'hegemonic, indeed ontological, association in the West of freedom and self-expression with choice'.[5] They seek to develop a specifically African understanding of democracy,[6] and they do this by questioning support in Botswana, a long-time multi-party democracy, for freely choosing leaders. First, they report significant support for the idea of a one-party state. This, they say, surfaced in 1974, after the country's third general election. Support for a one-party state was shared by opposition and government supporters: it was not engineered by party bosses, and its advocates insisted that one-partyism would bring a more participatory democracy.[7] The Comaroffs explain this as an expression of traditional cultural understandings of good government which, in their view, place great emphasis on traditional hierarchy.

While Botswana has held regular multi-party elections since independence, voters, the authors argue, believe they are electing a chief, not a president. Percentage polls drop dramatically when presidents seek re-election because part of the public believes there is no need to re-elect a president (chiefs are not re-elected) and so 'do not go to the polls until a new president is chosen'.[8] Voters also see no need to vote when they are happy with government performance, and low polls are therefore a sign of approval. Further evidence of Batswana voters' devotion to leaders is said to be a survey conducted by the authors which found that only 45 per cent of people questioned knew the name of their parliamentary representative. This is said to confirm that voters adhere to the Tswana tradition in which 'a leader is responsible for the personnel of his/her regime'.[9]

The Comaroffs are not trying to show that the Batswana are not ready for democracy. They want, they say, a '[re]turn to substantive democracy' and reject 'the chimera that freedom is the right to choose'. They therefore reject the 'Western model' and 'spoke of a specifically African alternative'.[10] But this claim is barely distinguishable from Lipset's. If we understand democracy as popular sovereignty, the Batswana voters described by the Comaroffs are not yearning for a fuller and richer share in decisions – they long, instead, for a social order in which they have far less right to decide. They are relinquishing their claims to sovereignty to a leader they want no part in choosing. If the authors are right, they are correct to insist that Batswana are rejecting the right to choose. What their analysis never shows, however, is why this should be a richer form of democracy rather than much less democracy – or none at all. If they are right, so is Lipset: Batswana have no wish to choose leaders, and their multi-party democracy is not an expression of their desire to govern themselves but a cultural imposition which ignores their wishes.

But the evidence shows that the authors are not right. Much of their argument rests on the claim that there is significant support for a one-party state in Botswana. But the only evidence cited is a discussion over 40 years ago. If Batswana really wanted a one-party state, they clearly did not feel strongly enough to demand it. No debate over the merits of one-party rule has raged in Botswana in the ensuing four decades. Nor do voters turn out in large numbers only when a new president is elected. In 1994, when President Ketumile Masire was re-elected, national turnout was 76.6 per cent, almost the highest since independence. Similarly, President Festus Mogae was re-elected in 2004 in a 76.2 per cent poll. The authors' argument is based on a single low poll – that in 1974, when only 31.2 per cent voted.[11] So there is no cultural tendency to avoid elections if a president is being re-elected. That only 45 per cent of voters could recognise the name of their representative may sound like a sign of indifference – until we discover that three-quarters or more of voters in two European democracies, Portugal and Spain, could not identify a single candidate contesting their elections. In that exemplary democracy Sweden, fewer voters than in Botswana – 33 per cent – knew the names of their representatives.[12] So Batswana voters seem more interested in their leadership choices than Northern voters do.

The Comaroffs' argument is more nuanced and less like Lipset's than this analysis has suggested. This is evident not only in other parts of the article, but also in a book chapter they published later which spells out their position in greater detail and responds to some points made here.[13] They argue that the traditional vehicle of Tswana democracy, the *kgotla* system, 'has remained a crucial element in the political *imaginaire* of Botswana'[14] – it shapes how citizens think about democracy. In their earlier article, they argue that the traditional Tswana view of democracy understands the relation between government and the governed differently to Western thought. It is marked by 'perfect freedom of debate' – all male citizens were entitled to a voice. A chief, the authors add, is meant to rule 'with' the people: the most quoted adage in the Tswana political lexicon is 'a chief is chief by the nation'.[15] Competitive politics was also reportedly a feature: 'support and opposition for the ruler tended to be articulated around identifiable *factions*'.[16]

They expand on this in the chapter, arguing that unhappiness with multi-party democracy in Botswana stems from a desire for a richer democratic system than that offered by multi-party democracy, which in their view reduces 'the Idea of Democracy to the exercise of choice'.[17] The *kgotla* was 'more than a forum for the discussion of social policy, although it certainly was that too'. It was also

> (i) a context for ongoing discourse about governance and sovereign authority
> – and, simultaneously, (ii) a space of contestation in which the powers of

a living ruler were negotiated and given social currency. Its primary constituencies were factions rather than political parties, one a chiefly bloc and
the other an opposition. These constituencies, patently, did not differentiate
themselves according to ideology or matters of principle ... In striking contrast to Western nation-states, where policy is seen from within to be the
provenance of partisan politics, here it was taken to be a *product* of public
discourse.[18]

So the problem is not that Batswana reject 'Western' democracy because it is too
democratic (in the sense that it does not show enough deference to leaders), but
because it is not democratic enough: it substitutes the occasional choice between
political parties for the richness of traditional democracy.

In their chapter, the Comaroffs answer the objection made here – that election
turnouts do not support their analysis. They say they did not conduct election
studies during 1994 and 2004, but they suggest that the turnout of over 76 per cent
was achieved in 1994 because 'President Quett Masire's regime was under fire for
its lackluster performance in office'.[19] The 2004 high turnout 'seems to have sparked
public interest largely because of internal politics within the ruling party, due in
some measure to the entry of Seretse Ian Khama, son of Seretse Khama, into its
leadership cadres – and the longer run prospect of a succession struggle that this
heralded'. They add: 'Both explanations would, if correct, be consistent with our
analysis'.[20] They do not say why, but the answer is presumably that, in the first case,
voters were acting on the custom of taking to task the performance of a chief who
was believed to be failing his people, while in the second they were moved by the
role of the son of the country's first president (who happened also to be a chief). But
they do acknowledge that Batswana electoral politics today is not the traditional
system grafted onto a constitutional shell: '[this] ... is not to say that the electoral
process mimicked the workings of the *kgotla*, past or present. The politics of the
nation-state were *not* those of the chiefship writ large, nor are they today'.[21]

The clarification is open to challenge: why would voters show their unhappiness
with Masire by going to the polls in large numbers to return his party to office?
Even if 2004 voters were expecting a succession struggle in the future, why would
this prompt them to vote? But this is far less important than the implication of the
Comaroffs' view for our understanding of democracy. Their critique of multi-party
democracy insists that traditional Tswana democracy was 'substantive' while that
in the West is purely 'procedural'.[22] But, while this may accurately describe how
some Batswana and some Westerners think about democracy, is the traditional
Tswana democracy they describe really inconsistent with Botswana's multi-party

arrangement? And, while Batswana may well reject democratic elitism's claim that choosing leaders is enough, why would they insist that democracy means not choosing at all?

We will discuss multi-party democracy and its critique by African political thinkers later. But it is difficult to understand what sets off the Comaroffs' understanding of Tswana democracy from that discussed here. With the obvious exception that chiefs were not elected, most of the uniquely Tswana perspectives they describe seem like standard democratic attitudes. The stress on the right to voice, the accountability and responsibility of leadership to the governed, and the right to form parties or factions (who do sometimes seek to remove chiefs and choose others) are all basic to democracy understood as popular sovereignty. Far from evidence of cultural exceptionalism, the fact that so many of the features which we associate with democracy were present in traditional Tswana polities seems to confirm that the demand to share in decisions is a human trait, not a cultural preference. It suggests that, like citizens the world over, Batswana want to be heard, and to hold their leaders to account.

Some of the forms democracy is said to take in Botswana may differ from practices in other democracies. The authors cite a 1980 account of Parliament which does not mirror the 'standard' multi-party form: the divide, they say, is not between government and opposition but between ministers and governing party MPs – opposition parties sometimes support the ministers they are meant to oppose. This is said to introduce into a multi-party assembly the patterns of the *kgotla*.[23] But this is not an exclusively African approach – members of the US Congress might oppose their own party and support colleagues in the opposition. Even if it is uniquely African, it is hard to see why this displays a different approach to democracy to that discussed here. Some other supposedly authentically African forms seem to differ little from practices in other democracies. Political parties are said to have little presence on the ground between elections, showing that they are really more like the factions which play a key role in the *kgotla*;[24] at governing party election meetings, '[s]peakers tended to line up into blocs of pro- and antagonists – the former being local party members, the latter, a coalition of dissent',[25] repeating the pattern of the *kgotla*. But Botswana is surely not the only democracy in which parties have little presence on the ground. On the contrary, complaints that political parties have become little more than vote-getting machines at election time are common in Northern democracies.[26] And Batswana are surely not the only voters to demand better from their MPs at party meetings.

Finally, the authors clarify their claim that multi-party democracy reduces 'the Idea of Democracy to the exercise of choice' by comparing the options which democracy offers to those offered by advertising to consumers.[27] But in what way is it possible for people to govern themselves without choosing who is to occupy government office? And why is choosing between political parties equivalent to shopping? People may choose parties because they are expressing their identity or demanding social justice or rejecting cultural domination. This is not only an exercise of popular sovereignty but an important form of self-expressions. In India, the poor vote more than others – research shows that 'the poor think of voting as a dignifying right'.[28]

Elections are not purely procedural. Voting can have a huge material impact on people's lives. We will see in a later chapter that many South Africans are alive today only because of voting, which shaped whether they would die of AIDS: that is surely as substantive as an outcome can be. The view that there is far more to democracy than voting in elections is not a challenge to mainstream understandings of democracy: it is widely accepted by the 'consolidation' paradigm, which would no doubt see Tswana democracy as a contradiction in terms. Democracy is never purely procedural – if it does not enable people to make substantive decisions about real issues, it is not democracy. Why does renouncing the right to choose leaders make democracy more 'substantive'? This is only one of the range of choices which are integral to democracy: in principle, citizens should be free to choose policies and how they should be implemented, engaging in precisely the deliberation which is said to be crucial to Tswana democracy. Without the right to choose, citizens will be dominated by elites who will choose for them – a richer and deeper democracy is one in which more people make more choices about an ever-widening array of issues.

The Comaroffs' critique is not aimed at democracy as it is understood here, although they dismiss democracy as a 'small idea'.[29] It is, rather, a response to a particular understanding of democracy. Northern democracy promoters do often appear to be peddling a political order which has very little to do with democracy as it is understood here, one in which citizens of the global South can choose any policies they like, as long as power-holders in the North like them too – we saw something of this in the mainstream's reaction to Palestinian democracy. It is this to which the Comaroffs' critique seems directed, not democracy. They note: 'Given their own conception of participatory politics, their own ideologies of sovereign authority, legitimacy, and accountability, it is obvious why so many citizens of Botswana were alienated by the Western model, *at least as presented to them*'.[30] This, of course, acknowledges that the hollowed-out procedural democracy against which Tswana thought is said to rebel is not necessarily the genuine article and is, rather, a caricature peddled by some in the North who are more interested in turning Southern societies into clones of their (imagined) societies than in empowering their citizens.

More importantly perhaps, they add that voices in Botswana 'called for a vernacular, indigenously rooted version of the kind of liberal democracy that Euromodernity has long idealized but scarcely realized – let alone implanted successfully elsewhere, especially when other interests have intervened'.[31] This gets to the heart of the matter: the issue is not the smallness or irrelevance of democracy, but that the version sold to or imposed on the South is a pale shadow of the genuine article. It is also that the peddlers of 'democracy' are more interested in selling a set of institutions and ways of arranging politics than with supporting the right of citizens to govern themselves. These important complaints about the way in which particular understandings of democracy are imposed on Africans and others in the global South should not be confused with a critique of democracy which implies that Africans – or anyone else – prefer being led to controlling their own lives, a claim for which no supporting evidence exists.

Dialogue of the Deaf?

A study of political culture in the Buganda region of Uganda by a student of the Comaroffs, Mikael Karlstrom, takes the cultural imposition argument much further and offers none of the nuance with which Batswana democracy is discussed.[32] It merits discussion here because it is more representative of thinking which belittles African democracy by claiming to validate it than the discussion of Botswana.

Karlstrom too does not want to argue that Africans are not ready for democracy – they are, in his view, 'by no means uninterested in democracy' – but he insists that they envision a democracy which 'does differ significantly from Western liberal conceptions'.[33] In his zeal to demonstrate this point, he unwittingly demonstrates that the Baganda's understanding of democracy may be more accurate and more consistent with the understanding of democracy discussed here than his own.

Baganda, he writes, understand democracy as 'freedom from oppression' which is 'undoubtedly' an outcome of the region's lengthy battle with the Ugandan state for the restoration of the Baganda kingdom. He asserts, without supporting evidence, that they see oppression not as freedom from 'excessive state power' but as a symptom of 'authority which has lost its anchor': 'Liberty in its most basic sense is thus a concomitant of a rightly ordered polity oriented around a properly and firmly installed ruler'. When asked to name the liberties which are central to the freedom they seek, Bugandans reportedly emphasise freedom of speech – but this 'is not speech directed towards a general audience of equals, but rather the speech of subjects directed towards their ruler'.[34]

This freedom of speech 'differs from a general Western liberal conception in that it is rooted, not in a model of politics as competition for power among the plural representatives of various political views, but rather in a model of legitimate *unitary* authority as founded on the willingness of power-holders to hear the voice of their subjects'.[35] Another key element in this concept of democracy is 'the fair and impartial judgment of disputes and court cases'. But this does not mean 'Western egalitarianism' – the concern is 'narrower': for a 'situational equality of subjects before a power-holder ... rather than an ontological equality of persons'.[36]

Further examples would belabour the point – that when Baganda talk of democracy they do not mean popular sovereignty, but their desire to be ruled by a monarch who is fair and listens to his or her subjects. This explains two other attitudes claimed by Karlstrom – disenchantment with political parties,[37] and enthusiasm for the then prevailing 'no-party' system of Ugandan president Yoweri Museveni which permitted elected representative government but banned parties. All Ugandans were assumed to belong to his National Resistance Movement and could stand for office, but not as party candidates.[38] This system, Karlstrom writes, fits Ugandan understandings of democracy. To reject it is cultural arrogance '[b]ecause the democratic project is everywhere emergent and incomplete, the West, despite its historical priority, can claim no monopoly of its current and future forms or definitions'.[39]

This defence of African political leaderships which limit democracy was born of an understandable desire to refute the charge that Africans and Asians were incapable of establishing democracies – or that only the Western democratic form is really democratic. But its effect is to legitimise power-holders who deny citizens the right to decide. It does not strike a blow at Western assumptions of superiority – it insists that Africans do not want to govern themselves, that they are indeed not ready for democracy (and perhaps never will be). But it produces no credible evidence in support of this claim.

The clash between democracy and African cultural understandings is as illusory in Uganda as in Botswana. Karlstrom makes no allowance for the possibility that people living in a political order in which parties are banned from contesting elections may not be entirely forthcoming when asked by social scientists what they think of parties. They may be saying what they feel the authorities would like them to say because they want to avoid trouble. Karlstrom's claimed consensus in support of 'no-partyism' fails to explain why, after multi-party elections were conceded by Museveni in 2006, there were significant claims of irregularity; the opposition candidate was jailed on charges widely assumed to be prompted by the fact that he was challenging Museveni at the polls.[40] If there was consensus in support of 'no-party' rule, none of this would be needed – the opposition candidate would have been shunned by Ugandans as an agent of division. Also, Karlstrom assumes that there is only one Baganda view of democracy which can be detected by anthropology – the possibility that residents of Buganda, like everyone else, hold differing views is not entertained. And so the consequence is a cultural stereotyping which is little different from that of those who make sweeping claims about 'African culture' and its presumed incompatibility with democracy.

The evidence marshalled by Karlstrom in favour of his claims suggests, ironic-ally, that popular enthusiasm for democracy is as strong in Buganda as in Botswana. Quotes from interviewees which he presents as evidence of cultural difference tell us that the right to be heard by power-holders and to receive an accountable response is essential to Bugandan understandings of democracy. Interviewees stressed the need to be heard, to 'have my ideas and they must be taken into consideration', that 'people must be entitled to speak openly and have your point answered'. Democracy, an interviewee sums up, means that 'we can stand up and say something and the authority listens to it'. Karlstrom claims that these understandings differ from those in the West because they are not directed towards an audience of equals 'but [are] rather the speech of subjects directed towards their ruler'.[41]

It is unclear why 'Westerners' are assumed to speak to equals rather than rulers. Some theorists of deliberative democracy might wish this to be so, but that does not make it real – others see democracy as a system in which citizens force gov-ernment to listen; witness Tilly's definition in chapter 2. And democratic elitists, who are impeccably Western, would find these Ugandan understandings of dem-ocracy too egalitarian because they do not show enough respect for the right of elites to rule. The Bugandan view Karlstrom describes would fit neatly into many 'Western' understandings of democracy. He distributes his cultural stereotypes even-handedly: just as he has no room for Bugandan residents who differ, so he assumes that all 'Westerners' view democracy alike.

This tendency to set up a reified and misleading set of ideas labelled 'Western democracy' and to contrast it with the opinion of Baganda interviewees is repeated when Karlstrom discusses ideas of justice and equity. Interviewees say leaders ought to be 'honest' and 'fair-minded', that democracy is a system in which people are not discriminated against by their ruler and in which 'you give an opinion and it is not ignored but *is also considered and a decision is made taking it into account*'.[42] Karlstrom claims these are not conventional 'Western' understandings because they 'presuppose the existence of a legitimate authority capable of dealing judi-cially with violations of certain basic norms and rights'.[43] Even a passing knowledge of democratic theory would question why any of this breaks with 'Western' understandings. Anarchism aside, no democratic theorists in the West or anywhere else would imagine that democracies could survive without legitimate authority able to deal judicially with rights violations. Karlstrom repeatedly cites attitudes among his Baganda interviewees which are regularly expressed by intellectuals and 'ordinary' citizens in North America and Western Europe, and then insists that, because they do not conform to his own abstract and often eccentric understanding of democratic thinking in the North, they express different values. Despite the trappings of cultural tolerance in which his argument is presented, it comes close to suggesting that his African interviewees are simply not available for a democracy in which authority is bestowed by the people and government requires a continuing popular mandate.

Why devote this much attention to showing that residents of African rural areas understand democracy far more accurately than some Northern scholars believe they do (or, perhaps, than those scholars do themselves)? Because the notion that certain understandings of democracy are foreign concepts imposed on other cultures is an oft-voiced complaint. As this discussion has tried to show, the notion has merit when it shows that some Northern understandings assume that the world must conform to a particular (but always undefined) democratic shape and form. But it often does not stop at making the point, made repeatedly here, that democracies can take on many shapes and forms as long as they enable popular sovereignty. It often lapses into denying that the desire for self-government crosses cultural boundaries.

It is no accident that these arguments are repeatedly made by Southern elites determined to protect themselves against popular sovereignty – Museveni has insisted that he was offering a more culturally authentic model of democracy. The key divide is whether it is assumed that human beings, whatever their beliefs and cultural practices, want a say in decisions which affect them. If they do, popular sovereignty is not a cultural imposition but a universal human need – and right – and no ruler can deny citizens their right to speak, act and choose by claiming to defend cultural authenticity. To insist that Africans embrace beliefs which recognise that leaders should deny them the right to decide endorses the denial to Africans – or whoever else is assumed to hold a cultural objection to deciding for themselves – of the right to be heard and to share in decision-making. Ironically, the desire to reject the thinking which leads Lipset to insist that hundreds of millions of people are not ready for democracy ends up making much the same claim.

POPULAR SOVEREIGNTY IN A LOCAL IDIOM

Given the arguments advanced here, it is no surprise that important African intellectual perspectives not only question the notion that African culture is not open to democracy, but also see these claims, by implication, as a convenient fig leaf for autocrats, and a denial of the repeated attempts by African citizens to exercise popular sovereignty.

First, they point out that appeals to 'African culture' ignore the diversity of cultures on the continent. Kwame Anthony Appiah points out: 'Whatever Africans share, we do not have a common traditional culture, common language, a common religion or conceptual vocabulary … we do not even belong to a common race'.[44] Much the same point can be made about Asian or indigenous Latin American (or European or North American) culture. The scholarship discussed here does not claim that political culture in Africa is uniform. But to assume a common set of political values and attitudes among particular ethnic or national groups (such as the Batswana or Baganda) may be as much a problem as the generalisations which Appiah rejects because that assumption, too, imposes a uniformity which ignores differing voices.

Analyses which claim that a 'pure' traditional culture is opposed to popular sovereignty also ignore the reality that there are no 'pure' cultures anywhere since 'foreign influences' have affected all cultures: 'Nobody reproaches Africa for importing its official languages, its main religions, its foodstuffs or its durable goods … and yet … people are offended by the idea of importing individual freedoms and democratic pluralism'.[45] The claim that indigenous cultures in the South have been able to shield themselves from Northern influence ignores the depth and breadth of colonialism. The anthropologist Maurice Godelier has analysed the degree to which the Baruya of New Guinea, who were not subject to Northern influence until 1951, 'were transformed into citizens of a new state that was a member of the United Nations, furnishing one further proof of the West's advance in that part of the world'.[46] The colonisation of the Baruya was relatively short and they were, before it, apparently entirely isolated. And yet, Godelier shows, Baruya culture has been deeply influenced by colonisation and has changed in important ways. If the culture of an isolated people can alter in two or three decades, it is safe to assume that everyone else's culture has also been altered by contact with others. Appiah thus notes that African popular culture 'is, like most popular culture in the age of mass production, hardly national at all'.[47]

This point acquires greater force when we note that some aspects of 'traditional culture' which are said to instil in people in the South support for hierarchy were created by the colonial power. Gender relations often seen as indigenous cultural expressions were imposed: 'many forms of inequality ascribed to "tradition" actually arose from colonisation'.[48] Ethnic identities were also in some cases hardened by colonial rule – most notably the difference between Hutu and Tutsi, which was transformed by Belgian colonisation from an ethnic to a racial difference, from a form of identity to a source of authority, with lethal effect in post-independence Rwanda.[49] Partha Chatterjee, among others, has drawn attention to how the colonial state in India shaped identities by classifying people ethnically: in the postcolonial period, this was instrumental in 'shaping the forms of both political demands and development policy'.[50] And hierarchical traditional authority, while not invented by colonialism, was given state sanction by colonial powers to impose indirect rule,[51] which inevitably reshaped these institutions and their cultural underpinnings. At least some of the cultural norms we are asked to accept as authentic were imposed by Westerners bent on dominating Africans.

Second, the cultural 'consensus' in support of 'African democracy' asserted by governing elites is rejected. Ake was not an uncritical admirer of Western democracy – he argued that a form of democracy which provided for group rights was more appropriate to African conditions than the liberal stress on individual rights. But, he insisted that democratic principles, 'widespread participation, consent of the governed, and public accountability of those in power' applied everywhere, including, of course, in Africa. Not only were democratic principles deeply rooted in pre-colonial African politics, they were at times more strictly applied than in the West. Chiefs were responsible not only for their own actions but for the workings of nature – floods, droughts and epidemics. If chiefs were found wanting, they would be forced into exile or 'asked to die'.[52]

Célestin Monga[53] argues that African citizenries have maintained a democratic culture – beliefs which underpin a desire for popular sovereignty – despite the efforts of authoritarian governments. This, he argues, expressed itself in repeated resistance, albeit not necessarily political action. The ways in which people talk about authority or how they stand, talk and sing expresses a rejection of domination.[54] Music and visual art are also a critique of power. Democratisation is seen not as a Western imposition but as a means of exerting popular sovereignty: 'the democratisation project in sub-Saharan Africa has not been perceived by the people as a cultural fetish used to disguise famine, misery and suffering. Rather, they see it is a means of expressing citizenship, confiscated and perverted by decades of authoritarianism'.[55]

We will return to citizens' defence strategies when they are denied popular sovereignty. But a rejection of illegitimate authority does not necessarily translate into political action. The single-party system, a Senegalese scholar observes, 'teaches the individual to act deceitfully, conceal his or her true feelings and to use stereotyped and conventional jargon so as to toe the party line and escape repression.'[56] Despite surface appearances, the attitudes and behaviour he and others analyse are not those of subjects content with rule by authority – they are those of aspirant citizens who see authoritarianism as illegitimate but lack the power to challenge it and may, therefore, pretend to support elites.

Third, despite much feigned compliance, collective action to make government more accountable and responsive to citizens has been far more common in the South – and Africa particularly – than claims of a deep-rooted respect for authority suggest. In response to analyses which see Africa's democratisation as a response to international events, in particular the end of the Soviet bloc, it should be noted that '[t]he opposition movements in Gabon, Ivory Coast and Zaire existed well before the collapse of the Eastern bloc regimes'.[57] Writing in 1993, Ake reported: 'Throughout Africa ordinary people are demanding a second independence, this time from the indigenous leadership ... The democracy movement ... expresses the desire of ordinary people to gain power and material improvement'.[58] Widespread mobilisation against African authoritarian governments questions the claim that citizens prefer strong leaders and reject the right to choose who rules.

It is not only in Africa that Southern citizenries demand popular sovereignty. In an influential study of popular politics in India, Chatterjee rejects what he sees as the liberal idea that the poor can exert influence by activity in civil society. He argues that the poor express themselves in 'political society' rather than in 'apolitical' engagement with authority in 'civil society' because this allows them to demand inclusion and participation.[59] Their claims are voiced, explicitly or implicitly, as a demand for rights: 'they make a claim to a habitation and a livelihood as a matter of right'.[60] While Chatterjee argues that the Indian poor's attempt to hold power to account and to force it to respond takes a very different form to that envisaged in liberal democratic theory, theirs is as much a demand for popular sovereignty as that of the 'classic' middle-class citizen of Western liberalism.

The claim that responsive and accountable government is a 'Western imposition' and that African citizenries do not believe they should govern themselves is far more the product of elites concerned to protect themselves from challenge than of popular preference: 'While the governed invoke rights and social justice, their rulers appeal to culture and custom'.[61] There is no evidence that Africans and Asians do not want to make political choices and are being dragooned into doing so by Northern powers. The evidence points in the opposite direction, showing that African citizens' views of what is democratic are shared with citizens in other parts of the globe. One analysis of opinion poll data observes that, in Africa, 'citizens make the same judgments about what is and what is not "democratic" as elsewhere in the world'.[62]

WRONGING RIGHTS

Just as democracy is said to be imposed on Africans, so are human rights. Critics see them as an attempt to mould the South to Northern cultural requirements, or a means by which the powerful wield power, or both. This challenges the view, argued here, that rights are a key ingredient of popular sovereignty since they are the grounds for the claim of each citizen to participate in collective self-government.

In Africa, the claim that human rights protect only the powerful enjoys significant intellectual support: 'Not surprisingly, rights-based discourses of citizenship are often viewed with scepticism by those who were excluded from civic citizenship under colonialism'.[63] The stress on rights is seen to emphasise the isolated individual rather than the solidarity of the group – 'what the liberal conception of citizenship as formulated in a rights discourse asks us to do is to block off issues of collective identity from democratic citizenship'.[64] Rights are also seen as an obstacle to active citizenship, as 'something that the government hands out to a passive citizenry instead of being dependant for its normative force on the engagements and commitment of an active citizen body ...'.[65]

The attacks on rights come in a variety of forms. Ake asserts that 'the idea of human rights really came into its own as a tool for opposing democracy: rights obstruct democracy because they protect the privileged from the decisions of the majority'.[66] A second view sees human rights as abstractions which do not address the material needs of citizens and so are, presumably, an indulgence of the more prosperous classes. Ake, again, insists that a 'relevant' African democracy would have to 'de-emphasize abstract political rights and stress concrete economic rights'.[67] In similar vein, Julius Ihonvbere, noting the poverty and underdevelopment which colonialism bequeathed to the continent, argues that 'human rights means very little within a context of mass poverty, unemployment ... and the general lack of basic human needs'.[68] Third, as suggested earlier, human rights can be seen as impositions on the sovereignty of African states and the cultural preferences of their peoples.[69]

The critics overstate their case for effect. Few if any dismiss rights out of hand. They seem, rather, to be criticising particular ways of seeing rights. Thus Ihonvbere's and Ake's concerns for 'concrete economic rights' are criticisms not of all rights, but of giving civil and political rights priority over social and economic rights. The former are seen as 'negative rights' which ensure 'that a person's freedom should be protected from the actions of other individuals, groups or the state', while the latter are 'more positive human rights regarding broader social justice'.[70] But the critics do see the right to vote, speak and act as insufficient to address the inequities to which Africans are subject.

We have dealt with one of these objections. While rights do limit majority rule, they make popular sovereignty possible because they offer every member of a political community the guarantee of full participation. Claims that rights have undermined democracy in the South are challenged by the frequent use of rights claims by citizens seeking to make power more accountable and responsive – whether actors in Chatterjee's 'political society' explicitly use the language of rights or not, their claims are made within an implied or explicit rights framework. It is this which prompts Arjun Appadurai to introduce a discussion of popular politics in Indian cities with this observation: 'There is some reason to worry about whether the current framework of human rights is serving mainly as the legal and normative conscience – or the legal-bureaucratic lubricant – of a neoliberal, marketized political order. But there is no doubt that the global spread of the discourse of human rights has provided a huge boost to local democratic formations'.[71] Rights have operated in the South not to protect the affluent, but to offer people who are dominated opportunities to make claims on power and to seek to force it to account to them.

Appadurai also suggests an equally important point – that, although rights are held by individuals, they are not necessarily expressed by 'isolated individuals' alone. Rights not only protect individuals from the state or social groups which seek to intrude on them (although this is important because it protects those who differ and are different from losing their freedom or worse), they also empower people to act collectively to change their circumstances and to challenge the exercise of power. We might all enjoy the right to speak our minds as individuals, but, if we want to be heard by power-holders, we join with others to speak in unison. The individual right to associate cannot, by definition, be exercised alone. And so the collective work of 'local democratic formations' is impossible without individual rights.

Scholars who privilege social and economic rights over their political and civil equivalents also seem to favour active engagement by citizens, particularly the poor, in holding power to account. But social and economic rights can only be the product of human action, of 'struggle from below' in Issa Shivji's terms, if people can exercise political and civil rights. If social and economic rights must take priority over their political and civil equivalents, what will grassroots citizens use to claim their rights? If they cannot do the claiming because they cannot be fully effective citizens until they have achieved social and economic rights, who will decide what form these rights will take in concrete societies facing resource constraints (as all concrete societies do)? Are we not ensuring that these citizens will be dominated forever because they will always be unable to say what they want and how it can be translated into concrete reality in their lives? Shivji thus urges that rights '[not be] theorised simply as a legal right … but a means of struggle … not a standard granted as charity from above but a standard-bearer around which people rally for the struggle from below'.[72]

What is a social and economic right and what is not is contested. How freedoms are to be realised is, we have noted, open to interpretation. But there is no debate among democrats over whether the vote or freedom of speech or assembly are basic rights. By contrast, there is no agreement on which social rights should be recognised, let alone on how they should be realised. Capitalist democracies cannot agree on whether a property right should be recognised, and there are inevitably debates within and between societies on which social and economic rights are fundamental: 'Some "rights" may be culture- and history-bound, while others may be temporally more universal'.[73] So, someone has to decide which rights should be pursued and which ignored.

Without political and civil rights, the poor and vulnerable cannot act to demand the social and economic rights which are important to them; the decision would be left to legal engineers, and this would impose precisely that charity from above which Shivji wants to avoid. The right to social and economic provision is meaningless without a right to participate in decisions on priorities. Citizens must also be able to ensure that the rights affirmed by courts or officials are realised in practice by holding governments to what the courts or policy have promised. None of this is possible unless the poor, with everyone else, enjoy the right, in practice, to speak, combine and act. Civil and political rights are not abstract indulgences – they are the means by which social and economic rights are realised and are, therefore, essential to social as well as political citizenship.[74] They are not a means of subordinating the poor but an essential foundation if poor people are to realise, and defend, their social and economic rights.

If we understand political rights in this way, there is nothing 'negative' about them. They function not only to protect individuals from state power, but also as a ground for active citizenship which makes claims on power. Viewed as enablers of collective action, rights are not bulwarks of social and political inequality, but essential to the activity which erodes it because they may ensure that collective action to influence decisions will not be the monopoly of the few. These rights are not handed down to passive citizens by charitable governments – they are claimed by collective action and they become essential ground for its continued use once rights have been formally won. If we all enjoy rights by virtue of our humanity, if they are as much ours as our bodies and minds, they can never be charitably bestowed. Power – public and private – cannot 'give' rights. It can only recognise or resist the rights we already have. Rights are not a substitute for political and social action, but their necessary precondition. The contrast between a view of democracy grounded in rights and one grounded in collective action is an illusion: the latter depends on the former. Western thought views rights as a product of the European Enlightenment, the French Revolution in particular. They were not universally applied – the vote was only gradually extended to working people and the poor, and women were excluded. They were also held not to belong to subordinated races – the US maintained slavery and legalised race discrimination with a bill of rights for decades; European democracies did not extend universal rights to their colonial subjects. As Mahmood Mamdani notes, within the colonised world, rights and the participation which went with them were the preserve of the coloniser.[75] But the claim to Western ownership is spurious. The idea that every human has an equal right to respect crosses cultural contexts. Witness the Basotho customary norm *Lekhotla ha le nameloe motho* – the court lends itself to no person– which 'recognised that all had equal rights before traditional courts'.[76] Notions of equality before the courts 'were evident in many traditional societies, including the Tswana, Sotho, Igbo and Akan'.[77] The interviewees cited by Karlstrom claim rights – to be heard and taken seriously by power, for example.

It has therefore been argued that those who reject rights as a cultural imposition may be reacting not to the notion itself but to the symbolism in which it is often cloaked:[78] the issue is not rights but portraying them as Western inventions. As long as the West insists that rights were created by French revolutionaries or American anti-colonials, Africans and Asians will see rights language as alien and imposed. Just as 'consolidation' scholars assume that democracy in its completed form exists only in the North, donor countries may present rights as a Northern product to be exported to a grateful South. But more may be at stake than cultural packaging. Rights can be realised only in specific contexts. In the North, they were embodied in a liberal democracy which may, as Ake suggests, assume elements which do not exist in (much of) the South today – 'a socially atomised society where production and exchange are already commodified, a society which is essentially a market'.[79] This means that rights need to be realised in different ways in the South. The key problem may not be that rights are clothed in Northern symbolism, but that they are attached, needlessly, to a Northern social form; critiques of rights may react to this form, not the substance of rights. It is crucial, therefore, to distinguish between the universal rights which underpin democracy and the culturally specific form which the attempt to realise them takes.

Civil and political rights do not impose colonial domination; they challenge it. As Mamdani and others point out, colonialism did not impose on the South rights which clashed with local culture – it denied rights to the colonised. To demand rights is not to embrace domination, but to rebel against it. The right to recognition regardless of race has been central to understandings of democracy in Africa (and elsewhere in the South). While there may be heated arguments over what that right means, it is close to an article of faith in Africa, cutting across most divisions. Rights were repeatedly invoked by some anti-colonial leaderships,[80] most notably in South Africa, where 'liberation movements' repeatedly invoked rights language to challenge the legitimacy of apartheid.[81]

That rights can enable people to challenge cultural imposition is illustrated by the rise of indigenous people's movements in Latin America: 'Challenging the historical image of Indians as a submissive, backward and anachronistic group … newly formed organisations have … mobilized around their indigenous identity. Their demands have included territorial autonomy, respect for customary law, new forms of political representation, and bicultural education.'[82] Rights played a key role in making this possible: 'increased freedoms of association, expression and the press, provided a changing political opportunity for legal popular movement organizing …', while increasing respect for civil rights and the ensuing political liberalisation 'enabled the potential development of … the politics of identity'.[83] For indigenous activists, rights are the key to expressing who they are and inserting their voice into national conversations. They are central to contesting precisely the imposition of identity on others which their critics claim they are meant to entrench. To insist that every human being, by virtue of being human, has a right to decide – and to enjoy all the rights which are needed to make this right real – is not to endorse colonial imposition, but to reject it.

THE DANGER OF DIVISION

If Africans, like human beings everywhere, want democracy, that does not necessarily mean that they want the version on offer in the West. Does Africa need its own democratic form and, if so, how would it look? Perhaps the most consistent alternative – and that most developed by African political thinkers – is the view that decisions should be taken by consensus; adversarial politics, marked by competition between political parties, is rejected as a Western imposition.

Advocates of consensus make two core claims – that it is deeply rooted in African culture because it reflects the way in which African political systems operated, and that it is best suited to African conditions because it is most likely to cure ills besetting African democracies, in particular ethnic conflict. The leading thinker in this school, Kwasi Wiredu, claims that '[w]here consensus characterises political decision making in Africa, it is a manifestation of an immanent approach to social interaction'.[84] For Wiredu, consensus is part of the DNA of African societies. Similarly, another advocate of consensus, Edward Wamala, seeks to show that it was intrinsic to African societies. Again the Ganda (Baganda) are used as a case study, and Wamala asserts that 'seeking consensus in traditional Ganda society … seems to have been at the heart of social and political organisation and the ethos of the people of Buganda' and was rooted in the firm belief 'that knowledge is ultimately dialogical or social, and in the collective responsibility of all for the welfare of the community'.[85]

Proponents of consensus also insist that it is a cure for the conflicts which have beset Africa. Wiredu argues that 'interethnic conflict and the problem of its contemporary reverberations … is one of the reasons why the idea of a consensual non-party system ought to be taken especially seriously in Africa'.[86] He and other advocates of consensus see political party competition, which they insist is a product of Western political culture, as a deeply divisive source of conflict. Political parties become vehicles for ethnically mobilising people against each other and, because the system is also majoritarian, of imposing the will of one ethnic group, through its party, over all others. Wiredu stresses that consensus can restore the right to a say of the minority, who are currently reduced to opposing the majority.[87] Consensus is thus the key to harmony and inclusion.

At first glance, this seems to be a fairly straightforward argument for a one-party state or other forms of non-democratic government in which people's right to form parties is suppressed. While some advocates of consensus do advocate a monarchy, Wiredu is alert to this danger and anxious to show that he is advocating another form of democracy, not a new justification for ending it. He rejects the one-party state as a form of sham consensus achieved by killing off opposition: 'In the one-party situation, the reason why no party loses is because murdered parties do not compete'.[88] One-party states are, for Wiredu, another form of party state, one in which the strongest party has eliminated all the others. He is, he says, advocating a no-party state.

This sounds very much like another academic rubber stamp for Museveni's 'no-party' state, and Wiredu is aware of the risk that he might be seen to be endorsing the one-party state in a new guise. To counter this, he endorses full freedom of association – the right of everyone to form associations to represent common interests and values – provided that these do not compete for political power: 'The crucial factor here is the absence of the rule of the sectional appropriation of power'.[89] In contrast to Museveni, Wiredu suggests that his favoured system should be established not by law and force, but by debate and persuasion: 'What we can legitimately do is to try to change … beliefs with argument and evidence', with the aim being a 'consensus that may be brought about by compromise'.[90] So Wiredu is not, he insists, seeking to rob Africans of popular sovereignty in the name of culture – he is proposing a different, more appropriate, form.

Other African political thinkers doubt whether the consensus proposal is consistent with popular sovereignty. Emmanuel Chukwudi Eze offers two key objections. First, he notes that consensus can be a valid decision-making principle only if there is an identity of interests between citizens. He doubts that this is so and argues that the claim that people share common interests is likely to serve power-holders who seek to dominate others rather than a common humanity. Second, he argues that democracy is a system which seeks to manage difference, not to dissolve it in consensus.[91] This is a key argument for democracy: difference is intrinsic to human beings and democracy is needed so that difference can be expressed politically rather than in violent conflict. Paulin Hountondji thus argues that pluralism, recognition of difference, is not only essential to modern Africa, but was also experienced in pre-colonial times. Hountondji dismisses as 'the unanimist illusion' the notion that 'in small-scale societies or so-called primitive societies … everyone agrees with everyone'. Pluralism is, he argues, 'valuable and fruitful': 'not only modern Africa but even the so-called traditional Africa have been experiencing pluralism over time in all domains'.[92]

In these views, consensus denies difference and is therefore likely to suppress it: people will continue to differ but will be unable to express themselves. Wiredu acknowledges that consensus may be impossible in modern society, and therefore suggests that elements of it could be introduced in a political system rather than insisting on it as the system's core feature.[93] But this significant retreat from the demand for consensus does not deter Wiredu in his later work – and other consensus thinkers – from arguing for a democracy founded on the consensus principle.

In similar vein to Eze and Hountondji, Emmanuel Ifeanyi Ani defends voting (which consensus thinkers reject, although Wiredu allows for it in extreme circumstances where consensus is impossible) as an intrinsic right for Africans and all humans: 'voting is a basic human solution to resolving intractability, and intractability exists everywhere. The very idea of voting cannot have been imported'[94] (to

Africa from elsewhere). Like Eze, Ani points to the impossibility of a society in which differences can be dissolved; they will always exist. Voting is essential to ensure that the majority view prevails. Again, consensus will not eliminate difference; it will simply suppress it.

That non-party consensus democracy may suppress rights is also a concern of Ademola Kazeem Fayemi, who points out that forming a political party is an expression of the right to associate with others in pursuit of common goals: 'people of like minds will always identify with one another and come together to discuss how their interests can be articulated and promoted ... Political parties in major-itarian democracies function primarily in like manner'.[95] He suggests that alliances which shared some characteristics with political parties existed in pre-colonial African political systems. A no-party system would thus suppress a right which is also rooted in Africa's past. Wiredu would no doubt answer that consensual democracy would need to be adopted voluntarily and could not be imposed. But Fayemi suggests that it would be impossible to maintain a system in which parties played no role without suppressing them. (Even if one generation agreed to forego parties, the next generation is likely to insist on them since human beings will want to join with like-minded people to pursue common goals.) So consensual democracy could be sustained only by abolishing a core democratic right.

The debate over consensual democracy has been discussed in some detail because it adds concreteness to an abstract discussion on how democracy may be made distinctively African. It also offers an insight into the issues at stake when proposals for indigenous and alternative forms of democracy are discussed. Wiredu believes his proposals would enrich and expand democracy – he is not using democratic arguments to smuggle in new forms of domination. This makes the debate between him and his critics pivotal because at issue is what qualifies as democratic. Both sides agree that democracy must be a system in which all enjoy a say – a system of popular sovereignty: they differ on whether consensual democracy would achieve that. This offers a framework for all debates on this question. As Ake suggests, the right of people to govern themselves is an essential feature of any democratic system. Africans have as much right to this as any other people. Proposals for more indigenous forms of democracy must, therefore, show that they recognise this right.

UNIVERSALLY RECOGNISING THE PARTICULAR

To insist that the right to decide crosses cultural boundaries is not to claim that those barriers are illusory, nor that new democracies can be built and deepened without taking the right to culture and identity seriously. Race, culture and identity remain important forms of domination in democracies, new and old. Indigenous people's movements are but one example of cases in which groups may be denied a share in popular sovereignty because of their identity, even where formal political equality is recognised. Formal democracy does not solve the problem of identity domination; it merely makes action to challenge it possible. The insistence on the universality of civil and political rights cannot serve democracy if it is used to suppress the identity difference whose free expression is central to an equal share for all in popular sovereignty.

Identity-based organisations and politics are not, as is sometimes supposed, a threat to democracy; they may help to realise it because they could enable citizens to overcome a key barrier to their exercise of sovereignty. In South Africa, the Black Consciousness Movement (BCM) proclaimed this principle under apartheid.[96] But it remains valid when formal equality is achieved because identity-based domination, and the attitudes of superiority and inferiority which underpin it, do not dissolve simply because a new constitution is adopted. If identity-based parties and associations – in South Africa, those which represent black people or women exclusively – recognise the civil and political rights of others, their existence is consistent with democratic principle, and, where they seek to overcome identity-based domination, they are an important source of democratic deepening and broadening.

Where rules and institutions are used, in an ostensibly race- or culture-blind manner, to deny dominated identity groups a full share in decisions, democracy is not advanced by sweeping this under the carpet by insisting that the system is colour-blind. Denying people their full rights and dignity is a form of domination, even when it uses supposedly universal rules. Democracy challenges all domination, and so the democratic response is to recognise identity domination and to seek to end it. If this can be achieved by creating political rules and institutions which recognise identity difference and offer it expression[97] in ways which do not deny a share in sovereignty to other members of the political community, this is precisely what deepening and broadening democracies in which identity domination survives requires. This is a crucial point in South Africa, where, after two decades of democracy, the minority domination which democracy was meant to end survives in new forms.[98]

In South Africa and elsewhere in Africa, voting and other forms of political action often express racial, ethnic and language identities.[99] This is decried by some students of African politics who look forward to the day when 'normal' voters will make their choice on 'bread and butter issues' alone rather than on identity. But this implied sense of shame at the continued importance of identity is itself a cultural prejudice. It assumes that 'normal' or 'sophisticated' voters base their vote on a 'rational' calculation of their economic interests; 'underdeveloped' voters prefer to express identity. It is often assumed too that only African voters express identity at the ballot box, yet another sign that they are 'not ready for democracy'.

But identity voting is common in the oldest democracies. The landscape of European democracies is strewn with parties organised around identities – Christian Democratic parties and regional parties in Scotland and Wales, for example. Claims that Barack Obama's election in the United State signalled the end of identity politics was contradicted by analyses discussing the role of race and gender in voting patterns.[100] Race was decisive in electing Trump. Even where no explicit identity parties exist, voters in particular regions of older democracies routinely return the same parties, confirming the key role of identities in shaping electoral choices. Monga thus asks of those who see identity voting in Africa as a sign of political underdevelopment: 'Why is the notion of an electoral base, accepted throughout the world and considered by Western political science as something every serious politician needs, systematically interpreted as a sign of backwardness when it comes to Africa?'[101]

Nor is identity-based collective action in the North restricted to voting. Much of the theorising on new social movements in the 1980s sought to understand how, in the view of Alain Touraine and Alberto Melucci,[102] the 'classic' Northern spur to collective action – class and social inequality – gave way to action demanding recognition of identities such as gender and ethnicity. In Melucci's view, even seemingly issue-based movements, such as ecology and peace campaigns, were expressions of new identities.[103] Mobilisation in support of identities is, therefore, not specific to particular cultures and levels of wealth. The claim that 'sophisticated' societies mobilise around class and interest, 'primitive' ones behind identity, is as culturally loaded as the 'consolidation' approach. There is no contradiction between identity politics and democracy – popular sovereignty is, in its ideal form, a vehicle for expressing identities in a manner which allows all to be heard and none to dominate. The inferiority complex which seizes some new democracies, South Africa's included, because identity shapes how people vote and organise is misplaced: a democracy in which people are concerned about identity is no less real than one (if one exists) in which material interests are the only spur to political behaviour.

Not only is identity a permissible form of mobilisation in democracies, it may be the most common and effective, even on material issues which are supposedly settled by contest between social and economic classes. Ashutosh Varshney, one of whose specialities is identity conflict in India, argues persuasively that people who experience domination are more likely to mobilise behind identities than any other form of difference. He adds that mobilisation against poverty is likelier if the poor share a common identity: 'not only is it easier to mobilize the poor as members of ethnic communities, but that is also how they often vote – along lines of ethnicity, not class. The dignity gains of democracy might be greater than the poverty gains'.[104] This last observation offers a hint at why identity mobilisation is so effective – because people's dignity is at stake. This further reinforces the point that identity mobilisation within democratic rules is a perfectly valid response to domination and thus a core democratic activity: one study argues that 'religious conflict [and] ethnic cleavages ... played a much greater role in Europe's democratisation than has typically been appreciated'.[105]

Some identities may seek different forms of expression to those to which liberal democracy is accustomed. Some indigenous organisations in Latin America 'demand multiple types of citizenship with boundaries that guarantee equal rights representation at the national level and recognize corporate indigenous authority structures in the indigenous territory. Such recognition requires that the law be configured on the basis of universal claims to citizenship and differentiated claims to difference'.[106] Understanding democracy as an always unfinished task in which everything – including the form of democracy itself – is open to debate, means that demands for new democratic forms which meet the needs of groups who believe their identities are not expressed in current arrangements is a deepening of democracy, provided that it does not deprive anyone of a say in decisions which affect them.

Devising forms which recognise the right of all to share in sovereignty but provide channels for expressing suppressed identities is a key challenge in the quest for stronger and deeper democracies. That democracy can take varying forms in the South should not need saying since it takes a variety of forms in the North. That experimentation is not only consistent with democratic principle but may be crucial to democracy's realisation is underlined by the fact that the two African states which have remained democracies since independence contain elements to which some liberal democrats would object – Botswana's continued use of *kgotla* or Mauritius's consociationalism. In Mauritius, ethnic groups are guaranteed representation in Parliament by a 'best loser' system in which the best-performing candidates of minorities are elected, regardless of their share of the vote.[107] This arrangement may support Ake's argument for a 'consocietal arrangement' in Africa, 'a highly decentralized system of government with equal emphasis on communal and individual rights'.[108]

A credible theory of African democracy needs, therefore, to recognise that the right to popular sovereignty is inherent to all, regardless of culture and identity, and that it must provide a voice to all cultures and identities. Since cultural domination is as much a threat to popular sovereignty as its economic equivalent, allowing all cultures and identities to be expressed in ways which do not entrench domination is a major democratic task.

The challenge is to distinguish between those forms – such as the one-party state – which deny popular sovereignty and those, such as the models tentatively discussed here, which respect it. This must begin by rejecting the claim that rights are a Western gift to Africa:

> by eroding the concept of Western 'ownership' of human rights, we may increase the possibility of real dialogue across cultures. With contributions from non-Western societies, human rights dialogue can more easily lose the stigma of having the West as the authoritative interpreter of human rights (thus eliminating the all too convenient 'cultural imperialism' excuse used by repressive regimes), and become part of a universal understanding not just of human rights standards, but even more importantly, of the implementation of these standards.[109]

But equally important is the delicate task of distinguishing between the core democratic principle – that each person has an inherent right to an equal share in popular sovereignty and to enjoy the rights which make that possible – and the various historical forms which the attempt to realise that right may take: 'by studying the evolution of systems of rights protection under differing cultures and historical situations, it may be possible to understand better the values to be protected'.[110]

New democracies in the South which succeed, through democratic politics, in shaping institutions which give concrete and sustainable form to popular sovereignty in their particular contexts will deepen democracy. They may also offer important lessons to other democracies and those who seek to understand the range of democratic possibilities: 'non-Western rising democracies are now well set to add their distinctive input to making … democracy more effective', and so they may contribute to a key task – democratising democracy.[111]

5

Another Lens: Collective Action and Democracy in Africa

How does the approach to democracy proposed here help us to understand democratic progress in Africa?

This chapter suggests a way of examining African democracies which moves beyond prejudice and generalisation to understanding.

This is not yet another of the reviews of 'the state of democracy' in Africa which are so popular among scholars[1] and 'think tanks'.[2] While these assessments differ, they are generally united by their endorsement of the 'consolidation' paradigm – the test is almost invariably how close African states are to resembling an idealised notion of 'Western' democracy. A detailed account of democratic progress throughout the continent using a different framework would add much to our knowledge but is well beyond the scope of this analysis, particularly since a meaningful assessment would not be possible unless it offered detailed and textured analyses of each country. Analyses which generalise about an undifferentiated 'African state' distort reality by ignoring important differences: often, they stigmatise rather than analyse.[3] New African democracies are not all the same and analyses which ignore their differences miss as much as they explain. The purpose of this chapter, therefore, is not to attempt a detailed appraisal of democratic progress on the continent but to offer a framework for looking at democracy's progress in Africa.

BEYOND LEADERSHIP

Mainstream discussion of democracy in Africa would warm the hearts of democratic elitists – it is preoccupied with leaders, not citizens. The claim that the root cause of Africa's democratic problems (indeed all its problems) is the quality of its leadership dominates mainstream thinking on the topic, regardless of whether the commentator is African[4] or Western.[5] The Mo Ibrahim Foundation, which expresses the mainstream view on governance on the continent, awards an annual leadership prize. However, in keeping with the rest of the mainstream, it is repeatedly disappointed and so often does not award the prize.[6] Even social and medical challenges – HIV and AIDS, for example – are said to depend on leadership.[7] Scholarly work on democracy in Africa is equally fixated on leadership – mainstream credibility requires that it be seen as the core of democracy's problems and possibilities. Thus, a discussion of Africa's 'waning democratic commitment' soon turns into an examination of the commitment of its leaders alone.[8] Richard Joseph, whose discussion of African democratic prospects was mentioned earlier, joins the consensus, offering this key to democratic prospects: 'What Africa greatly needs … is the emergence of a class of leaders determined to pursue policies that enhance growth, deepen democracy and enlarge security for most citizens'.[9] Citizens themselves, it appears, have no role in this solution at all. South Africa's mainstream debate, which often avoids endorsing current thinking on the continent, enthusiastically endorses this view – it was noted earlier that 'leadership' is repeatedly cited as the cause of and solution to all national problems.

The claim that leadership is the key to African failure or success is rarely if ever justified – it is simply assumed, without justification, to express 'common sense'. What it actually expresses is an unsubstantiated bias which assumes that elites matter and citizens do not, even though collective action by citizens plays a key role in even some mainstream accounts of how formal democracy was achieved in many African countries. It also makes little sense as an analytical judgment since it confuses consequences and causes. Why are African leaders inferior to those on other continents? As soon as we dismiss prejudices – the claim that Africans are biologically or culturally ill-equipped for leadership – no explanation is available. We are, therefore, left to assume that, through a process no one understands, Africans are somehow fated to suffer under 'bad' leadership until and unless 'good' leaders emerge.

One explanation which can be safely discarded is that autocratic leaders are so common because they are the sorts which Africans prefer. We have dealt with this issue in the previous chapter, but, to belabour the point, the Afrobarometer data quoted earlier support the view that most African citizens value democracy, not strong leadership, and want more of it. But what do respondents mean by democracy? Given constant stigmatising of Africans' enthusiasm for democracy, could it be that citizens are endorsing an attractive-sounding concept they do not understand? Afrobarometer findings[10] show that African citizens know what democracy is meant to offer. Thus 78 per cent reject single-party rule; 58 per cent see democracy as a system in which 'people choose government leaders in free and fair elections' and 'people are free to express their political views openly'. There is also majority support for democracy as popular sovereignty: 55 per cent agree that 'the government is like our employees. We are the bosses and should tell government what to do'.[11] Afrobarometer's Round 4 survey, conducted in 2008, found that 74 per cent agreed that '[p]eople should be able to speak their minds about politics free of government influence, no matter how unpopular their views may be', and 86 per cent agreed that news media should be able to publish whatever stories they see fit.[12] In sum, the surveys show that most African citizens understand – and value – democracy as popular sovereignty.[13] They do not support the claim that 'African culture' rejects democratic values. They suggest that, if African citizens are able to act collectively to decide their societies' futures, they are likely to support citizen participation in decisions and those freedoms which make it possible.

But if Africans don't want leaders who care more about themselves than their societies, why do they often get them? And, if a focus on 'leadership' tells us little about democracy's progress on the continent, what does? This chapter seeks to edge towards answers to these questions by offering a more concrete and socially rooted view of democratic possibilities and limits in Africa (and perhaps elsewhere too).

NEGATIVE AND POSITIVE

Two elements are essential if we are to assess the depth and breadth of any democracy through the prism of popular sovereignty: whether citizens' freedoms are respected, enabling them to participate freely, and whether they can actively share in the decisions which affect them.

The two must be considered separately because the dynamics which underpin progress are different. To insist that governments respect the liberties of citizens is to require 'negative liberty',[14] freedom from constraint. The question is whether governments choose or are forced to allow citizens the freedom to take part in public life. 'Negative liberty' is usually seen as a measure of whether citizens are left alone. But if we see democracy as popular sovereignty, these freedoms are not a way of escaping the reach of government, but a minimum requirement for participating in it. Participation remains an option, not a duty, but the freedoms must be fully available to all, whether or not everyone chooses to use them. Popular sovereignty, therefore, depends on everyone enjoying the 'negative liberty' which may enable some to participate even as it allows others to get on with their lives. If citizens shape decisions, they enjoy 'positive liberty', the capacity to use rights to influence public power. This requires a continuing relationship between government and governed.

The key difference between the two lies in what is needed to sustain them. While democracy is created and sustained by collective action, this does not mean that every aspect of the system is perpetually sustained only by continuing collective action. It means that democracies will not emerge unless groups with an interest in holding political authority to account engage in collective action, and will not broaden and deepen unless organised citizens engage in continuing action to ensure that they share in decisions. But 'negative liberty' will survive as long as governments choose not to enter areas of public life in ways which remove freedom. They may respect freedoms even if there is no collective action in their defence.

A key source of 'negative liberty' is the role of institutions, which can play their part in democratic systems only if they remain independent of political authority and are not expected to reflect majority opinion. The most obvious case is the judiciary. Democracy does not require that legal actions be settled by popular vote – on the contrary, it is central to the democratic legal order that legal disputes be judged by officers who reach decisions on grounds other than prevailing political opinion. The university is another such case: academic freedom rests on the recognition that intellectual inquiry in a democracy can play its required social role only if research findings and ideas remain independent of public opinion.[15] While neither these nor any other institution whose independence is essential to democracy's survival can be 'above politics', since they rely on human beings who are not politically neutral, they cannot do what they are meant to do if they tailor their findings to the needs of the political authorities – or of prevailing majorities.

Collective action does influence whether their independence is preserved: over time, institutions which rely on independence from political authority to perform their tasks will maintain autonomy only if a social consensus – or at the very least agreement among influential social interests – recognises that their independence is necessary and so chooses to support it:[16] independence is unlikely to survive indefinitely in the absence of this support. Autonomy exercised in a way which antagonises social interests may trigger collective action aimed at ending it. The independence of the courts may be challenged, as it has been among sections of the South African grassroots, by vigilantism or by citizens deciding that they know better than the courts who is guilty, and acting against those they blame.[17] The repeated use of courts in South Africa to settle political disputes also runs the risk of inviting collective action to limit their independence. This reality may have prompted Dikgang Moseneke, a former deputy chief justice respected for his independence, to warn against the pressure imposed on courts by the expectation that they substitute for democratic politics by resolving issues which it is meant to address.[18] If this happens, the institution's capacity to endure will depend on its ability to mobilise collective action in its defence. But this does not mean that judicial independence or academic freedom can exist only if there is collective action in their support – they may be sustained by an absence of action. Sustained collective action is not, therefore, routinely essential to their survival – it is likely to become relevant only when they are under threat.

Much the same point can be made about the freedoms democracy requires if citizens are to exercise popular sovereignty. While they are a consequence of collective action, and will not endure indefinitely unless citizens act collectively to enforce and protect them, liberties do not depend on continuous action to sustain them because, like the independent institutions, their survival requires only an absence of action by those hostile to them. They could, therefore, be respected, at least for a time, even if citizens do not act in their defence. This explains why respect for liberties is often achieved in Africa through influences other than citizen action – pressure from donors, for example. Because protecting freedoms from government action does not depend on organised participation, progress is possible even where citizens with an interest in democracy's survival lack the means to hold government to account (although, in the absence of sustained citizen action in defence of rights, freedoms will remain fragile and some rights will be largely theoretical for many citizens). Because freedoms may be established and maintained in response to a range of factors, respect for them, at least in form, is possible in societies in which the means of collective action are not available to most citizens who support democracy. 'Negative liberties' are, therefore, more likely because less is needed to sustain them. 'Positive liberty' – the capacity to exercise popular sovereignty by influencing law and policy – is inconceivable without an engaged and active citizenry. If sustained collective action to hold political authorities to account is rare and unevenly spread in most African countries, 'positive liberty' will remain sporadic at best.

An examination of Africa's democracies seems to support this analysis. The potential for liberties to be expanded was increased by a change in the global climate of opinion: since the end of the Cold War, Northern donor governments, no longer concerned to recruit allies in the conflict against communism regardless of the domestic practices of their governing elites, were more inclined to stress formal democracy in decisions on aid and other forms of approval. While this trend has been eroded[19] by a combination of factors, chief among them a rightward shift in Northern countries which championed democracy promotion, international disapproval of democratic lapses continues. The pressure to remain at least formally democratic has also shifted to regional and continental multilateral organisations such as the Southern African Development Community (SADC) and the African Union (AU).

For much of the post-independence period, the Organisation of African Unity (OAU) strictly adhered to the principle of non-interference in the domestic affairs of member states.[20] And so it showed no interest in member governments' attitudes to their citizens' liberties. Both the OAU's successor, the AU, and some regional forums have, at least in principle, abandoned this position and agree in principle that African governments ought to protect their citizens' freedoms. The AU's Constitutive Act, adopted in mid-2000, empowers it to 'intervene in a Member State ... in respect of grave circumstances, namely war crimes, genocide and crimes against humanity'.[21] In 2002, it also adopted the New Plan for Africa's Development (Nepad), which included a Declaration on Democracy, Political, Economic and Corporate Governance committing African governments to '[t]he rule of law, the equality of all citizens before the law and the liberty of the individual, individual and collective freedoms, including the right to form political parties and trade unions ...'.[22] Nepad introduced an African Peer Review Mechanism which encouraged states to submit to a review of their compliance with these norms by other African states. Civil society organisations in the country under review are expected to participate to ensure that governments are reviewed by their societies as well as their peers.[23] SADC communiqués have stressed its role in promoting 'democracy, good governance and respect for human rights'.[24] This does not, of course, mean that it has become a strong force for democratisation – Swaziland remains a monarchy and the military plays a direct role in government in Zimbabwe. But it does place some limits on what member governments can and cannot do: when the Zimbabwean military removed President Robert Mugabe in 2017, it insisted repeatedly that it was not staging a coup and Mugabe was not removed until the ruling ZANU-PF party voted to remove him. The effect is mostly cosmetic, but this may have ensured that the change in government was not violent.

According to Afrobarometer, the people best able to judge the state of civil liberties in Africa are reasonably satisfied. In its 2010–2012 survey, most (56 per cent) reported that governments 'never or rarely' silence opposition parties, and 63 per cent responded that their governments respected the law and the courts.[25] The expectation that respect for freedom would be uneven is also supported by the evidence. Data compiled by human rights monitors show that compliance varies within and between societies (Amnesty International and Human Rights Watch seem to prefer country reporting of abuses to tracking improvement or regression).[26] There are African countries in which few, if any, freedoms are recognised; in the rest, respect for freedoms varies considerably – as it does, of course, in many 'established' democracies. Thus Mauritius, probably closest to a 'model' African democracy, is accused of some abuses of liberty (as are the UK and US).[27] There are, however, also advances in countries whose democratic depth and breadth is generally poor. Civil liberties trends in Africa further support the view that dividing democracies into 'finished' and 'unfinished' products prevents an accurate understanding of their dynamics. Formal respect for liberties in Africa is fairly widespread and uneven. The material available on human rights compliance also provides ample evidence that formal democracy is no guarantee that all the freedoms a democratic order requires will be respected. But it shows too that democracy has brought more political freedom, opening new possibilities to citizens.

This judgment – that formal democracy has made significant progress in Africa – is not the mainstream view it might have been a decade ago. Scepticism about the health of African democracy is now more prevalent. But, while democracy has not taken root throughout the continent, the scepticism seems based more on inflated expectations and prejudice than analysis. One influential analysis, for, example, bases its pessimism almost purely on an analysis of one country – South Africa –and owes more to current media fads than serious analysis.[28]

Among the evidence produced for its assertion of democratic retreat is corruption associated with former president Jacob Zuma and the claim that legislation was passed preventing media from reporting on corruption. But the link between Zuma's behaviour and the state of democracy is unclear. There is no necessary connection between the health of a democracy and the behaviour of its senior politicians – if it was, American democracy might have collapsed in 1992 when hundreds of members of the US Congress were implicated in a banking scandal.[29] The legislation to which the article refers contains a lengthy section making it clear that it is not designed to ban reporting on corruption – it stipulates that anyone who uses it in that way is liable to prosecution.[30] It has still not become law despite being passed in 2012 because Zuma refused to sign it on the grounds that it was unconstitutional.[31]

The analyses also assume that the health of a democracy can be judged by the commitments of a country's leaders. South Africa clearly contradicts that view. Zuma's actions have been repeatedly struck down by the courts in judgments which have been accepted by government leadership (it has chosen to appeal against rulings rather than reject them); and citizens remain free to reject his party at the polls – its electoral majority is under threat for the first time since democracy was achieved. No African state has reached the (unattainable) levels of perfection demanded by the 'consolidation' paradigm. But citizens remain freer than in the past, and failure to recognise this has more to do with the paradigm's biases than reality. This is so even where there is no evidence of collective action to defend freedoms.

PARTICIPATION: GOVERNMENT BY SOME PEOPLE?

'Positive liberty' has proven far more elusive on the continent – a trend which is more uniform than the uneven spread of civil liberties.

Hard evidence on the degree to which African citizenries are able to influence decisions is not readily available. But there is widespread agreement that Africa's wave of democracy has not produced a concomitant rise in citizens' ability to shape policy decisions. There are obvious exceptions – one of which, South African activists' fight to win treatment for people living with HIV and AIDS, will be discussed in a later chapter. But the trend is that the ability to shape decisions remains the preserve of an elite. It is important to stress that this does not mean that elected African governments pay no attention to citizens' organisations. No government, democratic or otherwise, is free to ignore all social groups, a point to which we will return. Studies show that business and professional associations do influence decisions in African democracies.[32] What is absent in most of the continent's democracies is evidence that the ability to shape decisions is becoming more widely distributed. It is argued here that this is a consequence not of the quality of leadership or citizens' attitudes to leaders but to the limited leeway for using collective action to influence policy decisions. The problem is not that citizens are happy to leave decisions to leaders – it is that they lack the power to act together to force them to listen.

A flavour of the dynamics at play is underlined by a study of the relationship between official anti-poverty policy and participation in decision-making by independent citizen groups in nine countries which belong to the SADC.[33] While it was conducted a decade and a half ago, it is used not to make claims about today's realities but to suggest a different way of examining the problem.

The Poverty of Participation

Poverty is a key social issue in all the countries studied, and some participated in drafting Poverty Reduction Strategy Papers (PRSPs) in collaboration with the World

Bank and IMF, an exercise which was meant to rely on civil society participation to identify poverty reduction priorities. But, despite the extension of formal democratic rights, citizen influence on policy remained very weak. Anti-poverty policy documents were usually vague and general, reflecting international fashions rather than local realities. The lack of references to country-specific realities suggested a process in which domestic perspectives made little or no impact.

This was hardly surprising because policy, the research showed, was not the outcome of competition for public support between groups of organised citizens or bargaining and compromise between them: interaction between governments and international institutions was the key source of influence, and, to the extent that society participated at all, it was in a ritualised process incapable of yielding a democratic outcome.

Since opinions in society are never uniform, and the making of policy is an inevitable clash of interests and values, the will of the majority must be established in an open process in which conflicting views contend for support, and in which either a majority coalition is assembled which will ensure that its preferences are implemented or a compromise between contending positions is reached. None of this is possible in a formalised consultation process in which parties engage each other for a brief period and the 'view of society' is distilled from the discussions. Nor can the will of grassroots citizens be determined in a forum to which they have no access because they lack the means to organise.

These weaknesses ensured that engagement on poverty priorities did not endure beyond the consultation period mandated by the relevant international organisation. Even the generalised and vague commitments which these processes yielded were not translated into policy because there was little or no sustained pressure from organised citizens' groups to hold politicians and officials to their commitments. Of course, there may be little enthusiasm in society for holding politicians and officials to decisions which most citizens had no role in shaping. But, since citizens' organisations seemed to be ignoring the PRSP outcomes rather than mobilising in opposition to them, it seems likely that those groups with an interest in reducing poverty did not enjoy access to the collective action which may propel anti-poverty programmes to the top of government priorities. The processes failed to reflect citizens' preferences because social groups with an interest in change were unable to engage in sustained collective action to ensure that decision-makers endorsed their priorities.

This diagnosis is supported by the study's finding that successful advocacy on issues related to poverty reduction was rare in the societies studied. There were cases of successful advocacy and, as we might expect, these were in countries where respect for civil liberties was more pronounced – Botswana, Malawi and South Africa, rather than Zimbabwe or Swaziland. But cases in which governments altered a policy or law because the voice of citizens urged them to do so were very rare.

Advocacy, whether expressed in learned policy papers, heated public debate, petitions or non-violent street demonstrations, is the stuff of democratic decision-making, the key means by which citizens influence others to support their position and ensure that their government responds to them. If governments are not making policy and implementing it in response to citizen preferences expressed through advocacy, it is hard to see how policy could express the preferences of those who have assembled a majority in their support in contest with competing views. In the countries under discussion, responses to poverty were weak, half-hearted and often out of touch with available knowledge on grassroots wants and needs because citizens with an interest in programmes to fight poverty lacked the means to engage in collective action effective enough to ensure that governments took them seriously.

And, while there was some engagement between government and citizens' groups outside the PRSP processes, governments did not, in the main, see citizens' organisations as necessary, let alone desirable, participants in the policy process: 'there is good reason to question whether any of the societies of the region have reached a stage ... [at] which a vigorous and highly critical civil society is regarded by government as at worst an unpleasant fact of life rather than a threat', the study concluded.[34] If we assume that governments can ignore the need to deal with citizens' organisations until important sections of the citizenry manage to make themselves heard, this attitude persisted because citizens could not mobilise sufficient collective action to ensure that governments needed to deal with them.

This failure to mobilise sufficient citizen action to influence government decisions is not the result of a lack of capacity for mobilisation among citizens' groups. Indeed, one reason for governments' wariness was that citizens in the region do mobilise at times to demand accountable government. But, while citizens' groups in the countries studied had acquired the ability to act effectively to veto some unresponsive governments in exceptional circumstances, they were not able to ensure government responsiveness in a sustained way. They could, at times, block that which governments wished to do because, in times of 'national emergency', they could act with other interests who shared their concern to prevent the government from acting in particular ways. But they could not exert enough influence on routine decision-making to ensure that governments adopted their policy proposals. They could at times act effectively to prevent power-holders from imposing themselves on the people indefinitely, but were not yet strong enough to ensure that government decisions reflected citizen opinion.

This weakness stems mostly from inadequate access by grassroots citizens to effective collective action – the study found that, while action by citizens' organisations in most of the societies was independent and sometimes vigorous, they lacked an organised base at the grassroots.[35] The problem was not that organised associations were reluctant to challenge governments: rather, citizens' groups which engaged with public policy issues lacked a firm base among the grassroots citizenry. While organisations were capable of collective action, their base in society was far too shallow to force policy-makers to take citizen opinion seriously. While citizens' groups who are reasonably close to governments, share interests with them or are needed by them (such as businesses) may be able to achieve substantial influence with collective action which lacks a deep base among the citizenry, those which enjoy none of these advantages usually need to show that they are able to mobilise a substantial part of the citizenry if they want to influence decisions. Without that, they may be ignored.

Outside South Africa and Botswana, the institutions which invariably led attempts to hold governments to account for their responses to poverty were the churches, the major international denominations of Christianity rather than indigenous vehicles. These churches have often, in the recent past, been the most significant counterweight to authoritarianism in Southern Africa. Churches enjoy access to resources independently of governments through their international linkages. They are also underpinned by an infrastructure which enables them to sustain interventions. They therefore enjoy a strong capacity to become vehicles for collective action. They are also partly protected against reprisal by the high degree of legitimacy which religion enjoys on the continent: clergy who challenge authority may enjoy a degree of immunity from state action which, while not absolute, is substantial compared to that of others in civil society.

The church brings a set of resources – financial, organisational and moral – which enable collective action. It is this which enables it to articulate an independent vision, to seek to hold governments to account, and to provide at least some citizens with the means to express themselves to the authorities and to seek to ensure that power-holders respond to their needs. Where other means of collective action appear to offer this prospect, the church's role is diminished (although not entirely absent). But, where lack of resources and limited access to government decisions prevent most citizens from engaging in effective collective action, the church fills the gap.

Weaknesses in society's capacity to hold governments accountable may, on the surface, seem to serve the interests of governments since the fragility insulates them from effective citizen influence. This would seem to offer power-holders greater latitude to act as these weaknesses please. But these weaknesses also limit government effectiveness. Insulation from social pressures can also mean failure to penetrate society. Göran Hydén argued decades ago that many African states '[sit] suspended in "mid-air" over society and [are] not an integral mechanism of the day-to-day productive activities of society'.[36] While a lack of citizen action relieves governments of the need to account or respond, it also means that they lack the relationships with social actors which would allow them to implement programmes, since these invariably require co-operation from key social interests. As long as government remains above society, it can prevent social actors from influencing its decisions but is less able to get them to do what it wants them to do. It is, therefore, far better able to control than to initiate. And even control can be tenuous where links between government and society are weak. Where governments want only to extract resources from the public coffers, the arrangement works for them. But, where they seek to govern society, the distance between government and the citizenry caused by citizens' inability to act collectively in ways which would force governments to engage with them also ensures that government programmes are unlikely to be implemented.

The states which Hydén described were not democratic and it might have been assumed that democracy's advent would close the gap between state and society. But formal democracy has not necessarily achieved this. The notion of the 'capstone state' has been proposed to describe governments which are still, despite democratic elections, 'sitting over society' and have 'strong blocking but weak enabling powers'.[37] Because the government has not developed the links to the citizenry which would enable it to implement programmes, it remains far better able to prevent action than to enable it. The result is weak policy-making and implementation – so weak that, at times, as Thandika Mkandawire and Charles Soludo note, it entails 'the complete surrender of national policies to the ever-changing ideas of international experts'.[38]

Anti-poverty action by the post-apartheid South African government in the first years after democracy confirms these prognoses. Policy priorities were often inappropriate because they misread grassroots needs and desires – even where formal processes were created to negotiate policy. Housing policy illustrates the point. During the early 1990s, the government provided a model for negotiated policy-making between all social interests. The policy adopted by the post-1994 government was a product of one of a dozen social and economic forums established during the political negotiation period. Its participants included a wide range of interest groups, including several who were seen as representative of the poor, and one of its focusses was a lengthy negotiation between them and organised business on ways to ensure that mortgage finance reached the poor – although none of the participants asked whether poor people wanted mortgage finance.[39] But research suggests that several years were spent seeking ways of offering the poor something they did not want. Far from seeking mortgages, poor people who participated in nation-wide focus group interviews associated this form of housing finance with evictions and wanted to avoid mortgage commitments.[40] Organised social actors party to negotiations were not representative enough of the grassroots poor to know that they were negotiating a 'benefit' the recipients did not want.

More generally, government implementation priorities tended to reflect the concerns of affluent and well-connected groups rather than the grassroots poor, with a consequent weakening of both the quantity and quality of action against poverty. While social grants are the country's most effective poverty alleviation instrument,[41] there was, initially, little public discussion after 1994 of the degree to which grant payments are both efficient and tailored to the needs of beneficiaries. When the Department of Social Development vastly improved their distribution, ensuring that they reached millions who were entitled to grants in principle, this was a product not of public debate and political action but of a decision by the minister and his advisors.[42] Despite the increasing centrality of grants in the life of the poor, public debate on grants and their effects is often dominated by prejudices, such as the false claim that many teenage women fall pregnant to access grants.[43] It was noted earlier that mythology about social security is hardly unique to South Africa. But a grants programme which shapes the economic prospects of the grassroots poor and is greatly valued by them[44] is routinely undervalued because, while poor people participate in elections, they lack voice between them. This limits the government's ability to meet its stated policy goals.

Finally, tax collection experience suggests that, when the authorities did well at collecting revenue from the formal economy, they could not raise taxes from informal businesses. Since evidence suggests that tax collection is shaped by the relationship between government and citizens rather than by administrative capacity alone,[45] this indicates that the citizen–government interaction needed for effective taxation is limited at the grassroots.

These examples are particularly significant because the post-1994 government made public participation in development decisions a cornerstone of law and policy – albeit through formal forums rather than more open-ended processes in which citizens might engage freely with power-holders.[46] It has pursued a more active anti-poverty programme than most, if not all, other African countries. It also has access to far more domestic research on grassroots needs than any other African country. If anti-poverty policy fails to meet the needs of the poor in the country most concerned about both (formal) participation and poverty reduction, the pattern will be more pronounced in many, if not most, other African societies. While other African countries might cite financial constraints to explain their limited success in poverty reduction, this is not a tenable explanation in South Africa. And, while commentators invariably blame the technical incapacity of government officials, the gap between citizen preferences and government plans is the most plausible explanation for much of the relative ineffectiveness of anti-poverty programmes. Grassroots citizens' inability to impact on government through collective action is, therefore, also a key constraint on government's ability to fulfil its policy goals.

THE CENTRALITY OF COLLECTIVE ACTION

The chief constraint to popular sovereignty in Africa, then, is the ability of the state largely to insulate itself from society's scrutiny and influence, which limits governments' capacity to govern.

Besides obviously ensuring that policy reflects the preferences of the government and international actors, not citizenries, this is also a key reason for 'neo-patrimonial' or 'prebendal' forms of government, in which the state becomes a personalised vehicle for rent-seeking elites, not a means to realise democratic aspirations. Power-holders who are insulated from society will, of course, face few domestic pressures to account to citizens for how they use power. As long as those who govern newly democratic African democracies can continue to insulate themselves, democracy is likely to remain neither deep nor broad.

Over the past few years, there have been tentative signs that strategically placed groups in African countries, such as urban professionals, are beginning to engage in collective action which opens possibilities for deeper and broader democracy. Over the past decade and a half, citizens have mobilised to limit the power of office holders and to demand more freedoms[47] or have voted to remove incumbent governments.[48] But progress is partial and limited – if African citizens with an interest in democracy's broadening and deepening can now hold governments to account on some issues some of the time, they are far from being able to do so on most issues most of the time. Where citizens do demand and achieve change, action centres on formal politics, not social and economic change. A key reason may be that, except in rare circumstances, the spectrum of society able to engage in collective action remains narrow. The poor lack the means to act collectively to make government work for them – and so the gap between state and society has only been partly bridged, even in states in which collective action has enabled some interests to narrow the gap between government and society.

The incapacity of citizenries in post-independence Africa to engage in collective action capable of holding the state to account enabled elites to create the state in their image, making it serve their needs: citizens' capacity to do so in future will determine whether African states are remade in a more democratic image. And it is the continuing limits on collective action – its often shallow base which restricts participation to urban elites and its historic inability to mobilise enough power to force governments to account and respond – which slows progress towards deeper democracy. The outcome of pressures for democratisation will be shaped by the degree to which this latter constraint is overcome. As Moore shows, mobilisation by elites alone can enable democracy – only these elites are currently able to mobilise sufficient collective action to demand greater accountability, and it is probably they alone who can begin the democratisation of their societies. Where they win rules and institutions which ensure that all enjoy the formal right to participation, they may open opportunities for the grassroots to deepen democracy later.

In a celebrated study of post-independence Africa, Mamdani argued that, despite the end of colonisation, Africans remained 'subjects' rather than 'citizens' because they remained subjected to unaccountable power-holders.[49] While indigenous elites rather than colonisers now ruled, the patterns of power created by the coloniser, which denied the promise of citizenship, remained. The road to deeper and broader democracy – and, therefore, to states which seek to serve the people and are connected enough to them to be able to do so – depends on the degree to which Africans can become citizens. This demands that citizens also become subjects – not in Mamdani's sense, but as persons who assert their subjectivity: autonomous agents capable of actively shaping their societies rather than passive objects of power-holders; subjects who can make those who govern their societies objects of their will. To the extent that they can do this, they will ensure deeper and broader democracies and so build societies in which significant self-government becomes a reality. This may also ensure longer-lasting democracies because, if citizens are not sufficiently in control to hold power-holders to account, democracy remains vulnerable to anti-democratic shocks. For a time, rulers may endorse democratic rules to maintain international legitimacy. But, unless citizens can act collectively to ensure that power can only be exercised within the parameters they set, democracy's survival will be continually in doubt. Capacity to engage in collective action, therefore, determines not only whether democracies offer their citizens real progress to popular sovereignty, but perhaps whether they survive.

There is no reason to believe that this applies only to Africa. The creation, survival and deepening of democracy has always been the consequence of an ability by social groups to engage in collective action effective enough to constrain power-holders. Initially, those able to do this have been a relatively small elite. This limited the depth and range of popular sovereignty. But, in time, the limited accountability and responsiveness won by these elites was followed by enhanced organisation by labour unions and other popular organisations: the result was deeper democratisation and advances for popular sovereignty. Democracies become richer and more enduring the more citizens can turn their democratic rights into the capacity to hold leaders to their promises and to ensure that they act in response to the will of the majority. And the greater the capacity for collective action, the greater the ability to withstand authoritarian pressures when they emerge. In Africa as elsewhere, collective action remains the key to democratic quality, greater progress towards popular sovereignty and more enduring democracy.

6

Every Day is a Special Day: Collective Action as Democratic Routine

Why is access to collective action limited to a relatively small slice of African citizenries? Why, in other parts of the world where unaccountable governments decide on behalf of citizens – as many have done in Africa for decades – do citizens not combine their energies and efforts to make government work for them? Is it because people do not know how to act collectively? Because sustained collective action is the preserve only of those with particular resources or cultural attributes? Or because grassroots citizens want to act collectively but their circumstances make action difficult or dangerous?

For much of the political studies mainstream, collective action is an oddity, not a contribution to democracy. A once influential work on the topic, *Why Men Rebel,*[1] sought to understand particular types of collective action by inquiring into the mental and emotional state, the sense of 'relative deprivation', of people who engage in it.

This reflects an ideological choice. It signals that protest is odd, even pathological, and must, therefore, be related to something unusual happening inside the protestors' heads. Collective action, for writers who hold this view, is 'anomic, alienated and outside the polity'.[2] There is nothing self-evident about this: it might be equally valid to assume that normal people always engage in collective action and, therefore, to investigate the mental make-up of passive citizens to explain their alarming lack of civic activity. A detailed study of collective action by Barrington Moore focussed not only on why people rebel, but also on why they obey.[3] By examining the psychology of those who act rather than those who do not, *Why Men*

Rebel declares that passivity is the norm, and action to challenge power the exception which must be explained.

Popular collective action discomforts elites and may appear to them as a threat: to those who are challenged by collective action, it may, therefore, seem the product of a troubled mind. Psychological theories of collective mobilisation might reflect this bias. They may spring from the assumption that existing arrangements are so manifestly in the interests of all that anyone who opposes them must be dysfunctional. But simply to dismiss psychological explanations is to gloss over an important issue.

If citizens were as inclined to combine with others to express themselves as they are to engage in economic activity, collective action would not seem remarkable enough to require explanation. Whether we see it as a virtue or a threat, it is not generally seen as a commonplace. It is not routine for citizens to act in unison to hold power accountable. On the contrary, even where entire populations are dominated by power-holders who routinely ignore their concerns, it is often only a small minority who actively participate. Thus a paper examining an increase in protest politics internationally cites World Values Survey data which show that, even after a marked rise in protest, the highest reported percentage of respondents saying they had participated was 39 per cent.[4] While the participation of two in five adult citizens in protest activity indicates a very high level of engagement, it still means that most people do not participate. The 'default' position of most human beings seems to be to avoid collective action while they get on with their lives. Doesn't that mean that collective action – and, more generally, civic action – is always the preserve of a few zealots? And, if it is, how much sense does it make to insist that democracy rests on popular sovereignty – and that it can be sustained only by actions in which relatively few people engage? Is a stress on collective action not a new form of democratic elitism because it makes democracy the concern of only that select group which is willing and able to engage in civic action? Does this not condemn most citizens to remain passive spectators as a minority of collective actors decide on their behalf?

The questions are crucial to the way in which democracy has been understood in South Africa over the past two decades. Popular collective action played a key role in apartheid's defeat – this strongly influenced thinking on democracy in the period just before and after 1994. For a strong body of opinion within the political leadership which had led resistance inside the country, democracy required that activist groups enjoy a guaranteed say in decisions. This was challenged on the grounds that it gave a relatively small section of the citizenry who enjoyed access to the means of collective action greater power than everyone else.[5] But it is responsible for the fact that post-1994 South Africa introduced perhaps the widest array of participatory structures in the world – issues ranging from local development priorities through to crime fighting were to be decided by forums in which citizens who engaged in collective action would play the key role. The result was not the flowering of democracy but an attempt to channel citizen energies into avenues which were very convenient to officials but did little or nothing to enable citizens to shape decisions. It could be argued that these approaches assumed that a minority who engage in collective action has the right to decide for everyone else. Can a view which insists on the centrality of collective action to democracy avoid this trap?

These questions require two sets of answers, which will occupy this and the next chapter. First, we need to examine the collective action which sustains democracy – and to understand that protest is only one of many ways in which citizens claim a say in how they are governed. Second, we need to recognise that reluctance to act is not a product of human aversion to action, but of power relations which make it far easier for some to act than others. It follows that the collective action which is essential to democracy need not be the permanent preserve of a few, and that it may be possible for access to collective action, and, therefore, a share in popular sovereignty, to be widely distributed throughout the adult population, if the power relations which prevent most people from acting are altered. We will address this second theme in the following chapter. Here, we examine current understandings of collective action to understand how citizens act together to exercise sovereignty.

PROTEST AND BEYOND – HOPES AND FEARS

What would a society in which everyone had access to collective action look like? Would perpetual protest make society ungovernable? Or, as the South African activists who wanted those engaged in collective action to enjoy an extra say seemed to hope, would active citizens perpetually engage in civic activity, fulfilling the expectations of those to whom the ideal society is one in which all are always politically engaged?

The latter two questions express, broadly, the fears and hopes which are evoked by the prospect of a permanently mobilised citizenry – and both are hostile to broadening and deepening popular sovereignty. On the one hand, democratic elitism is only the most obvious example of widespread thinking which fears that 'excessive' popular participation would destroy democracy because it would soon submerge reasoned decision-making beneath a tide of pressure from a 'mob' determined to impose its will and to trample over any rules which stood in its way. In this view, if democracy is to grow and strengthen, participation must be channelled and limited. On the other, enthusiasm for active citizenship as a cornerstone of democracy produces unrealistic hopes and inevitable frustration as those who hold to this view find that most citizens – including the poor and weak, who seemingly have most to gain from collective action – have a limited appetite for the active exercise of citizenship and so are unavailable for projects which seek a permanently engaged citizenry. The first view threatens popular sovereignty by presenting it as a threat to democracy rather than its lifeblood, the second by expecting a level of citizen involvement which, if it was essential to democracy, would make even limited popular self-government impossible.

These fears and hopes must be addressed by a workable vision of democracy as popular sovereignty. The types of collective action needed for effective democratic citizenship are anything but obvious. First, it needs to be shown that collective action strengthens, rather than threatens, democracy. Second, we need to show that popular mobilisation, important though it is, is not the only form of collective action in which citizens engage to claim their share of a say. It is not even the most important mode because it is used rarely, is out of reach of many and is often not as effective as the less obvious forms of collective action preferred by the powerful. Given this, we need a broader view of collective action which can understand the full range of options used by citizens and hold open the possibility of a working democracy in which all would have a stake, whether or not they participate actively and regularly.

VALIDATING POPULAR MOBILISATION

Elitist doubts about popular mobilisation have been challenged by scholars who have sought to understand collective action and to show that it sustains and strengthens democracy. This school was a response to public mobilisation in the North in the 1960s, which focussed academic attention on collective action and 'contentious politics'.[6] American scholars such as Tilly and Sidney Tarrow led an attempt to understand afresh why people combined in social movements and their effect on democratic politics. In Europe, a belief that the 1960s initiated new forms of social movement activity which differed from the class-based actions of the labour movement prompted attempts by scholars such as Touraine and Melucci to explain the changed ways in which activists were said to express themselves in response to structural shifts in 'post-industrial' economies.[7] The result was a rich body of data and theory explaining collective action – or, as some scholars had it, the 'dynamics of contention'.[8]

The right to protest or to press power-holders to concede to demands is a key ingredient of democracy, one of the ways in which citizens seek popular sovereignty. This is ignored surprisingly often by accounts which see protest and mobilisation as a refusal to use democratic institutions. In an influential study of economic reform in new democracies, Luiz Carlos Bresser Pereira and his colleagues argue that, if reforms are to proceed under democratic conditions, all groups must channel their demands through democratic institutions and reject other tactics. They must be willing to accept defeats and to wait, 'confident that these institutions will continue to offer opportunities next time around'.[9] Democracy obviously cannot operate if those who lose arguments ignore or subvert democratic institutions. But the authors are not simply saying that people must accept democratic contest even if they lose arguments. They endorse the view of John McGurk, chairman of the British Labour Party in 1919, who declared: 'If we are constitutionalists … it is both unwise and undemocratic because we fail to get a majority at the polls to turn around and demand that we should substitute industrial action'.[10] For the authors, citizens whose party loses an election are undermining democracy if they mobilise before the next election. This implies that mobilisation is anti-democratic because it substitutes action by a minority for rule by the majority.

But why should this be so? Obviously, not all mobilisation strengthens democracy: 'mob rule', in which some impose their will on others, threatens democracy[11] because it silences people. Collective action has also been mobilised by authoritarians against democracy. But this does not mean that mobilisation always threatens democracy: in most cases, it is essential to its maintenance. It was noted earlier that elections cannot settle policy debates because a vote for a party or candidate does not necessarily mean a vote for a particular policy. Even if it could be established that most voters had endorsed a policy at the polls, opinions change. Contention over policy does not, therefore, stop between elections – it is a routine feature of a functioning democracy. If the purpose of industrial action, or any other popular mobilisation by supporters of a defeated party, is to influence public opinion, it cannot be an attempt to undermine or subvert democracy – it enables the system to operate as a vehicle of popular sovereignty.

The difference between action designed to sustain democracy and that which seeks to undermine it does not lie in whether citizens mobilise to make their voices heard. It lies, rather, in the way people mobilise, or use any other method of influencing political decisions. Mobilisation subverts democracy only when it seeks to impose the demonstrators' will on everyone else by force. Mobilisation is only one method which can be used to subvert an elected authority: elites who feel threatened by an elected government are likely, as Bermeo has shown,[12] to have other options available. Mobilisation in itself does not threaten democracy and avoiding it does not necessarily protect it. Where its purpose is to enable citizens to express themselves to power-holders within democratic rules, it is not a threat to democratic institutions, but one of their essential features. Participation in protests and other forms of mobilisation strengthens the system, provided that those who engage in it do not impair the rights of others. Protests may indicate not a rejection of democracy but its affirmation, because those who engage in it have enough confidence in the system to believe that collective action within democratic rules can influence decisions. Tarrow therefore remarks that the protests of the 1960s challenged the notion that 'a hard-and-fast-line could be drawn between social movements and institutional politics'.[13]

This may explain why a study of protest action by Eastern European citizens found a positive correlation between protest and the strength of democracy in the societies studied.[14] The authors suggest that protest strengthens democracy when it 'is employed as a means of bringing forward demands for reforms and not challenging the legitimacy of the regime'.[15] While the understanding of democracy which is advocated here would insist that citizens are entitled to challenge the legitimacy of a regime, this does make the point that most protest strengthens democracy and does not threaten it. The 'social movement' literature has played an important role in reminding us that popular mobilisation which seeks to use democratic rights and rules to influence decisions is not a threat to democracy, but a crucial source of strength.

PLACING DEMOCRACY (MOSTLY) OUT OF REACH?

As important as this scholarship was in highlighting mobilisation's contribution to democracy, its understanding of the role of collective action and contention in sustaining democracy misses a crucial element.

Invariably in this work, collective action and contention are equated with mass mobilisation, protests or demonstrations. Tarrow writes: 'The contentious politics of the late 1960s and early 1970s' shocked some scholars 'from the calm assurance that ideology and militancy were dead'; some 'now concluded that mass politics had run amuck and that democratic institutions were threatened...'.[16] Clearly 'contention' and 'mass politics' are here one and the same, a perspective shared by the literature on 'social movements' and 'contention'. Politics becomes contentious when people use protests to influence power-holders.[17] A key feature of this form of engagement is that it is unusual and remarkable, that it breaks the flow of 'normal' life even if it happens quite frequently – in this view, contentious politics is an 'episodic' form of collective action.[18] This school of scholarship does not agree that collective action is deviant – it agrees, however, that it is out of the ordinary.

But mobilisation is only one form of 'contention' and not the most common one. Politics becomes 'contentious' whenever opposing visions and interests clash – which is just about always. Democracy is a system in which contention – the clash of visions, interests and values – is not only recognised but celebrated, if it is channelled through institutions which protect the right of all to contend. Contention is the lifeblood of vigorous democratic politics. It is the refusal to acknowledge contention which characterises formalised 'public participation' processes. And it is the recognition that democratic politics is contentious that lies at the heart of the democratic critique of forums which insists that genuine participation requires the free expression of contention within rules which ensure that the right to contend remains open to all.

This does not mean that all democratic politics is about conflict and contention. There are democratic processes in which the participants share common interests and values and in which decision-making is an attempt to arrive at the best means to a common end. But in these cases, the decision on whether to hear all opinions or to leave the task to technically qualified people is a pragmatic choice, not one of principle. If all agree on goals, no one is disadvantaged if decisions on how to achieve them are left to technical specialists. 'Public participation' techniques which insist that poor people ought to debate the type of sewer which will be installed in their neighbourhoods, for example, assume that participation is always needed in every decision. In reality, we only need to participate when our interests or values are affected and this can occur only if there is disagreement. Wherever this is so, contentious politics is essential if all are to share in decisions.

Given this close connection between contention and democracy, contention cannot be reduced to social mobilisation alone because any free competition between contending ideas and interests must be understood as contentious. Tilly recognises this when he describes 'repertoires of contention' as 'the ways that people act together in pursuit of shared interests'.[19] And that means that fairly mundane activities such as casting a vote or attending a neighbourhood meeting, signing a petition, writing a letter to the press or lobbying a local representative are also examples of contentious politics. Tilly and David Snyder recognise this when they note that some contenders for power have 'routine means of influencing the government…'.[20]

The active democratic citizen is not only the person who joins a march or boy-cott, but one who engages in routine activities associated with citizenship. The division is not between those who demonstrate and those who do not, but between those who participate in public decision-making and those who do not. It is therefore significant that, when surveys measure participation by citizens, people are far more inclined to participate in more routine forms of collective action than mobilisation. So great is this change that participation becomes the majority choice, confounding the surface impression that most people's 'default' position is not to participate actively in exercising citizenship. A study which found that Belgians are the world's champion demonstrators, because slightly fewer than two in five say they have participated in protest, also reports data from that country's Flanders province showing that 97 per cent of respondents have voted and 76 per cent have signed a petition.[21] Where people can make themselves heard in ways which do not impose excessive costs on themselves, participation predictably increases dramatically, becoming the choice of the majority, not the motivated minority.

If mobilisation is not the only form of contentious politics, it is also not the only form of democratic collective action. The assumption that collective action consists purely of the exotic and unusual can be traced back to the view that 'collective behaviour' is unusual and outlandish – the 'panic, the craze, the hostile outburst, the norm-oriented movement and the value-oriented movement'[22] – in contrast to democratic commonplaces such as lobbying. Collective action is seen here as the unruly, which disturbs the smooth functioning of an orderly society. But orderly societies are underpinned by routine collective action. The form of collective action which maintains democracy is more mundane and is usually used by the affluent and the well connected. This masks the degree to which its use is a daily feature of any democracy.

The only difference between the letter-writer and the marcher is that they have chosen different ways to express themselves. If the former acts with others, she or he is engaging in democratic collective action. Just as the marcher or placard-holder is not an inferior form of democratic citizen, neither is the letter-writer or meeting-attender. Democratic collective action is the process in which people combine with others to use the rules and rights of democracy to influence power – regardless of the method.

This routine collective action is also often vicarious – people rely on others to speak or act for them. Most members of a business or professional or suburban ratepayers' association do not do the letter-writing or petition-drafting themselves – they rely on others to do it. Rational choice theorists overstate the case when they insist that this 'free riding' is the only rational way of engaging in collective action – if everyone relied on everyone else, no one would ever act – but it remains the most common, even among those who identify strongly with an organisation. The effectiveness of collective action does not rely on everyone undertaking all the tasks which make routine action possible. Citizens may participate in collective action without engaging directly in any action besides joining an organisation.

Much development thinking on participation fails to acknowledge this. It tends to assume that people are active citizens only when they attend meetings or take to the streets. And, since development thinking focusses on the poor, the effect is to demand of the poor and weak a level of engagement which the wealthy and connected avoid because they have others to undertake the tasks for them. The ability to act collectively to influence decisions is a right, not a duty. Most citizens do not regularly engage in routine collective action regardless of how connected to power they are: the test of a broad and deep democracy is whether all have access to routine collective action *when they need it*, not the frequency with which citizens act in concert. An account of democracy which stresses the central role of collective action must not become a double burden on the weak by imposing obligations to act which the strong can avoid. Often, it may be precisely the ability to engage in routine collective action without being constantly available for direct participation which determines the degree to which citizens enjoy a share in popular sovereignty.

While the routine form of collective action which does not require public mobilisation is less glamorous, it is far more frequent – and, usually, far more potent. Protest can often entail significant costs. And, while participants may derive personal satisfaction from participating in it – much the same 'pleasure in action' which, in the view of one study, prompted rural people to engage in guerrilla warfare in El Salvador[23] – it is the quiet, routine, collective action of the well resourced and well connected which has a far greater impact on concrete decision-making by power-holders.

Social movement theories offer valuable insights into how citizens mobilise to seek to hold power to account and to force it to respond. But their sole focus on mobilisation, protest and other forms of episodic and dramatic collective action risks misreading the role of collective action because it suggests that it is an unusual feature of democracy. Collective action is intrinsic to all democracies – the issue is not whether citizens engage in it but which citizens do and in what way. The action social movement scholars describe is not the only sort – nor is it the most common or influential.

This recognition that collective action is intrinsic to all democracies but that its impact is usually greatest when it is employed in an unobtrusive routine manner, usually by private elites, has important implications for our understanding of collective action's role in democracies – and of the change which is needed if grassroots citizens are to participate in the exercise of popular sovereignty.

WEAPONS OF THE STRONG: ELITE USES OF COLLECTIVE ACTION

On very rare occasions, business people and professionals can be seen demonstrating with their fellow citizens in support of democracy. Even more rarely, a business may, as a South African bank did in 2007, seek to mobilise citizens to press government decision-makers to act on their concerns.[24] These actions are very rare – the scattered examples excite comment precisely because they happen hardly at all.

But business people and other elites are acting collectively. Their public displays of voice are so rare because their engagement in collective action in pursuit of their interests is routine. Public attempts to influence decisions are unnecessary: elites do not take to the streets because they have no need. The forms of elite collective action are often not visible to everyone else: for example, lobbying and face-to-face meetings with decision-makers. But, since all require co-ordinated action to frame goals, make them known to public power-holders and seek their incorporation in law, policy and programmes, they are forms of collective action which seek a response from governments. They rely not on mobilisation but on organisation, which enables sustained influence and allows participants to benefit without incurring the costs of mobilisation.

This reality has been obscured by popular commentary and scholarship which tends to class this form of collective action as 'interest group' representation. In academic writing, interest group engagement is usually classed as 'pluralist' or 'corporatist' – the former is relatively unstructured, the latter formalised.[25] But these are simply different variants of collective action, a point recognised decades ago by the classic 'rational choice' theory of collective action, that of Mancur Olson.[26] Since this form of engagement between citizens and governments is acknowledged by scholars as a perpetual feature of all political systems, it follows that collective action is not an unusual event which requires explanation. It is an inevitable and routine feature of all political systems.

Routine collective action is more influential and more decisive for democracy's fate than is mobilisation. Interests which enjoy access to government decisions routinely are far more likely to enjoy sustained influence. Evidence is offered by a study of officialdom during the late apartheid era: a relatively small group of organisations who enjoyed ready access to government were identified by most officials as the prime sources of societal influence on its decisions.[27]

Groups which engage in this sort of collective action exert influence for four reasons which are not mutually exclusive. First, they find organisation far easier: Olson argued that it is easier to organise small groups than very large ones.[28] While the next chapter will reject his claim that people in large groups act collectively only when forced to do so, sustaining the organisation of a relatively small group of firms is easier than keeping tens of thousands of workers mobilised. Where interests rely for their influence on the reality that a small set of actors has access to much of society's resources, collective action is far easier. Small, powerful groups find it easier to influence public decision-makers than those who depend on mobilising large numbers to make themselves heard.

Second, resources – not only money but leisure time and 'cultural capital' – make collective action much easier. People who do not enjoy access to these goods are not necessarily excluded from collective action – if they were, democratisation would be impossible. Access to resources is not the prime determinant of whether people can participate in collective action. But it is a great deal easier for those who command resources to act collectively to influence public decisions; more affluent people are more likely to be able to hold government to account. In South Africa, attempts to broaden public participation in government often empower the affluent – who are, ironically, usually those who benefitted from racial oligarchy – not the newly enfranchised majority.[29] Access to resources may also enhance the frequency and influence of less organised forms of collective action, such as letter-writing campaigns, because participants have more of the resources required to make these possible and more of the access to decision-makers which might ensure that they are heard. In some cases, simply knowing who the relevant decision-makers are may offer some a possibility of effective collective action not available to others.

Third, some citizens enjoy access to already waiting organisational infrastructure – they can join, at minimal cost, associations which are engaged in collective action simply by occupying a job or living in a neighbourhood. Their collective action is also assisted by the reality that highly structured organisations, such as business and professional associations – and, where the right to participate is guaranteed by law or formal arrangements with employers, trade unions – require less effort from members. Since much of the influence is exerted by professionals hired to engage political authorities, no more may be required than to pay subscription fees. Contrary to Olson's claim that there is no reason why people would voluntarily join large organisations since the costs of doing so outweigh the benefits, the costs of participating in established, structured, organisations are usually low enough to make this an attractive option even to people who will derive only limited concrete benefits from membership.

Fourth, some groups acquire influence because they perform functions considered essential to society: decision-makers engage with them because, it is assumed, the system cannot survive without them. The example *par excellence* is business, whose resources are essential to governments presiding over market economies. This reality ensures, in the view of a celebrated study by Charles Lindblom, that business enjoys a 'privileged position' in formal democracies, even though all social actors enjoy equal influence in theory.[30] In societies which use corporatism – structured engagement between governments and interest groups – to make policy, producer groups such as unions and professional associations may also have greater influence. They can allow or prevent the production and distribution of goods and services and enjoy access to structured forms of collective action such as mandatory participation in policy processes, which are not available to consumer groups.[31]

In all of these cases, collective action does not necessarily entail popular mobilisation – although unions use this strategy if circumstances demand it. It may seem, both to those who engage in it and those with whom they engage, to be routine, an almost natural expression of daily engagement between citizens and public officials. This may be why it is usually studied not as a form of collective action but of interest group intermediation, or of lobbying.[32]

The collective action discussed here is a routine feature of any political system in which there is regular engagement between government and social groups. It is not an exotic element; it is the underlying pulse or heartbeat which keeps democracies and, to a degree, semi-democracies alive. Rather than seeing collective action as a rarity, engaged in only, or even mostly, when people take to the streets, we need to see it as a constant, the engine which drives the political system. As we focus on those who have fairly easy access to collective action in democracies, we come to recognise how 'ordinary' a feature of political life it is. This recognition also draws attention to collective action's role in reflecting and reproducing power – again, in a routine manner. The powerful's access to routine collective action does not guarantee influence over all decisions. But it does, as Lindblom's work on business–government relations showed, ensure a 'privileged' position.[33]

Research has confirmed Lindblom's finding that, if everyone in the US enjoys the equal right to act collectively to influence decisions, some groups, particularly business, enjoy greater access than others. A study in the 1980s of the nearly 7 000 interest organisations actively engaging with the political system in Washington, DC, found that '[a]lthough much has been made of the arrival in Washington of many new citizens groups over the past two decades, business interests are overrepresented among organized interests there in terms of the number of interest organizations and the structure of interest representation. This overrepresentation takes place at the expense of the representation of the interests of broad publics and the poor'.[34] The evidence supports EE Schattschneider's famous critique of the notion that, in (pluralist) liberal democracies, interest groups compete on equal terms for the ear of government: 'the flaw in the pluralist Heaven', he noted, 'is that the heavenly chorus sings with a strong upper-class accent. Probably about 90% of the people cannot get into the pressure system'.[35] Because some enjoy routine access to government while others do not, the universal right to collective action which popular sovereignty confers benefits the few who enjoy this access at the expense of the many who do not.

It is this which ensures that there is no automatic correspondence between the degree to which political institutions formally recognise popular sovereignty and the extent to which the principle is practised. The US again illustrates the point. Its institutions are often a model of popular sovereignty. Party candidates are chosen directly by voters in primary elections. Many of the posts which, in other societies, are allocated by processes in which citizens cannot participate, are open to public election. District attorneys and judges are examples: the US is reportedly one of only three countries where judges are subject to some form of election, and in the other two the practice is far more limited.[36] Key public functions such as education are often subject to control by elected councils. Citizens dissatis-fied with elected government's failure to adopt their policy proposals can force them to do so by drafting ballot initiatives for consideration by voters. Elected officials can be recalled by popular ballot before their terms have ended. More positions and decisions are open to direct decision by citizens than in most other democracies.

But popular sovereignty in the US is weaker than in many other democracies. We have noted state-imposed restrictions on the right to vote – they help explain why only 49 per cent of the adult population voted in the election of 1996.[37] This is substantially lower than the percentage of adults voting in other Northern democ-racies – and lower also than many democracies in the South.[38] While subsequent elections have improved slightly on this low, the percentage of eligible citizens voting has not reached 60.[39] Measures which ensure that minorities find it dif-ficult to vote remain a major block to participation in elections.[40] We noted that little over a third of North Americans believe their government reflects the will of the people. Despite formal democratic rights for all, racial minorities, the young, the less educated and less wealthy do not enjoy the same rights to decide as the mainstream and so citizenship rights are unevenly distributed.[41] The key reason is the phenomenon Lindblom identified – that some have routine access to political decision-makers which enables them to influence not only the decisions but the rules which determine how they are made.

In the US, this is more acute than in other democracies because restrictions on the use of money to influence political outcomes have either been defeated or have been ineffective: 'in the world of actual politics people confront one another in massively unequal power contexts – in the United States most obviously owing to the role of money in politics'.[42] Wealth is used to influence politics in a variety of ways, among them the routine access to political representatives enjoyed by those who fund the campaigns of elected office holders. The problem is not an absence of collective action but its unequal distribution, which ensures that the power wielded by the action of small groups with large resources, in routine engagement with government, far outweighs that of the rest of society, even when those outside the charmed circle are occasionally able to mobilise tens of thousands of people. But the problem is not unique to the US, even if it is most evident there: that some can routinely act collectively to influence political decisions while most cannot is a reality in all democracies.

The public mobilisation discussed in the 'social movement' literature is the sort to which citizens resort when the easier, more direct forms are not available to them. While people who engage in these more costly forms of collective action may derive from it a sense of their ability to become thinking, acting subjects, this does *not* mean that human beings engage in demonstrations because this is a satisfying activity. If it were, the affluent, whose access to resources offers them options not available to others, would engage in it regularly. Public mobilisation is usually the preserve of those unable to gain access to routine collective action; it is an important display of civic engagement but also a last resort to which people turn when easier, more routine action is unavailable or when it cannot influence powerholders. It is less a romantic form of engagement than a reflection of unequal access to collective action which influences decisions. Poor people are eager to engage in routine collective action when they get the chance: in India, the poor vote more often than other groups – not only because this is one of the few forms of available expression but because 'the poor think of voting as a dignifying right'.[43]

Routine collective action's central role means that democracy's deepening and broadening depends on whether it becomes widely accessible through organisation of the excluded or by the way democratic governments conduct their affairs. Societies are more democratic the more routine action is not the preserve of the few.

DEMOCRATISING COLLECTIVE ACTION: A CHIMERA?

How do poor people, who lack the resources and access which the affluent enjoy, take part in routine collective action?

It is rare for those who lack resources and skills to rely purely on routine collective action to be heard. Where they are able to get close enough to political authorities to use this action at all, they almost always need to combine it with public mobilisation by part of their constituency part of the time. Where routine engagement with public officials by grassroots citizens occurs, this is often a product of public mobilisation. Are there ways in which people at the grassroots can engage with public decision-makers in a routine way which holds out a reasonable prospect of influencing decisions, whether or not their members engage in (often costly) public mobilisation?

Some theories insist that this is simply not possible in unequal societies – which, thus far in human history, means all societies. Marxist theory holds that those who own the means of production also control the state: while democratic form may enable all to engage with elected representatives and officials, 'the executive of the modern State is but a committee for managing the common affairs of the whole bourgeoisie'.[44] That is, it implements the will of the property-owning class alone. In this view, while those who do not own productive property may enjoy the legal right to access the state, they cannot exercise it. Even if they gain access, they will be ignored if their concerns conflict with the interests of the owners, which they usually do. A variant of this view is argued in a study of mobilisation in the US by Frances Fox Piven and Richard Cloward.[45] While they do not argue that poor people cannot influence decisions, they do not believe the poor can advance their interests through routine engagement with political power-holders – if they try to do this, their interests will be shunted aside.

Piven and Cloward take issue with the 'dominant pluralistic tradition' and its claim that 'there is ample opportunity for the working class to pursue its interests through democratic institutional channels'.[46] But they wish also to challenge another assumption which is central to the argument proposed here:

> The presumption of most reformers and revolutionaries who have tried to organise the lower classes is that once the economic and political resources of at least modest numbers of people are combined in disciplined action, public or private elites will be forced to yield up the concessions necessary to sustain and enlarge mass affiliation ... The model has not succeeded because

it contains a grave flaw. The flaw is, quite simply, that it is not possible to compel concessions from elites which can be used as resources to sustain oppositional organizations over time.[47]

If this claim is accurate, sustained organisation of 'the lower classes' which would enable them to hold power to account in a continuing manner is impossible. The poor can be heard only through 'insurgency' – mass mobilisation – which is 'always short-lived'.[48] In sharp contrast to the argument proposed here, they insist that '[w]hatever influence lower-class groups occasionally exert ... does not result from organization, but from ... the disruptive consequences of protest'.[49] The challenge to those who organise the poor to exert influence, therefore, is that '[t]hey can only try to win whatever can be won while it can be won'.[50] Routine collective action, in this view, will get the poor nowhere. They can influence events, but only through a 'smash and grab' strategy in which short and rare bursts of mass protest win concessions which must be quickly seized before the moment passes.

But, if routine access to decisions really is impossible for workers and the poor, why would concessions won in mass protest endure? Elites would surely realise – probably sooner rather than later – that the poor cannot sustain collective action beyond the occasional burst. Rather than honouring concessions, elites would wait for the wave of protest to subside and then withdraw them. They might not even do that – if all the poor can muster is occasional bursts of mobilisation, elites might be better off sitting out the storm until exhaustion sets in. Elites, it might be argued, allow the concessions to remain in the hope of preventing more protest. But, if the poor cannot gain a routine share in decisions, they are likely to mobilise when-ever they have the energy to do so and elites would not be protected against new disruptions by honouring the concessions made in the last round. So, if Piven and Cloward are correct, we are asked to believe that elites honour concessions despite any incentives to do so. This is implausible, particularly since they see change as a product of social conflict, not elite goodwill.

Nor does this argument explain why organisations of the 'lower classes' endure – and influence decisions. Organisation, not mobilisation alone, enabled workers in Western Europe to elect governments sympathetic to their interests and to increase their incomes significantly.[51] Organisation built out of mobilisation enabled black industrial workers in South Africa to sustain lengthy battles for the recognition of their unions and to use the routine bargaining rights they won as bridgeheads to build a movement which also helped end minority rule.[52] In democratic and authoritarian conditions, organisation of the poor does endure and is some-times incorporated in structures which offer routine access to power – through corporatism or less structured forums, such as the National Economic Development and Labour Council (Nedlac) in South Africa. While Piven and Cloward would, given the gist of their argument, see these as processes in which poor people's organisations are offered the illusion of access, organised routine engagement has achieved a redistribution of power and resources which survives even though it has faced great stress.

REALISING POSSIBILITY: ROUTINE COLLECTIVE ACTION AT THE GRASSROOTS

If the labour movement was the only vehicle through which access to routine collective action could be democratised, prospects would be limited and declining. But routine collective action is possible for poor people who do not belong to trade unions. A later chapter will discuss the way in which people living with HIV and AIDS used their constitutional rights to engage in mobilisation and routine action. This section will examine some international examples in an attempt to understand how people at the grassroots might gain access to routine collective action which would enable them to press political authority to respond to them.

An example of how grassroots citizens can engage in effective routine collective action is discussed in a study by Richard Wood of faith-based community organisation among racial minorities in the US.[53] Their goal is not to campaign for particular policies but to ensure that political authority accounts to those on whose behalf it is meant to be wielded. When asked to identify the fundamental task of their work, 'holding officials accountable' was the most common response among leaders of the grassroots organisations he studied.[54] The purpose of the activity is to make democracy work by ensuring greater popular sovereignty. The organisations seek to do this through routine engagement with local government.

Grassroots routine collective action is, unsurprisingly, different from that of more affluent groups with their greater access to decision-makers. While it does mean negotiating with officials, it also uses mobilisation. But it seeks to ensure that addressing the interests of once excluded citizens is part of the routine functioning of government, not a special event. The difference between sporadic campaigns for change and routine collective action among the poor or weak is not that the one relies on gentle pleading with officials across boardroom tables while the other depends on displays of power. On the contrary, the collective action Wood describes is routine only in the sense that it is a constant feature of life – there is nothing 'moderate' about it. The organisations which he analyses aim to channel the energies of participants to gain constant access to the democratic system rather than to mobilise to win sporadic concessions from it. Wood therefore described this strategy as 'constructive use of political conflict to promote democratic engagement'.[55]

Equally important is that the organisations do not engage local government through formal public participation vehicles designed by officials. These forums structure participation through channels chosen by power-holders and have been labelled 'invited' spaces[56] since officials invite citizens to comment on their initiatives. This form of routine collective action is extremely popular among international development agencies and governments seeking ways of institutionalising 'participatory governance' to ensure that grassroots citizens comment on policies and programmes.[57] It was argued earlier that these forums cannot offer citizens the free exercise of popular sovereignty because they are heavily biased towards the better resourced and engagement occurs on the terms of, and in a manner convenient to, public power-holders. By contrast, the routine collective action in which the organisations discussed in Wood's study engage occurs on citizens' terms. They show that these spaces can become a routine feature of the way in which citizens engage with government. But they do so on terms they, not political authorities, choose.

Engagements between the organisations Wood discusses and local government happen at the behest of the organisations, at venues they choose – neighbourhood halls, not municipal offices – where the mayor and other officials are invited to hear citizen concerns and respond to them.[58] Civic power-holders are not granted special status at meetings – they are given a few minutes to respond and are cut off when they exceed their time: 'organizational discipline is used to prevent both manipulation by ambitious officials and spontaneous disruption by the audience'.[59] A sign that these exchanges are about the exercise of citizenship is an insistence by the citizens groups that the mayor arrive at a time set by the organisation: when he repeatedly indicated that he would be late for meetings, the organisation pressured him successfully to arrive on time.[60] That engagement between elected officials and citizens occurs on the latter's terms is explicit. A priest who, while chairing a meeting, cut the mayor off because he felt his answers were evasive, justified his actions thus: 'This is our meeting and our agenda; politicians want to make it their meeting and their agenda, and you can't let them do that.'[61] This does not mean that citizens have succeeded in ensuring that government serves them. But it does establish a pattern of routine collective action which makes deeper popular sovereignty possible. And it does this primarily because, in contrast to 'public participation' techniques, it makes engagement between citizens and government a consequence of a process in which citizens use the free exercise of citizenship to force government to account to them on their terms.

Nor does engagement consist solely of meetings at which officials are held to account in public venues. It also includes negotiation, and at times partnership, with elected politicians: 'We don't just go to people and ask for something once. We create an on-going relationship'.[62] Relations with officials are often contentious, showing that partnerships between government and grassroots citizens do not force the latter to give up their independence or their commitment to those they represent. And they are seen as sources of power: 'nothing happens now that [our organisation] is not sought out for advice'.[63] Wood compares this engagement to the work of 'lobbyists and political action committees' which, in the US, channel the collective action of the affluent into the political process and sees it as potentially 'a form of democratic pressure' in 'a site of elite manoeuvring at the heart of our democratic institutions'.[64] While the collective action Wood brands 'manoeuvring' is more integral to democratic institutions than he is willing to allow, the key point is that the monopoly of routine collective action by the affluent is now challenged, at least to a degree, by equivalent action among the poor and once voiceless, which forces government officials to account to citizens other than the elites to whom they usually respond. And, while it would take a far greater exercise of grassroots power to begin to match the influence wielded by elite collective action, it is a potential counterweight to it and so a means of deepening popular sovereignty by including more voices in government decision-making.

Although this example is drawn from a Northern country, it is hard to see why it should not offer a model for any democracy anywhere, if poor people can achieve sufficient organisation to make routine collective action possible. There is no reason why it should not be applied wherever authorities make routine decisions which affect people's lives. It is clearly a possibility in South Africa, where local government is elected and does have some power to respond to citizens.

Nor is the interaction which Wood describes the only form of contact between citizens living in poverty and government which offers citizens the prospect of routine engagement with the authorities on their, rather than power-holders', terms. Social audits, which were devised in India at the end of the twentieth century – and are now in use in South Africa – stem from a similar approach. The Indian audits became part of the official governance system in 2005, when the Rural Employment Act mandated states to conduct audits.[65] The audits were, however, initially a citizen initiative, and it is as this that they are organised in South Africa. Social audits begin when 'citizen auditors' gather information on the way in which governments implement development projects.[66] They then disseminate the information in house visits to citizens. This enables people to contribute information but also mobilises them to participate in the core event of the social audit process, the public hearing, at which officials are invited to hear citizens' perspectives and to respond to them. Where the process succeeds, the hearings initiate a procedure in which citizens engage with the authorities to ensure that proposals for change are implemented. In South Africa, social audits were first used by the Cape Town-based Social Justice Coalition.[67] Its initial project was hampered by the refusal of the Cape Town council to respond sympathetically to the audit,[68] but the audits have since achieved greater success in other municipalities.

The core principle of the audits is that citizens take the initiative in identifying the issues which concern them and placing them on the agenda. As in Wood's examples, citizens ask government to meet them at a place and on terms of their choosing. And again, if the process works, it can ensure that grassroots citizens engage in routine collective action to improve the way in which the authorities respond to them. They show that ideas which extend popular sovereignty to people at the grassroots need not always begin in the global North – there are, no doubt, other ways of channelling citizen engagement with government which could meet the same criteria.

These examples show what may be possible if we understand collective action as a routine feature of democratic government. The extension of popular sovereignty depends less on the occasional campaign or movement than on extending routine engagement with democratic institutions to all citizens, particularly those at the grassroots who are least likely to enjoy means of holding power to account. This does not exclude mobilisation – on the contrary, for the poor, it usually depends on it. But it builds on the passing gains won by mobilisation to secure perpetual access to decisions.

Wood's organisations also seek to hold private power to account by, for example, engaging with corporations: it seems inevitable that routine grassroots collective action will engage with private economic power-holders too. While the argument developed here concentrates largely on government, it does not deny the importance of unequal power in the private realm. But it does assume that popular sovereignty is exercised through public representative institutions, and that the test of the degree to which citizens are sovereign is the extent to which representative government does what most members of the political community want it to do – which may include regulating private economic power.

Routine But Not Regulated: Collective Action in the South

Further evidence that the routine engagement described by Wood is not a Northern experience unavailable to most of humanity is Chatterjee's study of popular politics in India, which was mentioned earlier. At first sight, the politics which Chatterjee describes seems to confirm the immense gulf between prospects for routine collective action in the South and the North, for it is almost the antithesis of that which Wood reports. Wood's American urban dwellers may be victims of racial and economic hierarchies which make it difficult for them to share in popular sovereignty, but everything they do assumes that they are rights-bearing citizens to whom public power ought to account. And, while municipal officials may not fully recognise them as participants in sovereignty, they acknowledge a duty to account and respond to them. They are, therefore, as Chatterjee points out, members of 'civil society', the realm in which rights-bearing citizens engage with public representatives in the exercise of popular sovereignty. Chatterjee, like Mamdani in the African context, reminds us that 'civil society' is a realm of collective action engaged in by people enjoying rights and therefore entitled to engage with political authority.[69] It is clear from the texture of engagement with local office holders which Wood describes that this is a form of civil society engagement with the state.

Chatterjee insists that this is not possible in India and, by extension, much of the rest of the world. While formally all Indians enjoy equal rights and a share in popular sovereignty, in practice most citizens 'are only tenuously, and even then ambiguously and contextually, rights-bearing citizens in the sense imagined by the constitution. They are not, therefore, proper members of civil society and are not regarded as such by the institutions of the state'.[70] This is so because they may live in 'illegal' settlements and make 'illegal' use of public services. The state cannot treat their claims as rights because this would 'only invite further violation of public property and civic laws'.[71] Chatterjee's city dwellers do not participate in civil society because the legal order denies their right to a say in decisions and power does not grant them the respect which would enable them to exercise their theoretical rights. They are not represented by government; they are 'looked after' and 'controlled' by it.

Chatterjee's analysis is based on observation of Indian popular politics – in Kolkata in particular. Given this, his claim that he is describing politics in 'most of the world' might seem to be purely a rhetorical flourish. But he does point to realities which exist beyond Kolkata or India. In much of the world, South Africa included, new or not-so-new democracies do not extend to many or most of their citizens the security of tenure which enables them to live legally in the cities or on their fringes. It is estimated that one in eight human beings, around a billion people, live in 'slum conditions';[72] most lack secure tenure. This means that they are 'illegally' occupying the places in which they live and that their use of public services is also 'illegal'. In South Africa, this applies to people living in many shack settlements – and to inhabitants of inner-city flat blocks in Johannesburg.[73]

This has significant implications for popular sovereignty: while their citizenship entitles them to make claims on public power, their status as 'illegal' residents and users of services disqualifies them. Even if they are not subject to official harassment (as they often are), they have no legal right to make claims on the state because they are not meant to be living where they are or using services there. As citizens, they enjoy a right to vote and so to share in popular sovereignty. But they may not make any of the claims associated with citizenship. In Africa, traditional power may also ensure that the formal share in popular sovereignty available at elections is denied for the rest of the time – it is this continued subjection to unaccountable power which, Mamdani argues, ensures that many Africans remain subjects even when democratisation makes them formal citizens.[74] Even if, as some in the international development debate insist, this problem could be solved by extending property rights to all[75] (a 'solution' far more complex in practice than it is in theory),[76] many people in the South may find that, even if they were miraculously granted security of tenure, their right to engage with public power would remain restricted to voting. So is access to the routine collective engagement with power which is essential to the exercise of popular sovereignty unavailable to most citizens of the South – and thus to most human beings?

It is obviously difficult to engage in routine collective engagement with authorities in the conditions in which most people live. But it is not impossible. The difference between Wood's bearers of rights and Chatterjee's victims of control may be less stark than it seems. Chatterjee's citizens may not participate in civil society, but their role as recipients of state welfare functions and objects of its control brings them into a political relationship with it, and impels them into regular engagement with it. This interaction between citizens and government officials, characterised by confrontation and negotiation, may not be based – as the routine collective action of elite groups is – on a recognition that the citizens enjoy a right to be heard. But because, as Chatterjee notes, they cannot be ignored, the effect is regular interaction nonetheless. While mobilisation is often an important feature, so too is the routine collective action on which elite groups rely.[77] In effect, collective action forces recognition of substantive citizenship, even when illegality would seem to formally exclude it, as residents of squatters' colonies manage to 'organize to get themselves recognised as a distinct population group that could receive the benefits of a governmental programme'.[78]

For Chatterjee, this form of engagement is not an exercise of democratic citizenship since those who make claims on public authorities in this way are not viewed as citizens. They are presumably seen by officials engaged in the technical tasks of governing as problems to be managed, not citizens bearing rights. And, for that reason, 'here there is no equal and uniform exercise of the rights of citizenship'.[79] An examination of the way many governments in the South (and, when confronted with similar problems, many in the North) engage with citizens tends to confirm this diagnosis. Government tasks are usually seen not as a means of realising the rights of citizens but as a means to solve technical problems. Government is hollowed of all democratic content – it is not about the exercise of popular sovereignty but about 'urban development' or 'effective public management'.

These attitudes are reinforced by the formation, within countries but also across borders, of mutually reinforcing 'epistemic communities'. These are networks of 'knowledge-based experts or groups with an authoritative claim to policy-relevant knowledge within the domain of their expertise' whose members 'hold a common set of causal beliefs and share notions of validity based on internally defined criteria for evaluation, common policy projects, and shared normative commitments'.[80] Officials talk to each other and to officers of international aid and development agencies, creating and maintaining shared understandings of social problems and their solutions which citizens have no role in shaping. Citizens appear only as problems to be explained and managed – usually in ways which misread social reality because they are based on conversations between technicians, not on an understanding of the world in which citizens live. But, while officials and technicians may not see interactions between citizens and officials as an exercise of democratic citizenship, this may be precisely what citizens have been able to fashion, despite authority's best efforts to prevent them.

While the 'equal and uniform exercise of the rights of citizenship' remains the democratic ideal, citizens rarely interact with elected government as bearers of rights, not causers of problems. Officials engage with Lindblom's privileged business people not because they see them as rights-bearing citizens but because it would be impossible for government to do its job if they did not. And, while business and even trade unionists may be treated with greater deference by officials engaged in corporatist bargaining with business and labour than the poor of Kolkata are treated by officials, the slum dwellers too gain access to routine collective engagement with officials because they can create problems for governments.[81] The similarity does not end there. Corporatist power-wielders are, like Chatterjee's slum dwellers, seen by officials as actors who perform a social function of concern to administrators, not as citizens claiming their right to a say. Popular sovereignty is not bestowed on citizens by officials – if it was, the result would be popular passivity, not sovereignty. Citizens gain access to routine collective engagement with government when they organise effectively enough to force the administration to concede it. Given this, Chatterjee's slum dwellers are engaging in the routine action which underpins democracy, however much their methods and dealings with officials may differ from that of elites.

A crucial element which makes this possible is that most basic element of democratic citizenship, the vote. Chatterjee argues that a key spark to the political engagement he describes was the defeat of Indira Gandhi's emergency in the 1977 general election, which 'established in the arena of popular mobilizations in India the capacity of the vote and of representative bodies of government to give voice to popular demands of a kind that had never before been allowed to disturb the order and tranquillity of the proverbial corridors of power'.[82] This widened 'the arena of political mobilization, prompted by electoral considerations and often only for electoral ends',[83] and gave further bargaining power to citizens claiming a share of decisions: 'They often make instrumental use of the fact that they can vote in elections'.[84]

Chatterjee insists that this is not a 'pure' exercise of citizenship: the slum dwellers are using the vote only 'instrumentally' and 'within a strategic field of politics'.[85] But citizenship is rarely exercised by people because they have a deep sense of democratic commitment rather than because it meets their needs. Some citizens, such as the identity voters discussed earlier, vote for parties because they express who they are. But the vote can be used in any way voters or groups of voters feel will advance their quest for a say in the decisions which affect them. The slum dwellers who promise to vote for a party in the hope of gaining a say in where and how they live are exercising the rights and privileges of citizenship in a manner which is as valid as the citizen who does so moved by a lifelong attachment to the rights of labour or a closeness to the party of Nelson Mandela.

The key implication is the continuing possibility electoral democracy offers for popular sovereignty. Lipset's assertion that political parties 'must be viewed as the most important mediating institutions between the citizenry and the state'[86] in a democracy needs rethinking where citizens find more effective ways than participation in parties to mediate that relationship but use parties as one among several means of making themselves heard. Chatterjee's analysis and evidence confirms that electoral democracy offers opportunities for collective action. While, contrary to Lipset's assertion, Chatterjee's citizens use parties to gain strategic leverage, not to express their interests, competition for their votes offers opportunities for engagement with political authorities which are absent in one-party or no-party systems. This explains why, in a multi-country study of citizen action to achieve national policy change, every case study – in Asia, Africa and Latin America – showed that electoral politics played an important role in opening opportunities for citizens to influence the policy they sought to change.[87] Piven and Cloward, despite arguing that American electoral politics could not deliver sustained influence to workers or black people, acknowledge the importance of parties' desire to court black votes to the effectiveness of the civil rights movement.[88]

This is particularly relevant since it is often claimed that societies need to move beyond electoral democracy if political communities are to govern themselves. It is claimed that democracy is undergoing a 'crisis of representation' in which electoral politics cannot enhance popular sovereignty:

> citizens across the world have shifted from older and traditional forms of representation, such as political parties and trade unions, to 'newer' modes such as social movements, informal citizen groups and non-governmental organizations (NGOs). Alternatively, taking the Eastern and Central European experience of the 1980s as a referent, theorists suggest that citizens faced with recalcitrant and unresponsive political institutions turn their back on the political domain and form self-help organizations in civil society to resolve their problems.[89]

In South Africa, the claim that people do not rely on political parties to express themselves to the authorities is contradicted by evidence. In townships and shack settlements, the ANC (African National Congress) has been, for much of the more than two decades since democracy, the dominant vehicle of political expression – so much so that conflict is often channelled through it: it is not uncommon to find grassroots protests in which local ANC structures mobilise against ANC-controlled local governments.[90] In the suburbs, the Democratic Alliance (DA) and its local structures are also often the vehicle through which citizens approach government.[91] It is too early to tell whether the decline in the ANC vote since 2014 indicates a decline in its dominance, but citizens' behaviour suggests that they still see parties as important actors.

In India, where the Indian National Congress's dominance ended decades ago, we might expect to find that parties wield far less influence. But in a survey conducted in Delhi in 2003, not a single respondent, when asked who they approached to solve their problems, mentioned NGOs: 36 per cent approached the government directly, and 28 per cent approached political parties.[92] Asked which organisations were concerned about their needs, 48 per cent felt that parties were. Only 41 per cent felt that neighbourhood groups, the supposed alternatives to parties, were concerned about their needs.[93] The survey's author, Neera Chandhoke, found not only a crisis of confidence in parties, but in other forms of representation too: 'In sum, the crisis of representation simply lies in the fact that no organization has been able to inspire confidence that it can represent people's needs adequately, or indeed press demands so compellingly that the government is necessarily obliged to do something about them'.[94]

While citizens prefer to approach the government directly rather than through parties (a finding consistent with Chatterjee's understanding of popular politics), parties play an essential role in enabling popular sovereignty. Citizens do not rely exclusively or even mainly on them to gain a say in decisions – most of Chandhoke's respondents say parties are not concerned about them. But they are more inclined to believe that parties care about their needs than to say the same about religious organisations, unions and neighbourhood associations. Chatterjee's analysis and Chandhoke's data show that parties have not been supplanted as vehicles of popular sovereignty in India.

The claim that parties are essential to the exercise of popular sovereignty because they make routine collective action possible does not mean that citizens necessarily rely mainly on parties – they do not inhabit Lipset's world, in which the party is the citizen's voice. But the existence of electoral democracy makes routine collective action, particularly by people at the grassroots, easier and thus more likely because it gives citizens bargaining power as competitors for political office seek their vote. Even if it could be shown that citizens hold parties in contempt, they might still be important facilitators of routine collective action because they allow for the strategic use of parties which Chatterjee describes. While the evidence does confirm that citizens cannot – and do not – rely on parties to convey their concerns to political office holders, it does show too that competing parties are important, if not inten-tional, facilitators of grassroots routine collective action, even when their role is to strengthen action by citizens who bypass parties in their dealings with governments.

NO (SOCIAL) MEDIA MAGIC

Another fashionable – and flawed – theory holds that all or some of the problems described here have been solved by social media. In this view, social media have removed barriers to collective action by making it easier for people to protest.[95] They have also made possible 'open and equal deliberation between citizens' representatives and policy-makers'.[96] So social media have made it possible for everyone to participate not only in the mobilisation discussed by Tarrow and his colleagues but in routine collective action. This optimistic view, common in the 1990s, was later countered by critics who argued that, far from challenging social hierarchies which denied most people a say, social media tended to entrench them, giving the better off and better connected yet another opportunity to express themselves while everyone else remained silent.[97] Some voices warned that social media would obstruct democracy because the voice of some would be passed off as the voice of all. Other sceptics have pointed to social media's capacity to strengthen partisan 'echo chambers' in which people talk only to those with whom they agree, polarising society and making dialogue and debate across political and social divides more difficult. And revelations about the use of social media to manipulate elections have, of course, prompted new fears about the damage which these media may do to democracy.

Because scholars and journalists are avid social media users – and research on social media is so easy because it does not require either to move out of their offices – the literature on social media and democracy is vast and comprehensive. For our purposes, the key question is whether their advent has made it easier for people to act collectively either by mobilising or by engaging in routine collective action. On the first score, claims, prompted mainly by the uprisings in the Middle East and North Africa beginning in late 2010, that social media made it possible for people to overthrow dictatorships and install democracies have been largely discredited by unfolding events. Despite the euphoria of the time, the social media 'revolutions' left virtually all the authoritarian states they were meant to replace firmly intact.[98]

Whether social media fuelled protest or, as some analyses suggested, merely provided a sharper tool for existing protest organisation, the indisputable reality is that they did not abolish the laws of politics and power. It still required organised collective action to remove authoritarians and build democracy, and, despite the use of social media, the protestors did not command enough of it to change their societies.

On the second score, there is little evidence that social media have made it easier for people who are excluded from routine collective action to force their way in. It has been argued that social media change the power balance by giving voice to views and news which would be ignored by the mainstream media.[99] In South Africa, as elsewhere, it has become common for media and social commentators to assume that social media reach everyone and that the views expressed through them are those of the entire society. This is in itself a form of elitism which excludes most people from the debate.

According to the South African Social Media Landscape Report for 2017, 16 million South Africans now use Facebook and 8 million use Twitter.[100] It seems likely that there is considerable overlap between the two and that virtually all the Twitter users are also registered on Facebook. Even if we assume that everyone who has signed up for these two outlets is an active user, which seems unlikely, the figures suggest that around two-thirds of the country are not social media users. So, while social media do enable some citizens to place issues on the agenda which might have been ignored before these media were invented, those who are enabled are at most one-third of the citizenry. It comes as no surprise, therefore, that the issues placed on the agenda are not those of the poor and the weak. The concrete example offered to support the claim that social media were breaking the main-stream media's silence was a speech by the late Allister Sparks, a liberal political commentator, which described the architect of apartheid, Hendrik Verwoerd, as 'really smart'.[101] This obviously deserved coverage which it may not have received were there no social media. But it hardly forced onto the agenda concrete issues in shack settlements. An examination of political discussion on social media shows that this was no isolated example. Not only are the topics discussed usually those of concern to the middle class, but, in most cases, users comment on items reported in the mainstream media to which social media are meant to offer an alternative. In the main, the new media offer another conduit to people who already enjoy access to routine collective action – they do not create new channels.

The fact that people can raise issues on social media does not mean that they are able to use it to influence the decisions of power-holders. There is little evidence in South Africa thus far that airing issues on social media prompts politicians to act. Perhaps the only issue on which this may have been so is the government's decision to introduce a bill that would curb hate speech – it might not have done this had social media not been used to express anger at racist behaviour and speech (some of it, ironically, aired on social media).[102] But, while citizens raised the issue, there was no campaign specifically for a law on the issue. So, while citizens may have placed the issue on the agenda, they had no influence on how it translated into policy and law. Routine collective action, by contrast, often entails citizens not only complaining about a problem but demanding a specific course of action – and retaining a say over how their concerns are addressed. None of this happened in this case, and there are no others on which social media can clearly be said to have prompted a particular decision or change. This confirms the point made earlier: social media might help existing protest organisation, but they are no substitute for the organised, routine, collective action that influences the way in which power decides.

INVENTED SPACES: AVOIDING THE STRAITJACKET

Insisting that democracy requires the participation of everyone, particularly the poor and weak, is open to a misunderstanding. It was noted earlier that development writing is filled with support for a citizen role in decisions, but that it tends to assume that this is best achieved by 'public participation' techniques and the creation of formal forums, such as the PRSP processes discussed earlier.[103] The stress on routine collective action as the key to extending popular sovereignty could be understood as an endorsement of formal participation forums and techniques designed to ensure regular engagement between office holders and the grassroots. But structured participation forums or techniques cannot ensure effective routine collective action which would deepen and broaden popular sovereignty.

Besides the other objections levelled against them here, structured forums tend to assume a false community of interest within society. If everyone shared the same interests, it would be possible to discover the opinions of entire 'communities' or societies. In reality, 'communities' inevitably include a range of differing identities and interests.[104] Gender is an obvious divide, but so is social class or interest divisions as basic as that between transport providers and commuters or differences of language or ethnic origin. It is impossible for 'communities' to express themselves in one voice. When 'communities' are said to speak, which of the myriad voices is heard? The not surprising answer is that those who have the resources – material, cultural and political – to present themselves as the voice of 'the community' speak for all: those who are already dominant reinforce their dominance. By assuming a uniformity and equality when reality is diverse and unequal, structured participation techniques give voice only to those whose dominance enables them to be heard and silences many in order to hear some.

A more sophisticated approach to participation seeks to extend voice to 'civil society'. Since this provides for more than one voice, it seems to avoid the problem of allowing some to speak for all. But it risks muzzling more voices than it hears. Despite the fact that definitions of civil society are hotly contested, much development literature assumes that the concept is self-explanatory because, for much development writing, it is: it refers to visible organisations which are available to negotiate with governments and aid donors – NGOs and community-based organisations (CBOs).[105] This, by definition, grants voice to the organised and leaves voiceless those who lack the means to organise. It assumes that the capacity to organise is evenly spread and that those who wish to organise can do so. In reality, capacity is very uneven, and, if voice is available only to the organised, the right to speak will remain highly exclusionary.

This approach privileges some kinds of collective action over others. Those who organise in a manner which enables them to sit at the negotiating table are heard; those who combine in other ways are not.[106] The 'civil society' approach privileges the sorts of engagement in public debate which demands cultural resources unavailable at the grassroots. To put it less abstractly, those who have access to people who can read and write complex policy documents and know the jargon of development may wield influence, but those who don't will not.

The assumption that 'civil society' can be heard by gathering a group of organisations around a table, hearing their views and then distilling them into a policy document also implies a unanimity which cannot exist since the right to organise which makes civil society possible must produce organisations expressing many voices. The forums might allow all organised voices to be heard, but, because they are always forced to distil a single view as 'the perspective of civil society', rather than to allow the various voices to continue the contest for public support, they inevitably suppress democratic contest between competing views.

The fallacy which underlies participation forums is highlighted by Jane Mansbridge.[107] Although her understanding of democracy does not rely on the clash between competing interests proposed here, she offers an important insight into why popular sovereignty cannot be extended through forums. If we all shared the same interests, Mansbridge points out, it would not matter who represented us – the only criterion for selection would be who was good at performing public tasks. But we hardly ever share the same interests and so it is important that we be represented by people who share our interests. To apply this to forums, if we all shared the same interests, it would make sense to hear everyone's suggestions and then summarise them as a 'stakeholder consensus'. But, since we do not, interests must engage with each other in a manner which allows the clashes and possible compromises which permit differences to be expressed and resolved. This requires a competition for influence governed by rules which ensure all a say, particularly those who might be too weak to speak without protection. Forums assume a community of interest which cannot exist in a society where resources are scarce and interests compete for them – which, at this stage of human evolution, means all societies.

Far from providing a vehicle for popular sovereignty, formal forums and participation techniques obstruct it by suppressing important voices and the democratic expression of important conflicts. Routine collective action which extends popular sovereignty must, therefore, rely on the free use by citizens of democratic rights to engage with office holders in the manner citizens choose, not that which power-holders confer – it requires the creation of 'invented', not 'invited', spaces.

A PART OF THE ACTION: DEMOCRATISING ROUTINE COLLECTIVE ACTION

This chapter has sought to show that the collective action which sustains democracy is not restricted to popular mobilisation and that it includes routine collective engagement between citizens and governments. While the use of democratic rights to engage in mass protest and other forms of collectively raising voice remains a crucial instrument in citizens' armoury, these occasional expressions play far less of a role in conveying citizens' wants and needs to government than routine engagement between groups of citizens and holders of public office.

We have noted that this routine collective action is found in all democracies (and in all societies in which at least some citizens enjoy access to public office holders). The degree to which democracy deepens and broadens and thus the extent to which a society is moving closer to popular sovereignty is determined not by whether there is collective action (because there always is) but by who can engage in it. While some analyses of democracy base their diagnosis and prognosis on whether 'civil society' is engaging with government,[108] implying that it is possible to imagine a society in which organised groups of citizens do not engage with governments, we come closer to reality when we ask not whether citizens are interacting with government, but which citizens are doing so and how they are doing it. The more open the engagement and the wider the range of citizens able to engage in routine collective action, the further along the road of democratisation a society is.

The deeper and broader the range of interests able to collectively engage with government as a matter of routine, rather than only when they can muster the resources to take to the streets, the more citizens are able to share in popular sovereignty. The key test of democratisation, therefore, is the degree to which people who had not previously engaged collectively and routinely with government are able to do so and how deep and broad the engagement is. The ideal democracy in which all citizens are engaging routinely and collectively with government will never be achieved – but we measure societies' progress towards that ideal by the extent to which routine collective engagement extends from elites to society's grassroots.

7

Power is Theirs? Why Collective Action is Usually the Preserve of the Few

If collective action is the engine of democracy, why do only a minority use it in a way which gives them influence over decisions?

Several theories try to answer this question. For one, to engage in collective action is irrational – the reasonable person, it claims, leaves it to others to act on their behalf. For another, lack of interest is the problem – most people do not see any value in acting. For still others, ignorance of the opportunities for action and its power to advance interests explains inaction – a variant of this argument holds that people believe that there is no need for action because power-holders know better what their political community needs than they do. In all these explanations, the failure to act is a freely taken decision. They all insist that people do not use collective agency to claim a share in decisions because they do not wish to do so.

This chapter rejects this view. It argues that, in the main, citizens refrain from collective action not because they do not wish to speak but because they cannot – or because they believe they will be unable to make themselves heard. It notes that people with more resources are better able to act, a reality stressed by social movement theories. But it insists that access to resources, while it matters, is not the chief reason why people who enjoy formal democratic rights do not act to challenge power. Whether people act is shaped by access to power: people avoid acting when they believe they are powerless. They fear that the powerful will punish them or ignore them.

Their perceptions of powerlessness are not necessarily accurate: people may underestimate their power and so may avoid action which could gain them a share in decisions. But their failure to act is not a preference. In the main, people know that those who wield power over them ought to account and respond to them, but they avoid acting to achieve this accountability because they believe themselves too weak to achieve the share in decisions to which they know they are entitled. Before discussing the evidence for this claim, this chapter will discuss the rival explanations for the inaction of the many.

THEORIES OF INACTION

A celebrated explanation for limited participation in collective action is Olson's rational choice theory, mentioned in the previous chapter.[1] Olson argued that it was irrational to engage in collective action in large groups because, once a group grew to a certain size, the action of one member would not make a difference to its ability to achieve its goals. It was, therefore, rational to 'freeride': to accept the benefits of the actions of others while not acting oneself. For this reason, large groups – such as trade unions, the example to which Olson devotes most attention – can ensure that their members continue to belong and so to participate in routine collective action only if they force them to belong or offer them 'side incentives' to persuade them to stay. This explained, he argued, why unions use closed shops – agreement with employers that only union members could work in the firm – and offer benefits to members.

Olson's critics have shown that larger groups do not necessarily create any greater barriers to collective action than smaller ones.[2] They argue, too, that 'side incentives' do not solve his purported collective action problem since someone has to pay for them and can do so only by engaging in collective action.[3] Still others have argued that Olson's approach has too narrow a view of human motivation, ignoring the importance of what one scholar has called 'pleasure in action',[4] the positive emotions many people experience when they work with others towards a common goal. Motives such as solidarity or altruism do not, critics note, feature in Olson's theory (although he did try later to adjust it to provide for them).

But perhaps the strongest objection to Olson's theory is that it does not explain why, in the absence of compulsion or side benefits, people engage in collective action, sometimes at great personal cost. Olson himself noted that workers engage in strikes for union recognition[5] – obviously before membership has become compulsory. Why do they do this, if collective action is irrational? And who decides to impose the compulsory membership or offer the 'side incentives' in the first place? Unless we claim that people engage voluntarily in collective action until their group reaches a certain size, at which stage they recognise that the incentive to participate has evaporated and that they need to force themselves and others to act, we must recognise that at least some people are capable of acting collectively in large groups without being forced. Olson does not assume that rationality is available to some human beings only, nor that what is rational for some is irrational for others. So, if some people find voluntary collective action rational, then everyone is presumably capable, given the appropriate conditions, of finding it reasonable to combine freely with others to pursue common goals.

While Olson's theory cannot explain why people do or do not engage in collective action, it makes an important contribution by warning that there are constraints to collective action. Before his book appeared, scholars had assumed that it was natural and normal for people who shared common interests to act together to realise them.[6] Olson advanced our understanding of collective action by showing that there was nothing automatic about it – that people may need to overcome obstacles if they are to act together in pursuit of common interests.

Theorists who argued that collective action was natural and normal knew that it is often the preserve of a small minority. But a failure to act collectively was explained by assuming that those who remained inactive felt no need to act: since they could participate in collective action if they chose, the fact that they did not act meant that they did not so choose. Dahl, in his study of politics in the American city of New Haven, declared that '[t]he independence, penetrability and heterogeneity of the various segments of the political stratum all but guarantee that any dissatisfied group will find a spokesman …'.[7] Those who did not find one could, therefore, not have wanted one. For Dahl and other pluralists, people did not act because they did not see collective action as a priority – for them, 'political action will seem considerably less efficient than working at [a] job … planning a vacation … or coping with an uncertain future in manifold other ways'.[8] Like Olson's rational actor, the pluralist non-actor weighs the costs and benefits of action and usually decides against it. But, while Olson's actor always – in principle – rejects action because it is more rational to leave it to others, Dahl's acts only when so dissatisfied that the need to act outweighs other priorities. Inaction is therefore a choice by people satisfied enough with their circumstances to conclude that doing something to change them is not worth the effort.

The view that people do not act because they accept things as they are is not restricted to pluralists who believe that all have an opportunity to be heard. It is also held by some radicals who believe pluralist democracy is a facade for rule by the economically powerful: in their view, the acceptance, and the inaction it produces, are based on a misreading of reality encouraged by power-holders. The willingness of people excluded from economic power to accept this fate is not an 'objectively' accurate understanding of their interests: they have no reason to be satisfied with their lot and, if they fully understood their situation, they would act to change it. But power-holders have deluded them into accepting that the exercise of power by others is in their interests and that they have no need to demand a say. That people may decide not to act in defence of their interests, even when they are victims of great injustice, because they have been fooled into believing that the *status quo* is just lies at the heart of the notion of 'false consciousness'. In other words, people oppressed by the social order may accept that this is fair because they cannot understand their own interests.

The most obvious problem with this idea is that it can be – and has been – used to legitimate the right of an elite to decide on behalf of people because some know what others' 'real' interests are and so what their 'real' consciousness should be. It is found on the left in the idea that an elite understands the interests of the people better than the people themselves. Since there is no 'objective' way of deciding what anyone's interests are, 'false consciousness' subverts democracy by providing a reason for an elite to exercise sovereignty on behalf of those whose 'real' interests it claims to understand. This not only denies the need for free expressions of the popular will, but also seeks to abolish politics, if by 'politics' we understand the free contest of opposing interests and positions within agreed rules. If there is only one 'objective' interpretation of everyone's interests, decisions should be made by those who know 'the truth' – contention between rival positions opens the door for false understandings of people's 'real' interests. And so politics is collapsed into administration, the 'scientific' management of society by those able to steer all towards the realisation of their 'true' interests.[9] There are also similarities between this approach and the oft-criticised tendency of the welfare state to rely on the technical expertise of planners and public servants, rather than the agency of citizens, to address poverty and inequality.[10] Again, it is assumed that people require the guidance of those who know what they need better than they do. But the idea that citizens act or do not act because they do not understand reality is, as we shall see, hardly a left monopoly – it underpins some very mainstream understandings of how to promote democracy.

The view that people do not act because they do not know their best interests assumes, with understandings of collective action before Olson, that people do act collectively in pursuit of their interests when they are convinced that there is a need to do so. While the 'false consciousness' view assumes that people are deluded in choosing not to act, and more conventional understandings assume that inaction means that society has met the needs of the inactive, neither see failure to act as a consequence of constraints which obstruct action. People do not act because they do not want to, not because they cannot.

It will be argued here that people refrain from acting not because they are un-aware of their interests or of the benefits which they might gain from action, but because they believe they cannot act: failure to engage in collective action is a consequence of constraint, not choice. But what are these constraints? What convinces many people that they cannot act to claim their share in popular sovereignty?

MOBILISING RESOURCES: A PARTIAL EXPLANATION

One explanation argues that the barrier to collective action is lack of access to resources. The argument is straightforward and has underpinned a school of American social movement research: the 'resource mobilisation' approach, which, while it analyses social movements rather than routine collective action, applies to both since the activity it addresses includes the routine action discussed in the previous chapter. This school focusses on the resources which movements need to engage in sustained collective action – quality of leadership, capacity for forming organisations which could ensure continued activity, and access to funding are among the assets considered necessary.[11] It rejects the view that action is unnecessary or irrational – it accepts that there is always enough discontent in any society to supply grassroots support for a social movement if it is effectively organised and enjoys access to resources.[12] It also, by implication, challenges the pre-Olson view of collective action in which any group of people who hold a collective interest or grievance will act collectively; if people need resources before they can act, they may harbour very strong grievances but remain inactive if they lack them.

So resource mobilisation does go some way to explaining why some engage in the action which influences decisions while others do not. Access to resources does play an important role in determining who can and cannot act. A key flaw of approaches to democracy and development which place a heavy burden on the active citizenship of the poor – which rely, for example, on grassroots citizens to play an active role in making technical decisions – is that they ignore the crucial role which resources play in deciding who can act. Collective action is not purely a product of the will. It requires time, which the poor often lack, and access to skilled organisers or negotiators, which are almost always beyond the grasp of the people who need them most. Poor people may be expected to show great capacity for collective action in contexts where it is unreasonable to expect this. An understanding of democracy's limits and prospects needs to recognise that lack of resources is a significant obstacle to collective action and that capacity to act is not spread evenly through society.

Nevertheless, reducing the barriers to action to access to resources underestimates the obstacles to routine collective action for poorer and weaker citizens. If access to resources decides whether people act collectively, why do some people with access to very meagre resources act? John Gaventa asks: 'If most [American] blacks are of a relatively low socio-economic status, why did a highly organised civil rights movement develop, and itself alter patterns of political participation?' Some groups with very limited resources act while others do not – an explanation based simply on resources cannot explain this.[13]

Concentrating solely on resources also assumes that, regardless of social context, any group which enjoys access to the required skills and funds can engage in collective action: the distribution of power in society plays no role in determining who acts. This denies an almost self-evident truth, that power is central to politics: 'political theorists from Plato to Foucault have often noted that the ineradicably hierarchical nature of much social life makes power relations ubiquitous to human interaction'.[14] And yet none of the theories of collective action we have discussed make room for the possibility that some do not act because those who have more power than them prevent them from doing so. Whether we assume that people do not engage collectively with political decision-makers because it is irrational for them to do so, because they are content with their decisions (whether they ought to be or not) or because they lack resources or access to someone who has them, we ignore the possibility that a core political reality, the exercise of power by some over others, shapes who can act and who cannot.

The resource mobilisation approach does recognise external constraints and does not insist that anyone with resources can act. While insisting that money and labour are crucial to social movement activity, it recognises that more may be needed if citizens are to combine in action:

> The resource mobilization approach emphasizes both societal support and constraint of social movement phenomena. It examines the variety of resources that must be mobilized, the linkage of social movements to other groups, the dependence of movements on external support for success, and the tactics used by authorities to control or incorporate movements.[15]

The 'costs and rewards' of collective action are, the authors add, 'centrally affected by the structure of society and the activity of authorities'.[16] This recognises that power may constrain collective action. But power is not the resource mobilisation approach's central concern. It remains primarily concerned with the way movements use resources to make claims on political power-holders, rather than with how power relations shift to open opportunities for action for those deprived of them. It also, crucially, wants to explain the appearance of social movements rather than the distribution of capacity to act within societies. John McCarthy and Mayer Zald, whose work is quoted here, link the size of the social movement sector, and hence the extent of collective action, to the availability of resources: 'The greater the absolute amount of resources available to the [social movement sector], the greater the likelihood that new [social movement industries] and [social movement organisations] will develop to compete for these resources'.[17] This may predict how new organisations might be formed, but it says nothing about the distribution of collective action because it does not predict that more people would act if more resources were available (only that new organisations would be formed). Because it focusses on visible organisation, it is far better able to explain why people act than why they do not. While it offers important insights into some of the organisational dynamics of social movements, it offers little which could help us understand how unequal power relations prevent people from acting and how changes in the distribution of power might prompt them to act.

The problem of power is confronted directly by Tarrow and other authors in the 'political opportunity' tradition who stress the 'mobilization of resources *external* to the group'.[18] Tarrow proposes the idea of the 'political opportunity structure': the 'consistent – but not necessarily formal, permanent or national – dimensions of the political struggle that encourage people to engage in contentious politics', which enable contentious politics to emerge when 'ordinary citizens, sometimes encouraged by counter elites or leaders, respond to opportunities that lower the costs of collective action', and which are to be distinguished from constraints such as 'repression ... [and] ... authorities' capacity to present a solid front to insurgents ...'.[19]

In this view, action depends not on whether resources are available but on whether circumstances in society deter or encourage action. This allows us to consider the obstacles to action which powerless people face. Tarrow rejects the claim, implicit in the pluralist framework, that people are more likely to act the more they are disaffected – threats to people's interests are, he observes, likely to 'produce sullen resentment as easily as collective action'. People act when they are given an opportunity to do so.[20] Only when new opportunities remove old constraints does action becomes possible. Like the other social movement theorists, Tarrow wants to explain mobilisation, not routine collective action – his discussion of opportunities begins by asking, 'When will ordinary people pour into the streets, risking life and limb to lay claim to their rights?'[21] But this explanation applies to all other forms of collective action too. While Tarrow does not explicitly mention shifts in power relations as a change in political opportunity structures, the processes he describes imply this. Among the factors which change opportunity structures, in his view, are liberalisation of repressive political orders, divisions among elites and opportunities for actions offered by elections.[22] In all of these cases, a power balance shifts: elites either becomes less able to suppress collective action or they seek the active consent of citizens. The result is that a constraint on collective action imposed by one group on another is eased, shifting the power balance and making action possible.

The forms of power Tarrow identifies are, by implication, found in authoritarian regimes only, and so he does not offer much help in identifying constraints to action in democracies. To explain how power inhibits collective action where citizens are allowed to act, we need to look beyond the literature on opportunity structures.

BRINGING POWER BACK IN: CONSTRAINTS TO COLLECTIVE ACTION

An important insight into how power restricts collective action is Gaventa's study of organisation among white mine workers in America's Appalachian valleys during the 1970s.[23] The miners enjoyed, at least in principle, full political rights. They also experienced considerable social deprivation. And yet they did not engage in collective action – or, at least, not as much as many other citizens did: the region had a higher percentage of non-union or 'company union' miners than any other unionised area of the eastern US.[24] Gaventa argues that their failure to act to seek an improvement in their conditions was a consequence not of choice, but of power's capacity to prevent them from acting.

Gaventa wants to show a possibility not addressed by the literature we have discussed thus far – that power may be exercised even where it seems absent and that what seems to be a product of choice may reflect power. Following Steven Lukes's assertion that power can be expressed by A over B 'by shaping, influencing and determining his [sic] very wants',[25] he suggests that visible power (which Tarrow discusses) is only one of three dimensions in which some exercise power over others. Power may also be wielded in ways which are not immediately visible – it shows not in what happens, but in what does not: 'the power process involves a non-event rather than an observable non-decision'.[26] This challenges the pluralist view that non-action is a choice. Instead, Gaventa argues that inaction is a consequence of powerlessness. People are refraining from acting not because they are satisfied, but because someone wields power over them. And so, by implication, the distribution of collective action in any society – the reality that some engage in action while others do not – is a product of its distribution of power.

How does power prevent action where it cannot be directly seen? In the second dimension, Gaventa, following Peter Bachrach and Morton Baratz, and Schattschneider, says that power relies on a 'mobilization of bias': 'a set of predominant values, beliefs, rituals, and institutional procedures ("rules of the game") that operate systematically and consistently to the benefit of certain persons and groups at the expense of others'.[27] Powerful actors use political rules or cultural symbols to suffocate action before it occurs. The third dimension, which Gaventa says is 'the least developed and understood', is one in which 'power influences, shapes or determines conceptions of the necessities, possibilities and strategies of challenge in situations of latent conflict'.[28] Power may be wielded through social myths and symbols or the communication of information. Following Lukes again, A gets B to act and believe 'in a manner in which B might otherwise not, to A's benefit and B's detriment'[29] because 'B's conception of self, group or class may be such as to make action against A seem inappropriate'.[30] In this dimension, power ensures that people do not act because it convinces them that it is entitled to treat them in the way in which it does.

Much of Gaventa's study shows how power acted on the miners to encourage – and at times ensure – inaction. The most obvious bar to action was economic power. Many miners and their families were tenants living in 'company controlled communities'. Predictably, it was among people in this situation that the 'highest rates of non-unionism and the most claims of quiescent populations were found'.[31] The economic power of the mining company was pervasive, prompting Gaventa to describe the region as a 'company valley'. Unlike Dahl's non-activist citizen, the miners were refraining from acting not because they were busily planning holidays (they seem unlikely to have been able to afford any) or having a good time, but because the company's economic power over them strongly deterred action. Their exclusion from economic power prevented them from acting collectively.

Economic power had other consequence which obstructed miners' collective action. One was economic elites' influence over the media – presumably through ownership, command of resources which newspapers needed (such as advertising revenue) or contacts between the company and media. Some newspapers in the area were, Gaventa suggests, able both to frame social reality in a way which deterred action and to control the flow of news to deprive the miners of information which might prompt action.[32] The first goal was achieved by labelling opinions which might lead citizens to act collectively 'foreign' to society's values – that is, as 'communist' in a society in which communism was seen as a threat. The second entailed keeping from public view information about power-holders which might prompt action or, when relatively powerless people do act, creating the impression that their action is futile by ignoring or minimising its impact – for example, by repeating unsubstantiated employer claims that union action is not damaging company profits. Elite bias, which focusses on the collective action of well-connected actors and ignores that of the grassroots, or reduces poor people to passive victims, is an everyday feature of media coverage – it affects not only how the poor are covered within particular societies, but the way the poor of the South are viewed by the media in the North.[33]

Another source of power is the affluent's access to the instruments of government, discussed in the last chapter. This can ensure that seemingly neutral laws deter collective action against power-holders (the use of trespass laws against union activists, for example). Links between economic power-holders on the one hand and the police and judiciary on the other can ensure that law enforcers and judges act against the use of collective action by the dominated. In Gaventa's study, judges who jailed strikers had direct interests in the coal companies.[34] Usually the links are not that obvious. But the fact that economic power-holders are likely to be seen as 'pillars of the community' deserving of respect may ensure favourable treatment by law enforcers, who may deter action by the relatively powerless simply because the powerful's status makes their interests seem to be those of the society, and those of the people who challenge them to be threats to the established order.

These patterns of power will be familiar to critics of formal democracy – and anyone aware of the exercise of power in the South. That private economic domination can undermine the practice of democracy has been recognised by mainstream scholars[35] as well as radical critics. Gaventa shows that it does this by deterring collective action by the weak, ensuring that government accounts only to the more affluent and better connected. That power can obstruct the use of collective action by the relatively powerless is often ignored by studies of democracy. Gaventa's work is an important warning that building, sustaining and deepening democracy is possible only if power relations which restrict access to routine collective action change, so that the range of citizens able to engage in it to hold government to account and make it respond is greatly widened and deepened. Tarrow's criticism of 'the inherited notion that movements attracted only the alienated and the oppressed'[36] is valid – it is not the exploited and powerless who are likely to form movements, but the organised and connected. The same point can be made about routine collective action. It is generally the preserve of those who wield power, not those who lack it.

But Gaventa leaves an important question unresolved: the way in which power acts to deter collective action. Do dominated people not act because power persuades them that it is legitimate – because they suffer from 'false consciousness' – or because they know it is being used illegitimately but are powerless to do anything about it? The idea of 'false consciousness' is no longer the sole property of the left. It underpins the view of anyone who believes citizens do not exercise their rights because they are ill-informed or harbour a misguided regard for authority. Conservative white South Africans dismayed by black voters' support for the ANC repeatedly bewail their claimed tendency to support a party which does not serve their interests. This view is based on prejudice rather than evidence[37] but is a right-wing variant of the 'false consciousness' explanation.

It is this assumption which underpins the democracy education programme of Northern aid donors and activists: the view that people need to be 'educated' because they do not understand that they ought to hold power to account is often held today by elites across the political spectrum. 'Civic education' or other forms of instruction which seek to show people why they ought to hold power to account is often popular in Northern democracy-promotion programmes. 'Civic education is important', proclaims one enthusiast: 'If citizens are to practice democracy effectively, they must possess the skills ... that accord with democracy' – they must learn a 'sense of political efficacy'.[38] If powerless citizens have been deluded into inaction by power-holders, the remedy lies in educating them out of the delusion. This belief is not restricted to importers of democracy. It is often shared by activist groups in the South – it was popular across the political spectrum when South Africa became a democracy.[39]

A counter to this view argues that powerless people know that they are subject to injustice – and would like to do something about this if they could. They do not act not because they are ignorant but because they believe that the power arrayed against them is too great and so action will be futile and costly. If democracy's core principle is that no one can claim to know what is in another's interests, to claim that some know better than the powerless how power works on them is deeply anti-democratic. What, besides the prejudices and preferences of elites, establishes that people who choose not to hold private or public power-holders to account are deluded and in need of education? Why could their inaction not stem from the perceived consequences of action?

Even if it could be shown that citizens choose not to hold power-holders to account because they believe power is wielded legitimately and wisely, this too would be a valid choice, not one which requires remedial education. If Botswana voters or Buganda subjects really did believe that hierarchical power must be defended, they would be right to reject attempts by aid donors or civil society activities to 'educate' them out of their firmly held beliefs. But the evidence shows that citizens want to hold public power to account and force it to respond. They are not in need of 'education' but of the means to turn their desire for a say into reality.

If the powerless know they are victims of injustice, 'education' will tell them what they already know. If they are not acting because they feel the power balance is tilted against them, they need more power, not more teaching. This does not necessarily mean that dominated people really are powerless. Appalachian miners or poor people in the South may, like heads of government or business executives, underestimate their own power. But there is a great difference between knowing that power is unjustly wielded and being overly pessimistic about our ability to challenge it versus believing that the power to which we are subject is just. While people who do not act because they believe they can do nothing may need information on possibilities for action of which they were unaware, they do not need to be 'taught' that action would help since they already know this. Information is a resource which enables people to do what they want to do; 'education' is an attempt to tell them what they should want to do.

Were Gaventa's miners not challenging power because they have been duped into believing it is just – or because they know it is unjust but believe there is nothing they can do about it? He rejects the notion of 'false consciousness', but he does suggest that the powerless may express interests which are not really their own and that they come to share belief systems which serve the interests of the powerful.[40] He argues that if consciousness cannot be false, consensus may be the 'internalization of roles or false consensus [which] ... lead[s] to acceptance of the *status quo* by the dominated'.[41] This could mean that people claim to accept a consensus because they feel they have to pretend to do so or that they have been deluded into accepting it. Gaventa's reference to 'myths' and the 'internalization' of roles indicates that, in his view, delusion plays a crucial role.

Elsewhere, he suggests that the exercise of power by union leaders over members is possible because of an 'internalized understanding by membership of the appropriate relationship to their leaders'[42] – the powerless are 'shaped' to 'accept' power's version of reality. If action can be stopped by labelling it 'communist', the powerless must accept the view of the powerful – they could just as well conclude that collective action expresses the values in the American constitution. Labelling the civil rights movement 'communist' failed to deter action for racial inclusion since Martin Luther King Jr and other leaders of the movement insisted on framing their claims in terms consistent with values purportedly contained in the constitution.[43] Miners could also have insisted that there was nothing wrong with being a 'communist'. So Gaventa's treatment of power does suggest that people may remain passive because they endorse the world view of those who dominate them.

But Gaventa offers repeated explanations, often backed by evidence, to support the second view – that power convinces the powerless that action will be futile because the odds are too decisively stacked against them. He argues that 'acceptance of a state of powerlessness may occur as an adaptive response to the exploitative situation'.[44] Elsewhere, he observes that 'it is not the actual exercise of coercion but the constant possibility that it might be exercised that supports the routines of non-challenge',[45] and similarly that fear of power can convince the powerless that action is futile and only adaptation make sense.[46] He describes how past defeats of organisation may prompt the powerless to doubt that action would have better prospects in the future.[47] These explanations suggest that the powerless may know that the power to which they are subject is unjust. They are convinced that there is nothing they can do about it because the power-holders will defeat them if they speak and act.

Gaventa therefore endorses both views described here: power inhibits collective action by persuading the powerless to accept norms which will keep them from acting, and by convincing them that, if they do act, they will lose more than they gain. The two analyses seem contradictory: if people have been persuaded that the power to which they are subject is just, why would they contemplate collective action at all? The attitudes which people in real social situations actually hold are never as neat as social theory claims. It is possible for people to believe that collective action is acceptable only within limits – to challenge power at the ballot box but not in the streets, for example – or that power is justified but not when its exercise exceeds deeply held understandings of the limits which it should respect.[48] In these cases, people may believe that only some forms of collective action would be acceptable, but that even the limited range of actions which are permitted may be dangerous and futile. Gaventa's aim is to challenge the pluralist view that people choose not to act, not to offer a detailed account of how power prevents people from acting, and so he does not analyse the relative roles of imbibed choices and external constraints.

But the distinction is crucial because the two views yield very different understandings of the problem and its potential remedies. Other academic work, discussed below, shows that the second view of how power is exercised explains the highly uneven distribution of routine collective action and, therefore, democracy's frequent inability to include society's grassroots in the exercise of popular sovereignty. It shows that the obstacle is not the attitudes the powerless absorb from the powerful, but their belief that acting in the face of what they see as overwhelming power would incur costs but no benefits.

THE BETTER PART OF VALOUR: THE STRATEGIC CALCULATION OF THE POWERLESS

Perhaps the most important challenge to the notion of 'false consciousness' – and, by implication, theories which suggest that the powerless avoid collective action because they accept that the power to which they are subject is just – is James Scott's study of responses to power among the Malaysian peasantry, *Weapons of the Weak*.[49]

Scott's study, based on fieldwork in a Malaysian village, finds that peasants who appear to accept the authority to which they are subject, in reality reject its moral legitimacy. Statements of support for the existing order, he shows, reflect not what the powerless believe, but what they feel they have to say when the powerful are in earshot. Among themselves, the powerless ridicule power-holders. They may use 'onstage' linguistic terms to describe existing social arrangements as fair and just. But they may also use 'cynical and mocking' terms behind the backs of the powerful to describe the practice of power and the moral failings of those who wield it. What the powerless say to each other is 'plausible evidence that their claim to land, to interests, to rents, and to respect is at least contested at the level of consciousness, if not at the level of "onstage" acts'. In addition, those who curry favour with elites are ostracised: peasants 'are hardly in the thrall of a naturally ordained social order'.[50]

Theories of 'false consciousness' take at face value what the powerless say in public. Scott challenges this by introducing the idea of 'hidden transcripts' to describe what the powerless say to each other when the powerful are not listening.[51] To assume that what the powerless say in public is what they really believe is to ignore the reality that

> the exercise of power nearly always drives a portion of the full transcript underground … the weaker party is unlikely to speak his or her mind; a part of the full transcript will be withheld in favor of a 'performance' that is in keeping with the expectations of the power-holder … much of the ethnographic material supporting the notion of 'mystification' and 'ideological hegemony' is, I suspect, simply the result of assuming that the transcript from power-laden situations is the full transcript.[52]

The claim that the powerless accept the authority to which they are subject 'ignores the extent to which most subordinate classes are able, on the basis of their daily … experience, to penetrate and demystify the prevailing ideology …'.[53] Quiescence is explained 'by the relationships of force … not … values and beliefs'.[54]

The Marxist theoretician Antonio Gramsci is mistaken when he claims that the radicalism of subordinate classes is to be found more in their acts than their beliefs: '[they] are likely to be more radical at the level of ideology than ... behaviour, where they are more effectively constrained by the daily exercise of power'.[55]

The powerless, who reject the morality of the existing order but recognise that the powerful can thwart organised collective action, engage in acts of resistance whose purpose is to be misunderstood by outsiders. They may not appear overtly political and are usually ascribed to the cultural deficiencies of the powerless:

> Here I have in mind the ordinary weapons of relatively powerless groups: foot dragging, dissimulation, desertion, false compliance, pilfering, feigned ignorance, slander, arson, sabotage and so on ... They require little or no coordination or planning; they make use of implicit understandings and informal networks ... they typically avoid any direct, symbolic confrontation with authority.[56]

If routine collective action is the weapon of the strong, these acts of defiance or disobedience are the weapons of the weak. This realm of resistance is 'shadowy and individual – it includes a large variety of thefts and the murder of livestock'.[57] Where the consequences of open worker collective action 'are likely to be catastrophic in terms of permanent dismissal or jail, the work force may resort to a slowdown or to shoddy work on the job'.[58] Covert resistance may be directed at public power too: 'Small wonder that a large share of the tax receipts of Third World states is collected in the forms of levies on imports and exports; the pattern is ... a tribute to the tax resistance capacity of their subjects'.[59] This coping with power may entail avoiding rather than subverting it: Moore notes that the 'common man's [sic] most frequent and effective response to oppression has been flight'.[60] Piven and Cloward make a similar point about resistance to power in the US:

> [E]ven some forms of defiance which appear to be individual acts ... may have a collective dimension ... massive school truancy or rising worker absenteeism ... or spreading rent defaults rarely attract the attention of political analysts. Having decided by definitional fiat that nothing political has occurred, nothing has to be explained, or at least not in terms of political protest.[61]

These acts of disguised resistance are not cost-free. But the costs are much lower as long as this indirect resistance is not seen as a challenge to power – if, as is likely, it is viewed as confirmation of the powerful's view that the powerless are lazy, incompetent or dishonest. The powerful are unaware that what they interpret as stupidity or cultural backwardness is, in fact, resistance. But these disguised resistance strategies are also, Scott asserts, appropriate if people lack the resources to engage in collective action: 'Being a class ... lacking the institutional means to act collectively, [the peasantry] is likely to employ those means of resistance that are local and require little coordination'.[62] As a result, 'examples of ... resistance abound. They ... reflect the conditions and constraints under which they are generated. If they are open, they are rarely collective and, if they are collective, they are rarely open'.[63]

Failing to see these acts as resistance undervalues the consciousness and action of the powerless: 'Formal, organized political activity ... is typically the preserve of the middle class and the intelligentsia; to look for peasant politics in this realm is to look largely in vain. It is also – not incidentally – the first step towards concluding that the peasantry is a political nullity unless organized and led by outsiders'.[64] But this tactic of challenging power without being seen to do so can be politically effective. Hydén, writing about Tanzania, notes that the African peasant 'by using his [sic] deceptive skills, has often defeated the authorities'.[65] The resistance of the weak does not hold power to account. But it is potent at times because it frustrates power-holders' plans.

The powerless do sometimes engage in collective action despite the power arrayed against them. Scott believes that, given the cost-benefit calculations which confront the powerless, collective defiance is most likely when the behaviour of the powerful 'decisively destroy[s] nearly all the routines of daily life ...'.[66] Because they fear the costs of challenging power, the powerless are most likely to act collectively not to improve their conditions – because they believe this to be impossible – but to keep what they have. When their lives are changed radically in ways which threaten familiar patterns, Scott argues, they may act to conserve what exists.

Scott's explanation should strike a powerful chord for South Africans. The resort by the powerless to covert, individualised attempts to exploit the system or nullify its effects on them, not to challenge it, are familiar in societies marked by racial domination, where they are routinely explained as evidence of the inferiority of the powerless. White South Africans' constant complaints that black people 'fail to answer simple questions' ignore the possibility that the 'ignorance' is a resistance strategy. (In a radio discussion, a white caller complained that black people in the Eastern Cape, when asked for directions, 'don't even know the way to their own village'. This begged the question of how they managed to leave it and return each day. The possibility that they knew perfectly well where their village was but were not willing to tell someone whose manner betrayed deep contempt for them escaped him.) The effect is to set off a vicious cycle in which racial oppression prompts its victims to act in ways which serve only to confirm the prejudices of the powerful. Many of the 'cultural' patterns dominators cite as evidence of the 'backwardness' of the subordinated group are a product of the patterns of behaviour Scott describes. What begins as the weak's way of resisting the strong becomes yet another means for the strong to deny the claims of the weak. It is this which prompted theorists of black consciousness to explore ways of freeing the dominated from the assumptions of powerlessness which feed the cycle.[67]

A feature of labour relations in South Africa (and elsewhere) is the tendency for workers unable to engage in collective action to resort to absenteeism, theft and feigned inability to understand instructions to damage economic power-holders they feel too powerless to challenge. Societies in which access to collective action is restricted to the few pay a high price in lost productivity for their refusal to accord to all the right to act collectively. Most importantly, Scott's work explains the uneven distribution of collective action not by access to resources or choice, but by conscious calculations not to challenge a power whose moral pretensions the powerless reject but whose power they are forced to acknowledge.

Fear and Inaction in an Older Democracy

Support for Scott's explanation can be found in several other sources. For example, a study of black voting patterns in the US southern state of Mississippi found that fear, not apathy, explained low turnout. The authors, Lester Salomon and Stephen van Evera, note: 'In a rare show of unanimity, political scientists have generally taken as given that nonparticipation in politics is a result of disinterest or apathy ... [this] assumes that people fail to participate in politics chiefly because they do not think it is worth the time or because they fail to understand what is at stake'.[68] But a national civil rights group's checklist of reasons given by black voters for not voting listed 'economic pressure' as by far the most often cited.[69] Comparing turnout in the state's various counties, they found that it was lower 'where blacks are most vulnerable to economic intimidation',[70] where people were most dependent on the decisions of economic power-holders (because they did not own their homes or did not have secure sources of income, for example). Those who were most dependent were least likely to vote, indicating that people failed to vote chiefly because they feared the consequences. They note that fear may not be prompted by immediate violence and intimidation, but that memories of both can deter voting as much as two decades later.[71]

Their study found that organisation could reduce fear and that this was a chief goal of civil rights organisers: 'According to … two civil rights organisations … the major consequence of … organizational development was to enable individuals to "manage their fear" through group solidarity'. This finding is consistent with Scott's analysis since he too discusses periods in which peasants could overcome fear of power enough to engage in collective action. But they note too that fear means that 'organization which would permit mass action would probably never develop spontaneously', and that organisation must be built by people who are not subject to the power relations which inhibit action.[72] This points to a key flaw in Olson's approach – it has no room for power as a deterrent to action. It assumes that everyone has a free choice between action and inaction, and that the latter stems from a freely made calculation. The work discussed here suggests that cost-benefit calculations may inhibit action, but that they stem not from a desire to shift the burden onto others but from a calculation of the likely cost of antagonising power. It also offers an alternative to resource-based explanations of failure to act: the poor and vulnerable fail to act not because they lack the resources to do so but because they fear the response of power-holders.

Further confirmation that it is a sense of powerlessness that deters action can be found in Mansbridge's study of a form of routine collective action which seems to be the essence of democratic citizenship – participation in the 'town meetings' which residents of New England towns convene annually to discuss the issues facing them and to elect their leadership.[73] Mansbridge explains non-participation not as a response to power, but as evidence of people's aversion to 'adversary' democracy which is premised on conflict and contention: 'face-to-face conflict in town meetings creates fears of which I had not been sufficiently aware',[74] and '[e]ven in a representative democracy, nonvoters avoid politics because it involves conflict'.[75] In this view, people do not participate because they fear conflict, not power. But her work presents compelling evidence that it is fear of power which deters collective action.

Mansbridge reports that, while town meetings are often celebrated as a model exercise in participatory democracy, participation is uneven. Not everyone attends and those who stay away are usually poorer and less educated. So non-participation seems more a product of poverty since there is no reason why poor people should be more averse to conflict. Some of her interviews suggest that submissiveness is a reason for failure to participate: some poorer residents said they stay away from meetings because they assume that others are better able to decide what is good for the town than they are.[76] But, beneath these 'onstage' responses, her interviews suggest a 'hidden transcript' in which respect for the capacities of the more affluent and better connected may be based more on fear of power than on esteem.

Fear of the consequences of participation feature prominently in the responses of poorer and less connected residents. One reports feeling 'intimidated': 'If you go there, and you speak up, they make fun of you for speaking up and so on, and I guess people just don't want to go and be made fun of'.[77] This may indicate conflict aversion. But it is safe to assume that those who will be making fun are more powerful, while those who will be made fun of will be weaker. It is also important that those who stay away are more likely to be women than men since women are more likely to expect to be ignored or ridiculed. People on the wrong end of power seem to recognise the capacity of the strong to use ridicule to wield power – and to calculate that, in light of this ability of power to ensure that the powerless are not taken seriously, participation is pointless. Mansbridge, while defending her view that adversarial democracy deters participation, acknowledges that practices which repress conflict work against the least powerful.[78] She concedes too that '[n]ot bringing conflicts into the open ... usually gives more power to the members of whatever inside group settles things informally before or after the meeting'.[79] It is hard to see why poorer and weaker residents would want to participate in a process which will produce only outcomes selected by the powerful.

Some poor respondents are explicit about their sense that participation will achieve nothing because of power imbalances. One, who avoids meetings because she believes people would call her a fool, told Mansbridge: 'Well, I've heard a lot of people say ... "the main ones ... at town meeting, it always goes the way they want it. They would make the same decision whether I went or not" '.[80] Asked whether she would do anything to change a law she disliked, she said: 'They'd say ... she ain't nothing!' This is not the view of a person who believes the powerful know better, but of one who believes they do not take the powerless seriously.

These responses may also offer a clue to one way in which power deters collective action in democracies. Unlike Scott's peasants, the poor of Mansbridge's New England enjoy democratic rights and, in principle, are protected if they speak and act. But for them, a sense that some people are taken seriously while others are not – and that this reflects who holds power and who does not – operates in much the same way as fear of punishment in Scott's case. Power's effect is far more subtle, but its impact is no less clear. Mansbridge recognises this: 'Removing the legal barriers to influence ... will not by itself produce either the political equality theoretically required by adversary democracy or the widespread participation and equal respect which sustains a unitary democracy'.[81] So the issue is less whether democracy is practised in a way which convinces those who fear conflict that they can participate in a calm environment than whether power balances are changed to ensure that the poor and weak believe they will be heard – and will not face reprisals from power-holders.

Beneath the Surface: Power and Apparent Submission in Africa

'Apathy' among African-American voters or New England townsfolk is an expression of fear of, or resignation to, a power which the powerless see through but feel unable to challenge. Similarly, writing on postcolonial Africa suggests that the apparent willingness of Africans to accept or celebrate unaccountable power masks another 'hidden transcript' in which people seem to be endorsing power while in reality rejecting its legitimacy. Perhaps the one difference is that, while Scott's peasants speak from their hidden transcripts while power is not listening, Africans subjected to unaccountable rule do so in power's presence, albeit in ways which elude its gaze.

We noted Monga's critique of the claim – made, ironically, in the name of rejecting cultural colonisation – that one-party states and other limits on popular sovereignty reflect African cultural choices, not the effects of power. He supports his view that African citizens want democracy but are denied it by power by describing patterns of resistance to authority which disguise themselves not because they believe power is being wielded legitimately, but because self-preservation tells them it cannot be challenged. While the form may differ, the patterns, and the rationale for them, are the same as those of the Malaysian peasants studied by Scott:

> Realistically, African peoples are in a position of weakness, hence resistance must take a subtle form. Frontal assaults are avoided. Suicidal methods that might reveal the collective strategy are proscribed. Instead, a more insidious approach is adopted ... that may take the form of a play on words, a theory of derision, a deformation of the established rules, a refusal to follow instructions, or an irreverent attitude toward the hierarchy in place.[82]

To Monga, these responses to power are acts of resistance, even though weakness ensures that they cannot translate into a challenge to power: 'Surreptitiously, in the small events, gestures, words and actions of daily life, there has evolved a true ethos of resistance, a subtle sort of civil disobedience that cannot be described in the language to which we are accustomed ... if African peoples are adroit with words, they are also quite skilled in the use of silence ... to convey their defiance of political authorities ...'.[83] Nor is this response purely an act of protest – it can undo or subvert power's plans without directly challenging them: 'Apparently submissive and even consenting to their subjection', Monga writes, 'African peoples nevertheless often transformed the laws imposed on them into something quite different to what their leaders had in mind … To use de Certeau's words, "Their use of the dominant social order deflected its power, which they lacked the means to challenge" '.[84] Public policies are 'invalidated daily by collective indiscipline'.[85] The compliance with hierarchy – traditional or otherwise – is a survival strategy and is revealed as such by the gap between what people say about power and what they do about it.

This pattern, in which people ostensibly endorse power but ridicule it at the same time, is also described by Achille Mbembe's writing on the 'postcolony'.[86] Unlike Monga, Mbembe does not describe responses to power as resistance. He argues that 'the postcolonial relationship is not primarily a relationship of resistance or of collaboration but can best be characterised as illicit cohabitation …'[87] because 'the practices of those who command and of those who are assumed to obey are so entangled as to render them powerless'.[88] But that does not mean that African subjects are acquiescing to power – in Mbembe's view, we must avoid seeing postcolonial relationships through the 'binary oppositions usually adduced in conventional analyses of movements of indiscipline and revolt'.[89]

The responses of Africans subjected to unaccountable rule do not replace the power of the elite with that of the people. Rather, they neutralise the power of those who rule but become powerless in the process. This may explain why postcolonial African states have often been unable to govern effectively – their relationship with those they govern enables them to use force or extract resources but not to shape society. It may also explain why resistance to power in Africa has often been unable to alter it, why it has often centred on ways to avoid or subvert power rather than to change it. But here, too, subjects do not accept power's pretensions – on the contrary, they mock them while seeming publicly to endorse them. Thus Mbembe identifies the frequent use of ridicule as an expression of powerlessness: 'It is with the conscious aim of avoiding … trouble that ordinary people locate the fetish of state power in the realm of ridicule … Those who laugh … are not necessarily bringing about the collapse of power or resisting it. Confronted with the state's eagerness to cover up its actual origins, people are simply bearing witness, often unconsciously …'.[90]

Often, Mbembe asserts, this ridiculing of power occurs precisely when people seem to be validating it – under one-party rule, apparent chants of praise for the ruler are subtly changed so that they express mockery, disguised to fool power. Mbembe cites work on Togo by Comi Toulabar,[91] which shows how 'under one-party rule, people developed … a whole vocabulary, equivocal and ambiguous, that ran parallel to the official discourse'.[92] Often this mockery uses obscenity and the grotesque to make its point, partly confirming the claim of the literary critic Mikhail Bakhtin that they are a means by which 'ordinary people' resist the dominant culture by holding officialdom up to ridicule.[93] What appeared to the untrained eye to be an enthusiastic public endorsement of unaccountable power was its opposite: 'there remained considerable disparity between the images that the state projected of itself ... and the way people played [with] and manipulated these images – and people did so not just well away from officialdom, out of earshot, out of sight of power but also within the actual arenas where they were gathered publicly to confirm the legitimacy of the state' – by, for example, parodying the party slogans they were expected to shout.[94] Postcolonial subjects, Mbembe reports, invent multiple identities – the publicly visible, which ratifies power, is only one of several. Analyses which focus only on the identity which subjects present to power offers a distorted image because what people who consider themselves powerless say is not necessarily what they mean, but what they feel they need to say to survive.

Whether we see these responses to power as expressions of resistance or as cohabitation between power and powerlessness, they confirm the key argument of this chapter – that, where the poor and weak avoid collective action, they do so not because they accept the legitimacy of power, but because they believe they are too weak to challenge it. Whether they drop out, as in Mansbridge's town meetings, or mock power behind its back or in code in plain view, the powerless do not accept power's claims to legitimacy; they challenge it with whatever is at their disposal given their reading of the power balance.

Frequent monopolisation of routine collective action by the powerful is not a product of 'false consciousness' or a 'civic education' deficit. It stems from a power deficit. But this rejection of 'false consciousness' does not mean that dominated people can never be manipulated. Media can offer people a misleading account of why they are being dominated. This was a key factor in the 2016 British referendum campaign which led to that country leaving the European Union, primarily because many voters believed that this would end immigration to Britain – this included many working-class voters who blamed their declining living conditions on migrants. A study of media coverage of the campaign showed that media had stressed the threat posed by immigration: much of the coverage labelled immigrants as 'job stealers' who received benefits for which British taxpayers had paid.[95] These claims were untrue,[96] but they may well have persuaded many voters that their declining living standards were the result not of policies which favoured the rich, but of immigration. But this is not 'false consciousness'. The working-class voters did not accept their circumstances as part of the natural order – on the contrary, they rebelled against them. Because they were fed a steady diet of false 'information', they blamed the elite for admitting immigrants, not for cutting social services. They were misled into blaming the wrong cause – but they did not accept the circumstances in which the decisions of economic power-holders had placed them. The capacity of media and politicians to manufacture 'news' which prompts people to misread the causes of their domination does not mean that they accept being dominated. It is power (in this case the power to frame the problem in a misleading way), not 'false consciousness', which guides the actions of the dominated.

SUBSTANCE AND FORM

The conclusion that powerlessness deters collective action has practical as well as theoretical implications. If broader and deeper access to collective action – and, therefore, democratisation – stems not from educating the relatively powerless but from changing power relations, people do not need to be told by 'civic educators' that power ought to account to them. If they are to become citizens, they need tools which enable them to hold power to account. The history of the poor people's movements discussed by Piven and Cloward – in particular of the labour movement, which has perhaps been the most effective in changing power relations – shows that the power which prevents collective action can be challenged only by that action. At first glance, this seems an insoluble paradox – how can people who believe they cannot act because power is arrayed against them become able to act to change that reality? It is not – the literature on collective action shows that it is possible to change both the perception and reality of the power which prevents collective action.

Tarrow's opportunity structure is relevant again because it aims to show how power relations are shifted by new opportunities. But his treatment of the topic ignores the difference between two types of opportunity: 'subjective' and 'objective'.[97] The latter is beyond the control of potential collective actors – it refers to social and economic trends or shifts in elite politics which are not directly prompted by the powerless. If this were the only sort of opportunity, the notion of 'political opportunity structure' would mean that realities beyond their control decide whether the powerless can act. They would remain powerless unless opportunities for action open and are seized. The best they can presumably do is to be aware of the opportunities when they open up.

By framing collective action as a response to external events, Tarrow reinforces this view. He does devote some attention to 'making opportunities' – how the powerless can open space for collective action by their own efforts. But in the main he explains how citizens can use those which emerge, not how they can create them. Many of his examples, however, show that collective action by the dominated can open up opportunities. This is either explicit – when strikes by coal miners are said to aid action in the former Soviet Union[98] – or implicit – when collective action in Italy is said to have been helped by the presence of the Socialist Party in government,[99] which happened because citizens used collective action to elect it. And, while he quotes Piven and Cloward's analysis of how electoral politics created opportunities for the US civil rights movement,[100] Tarrow does not mention that this was at least partially a response to collective action, which began with Rosa Parks's refusal to accept bus segregation.[101] These examples show that the powerless are not doomed to exclusion from collective action unless events create opportunities for them: they themselves can create opportunities.

External factors do play a role in shifting power balances and opening up opportunities. These 'objective' factors must be acted on if collective agency is to be broadened and deepened, but they cannot be created by the powerless. The apartheid state began running out of skilled white labour in the early 1970s – this forced the employment of black workers in more skilled positions, enhancing their bargaining power, and raised the costs of suppressing collective action.[102] Tarrow points to the role of economic booms in fuelling worker bargaining power and, therefore, militancy,[103] while Piven and Cloward see economic modernisation as a key driver of action among black people who joined the civil rights movement.[104] Elites may also open spaces for collective action not because they are forced to do so by the excluded, but because other considerations propel them in that direction: Tarrow notes that the liberalisation which opened avenues for action in the former Soviet Union began with differences within the elite.[105] A coherent theory of how power balances change to allow an extension of collective action must address both 'subjective' and 'objective' dimensions.

Another key implication is that, contrary to Mansbridge's position, the form democracy takes is far less important than whether it is deepened and broadened by the spread of collective action. Just as she acknowledged that both the unitary democracy she preferred and the adversary democracy she hoped to transcend could not ensure equal participation if power was not distributed equally, particular democratic institutions cannot guarantee broader or deeper democracy if access to collective action remains unequally distributed. This has two further implications.

One challenges scholars and activists who insist that democracy's quality and survival depends on its design. Many lawyers and political scientists devote their energies to devising rules of the political game which can guarantee democracies that work and survive. But these institutions cannot decide democracy's fate nor can they ensure its depth or shallowness if power, and the powerless's perception of it, excludes most citizens from collective action. Institutions are not irrelevant, but their role must be placed in context. Whether they can deepen democracy depends on whether they help or hinder collective action by the powerless and weaken the power which obstructs that action – whether they, in Shapiro's terms, erode domination.

The other rejects the claim that popular sovereignty is blocked by representative democracy. Proposals for participatory democracy take many forms, one of which is the claim that forums, not representative democracy, offer a route to greater popular sovereignty.[106] It has been argued here that the rules of representative democracy are indispensable to popular sovereignty; it is power relations in society, not the rules of representative systems, which ensure that only some can participate fully. This suggests that the route to broader and deeper democracy lies not in abandoning the rules of representative democracy, but in ensuring that all can use them to claim a share of popular sovereignty.

Both points – that the powerless can organise to claim a say and that the rules of representative democracy enable them to do that – require more discussion. The next chapter will offer this by exploring a case which illustrates both points: the fight for a comprehensive policy to tackle HIV and AIDS in South Africa.

CHAPTER

8

Collective Action as Democratic Citizenship: The Treatment Action Campaign[1]

How do powerless people use representative democracy and the rights which support it to protect their interests and demand a say?

In early 2001, when many believed multinational corporations were invincible, and South Africa's new democratic government was so firmly entrenched that it did not need to listen to the voice of citizens, a group of activists was able to pressure international pharmaceutical firms to abandon a court action which sought to prevent the government from importing cheaper medicines.[2] In August 2003, a coalition of organisations and individuals won their sustained campaign to press a resistant government to approve a comprehensive AIDS treatment plan which included the distribution of anti-retroviral medication (ARVs) to people living with the virus.[3]

The common thread between the two events was the pivotal role of the Treatment Action Campaign (TAC), which was responsible for the 2001 demonstrations and also led a fight for access to ARVs as part of its campaign to win adequate treatment for people infected by HIV and AIDS. This second victory helped confirm TAC's iconic status internationally and at home. It and its former chair, Zackie Achmat, have received international awards and were nominated for the Nobel Peace Prize.[4] Besides playing a major role in prompting the corporations' 2001 decision not to contest the case, TAC, supported by key international NGO allies and influential civil society figures, was pivotal to the campaign which forced the government's reluctant policy change.[5] While this did not initially produce a dramatic increase in the number of South Africans receiving treatment, the number who receive free ARVs has steadily risen: by 2016, 56 per cent of the 7.1 million people living with HIV and AIDS received them, as did up to 95 per cent of pregnant women, whose medication prevented mother-to-child transmission.[6] Millions of people are alive purely because of this shift.

TAC has played a crucial role in forcing the South African government to heed the concerns of an important constituency – people living with a deadly virus. These gains have been won not for the affluent or people who enjoy access to government – most TAC members during the campaign were unemployed black women. It has, therefore, given voice to people who would not otherwise be heard. And it has forced an elected government to respond, making the democratic system more account-able and enabling hitherto voiceless citizens to gain a share in popular sovereignty. It has strengthened democracy, enhancing its depth and its survival prospects.

TAC's experiences, its limits and its possibilities are an important indicator that formal democracy does not obstruct policy which reflects the concerns of the poor and weak – that, if people at the grassroots can engage in collective action, they can use its instruments to win gains. They support the argument that, where formal democracy has failed to produce greater equity, this is not because the system cannot do this, but because citizens with an interest in a redistribution of resources have lacked the access to collective action needed to achieve change.

TAC's campaign also provides concrete support for many of the points argued here. First, it emphasises the role of collective action in deepening democracy and enabling citizens to claim a share in popular sovereignty. The advent of democracy in South Africa in 1994 did not automatically ensure citizens a share in popular sovereignty – it seemed initially that the government would remain largely immune to citizen pressure. The campaign for a comprehensive HIV and AIDS plan showed that citizens could imprint their stamp on decisions provided they organised and acted collectively. It also showed that power's restraint on action can be broken by effective organisation which can persuade at least some of the powerless that col-lective action can produce concrete policy change.

Furthermore, the campaign showed that democratic rights can be used to force the government to respond to citizens. The campaign used constitutional democ-racy to pressure the government to concede a treatment programme, and it showed that the obstacle to the exercise of popular sovereignty is not the rules of formal democracy but access to the means to act collectively. It showed that the use by citizens of the rights to mobilise bestowed by formal democracy to mobilise is a surer route to broader popular sovereignty than formal forums designed to advance 'participatory governance'.

It illustrated the importance of routine collective action: while the campaign relied on mobilisation, ensuring that the change of policy was implemented relied on routine engagement with government. This does not mean that mobilisation is unnecessary, but it does show the importance to citizens who seek a share in popular sovereignty of routine engagement with political authority.

Finally, the campaign suggested tactics which might ensure collective action that forces power-holders to respond, even where the power balance seems to preclude this.

THE CAMPAIGN AND THE CAMPAIGNERS

Launched on 10 December, International Human Rights Day, in 1998, TAC was a response to the HIV and AIDS epidemic whose impact, obscured as a public policy issue by the pressures of political transition, was becoming apparent. TAC was created to campaign for affordable treatment for people living with the virus, in particular for access to ARV therapy. In TAC's own words, it sought to 'campaign for greater access to treatment for all South Africans, by raising public awareness and understanding about issues surrounding the availability, affordability and use of HIV treatments'.[7] Its founders were two former anti-apartheid activists, Achmat (who is HIV-positive) and Mark Heywood; they sought to use techniques developed in the fight against apartheid to press pharmaceutical firms to offer affordable medication to people living with AIDS.[8]

TAC's methods ranged from civil disobedience and street demonstrations to action in the courts to pamphlets spelling out scientific arguments. While it was not an entirely conventional membership organisation, recruitment of members was an important route to participation. In 2005, membership was said to be around 12 000[9] – a very small percentage of the population living with HIV and AIDS. Activists pointed out that the numbers participating in TAC marches – estimated at up to 15 000 – indicated an ability to mobilise people in excess of its membership.[10]

TAC was not affiliated to a political party and members were said to support a variety of parties. But most were ANC supporters[11] – as they would have been in most membership organisations, given the size of the ANC's electoral majority at the time. Achmat's frequent insistence that he was a 'loyal member of the ANC' was criticised by activists in other social movements.[12] So, despite its political independence and diversity, TAC, unlike most other social movements, had a political identity which made a relationship with the government and ANC easier. Nevertheless, its relationship with the ANC was more conflicted than Achmat's statement might suggest: he accused it of largely ignoring civil society and founded a network of ANC voters committed to moving it in a more 'progressive' direction. In an interview before the 2004 election, he suggested that '[t]he ANC would like TAC to endorse a boycott of elections so that we can lose legitimacy',[13] suggesting that the party of which he was a loyal member was seeking to weaken TAC and its campaign. ANC support within TAC did not dissuade it from launching a civil disobedience campaign in which it attempted to charge two government ministers with culpable homicide. And, while the ANC expressed the political identity of many TAC members, this did not prevent government resistance to its campaign. Nor did it prevent TAC activists from experiencing considerable pressure within the ANC.[14] TAC's experience confirms, therefore, that citizens may see political parties as important, but might still not view them as the vehicle through which they seek to advance their immediate interests.

Since TAC's key concern was to win effective treatment for people too poor to afford it from private sources, it is perhaps inevitable that its grassroots branch membership was composed largely of poor black people. According to Achmat, during the campaign: 'The demographics of TAC are 80% unemployed, 70% women – the group most affected by HIV, domestic violence and violence in schools – 70% in the 14–24 age group and 90% (black) African'.[15] Most members were women, who are far more likely to be infected by HIV.[16] They are subject to domestic abuse and violence compounded by the advent of HIV, which gave them an added incentive to participate. They also seemed to be more active participants in TAC activities.[17] Most office bearers were, however, men.[18]

Collective action enables citizens to combine to speak to political authority – but only if they enjoy a voice within the organisations through which they act.[19] The degree to which campaigning organisations are internally democratic is, therefore, important in determining whether campaigns really offer a share in popular sovereignty. To what extent did TAC's campaign offer its participants a voice? Some of its strategies required technical knowledge which was not available to grassroots members who lack formal education. But its structure did provide for internal representative democracy. Members were free to speak openly and democratic structures ensured members retained a voice.

It was argued earlier that popular sovereignty requires more than that citizens enjoy a say in the organisations to which they belong, that it is necessary too that participation enables them to influence the exercise of power. TAC leaders believed that the organisation enabled members to become actors rather than passive recipients of decisions: 'Our members are not used to thinking of themselves as people with agency and power. Participation in TAC makes them aware of what they can do'.[20] The trade union movement, too, sought to instil a sense of political efficacy in members. Its experience seems to confirm collective action's ability to do this: opinion surveys conducted in the early years of democracy showed that union members held higher expectations of government and were more inclined to believe that change is possible than other groups.[21] Participation in TAC may also have convinced members that they could hold power to account using democratic means, enabling democratic citizenship more effectively than the associations which Putnam believes to be essential.

The Campaign: A Brief Biography

The campaign to change government policy on HIV and AIDS began in earnest in early 2001 with the successful action against international pharmaceutical firms, whose retreat was also a government victory: TAC's role in embarrassing the companies may have been decisive. Civil society organisations supported the government's position, but on citizens' terms and in their own way, without any agreement to co-operate. Co-operation between citizens and democratic government does not exclude mobilisation by citizens – in this case, and no doubt in many others, the two were complementary.

The companies' attempt to prevent cheaper drug imports was the sort of issue TAC had been created to fight. Its activists assumed that a government victory would bring much cheaper AIDS treatments, in particular that ARVs, then available only to people with medical insurance, would be imported and distributed to those unable to pass on the cost to an insurer. When, after the legal victory, the firms cut the costs of key medicines in an attempt to repair a public image battered by activist campaigns, the way seemed open for the distribution of ARVs to the poor through the public health system. But the government did not use the victory to extend affordable AIDS treatment to its constituents. Instead, President Thabo Mbeki led a government response targeted not at fighting HIV and AIDS, but at discrediting both the medication needed to combat it and the scientific theories which sought to explain it.

The government never adopted a policy rejecting ARVs. But it did refuse to distribute them in public health facilities. It presented a range of reasons, chief among them the claim that it was piloting their use and did not yet know whether they worked. Because it was not policy to distribute them at public hospitals and clinics, doctors in the public sector who prescribed them faced disciplinary action.[22] The minister of health, Manto Tshabalala-Msimang, with Mbeki's approval (he reappointed her after the 2004 election), repeatedly claimed that better nutrition was a surer antidote to AIDS than ARVs [23] and consistently undermined the notion that ARVs were a cure. In his regular reports to Parliament on his government's progress and plans, the president kept references to AIDS to a bare minimum.[24]

It became clear to ANC politicians that publicly differing from the president and minister on AIDS would be viewed as disloyalty. Most, hoping to protect their careers but to avoid alienating their support base and violating their consciences, stayed silent. The effect was not only to deny treatment to people living with AIDS who could not afford ARVs (the vast majority), but also to obstruct a coherent national response to the virus: mixed messages from the government ensured that there was no consensus on what should be done and how to do it. Activists claimed that the dissident message made it more difficult for people to protect themselves against AIDS: people did not, they said, abandon risky behaviour, because the government message suggested, or was interpreted to suggest, that individual behaviour had no effect on vulnerability to the virus. The government seemed to have placed millions of lives at risk, causing as much damage as if it had explicitly rejected the scientific consensus on AIDS and its treatment. TAC and others concerned for people living with AIDS soon found themselves locked in a battle with the government, which they pressed to launch a comprehensive response to the virus, including distributing ARVs at public expense.

TAC's founders did not expect conflict with the government – they anticipated campaigning against the companies.[25] But before long, the campaign to change the government's attitude overrode the fight against the firms (although they remained a target).[26] Initially, activist criticism hardened the government's attitude. Tension between it and civil society organisations escalated, prompting a public display of conflict at a major AIDS conference;[27] the government responded by excluding critics from AIDS decision-making. AIDS became a major political liability for the Mbeki administration. It found itself increasingly isolated on the issue as support, domestic and foreign, coalesced around a campaign for a comprehensive government response which would respect the scientific consensus. Critics included Nobel Peace Prize winners – former president Nelson Mandela and Archbishop Desmond Tutu – and other notables. Medical professionals, NGO activists, the media and civil society organisations were dismayed by the government stance, as were international organisations. While Mbeki would have faced criticism on AIDS even if TAC had never existed, its presence ensured that pressure for a policy shift was sustained by a broad alliance. It was also primarily responsible for keeping the issue in the public eye.

In July 2002, the campaign won a breakthrough when the Constitutional Court declared the government's failure to provide a comprehensive programme to prevent mother-to-child transmission of HIV 'unreasonable and unconstitutional', and ordered it to supply the ARV nevirapine to prevent transmission of the virus by mothers to newborn children.[28] By August 2003, TAC and its allies had won a commitment by the government to a comprehensive AIDS strategy which included the distribution of ARVs at public facilities.[29] The government agreed to appoint a task team to devise this and in November adopted a detailed plan to combat AIDS. 'Activism', the then deputy minister of health confirmed later, 'did force the government to alter course – partly by strengthening differing voices in government'.[30]

USING DEMOCRACY'S RULES: TACTICS AND STRATEGY

TAC was able to achieve policy change partly because of the way in which it related to the political environment – and specifically because it saw formal democracy as an essential means to influence.

While many activists are sceptical of the opportunities created by constitutional democracy, TAC was not. Its activism sought to use the levers which democracy offers – the courts and independent media – and the rights it entrenches – the right to assemble and express grievances chief among them. It also accepted, implicitly and at times explicitly, the constraints imposed by constitutionalism, including respect for (rather than obedience to or endorsement of) elected authorities.[31] TAC activists saw the Constitutional Court as a strategic resource: 'the government is afraid of the court'.[32] A social movement activist critical of TAC's use of the law conceded that it 'managed to find a balance between the legal [in the courts] and the masses in the streets'.[33] The campaign also enjoyed the support of allies in the government despite the conflict between activists and political authorities.[34] This would not have been possible before democracy was achieved.

Democracy also created new strategic challenges for activism. The legitimacy of the government and the support enjoyed by the ANC were realities which activists tackling government policy forget at their peril: 'A major tactical error would be to lose support among our members as other social movements have done when they are seen to threaten democratically elected leaders'.[35] TAC seemed unusual among South African social movements in appreciating the need to change strategy to adapt to the environment created by democracy. Thus its civil disobedience campaign in 2003 in response to the government's failure to sign its agreement to an AIDS treatment plan caused much internal debate, precisely because some in TAC – and the broader alliance seeking change in AIDS policy – were concerned that defying a legitimate democratic government would damage its credibility. But civil disobedience is not inconsistent with respect for constitutional order if those engaging in it recognise the right of the state to arrest them for peacefully breaking the law and accept restraints consistent with democratic principles such as respect for the rights of others – all of which TAC attempted to do. TAC activists were participating in democratic governance, not only by respecting the rules which underpin it, but by using collective action to force public officials to engage with citizens on framing and implementing government policy.

More specifically, two approaches adopted by TAC illustrate the strategic potential for effective collective action which democracy opened.

The Politics of the Moral High Ground

TAC's leadership readily acknowledge that it did not win gains because of strength in numbers. While it had a larger membership and a more organised structure than many other social movements, they insisted that its power lay elsewhere.

According to Achmat, morality was a key source of TAC's influence: 'TAC is not a numbers game. It is more about the ability to create a moral consensus. Morality is usually left to churches but we all have a duty to be moral. The left needs to give a sense of morality to politics'.[36] Morality is thus both a principle and an important strategic weapon which is often ignored as an asset of organisations engaged in collective action. It is assumed that there is an unbridgeable conflict between those who wield power and those over whom they wield it, so the weak can gain power only by forcing the powerful to concede it. Power is, in this view, force, not moral persuasion. But building moral support can itself be a source of power. A broad moral consensus in society may force power-holders to listen and moral argument may create divisions within the group which wields power. TAC's experience suggests that the ability to persuade a range of audiences that the actions of a power-holder are immoral is a vital source of power.

This may seem obvious: all movements claim their demands are moral. But TAC's approach understood morality in an unusual way. If power can be redistributed only by mobilising the powerless to force the powerful to concede, movements might see morality as no more than a convenient 'weapon' which can rally their constituency, since the powerful are assumed to be beyond moral appeal. Morality would seek to persuade poor people living with HIV and AIDS that they ought to support TAC because the government for which they vote is behaving 'immorally' while ignoring other constituencies or branding them immoral. Morality here is a tactic and is not central to the movement's manner of operating. It polarises the 'moral' and 'immoral' and so cannot build common moral understandings across society.

TAC's goal of a 'moral consensus' was far more ambitious – it assumed that it is possible to build a common moral understanding across social divides, not necessarily on all issues but in support of particular campaigns. Thus a government could be morally weakened because important international or domestic constituencies on which it relies are persuaded that its conduct or position on an issue is immoral. This may be damaging not only because it might isolate the government from important constituencies, but it may also affect the moral self-understanding of power-holders. Human beings want to believe that their actions are moral – why else would authoritarians insist on surrounding themselves with people who assure them that they are doing good? A moral consensus may damage the self-esteem of key members of the powerful group. The TAC approach assumed that it is possible for a small movement to compensate for its lack of brute force by appealing to a sense of compassion and fairness across social barriers. But for this to be possible, morality must become a permanent and indispensable element of the movement's campaign, not a tactic to be used or discarded depending on circumstance. Morality may be most effective as a strategy only when it is seen not as a strategy, but as an indispensable principle of a struggle for rights or entitlements.

If morality is integral to how a campaign operates, it must become an essential feature of all activity, from financial management and commitment to internal democracy to the way in which action is designed, since losing the moral high ground is to lose one of the campaign's reasons for existence. This means accepting constraints which do not apply when morality is seen only as a strategic device. One example is Achmat's decision not to take ARVs while other people did not have access to them, which threatened to cost him his life. In his view this is one of a number of cases which demonstrated 'a distinct tension between morality and strategy'.[37] The politics of the moral high ground means that tactics must be evaluated not only by whether they enhance the movement's ability to force others to do what it wants, but also by whether they will retain the movement's moral power: 'Tactics which show militancy but alienate people destroy a moral consensus'.[38] As the debate over civil disobedience showed, this is not a rejection of militancy, which TAC frequently used, but a recognition that collective action does not achieve change by force alone: action must be morally justifiable to far more people than just the core of committed activists. This strategy requires a constant effort to communicate goals and principles – through the media, where possible: 'TAC has managed to keep the media on its side – even when they brought in drugs illegally'.[39]

It could be argued that this approach works only on this issue: a moral consensus can be built over the denial of medication to people infected with a deadly virus, but not over issues which directly affect the interests of the affluent such as land redistribution. TAC could build a moral consensus, this position argues, because it campaigned on a morally clear-cut issue, making it easy to win mainstream sympathy. But it was hardly guaranteed that the campaign for treatment would win the moral support which it did.

The campaign's opponents could have painted the demand for cheap ARVs as an attack on intellectual property rights and so too the search for medication to fight the virus. They might also have blamed the sexual morality of people living with HIV and AIDS for the virus. The racial element in attitudes to HIV/AIDS – while the virus knows no racial barrier, racists tended to label it a 'black disease' – may have given the South African government a powerful incentive not to stigmatise victims, but might also have given others a reason to see HIV/AIDS much as many bigots see war and conflict in Africa, as a sign of African backwardness. That denying treatment to people with AIDS came to be seen as morally repugnant by conservative as well as liberal or left world opinion was a result of the moral campaign waged by organisations and movements, into which TAC effectively tapped. It was hardly inevitable that HIV/AIDS would be seen so widely as a cause for sympathy[40] – it was made so by the collective action of campaigners. Since this may be possible on other issues too, morality could become a key element of the campaign for social and economic equity in new democracies.

The consensus on rights in the new South African policy elite was a crucial element of TAC's success: it understood that rights appeals in the post-apartheid environment were powerful since the fight against racial domination succeeded partly by using the language of rights. Nor is rights language powerful only in South Africa. Chatterjee has pointed to its use by the poor in India. While using the language of rights is not always effective, this illustrates a wider point – the need for campaigns to find moral language which strikes a chord in their society.

Thinking Alliances

Perhaps predictably, TAC's interest in crossing social divides means that it also saw alliances as a means of pursuing its strategic agenda.

There seems to be nothing exceptional in deciding that a campaign would be more effective if fought alongside others. But alliance politics is not simply about accepting the support of those who agree. It requires an acknowledgement that no interest group in a democracy ever commands the power to win an issue on its own, and that the support of others is therefore essential. This means rejecting a purism which insists on working only with natural allies: it assumes that common ground can be found with those who are assumed to differ as well as those known to agree. It also recognises that alliances – like morality – are not cost-free since they require compromise.

In TAC's case, this was so even in the case of a like-minded ally such as the Congress of South African Trade Unions (Cosatu), which refused to support its civil disobedience campaign. It obviously applied even more to groups with differing perspectives: TAC worked with a counselling group which was supported by a drug company and with the Catholic Church, which opposed condoms, which were considered by TAC essential to curb the spread of HIV and AIDS. Alliances of this sort do not wish difference away: Achmat insisted that his activist past taught 'the development of united fronts despite differing views'.[41] Some government politicians and officials were TAC allies, even when the movement was in conflict with the ANC and the government, as were some corporate executives (outside the pharmaceutical industry).[42] Relying on alliances does not, however, mean working with everyone on any terms. TAC was selective in its choice of the movements with which it worked.[43] Almost by definition, alliances entail conflict and co-operation. They also require a strategic appreciation of who, on any issue, is an ally or opponent.

TAC leadership seemed to approach issues in a way which can be described as 'thinking alliances'. Indispensable to the planning of any campaign was considering where support could be sought from important constituencies, including unlikely ones. Thus, one rationale behind a proposed People's Health Campaign was the expectation that the middle class has a strong interest in health reform and that the campaign would attract its support.[44] This approach starts from the assumption that winning strategic allies is crucial to successful collective action. Absolutely indispensable to this is openness to the possibility that interests which may oppose a campaign on one issue may be allies on another.

'Thinking alliances' is particularly important in campaigns for social policy change. It was noted earlier that targeting anti-poverty programmes so that 'the non-poor' do not benefit politically isolates the poor by creating conflicts over resources between them and the less poor. This prevents the formation of broad alliances in support of redistribution.[45] Strategies are likely to strengthen the voice of the poor only if they enable poor people to find allies among those with potential leverage. The more campaigns for social equity are restricted to the weak forced to act on their own, the likelier is it that they will be ignored. In principle, TAC, by 'thinking alliances', opened new potential frontiers for action against poverty and the inclusion of the hitherto excluded in the exercise of popular sovereignty. The TAC experience suggests that campaigns which do not 'think alliances' are likely to remain isolated and weak.

TAC's most strategically important alliance may have been that with international allies. This seems to have been important in two ways. It placed pressure on multinational pharmaceutical companies because their head offices feared being portrayed as irresponsible or unsympathetic to the poor.[46] And it may have hurt a government which wanted foreign approval. While globalisation is frequently seen as a constraint to collective action, it may also be a resource. Advances in communications technology make alliances between local and international activists much easier. A key feature of international alliances in the era of electronic communication is that they can be sustained without using significant resources.[47] An environment in which a company official can face immediate unfavourable publicity in America and Europe because of a dispute in Africa offers considerable scope for collective action.

THE QUEST FOR ROUTINE ACTION: AFTER POLICY CHANGE

The AIDS campaign was a model of mobilisation, not routine collective action – where a government is hostile to a campaign, there will be little or no routine engagement between campaigners and the government.

But routine collective action is possible during a campaign. Even during the phase of mobilisation to win policy change, TAC engaged with anyone in government willing to engage with it. This became far more of an option when the government agreed to distribute ARVs and allowed TAC activists to serve on the South African National AIDS Council (SANAC), established to advise it on AIDS. Routine collective action is not a synonym for cosying up to political authorities: it is a means of expressing and channelling conflict, not ending it. A distinction between lobbyists who make useful suggestions to governments and activists who mobilise power in the streets to confront office holders ignores routine action's capacity to express conflict and mobilisation's power to make government work better. But routine engagement does require channels between government and citizens engaged in collective action which ensure that the two talk directly rather than only across an actual or metaphorical picket line.

At first glance, the 2003 policy change should have opened an opportunity for far more routine engagement. TAC was open to this since it needed an effective government response to the virus; it insisted repeatedly that it saw itself as an enthusiastic government partner in this venture. This routine action was not expected to be conflict-free. TAC knew that the government was reluctantly responding to pressure; ensuring that people entitled to ARVs would receive them needed continued activism, much of it adversarial. Governments which concede policy change under pressure do not eagerly set out to implement what they have conceded: they must be pressed to do this, and campaigns to secure implementation of policy gains are often as important as the activism which won the gains. The partnership TAC wanted was meant to hold the government to its stated intentions. This could mean further campaigns, confrontation and court action.[48] It might be accurate, therefore, to see it not as an abandonment of mobilisation but as mobilising on a new terrain. Yet, despite a history of conflict, once the government said it was committed to distributing ARVs, it was possible for campaigners to engage it on how it was implementing its commitment. Mobilisation, in effect, won for TAC the right to engage in routine collective action.

After winning the change, TAC campaigned to ensure that the promises made in 2003 were kept. It achieved some success in swelling the number of people benefitting from publicly supplied ARVs. In the two wealthiest provinces, Gauteng and Western Cape, it participated in provincial efforts to distribute ARVs and to enhance AIDS-prevention efforts.[49] Partnerships were formed with public health facilities to enhance efforts to fight AIDS.[50] Key figures within government retained contact with TAC, albeit in secret discussions.[51] Not only were tens of thousands of lives saved, but progress was made in winning support within government despite intense pressure on ANC politicians and government officials to avoid working with TAC. Evidence that TAC was winning the battle to persuade grassroots ANC members rather than senior politicians was, according to Achmat, an internal ANC survey which found that most party members supported TAC's position and wanted the government to do more on AIDS.[52]

The anticipated shift to more routine engagement was only partial – because the government shift on HIV and AIDS was only partial. Despite a formal policy change, national government hostility to TAC – and reluctance to distribute ARVs even though it was now policy to do so – did not end. Many provincial health departments refused to work with TAC or to implement AIDS programmes.[53] A memo from the presidency was said to instruct government officials who were ANC members not to talk to TAC.[54] Most important of all to activists, senior government figures seemed to be actively trying to undermine the fight against AIDS. These suspicions centred on claims of government support for Mathias Rath, who marketed vitamins to people living with AIDS as an alternative to ARVs and who, with other AIDS 'denialists', ran an aggressive campaign to persuade people living with AIDS to abandon ARVs. Despite gains after 2003, activists insisted that both the president and the minister of health remained hostile to the commitment and were working to undermine it. In late 2005, the deputy minister of health reported that 'we still hear about nurses refusing to give women nevirapine. In the Eastern Cape it is claimed that 90% of mothers are not getting it'.[55] Activists complained also that AIDS-prevention efforts were failing.[56]

The policy change of 2003 did not prompt enough of a shift to routine collective action to present TAC with a new strategic challenge: how to remain independent enough from government to represent its constituency while working with power-holders to ensure that policy was implemented. The conflict which had made mobilisation necessary continued and so the TAC–government relationship after the formal shift of 2003 was not qualitatively different from that during the campaign for a comprehensive treatment plan. A new form of engagement emerged only in 2006 as a response to broader political trends.

Creating Political Opportunity: The Thaw of 2006

A shift in government attitude in 2006 which allowed for more routine engagement with TAC is a prime example of the change in political opportunity structure Tarrow discusses. But it illustrates too that changes in opportunity structures are often a product of collective action. In this case, the action was not only or even mainly TAC's.

Change was signalled in November 2006, when two politicians with responsibility for AIDS, then Deputy Minister Nozizwe Madlala-Routledge and Deputy President Phumzile Mlambo-Ngcuka, 'emerged from the shadows' to take a leading role in the government's response to the virus.[57] The deputy president, who had been nominally responsible for the government response to the virus but had played a marginal role, took the lead, urging TAC and other activist groups to co-operate with her government and committing it to a plan which initially aimed to treat 650 000 people with ARVs and to distribute 500 million male condoms a year by 2011.[58] The deputy minister, who was committed to addressing the virus from the outset, was allowed to speak publicly in support of more energetic action and a partnership between government and activists. Although she was fired in 2007, in what was widely seen as a punishment by the president for her position on the virus, government willingness to tackle AIDS continued to grow, which triggered co-operation between activists and the government.[59]

Activists were not convinced that the government had changed course fundamentally. But that there was a change is clear – one immediate consequence was more routine forms of collective action as TAC activists and government officials co-operated to implement the changes for which TAC had fought. The shift was a product of a change in the political environment: by mid-2006, tensions within the ANC triggered a growing challenge to Mbeki. At an ANC conference in mid-year, his critics won important battles. This caused many ANC politicians to abandon their assumption that he could not be opposed and prompted open questioning of Mbeki and his ministers by ANC activists and parliamentary committees.[60] HIV and AIDS was one issue on which opposition crystallised,[61] suggesting that TAC's collective action had at the very least an indirect impact on events. Mbeki's response to AIDS reflected for many of his opponents a leadership style which they resented – in their view, an aloof refusal to hear the voices of the grassroots and an insistence on imposing the presidency's view on everyone else.

So AIDS became one of the issues on which a beleaguered national leadership felt it needed to make concessions to activist opinion; that this would also help to defuse international criticism must have made the strategic decision easier. Change was accelerated when Mbeki, after losing the ANC presidency to Jacob Zuma, resigned at the ANC's behest in September 2008. The new ANC leadership was committed to fighting HIV, and a cabinet reshuffle installed a new health minister, Barbara Hogan, committed to treating HIV and AIDS. In 2009, after Zuma became president, Hogan was replaced by Aaron Motsoaledi, who has actively promoted the response to treatment advocated by TAC. Although TAC continues to exist, much of what it campaigned for has been achieved. Routine engagement played an important role in this achievement.

These events show that Tarrow is right to point to political developments' role in opening opportunities for activism. The changes in ANC leadership were crucial to winning the fight for comprehensive treatment. But they do not mean that activists are always passive recipients of 'opportunity structures' which others make for them. The change in ANC politics which opened new opportunities for the AIDS campaign may not have been directly the result of AIDS activism. But HIV and AIDS would not have played a central role in the internal ANC controversy if sustained activism had not raised its profile.

It was noted earlier that routine engagement and mobilisation are not stark alternatives and may co-exist in the repertoire of activists. And so the shift of 2006 did not move TAC from pure mobilisation to pure routine engagement. Even before this change, TAC had allies in government, some of whom were willing to express their approval openly. TAC made presentations to parliamentary committees 'in a friendly environment' and advised the Department of Trade and Industry on responses to international trade regimes.[62] The ANC government of Gauteng in late 2005 invited TAC activists to address a major AIDS meeting.[63] TAC was seen by the Western Cape government as a partner in fighting AIDS.[64] Up to half the national cabinet was said to support the campaign even while government was resisting it.[65] Senior politicians and officials in government continued to meet campaigners privately to compare notes and exchange ideas[66] – at none of these meetings did the government suggest that TAC tone down its campaign.[67] A provincial health minister endorsed TAC publicly, while a national health department official said the government needed its co-operation to launch an effective prevention campaign.[68] This was greatly helped by the fact that what TAC was asking the government to do was official policy, albeit one resisted within government. But these examples show that, during a mobilisation campaign, routine engagement between collective actors and office holders is possible and that it may strengthen the campaign.

It was also noted earlier that routine engagement is another way of engaging in conflict. Similarly, mobilisation often makes democratic governments work better by ensuring that their actions reflect citizen demands, enabling them to win co-operation in society. This was tacitly acknowledged by officials and government politicians who recognised that working with the campaign could, at times, benefit them as well as the campaigners. Government policy gave them space to act and collective action created pressures which enabled them to do so. A provincial politician who wanted to build momentum for more energetic responses to AIDS was said to have told TAC that 'every time we demonstrate, we make his job easier'.[69] A senior provincial health official worked with TAC, co-ordinating its protests with his efforts. There are circumstances in which politicians and officials have clear incentives to work with campaigners even where they are publicly in dispute. The costs of doing this can be reduced if officials can rely on gaps or ambiguities in policy to insist, if challenged, that they were doing their jobs by working with 'the enemy'. The AIDS case created particularly favourable conditions for this because working with campaigners could be justified as a zealous attempt to implement government policy. Conflict and co-operation were not stark alternatives – they complemented each other.

More generally, citizen campaigns for social change can be an important resource for governments in the global South concerned to win greater equity: campaigners can place pressure on Northern governments and businesses in a way governments cannot, and campaigning can strengthen politicians' hands by portraying them as prisoners of popular pressures. In the AIDS case, this was shown by activists' role in the court case brought by pharmaceutical companies.

Governments rarely recognise this – activism seems to be too much of a threat to be viewed as an asset.

But some government officials and politicians did see the AIDS campaign as a resource. This may not have happened if TAC had not sought partnerships with sympathetic people in government – a strategy it justifies not only pragmatically but also because the role of campaigners is to make elected government do what democratic principle says it should do.[70] Co-operation between people in government and campaigners is, therefore, a consequence not only of openings within government but also of the strategies of the campaigners. Willingness to seek alliances with sections of government does not mean muting criticism – TAC's approach sometimes seemed calculated to anger government, not win its support. It does mean assuming that confrontation and willingness to co-operate can accompany each other and that it is possible to confront some in government while working with others.

A Means, Not an End: TAC and Forums

As part of its engagement in routine collection action, TAC used formal forums, notably SANAC. Where provincial government was sympathetic, activists served on provincial AIDS councils[71] or in more broadly based participation initiatives.[72] Participatory structures such as district health committees and hospital and clinic committees, designed to give citizens a say in health issues, also offered opportunities for influence and TAC used them[73] – at times it helped local hospitals or clinics to set up a committee.[74] But its activists saw forums created by the government as a complement to gains already achieved, not as a way of winning key advances.[75]

TAC illustrates the degree to which citizens can turn 'participatory governance' from a model in which government creates forums for citizens into one in which people use the rights democracy bestows to engage with government on their terms. TAC insisted on engaging with government on the campaign's terms – using a distinction mentioned earlier, it 'invented' spaces of engagement rather than waiting to be 'invited' into them. And it invented its spaces firmly within the norms and values of constitutional democracy. Despite its willingness to serve on forums, TAC's influence over government was wielded overwhelmingly outside them.

TAC has therefore shown that the most effective means of participatory governance in a formal democracy is not the channels established by governments, but the rights entrenched by constitutions and the democratic context which sustains them. Its experience suggests that real participatory governance is most likely when citizens actualise their democratic rights in ways which they choose, and the government then responds. Forums may enable activists to turn mobilisation into routine collective action. But they cannot create voice.

TAC's experience showed that, while forums cannot extend access to popular sovereignty, they may become a strategic resource to organisations which are deepening access to it in other ways. Forums cannot extend participation in government, but they may act as a strategic bridgehead for collective actors who are organised enough to win participation and use it to consolidate influence. Viewed this way, they are a supplement to the collective action of the already organised. TAC's presence in participatory governance forums was a consequence of its influence, not a cause.

MAKING DEMOCRACY WORK FOR THE WEAK

Democracy was crucial to the campaign's success. Confirmation that it opened up opportunities for influence is the fact that the AIDS campaign, which was far more concerned to use the instruments offered by constitutional democracy than were any other campaigns for change in post-apartheid South Africa, was also far more successful than campaigns which largely avoided use of constitutional democracy's levers.

Democracy offers greater opportunities for mobilisation – while marches on Parliament by AIDS activists might have been allowed before democracy was achieved, civil disobedience may have met a sterner response and activity at the grassroots may have faced far more repression. The introduction of a bill of rights in 1994 opened opportunities to challenge government action in court. But, while these are often the factors stressed by campaigners, particular levers may be less important than the reality that democratic governments face constraints which authoritarians do not. The most obvious is that voter opinion does matter – even the ANC, whose electoral victory then seemed guaranteed, could not ignore the demands of people who support it without risking electoral setbacks. TAC also found that, although the provinces' powers are limited, a substantial opposition presence in two provinces did aid the campaign, thereby raising the costs for provincial ANC politicians of ignoring demands for treatment.

Democracy also establishes checks on power which prevented Mbeki's 'dissidence' from taking root because it was constantly resisted. An activist argues that democracy created an environment which may have saved the AIDS campaign from defeat: 'The best analogy to what we are fighting is Lysenkoism in Stalin's

Soviet Union – a case in which a ruler of a modern state with a pseudo-scientific view courts scientists with similar beliefs. Fortunately, we live in a democracy in which the media and civil society can challenge this. Our success is closely tied to the survival of democracy'.[76] By creating checks on government power – not least among them accountability to citizens – democracy ensured that 'pseudo-science' was challenged.

Democracy brings new strategic challenges for activism: as noted earlier, public opinion comes to matter in a way in which it does not when populations unite against undemocratic rule (and majority opinion is likely to sympathise with anything activists do). Activism which worked in the fight against apartheid may fail if it alienates citizens. But claims that democracy cannot provide a workable channel for action by the poor and weak to claim popular sovereignty and win more appropriate policy are contradicted by TAC's experience.

TAC's activism showed that people excluded from decisions – and control over their lives – can use rights and democratic institutions to win greater equity and a fairer distribution of resources, as well as a share in popular sovereignty. This is possible because, as the case again shows, some of the distinctions made by democracy's critics are false. Just as TAC recognised no distinction between mobilising and using democracy's institutions, it rejected the equally misleading distinction between routinely engaging with government and challenging it. The question is not whether those who seek to speak for the weak can use democracy – it is how they can use it to channel their collective power into a share in popular sovereignty. TAC's form of campaigning offers not an alternative to representative democracy, but a means of realising the rights it promises in collective action capable of winning policy change. It is an example of the exercise of democratic citizenship and how it may be deepened and preserved.

This is also an answer to 'new social movement' theories which argue that 'normal' democratic engagement with the state cannot deliver gains for the poor and that something new is needed.[77] If the most successful of the movements in democratic South Africa used democracy and did not transcend it, TAC's experience is not a sign that an alternative to representative democracy is needed, but a graphic illustration of the need to make it work. While its stress on the moral high ground, its use of alliances and its tactical flexibility were all important assets which may provide useful pointers to more effective action for equity, none suggest that a new form of activism emerged in TAC. It remains possible through organised collective action to use the rights guaranteed and institutions created by democracy to win advances for the poor and weak. No new form of action is needed.

The Politics of Enhanced Possibility

What does the campaign tell us about the possibilities for effective campaigns to win greater social justice? The most obvious point is that TAC did win a concrete change for poor and weak people who desperately needed it. It was suggested earlier that success was hardly foreordained – TAC's campaign could easily have been stigmatised, as the demands of poorer and weaker groups often are when they lack the means to hold power accountable. There is no evidence that the fight for treatment for people living with AIDS was any more winnable than any other campaign for social justice. At the very least, the case shows that the use of collective action in formal democracies, using democracy's rules, can ensure that poor people win some gains on some issues.

The case invites those who expect collective action in democracies to produce fairer, more caring societies to expand their sense of possibilities. Despite gloomy talk of 'globalisation' and the constraints it places on campaigns for greater equity, a key feature of this campaign is the opportunities offered by advances in communications technology for pressure on power-holders. The campaign also showed that the range of potential supporters – and the scope for exposing power-holders' moral weakness – were far greater than campaigners often assume. This was demonstrated by the wide range of the coalition it assembled, isolating a government supported by more than two-thirds of voters.

The campaigners also understood that, where social justice campaigns focus on particular issues, the powerful – private as well as public – are not necessarily united. There are many cases in which wealthy interests endorse campaigns aimed at other wealthy interests – demands for lower medical costs might antagonise private doctors and hospitals but win enthusiastic support from medical insurance companies. In any market economy, there are issues which affect the interests of all wealth holders, and others which affect only some. These differ between societies. In South Africa, land redistribution may be seen by most affluent people as a threat; in Taiwan, it was seen by urban businesses as essential to growth. The scope for building support, the AIDS campaign suggests, is significant despite the reality that power-holders' interests may often inoculate them from moral appeals.

This finding confirms only that some single-issue campaigns can win gains for the poor in democracies. It says nothing about the constraints which would face an attempt to implement a broad programme to alter the distribution of wealth and power, such as those associated with the ascendancy of social democracy in the North after the Second World War. Were a campaign to be launched more broadly against social inequality, it seems unlikely that it would enjoy the same advantages as the AIDS campaign. But this may be less important than it seems. While effective action against poverty may require structural change rather than single-issue reforms, the political context which is required for this is not yet present, and campaigns for equity are likely to centre on particular issues for some time. The South African AIDS case suggests considerable scope for winning greater equity on particular issues. It is also important to stress that campaigns for structural change do not emerge fully formed out of a vacuum. They are a cumulative result of campaigns to win reforms on particular issues – the fight for social democracy began with attempts to win an eight-hour day. It is through single-issue campaigns that the poor and marginalised gain the organisation and sense that they can make a difference, which makes more ambitious attempts to use democratic rights to win equity possible. If the lessons drawn here show only how the preparatory campaigns might succeed, they may also point to the beginnings of a sustained attempt to ensure that formal democratic rights are turned into policy changes which create a more just society.

9

Towards Popular Sovereignty: Building a Deeper and Stronger Democracy

What does the argument presented here tell a South Africa that is faced with the challenge of building a deeper and broader democracy which can offer citizens a share in the decisions that shape their lives?

Of course, not all South Africans agree that building a democracy is a priority. They are not alone. Doubt about democracy's benefits is common across the globe, particularly in new democracies. Indeed, O'Donnell and Schmitter coined the term *desencanto*[1] (disenchantment) to describe the doubts about democracy which emerge when the system is achieved, often after long and bitter struggle. This book has tried to show that South Africans, like everyone else, need democracy not only because it is the only system which can allow people to control their lives, but also because it does offer the tools needed to fight for a fairer society. It has argued, in effect, that those who suffered and died to achieve democracy did not waste their lives, and that the system established in 1994 opens possibilities which may still be realised.

It has also rejected the view, still stubbornly embraced by those who mourn the passing of apartheid, that democracy must fail here because South Africa – and South Africans – have not developed to an economic or cultural stage where the system could work. Democracy can survive and grow here and in the rest of the continent. Everyone everywhere is 'ready for democracy'. Whether democracy is ready for them is a more difficult question. In South Africa, as elsewhere, the system works well for some but not others – for those who enjoy access to collective action but not for those who don't. The effect is to repeat many of the divisions created by apartheid.

This is so, however, not because the constitution imposed on the country an alien form of government which traps many of its people in servitude. Democratisation does not mean foisting a template on societies. On the contrary, it means empowering and enabling people to reject the templates which do not work for them and to choose the social forms which, in their view, do. And it means overcoming the powerlessness, real and perceived, which prevents most citizens from engaging in the collective action that holds power to account and ensures that decision-making is as much as possible an expression of popular sovereignty rather than elite preference.

If we want to understand whether South African democracy is likely to survive and deepen, this book has argued, we must look at who can act and who cannot – and particularly at who can influence decisions without having to pay the costs which are often presented as the price the poor must pay for a say. And, because it argues also that people refrain from collective agency where perceived power relations dissuade them from acting, building democracy also means identifying and reducing those exercises of power blocking action to claim a share in decisions. It also means encouraging people to organise so that they can develop a sense of their ability to change their society.

This has implications for democratic strategy, whether it is pursued by the government, those engaged in promoting democracy, or citizens. It argues against strategies which try to ensure that citizens embrace idealised replicas of Northern democratic form and assume that they must be 'taught' to participate. It argues for strategies which expand access to collective action – and so to a share in decisions, which is the essence of popular sovereignty – to the grassroots. But how might that be done? What will build deeper and wider access to collective agency? How can citizen action impact on public decisions to ensure that what democratic governments decide is what most citizens want? This concluding chapter will try to add some concreteness to the discussion by proposing, tentatively, an alternative approach to protecting and building democracy.

The core problem facing democracy is the uneven spread of access to collective action. While, since 1994, it has been fashionable to declare South African democracy doomed (because its people 'are not ready' for democracy?), it is in surprisingly good health. This was illustrated vividly by the Zuma era. The damage which might have been done to society was greatly reduced because the institutions of democracy – free elections, an independent judiciary, and freedom to speak and organise – ensured that attempts to turn the state into the property of the few were constantly frustrated. Democracy secured the president's removal from office, creating the possibility of a government more in touch with and responsive to citizens.

But the spectrum of society which held public power to account was extremely shallow. While election results show that disaffection with the government was shared by grassroots citizens, they were not part of the discussion which defined what was amiss and what ought to be done about it (at no stage did any anti-Zuma demonstration attract more than a few thousand people). The vast majority of citizens were reduced to spectators as the minority who enjoyed access to organisation fought public power, ostensibly on behalf of the people.

This illustrates a wider problem – that the key divide in South Africa is between those who enjoy access to routine collective action and those who don't. The former live in suburbs; their voice is always heard. The latter live in townships and shack settlements: theirs is rarely if ever heard.[2] Inevitably, the former can hold the government to account through routine actions (such as e-mailing the authorities to complain) which are not available to the latter. This largely duplicates the divide under apartheid[3] not because the law or policy says so, but because some can use routine collective action to ensure that government serves them and others cannot. Democracy works well for the minority who can make themselves heard, but not for the majority who cannot, and, as long as this persists, the democratic project will be stunted. Change lies not in tinkering with the constitution or in the advent of a new Mandela, but in finding ways which ensure that more and more citizens can act collectively to force public power to hear them and respond. How could this be achieved?

A WAY FORWARD?

The most obvious starting point is recognising that the appropriate strategy rests on creating conditions in which as many citizens as possible can act freely within agreed rules to claim their share of popular sovereignty. It must aim to stimulate opportunities which will enable all to speak freely to power-holders and fellow citizens and to act to influence policy on their own terms, constrained only by laws which protect the rights of others.

Refusing Artificial Substitutes

Frequently, support for more active citizen engagement in politics translates into enthusiasm for new governance technologies which are said to include citizens more directly in decisions. These mechanisms constitute, it is said, 'a new architecture of democratic practice', a 'deepening' of democracy.[4] Such instruments seek to restore the right of participation in shaping decisions that affect their lives to citizens who, in liberal democracy, are required to delegate this right to elected representatives. In some contexts, citizens become part of 'the state' such as initiatives in which citizens become part of deliberative institutions that make certain allocative decisions ... In others, devolution of statutory service delivery functions to citizens has created new arenas outside the state for citizen engagement in provisioning.[5]

These innovations are said to improve the depth and breadth of democracy by improving on the forms of participation allowed by the liberal democratic state. At first glance these purported breakthroughs seem neither new nor more democratic, since they bear an uncanny resemblance to the structured participation forums criticised earlier. Scholars who insist that they offer a more participatory form of democracy claim that they do not simply duplicate the forums – structured participation has now become a means to share in popular sovereignty, not a diversion from it: 'What participation comes to mean in these kinds of settings goes beyond older practices of consultation to open up new possibilities for voice, influence and responsiveness....'[6]

These channels for participation are said to differ from older forums because they offer a say in decisions rather than mere consultation. They are also said to offer real power because, while older forms of structured participation were seen as a substitute for a strong democratic state (and so left the essentials of power intact), in these newer mechanisms 'the [reconstituted] state is positioned at the centre rather than rolled back to the margins'.[7] They are also said to be framed, as the forums discussed earlier were not, as realisations of rights, mechanisms of democratic participation, rather than mere techniques to legitimise that which power-holders had already decided:

> This turn to rights recasts 'the people' or 'the poor' as neither passive beneficiaries nor consumers but as agents. This shifts the focus from invited participation in the planning and implementation of service delivery to the enhancement of people's capabilities to advocate for their entitlements ... and the right to participate more actively in determining the shape of those services.[8]

In this view, South Africa's initial enthusiasm for forums is not the problem – it is the type of forum chosen. But turning forums into decision-making vehicles and changing the language used to describe them does not transform them from obstacles to enablers of popular sovereignty. They still channel citizen action into paths chosen by political power-holders; participation still depends on selection or invitation rather than the free exercise of rights (which makes them less accessible than the much-maligned vote); and they still reinforce rather than challenge unequal power relations by providing a platform for those who are already organised and able to participate at the expense of those who cannot. They do not minimise domination, they reconstitute it. An attempt to simulate free routine collective action cannot hold power to account, whatever its formal powers. The key difference between the old forums and the new technologies seems to lie less in their intrinsic properties than in the fact that they were instituted by left governments.

A more complex rationale for this approach is offered by Avritzer, whose critique of democratic elitism was mentioned earlier. He offers an alternative to elitism by proposing the idea of 'participatory publics': these involve 'the formation at the public level of mechanisms of face-to-face deliberation, free expression, and association' which make it possible to address politically 'specific elements in the dominant culture'.[9] They are created when citizens' groups address contentious issues which were beyond public influence; what elites preferred to keep beyond contest and challenge is now open to both. The citizens' groups do this by engaging with government in forums which make them party to binding decisions and to monitoring their implementation.

Avritzer's 'participatory publics' are created when citizens engage in collective action to hold power to account and then find that they need to build on gains by insisting on a continuing role in public decision-making. Where this is conceded, the presence of 'participatory publics' is said to broaden and deepen democracy by providing new channels for participation by more citizens. Avritzer cites two Latin American examples. One is the celebrated example of participatory budgeting in Brazil, in which a section of the municipal budget is decided by a participatory process in which citizens set priorities. The other is the Mexican Instituto Federal Electoral (IFE), which organised elections and included citizen representatives in response to a campaign against electoral fraud.[10] Avritzer sees both as processes in which decisions which were an elite preserve beyond challenge – deciding on the budget and running elections – were subjected to deliberation by citizens and became open to popular sovereignty in a way in which they were not before. In both, citizens found that their gains might not endure unless a vehicle ensured that their victory would have binding consequences and that what the elite conceded would not be removed from their grasp. In his view, presumably, an expansion of popular sovereignty which did not become embedded in the routine practices of government would not last long. The only way to turn an immediate gain into a lasting one is to demand governance vehicles which institutionalise this expression of popular sovereignty. Avritzer's participatory publics do what TAC did: they seek to ensure that gains for popular sovereignty survive by participating in forums which make their engagement with government routine.

But, while citizens do need an institutionalised means of ensuring that their will is translated into reality, it is unclear why they need to participate directly in government to achieve this. The challenge of ensuring that changes in law or policy become concrete realities because they are effectively implemented is an enduring and inevitable task for citizens' groups whose collective action persuades power-holders to do what they did not want to do. Winning a new law or policy, it was noted earlier, is usually only the beginning of changing social reality: lengthy and difficult campaigns to ensure that changes in principle do reshape the world are often necessary. This also requires that implementation or its lack be monitored carefully. But citizens need not participate directly in government to ensure that governments do what they promised to do. And while citizens do need routine collective action to engage with power, institutionalised channels are not essential to this – affluent power-holders do not need structures to engage with governments. Routine collective action requires constant access, not direct participation in government functions. It does not follow logically that gains for popular sovereignty require that citizens groups participate directly in government.

It was acknowledged earlier that participation in structured forums can enhance the influence of citizens' organisations by consolidating gains won through action – but only if the forums are supplements to, not a substitute for, free collective agency. Just as labour militancy does not achieve lasting worker gains unless bargaining forums ensure that agreements are negotiated and implemented, citizens campaigning for free elections or for treatment for people living with AIDS or fair elections may find that their gains are most likely to become enduring if they join a forum. But there is an important difference between seeing these platforms as a source of strategic leverage for organised citizens seeking a share in popular sovereignty[11] and viewing them as enhanced forms of democratic participation. Citizens enhance their share in decisions – and so exercise popular sovereignty – through free collective action, not structured participation. Structures are one means by which citizens whose collective action has won gains for popular sovereignty can consolidate those advances while continuing to choose, within agreed rules, their own means of acting collectively to engage power. But that does not mean that they are, in themselves, advances for popular sovereignty: they are strategic tools in particular circumstances.

The participatory publics Avritzer describes are a minority. Despite the romanticism associated with participatory budgeting, the proportion of citizens who actually participate in deciding the limited budgetary choices is small – usually less than 15 per cent of the voting population, according to a source sympathetic to the practice.[12] The percentage of citizens represented by those who served on Mexico's IFE is even smaller. So it is not 'the people' who gain a share in sovereignty through these innovations – it is some people. Elections, for all their limitations, remain the only form of democratic participation available to all, and the free collective action which the enjoyment of rights allows is the only form of participation open in principle to all. While the governance instruments which participatory publics create may have had the beneficial effects Avritzer describes – opening new issues to deliberation and ensuring more accountable processes – they are not vehicles for substantially deeper and broader popular sovereignty. It is not achieved by 'improving on' the vote and citizenship rights by allowing organised groups a say in decisions denied to grassroots citizens. Advancing popular sovereignty requires, rather, enhanced access to representatives and increased use of the rights it promises. The route to deeper and broader popular sovereignty lies not in bypassing representative democracy, but in making it work by ensuring that more and more citizens enjoy more and more access to it.

Only contentious politics – a free contest for support between contending interests, in which alliances play a crucial role in building majority coalitions – will guarantee the deeper and broader access to collective action which can sustain democracy, extending its reach into society. Where citizens cannot turn democratic rights into a say in decisions, the problem lies not with representative democratic institutions, but with factors which block their access to the collective action which ensures that office holders respond to them. Remedies lie not in re-inventing representative democracy, but in making it work by ensuring ever broader and deeper access to it.

Citizens who are excluded from active engagement in democratic politics do not need to be taught to become democrats: they need the means to realise their rights in action, through mobilisation or routine collective action or both. This engagement does require that the rights of others be recognised. This is not so self-evident that it does not need to be learned. Elites do not automatically accept that they ought to consent to limits on their exercise of power; citizens, too, will not automatically be willing to act only within rules which allow others to do so freely too. But these realisations are not learned in a civic education programme – they are developed in action as social actors work to claim their share of a say in decisions and the obligations these entail.[13] Democracy will be built and strengthened not by more democracy education, but by expanding and deepening access to collective action within democratic rules. It is access to power which determines how broad and deep a democracy is. It is to the inequality of access to collective action that any attempt to understand the constraints facing democracy must direct its attention. It follows that strategies to deepen and broaden democracy must assume that access to collective action by people at the grassroots is hampered by severe constraints which policy and strategy must recognise and seek to overcome.

At first glance, the answer might seem easy: the poor and weak need to be organised – or to organise themselves – to ensure that they acquire a share in sovereignty. The previous chapter discussed how that might be achieved. Further illustrations could be offered by a study of the trade union movement and other examples of collective action by the hitherto excluded which have not only achieved formal democracy here and elsewhere but have assured its deepening and broadening too. The TAC case was chosen because it offers some insight into how the poor and weak might organise to force their inclusion in decisions – and, therefore, their share in sovereignty – in conditions less favourable to popular collective action than those under which the labour movement was able to grow. This is only one example of ways in which the weak, although deprived of the advantages which made the labour movement possible, might organise effectively to achieve greater equity.[14]

The conditions which enabled organised labour to lead the fight for inclusion and democratic deepening no longer exist.[15] But this does not mean that the often successful fight by unions to force democracy to include the poor should be relegated to a quaint historical footnote: it has much to teach those who seek broader and deeper democracies about how people who were excluded from decisions can organise to force themselves into the conversation – and, at times, into a position to influence the policy agenda. The TAC case suggests that some of the important lessons of the trade union experience can inform attempts to organise for a share of popular sovereignty by groups outside the workplace.

Precisely how access to collective action becomes more widely distributed in society is more complicated than organising manuals might suggest. It was argued earlier that people at the grassroots refrain from action because they believe that the power balance is stacked against them. Broader and deeper collective action requires that people who believe themselves to be powerless come to see that they do wield power – a point most organisers would readily accept. But it means also that collective action becomes more possible when shifts in the balance of power reduce the cost of action to the weaker and relatively powerless: democratic governments should be judged by the degree to which they make routine collective action more feasible for more people. Governments cannot organise the action which is meant to hold them to account: authoritarian governments organise collective action, democracies leave the task to citizens. But the government can create circumstances in which collective action is more possible and so more likely.

It is sometimes claimed that governments have little influence on the associational life of citizens and the collective action which flows from it because the dense networks of informal association in which many engage are impenetrable to state institutions. But a study of collective action by informal traders in Johannesburg suggests that informal organisation is shaped by government actions in crucial ways. Directly and indirectly, government policies and actions largely shaped the form of collective action in which traders engaged despite informal networks and power structures.[16] Governments can encourage or retard access to collective action, and they can be held to account for the extent to which they make it more possible.

A HOT LINE TO POWER? CREATING LINKAGES BETWEEN THE GRASSROOTS AND POWER

Developing strategies to encourage democratic collective action among people who have been unable to act seems logically impossible: the grassroots need to organise to claim a say in decisions, but no one can organise for them. Democratic deepening would seem to depend on the unlikely expectation that people excluded from collective action will, despite their lack of access to the means to act, organise themselves sufficiently to begin acting.

A study of civil society and poverty reduction, discussed in Chapter 5,[17] suggests that the puzzle may be open to a solution. It creates the possibility of stimulating grassroots collective action but does not impose choices on citizens because it starts from the organisations which the voiceless have already formed rather than seeking to build new ones. The key starting point is an often ignored reality: while the grassroots poor may not organise to speak to power-holders, they do associate and organise, even where there is no visible sign of people combining to engage with power. One form of grassroots organisation is what we might call 'survivalist' associations or organisations 'of collective sustenance'.[18] They address common social and economic tasks such as the care of people living with AIDS, or income-generating activities such as pooling savings (*stokvels*), producing crafts or channelling youth energies. They do not influence public policy and are invisible to the policy debate.

Why do these organisations not make demands of the government? In many cases, they may choose not to – participants might feel that speaking to power will not improve their circumstances. In that case, intervention to encourage them to speak would be pointless. But others may be willing to engage with power-holders if the opportunity presented itself – and may not have done so not because they have decided against action, but because they have no means of engaging in it. A study unearthed evidence that associations may avoid opportunities for participation not because they have chosen not to take part but because they believe the available avenues for engagement are not meant for them.[19] More commonly, citizens may be unaware of how to identify and engage those who command power and resources: they may not know who makes the decisions which affect their lives and where they might be found since no one may have told them. If they could engage with those who make decisions, they might use the opportunity to convey concerns and grievances. And, if they did this in the company of organisations whose resources could be useful to them, they might begin acquiring not only the opportunity to express voice through collective agency, but some of the capacities needed to do this. Stimulating a voice for the poor may be best achieved by linking grassroots 'collective sustenance' organisations to government and to private power-holders such as business as well as NGOs and citizens' groups in engagements which would enable them to speak, but would not, unlike many other initiatives which seek to bring citizens in contact with governments, commit them to partnerships or co-operation – or to any preconceived outcome. The effect could be to trigger engage-ment between grassroots organisations and power-holders, which could show the effectiveness of routine collective action and so spur wider engagement.

A key difference between this approach and structured forums is that it does not presuppose an outcome: it is not meant to produce a plan, a concrete deci-sion or agreed projects. It simply places associations in contact with power-holders and leaves the engagement to develop in ways determined by the participants. It assumes that, if grassroots organisations want to engage, this process will enable participants to choose their means of engagement – provided that they, and the process itself, receive support to ensure that they can continue to participate (since the power balance will be unequal, effort is needed to enable the weaker party to speak and decide freely). It might begin with an open-ended dialogue on the challenges facing citizens and continue until it dissolves or participants decide on action. Nor is it seen as a substitute for free political action: it may be a catalyst for it. The key ingredients would be open-endedness and an assumption that mobilisa-tion and engagement can be pursued simultaneously. The process could encourage grassroots groups to engage power-holders across a meeting table at the same time as they mobilised support on the ground. The sole purpose would be to ensure that those who lack power gain access to those who wield it – it would aim to open opportunities for engagement, not to close them by insisting that the process take a set time or yield a particular result.

This approach also differs from conventional participation strategies because it does not rely on handing out resources to grassroots organisations. Simply injecting money into organisations is unlikely to strengthen them and may well damage them. During the research project on civil society and poverty reduction mentioned above, interviewees who then participated in grassroots associations insisted that an infusion of money would damage the relationship between members of their organisation.[20] Rather, the approach outlined here relies on willingness by those with resources to place them at the disposal not of organisations but of a process – one without a defined outcome, whose destination is to be shaped by participants alone.

A GOVERNMENT ABLE TO HEAR

The idea that governments can encourage routine collective action among citizens who do not normally engage in it is hardly novel. It underpins the enthusiasm for 'participatory governance', the provision by governments of structured channels which enable citizens to engage with them.

The rejection of formal forums proposed here suggests a need to redefine the notion of participatory governance in a way which is consistent with the free exercise by citizens of their rights to engage collectively with democratic government. Rather than seeing it as a process in which governments create the means to include citizens in decisions, we need to view it as one in which citizens, on their own terms, use their capacity to organise and mobilise to claim a say in how they are governed, and in the decisions which democratic governments make.

This does not mean that government has no role in encouraging participation. It can help to provide channels for routine action by making itself accessible to citizens in general and to the poor in particular, and can make citizen activism more possible by responding to it if citizens engage in it. One approach which would make responsive government more likely is the 'linkage' strategy proposed above. By identifying grassroots organisations and seeking to engage them on their concerns and needs in an open-ended way, government could establish means of participation far more conducive to democratic citizenship than the channels currently on offer.

A similar proposal is that of Jeremy Cronin, who argued some years ago for an approach in which government would become aware of, and build on, examples of citizen activism and seek to form partnerships with activists to address social challenges. Using transport policy as an example (he was then chair of Parliament's transport committee), he argued that initiatives – ranging from spontaneous policing arrangements devised by train commuters through to union campaigns for safer trains to radio phone-in shows in which commuters can call in complaints which are then relayed to officials – can become seeds of partnership between government and citizens which would allow 'popular power at community level' to become a key influence on transport policy and programmes.[21] Some of his proposals would see citizens implementing policy rather than framing it, which is not conducive to popular sovereignty since it casts citizens not as decision-makers but as implementers of others' decisions. But not all would – there is room in this model for direct and effective citizen voice and routine collective action.

Information can play a crucial role in making possible routine collective action for those denied it.[22] Governments seeking to encourage grassroots participation could concentrate on fully informing affected citizens, particularly the poor, of their plans in ways which explain options and invite choices. Strategies which aim to ensure that all citizens are informed of their policy options in ways which allow them to choose between alternatives may trigger broader participation and an extension of access to routine collective action. There is an important difference between informing citizens and 'civic education'. The latter assumes that citizens need to be 'taught' how popular sovereignty works; the former that citizens know the value of governing themselves, but are unable to do so partly because they lack the information that would tell them which channels are available to them and enough about what government is doing to judge its actions. The accent here is on informing people in ways which enable them to take decisions and act on them.

This strategy is not as simple as it sounds. Ensuring that those who are usually denied access to information receive it may require capacity to reach the grassroots which has thus far eluded government. The narrow view of communication which has prevailed is perhaps best summed up by the fact that local governments are legally mandated to communicate with citizens only through newspapers (to which many citizens do not enjoy access) and radio.[23] There is no provision for direct contact with voters. Bringing adequate information to the grassroots would need sustained government commitment.

A second challenge is that officials who communicate with beneficiaries of development programmes usually succumb readily to the temptation to 'explain' options in a way which predetermines choice. They stress the advantages of the route they prefer and the disadvantages of the other choices – this is most likely when technical information is conveyed to lay people. The effect is not to empower people to choose, but to impose choices on them. Since government officials are meant to serve citizens, they should convey choices in a way which enables listeners to understand their options but leaves the choice to them. The more official approaches begin to hold this out as a goal, the more likely is it that decisions will reflect what citizens want. There is far more to providing citizens with information which enables them to choose than preventing officials from imposing their preferences. It would, for a start, require continual and direct dialogue between government and citizens, not the occasional communications campaigns, and so it would also need an approach to governing grounded in maintaining close and continuing links between government and citizens.

The more governments can form links with, and remain in contact with, those they inform, the more likely is it that they will receive a coherent response. Pamphlets dropped over a neighbourhood or an announcement on radio will have far less effect than direct contact. The key is an attempt to establish a link between officials and grassroots citizens. Official information is a continuous process dependent on routine contact between government and citizens, not a sporadic attempt to let citizens know what government has planned for them. It implies that information be made available before government decisions are made, not presented as explanations of what has been decided. And it suggests that information must be seen as a means of enabling citizens to claim their share of popular sovereignty, not a way of enhancing government popularity. The contrast between this approach and that which the government now uses is stark.

If this approach is adopted, and poor citizens begin responding, the reaction of officials would be crucial. While channelling responses into neat and structured channels might best suit administrators and the politicians they serve, citizens, particularly at the grassroots, might prefer less structured engagement, including the expression of democratic rights through peaceful public protest. If policy is to be informed by the voice of the grassroots, it cannot be stilled by straitjacketing it into forms chosen by officials. Engagement may develop along the lines of the routine interactions discussed earlier, in which citizens insist that government engage with them on their terms – by, for example, appearing at a meeting at a local hall at an appointed time at a meeting run by citizens, allowing citizens to decide how to speak to power. It would enhance popular sovereignty if office holders began to learn to allow citizens to choose how they engage.

A new orientation from the government is needed: one which recognises the organised, politically effective voice of citizens, and the open, often conflictual politics which it would prompt, as indispensable assets to effective governance; one which seeks not to artificially create citizen voice but to encourage its emergence – and to engage seriously with it if it emerges. A key ingredient is acknowledgement that democratic government exists to serve citizens and that the degree of democracy in any society is determined by the extent to which citizens, shape decisions. It follows that governments which seek to become more democratic need to recognise that it is government's task to enable the freest possible expression of citizen voice, and to make the adjustments to citizens' needs and preferences which this entails.

If government is to play a role in opening channels for citizens to be heard through collective action, it needs to understand more about their impact on informal social actors and associations. Finding strategies which will strengthen democratic collective action will require governments to understand far more about grassroots associations and social dynamics. Experience in development negotiations suggests that power relations in informal settings are not always visible: attempts to include the excluded are more complex than they seem and may have unintended consequences, such as strengthening local power-holders who present themselves as the voice of 'the community'.[24] Unless governments develop deeper understandings of these dynamics, they are likely to find that, if they wish to deepen access to decisions, they are obstructed by power-holders.

A key cause of informality which governments can do much to influence is citizenship and immigration status. It was noted earlier that the apparently common-sense link between nationality and voting rights is not nearly as automatic as it seems. Governments can move beyond the granting of formal rights and can also create openings which make it more likely that immigrants will participate in collective action. In the Johannesburg case mentioned earlier, the local government's insistence that it wanted to talk to representatives of all informal traders (immigrants had been excluded from trader associations) prompted a significant change in organisation: immigrants acquired at least a potential voice when the associations were opened to them.[25] These basic measures do not encompass all that governments can do to include immigrants.

The Citizen as Governance Tool

The previous section might seem naive. Why suggest that governments, even if they are democratic, will want to stimulate collective action which will make it easier for citizens to hold them to account? Surely they will concede ground only when faced with citizen organisation initiated despite, not because of, their actions?

The model proposed here is not, despite its stress on collective action, based on the crude notion that deepening of democracy is possible only when those excluded from access to power use sheer force to impel themselves into the conversation.

TAC's stress on building broad moral agreement shows that factors other than pure muscle can prompt broader and deeper access to decisions. While power is a crucial determinant of who participates in collective action and, therefore, popular sovereignty, it takes far subtler forms than purely conflict-based theories suggest. TAC's collective action succeeded at least partly because people in positions of power do care about how others see them. Power-holders, private or public, are not always motivated purely by a desire to maximise their power, and may be moved to act by a desire to be seen to be doing good (even if we understand this purely as a desire to enhance their self-esteem). This is particularly so when they are asked to support democracy: power-holders want to be seen to be democrats. Governments do not use structured participation because they want to delude citizens into believing they have a say when they do not – they are trying to open opportunities for citizen voice, but in a manner which suits them. Within limits, it is plausible to imagine people in positions of influence seeking to promote collective action because they want a deeper democracy.

This approach is also likely to make governing easier. Understandings of power tend to distinguish between two types – that which enables actors to impose their will on others, and that which enables them to harness others' energy in co-operative endeavours by reaching agreement 'upon a common course of action in unrestrained communication'.[26] Effective government needs the second form. While governments could not govern without relying on coercion to impose order, the familiar Weberian insistence that governments monopolise access to the legitimate means of force cannot be the sole or even the main means of government: 'force is certainly not the normal or the only means of the state'.[27]

Democracies limit the use of force, and so political authorities need the compliance of citizens: even as coercive a function as tax collection is influenced by citizens' attitude to compliance.[28] While unequal access to the means of collective action provides power-holders in formal democracies far greater latitude to ignore popular sentiment, democratic governments are forced to seek the co-operation of citizens if they want to implement their programmes. And, whether or not a political system is formally democratic, a lesson of Scott's work is that citizens who feel powerless will use the 'weapons of the weak' to negate decisions they feel they cannot oppose. Governments which do not wish to be undermined or frustrated may find an active citizenry, willing to talk to power-holders openly rather than to subvert them, essential to effective governance: hearing voices they would prefer to ignore may be unpleasant but is likely to make it easier for them to pursue their agendas. The 'suspended state' Hydén identified is a consequence at least in part of thwarting the engagement between citizens and state advocated here. Governance which relies on coercion, not engagement with citizens, may find itself exerting (in theory) more and more control over (in reality) less and less.

Relying on coercion may help governments control populations but cannot trigger development, particularly in the context of a global power balance which remains highly unequal. TAC's experience showed that governments which want a fairer share of global resources may find collective agency by citizens pursuing the same goal a crucial asset, if they accept that organised citizens who act to support government plans on some issues will act just as vigorously to oppose them on others. In theory, the government has not relied on force to impose development. But some of its methods have this effect. Often, they rely on government by 'expert' and a tendency to see government as producers and citizens as consumers of development – reducing inequality is seen as a technical task whose cure lies in more administrative and policy-making capacity in the public service. In South Africa, the relationship between government and citizens is seen as 'service delivery'.[29] The government is a provider, and citizens are consumers who judge it not on whether it offers them a share in popular sovereignty but on whether it 'delivers' goods and services to them. Thus, the citizen is excluded from decisions on what is to be provided and how provision happens, exercising agency only when the resultant product is not to her or his liking. Effectiveness is assumed to stem not from a relationship between government and citizens in which the latter decides and the former implements, but from recruiting the 'experts' necessary to decide what 'solutions' to impose on citizens. It is coercive because it reserves to government the right to decide what should be done and how to do it, reducing citizens to passive adapters to that which is provided them – or protestors who can react to, but not determine, the developmental path.

This approach violates the principle of popular sovereignty. It also makes governance ineffective because the technicians are usually obliged, in the absence of an active government–citizen relationship, to rely on abstract reasoning to imagine the likely response of citizens to initiatives, and they most often misread what is required.[30] It also cannot elicit the co-operation which governments need if they want their intentions to become reality. That citizens use the 'weapons of the weak' to frustrate government plans is confirmed by considerable literature on ways in which development initiatives are diverted by grassroots citizens into paths their architects did not intend.[31] If the government wants to govern effectively – and to become an agent of development – unstructured although rule-bound collective engagement between citizens and officials may be essential.

Crucial to this is a recognition by elites of democracy's worth as a system which offers citizens a means of expressing themselves and resolving society's inevitable conflicts without violence. This approach sees value in strengthening and deepening democratic institutions and practices because the most effective guarantor of effective government is the active citizen, holding government to account with other citizens and operating within democratic norms. This requires, too, a willingness by the governing elite to see independent advocacy by citizens as a vital asset, not a threat. In sharp contrast to approaches which reduce citizens' organisations to partners in the implementation of official plans, it would see independent collective action to hold power to account and force it to respond as a key to government effectiveness.

A key feature is invigorating the representative function and the legislatures which make it possible. Democracy-promoting donors, public commentators or political actors within new democracies often reduce government to the bureaucracy and the executive: the legislature and its elected representatives are seen as at best irrelevances, at worst as obstacles to effectiveness. An example is debate on provinces in which their role as 'deliverers' of services is stressed, but the function of their elected representatives as potential vehicles of citizen oversight over government is never acknowledged. In this view, making government more effective means strengthening officials, not elected representatives. But, while popular sovereignty cannot be reduced to the legislative function, it is impossible without it. Opportunities for grassroots participation in popular sovereignty are likely only if representative institutions are strengthened and their key purpose is to provide a platform for the exercise of popular sovereignty, not support for the executive in its attempts to implement plans drafted by technicians. It also requires strategies to make these institutions more powerful and more accessible to citizens. It is more than three decades since John Keane argued that more effective parliamentary institutions were a key to a more vigorous democracy.[32] But his point remains valid. This may need not only reforms enhancing legislatures' power, but also far more resources for legislatures. Part of the answer may lie in a political culture in which elected representatives take the trouble to find out what constituents want and to work to achieve their constituents' goals, and in which they are judged by how well they represent voters. This may seem trite, but it is far more common for elected representatives to be judged on their capacity to assist officials or party leaders.

The role of provincial and local government may be important here. While enthusiasm for 'democratic decentralisation' often ignores the degree to which local and regional power can suppress collective action and entrench the power of elites, it is essential to popular sovereignty that as many opportunities as possible be created for decision-making by elected legislatures rather than officials. And, they are created, legislatures should have decision-making powers rather than the 'right' to implement the plans of national and local officials. These units of government must be judged not by technical criteria but by their capacity to offer maximum representativeness. To do this, they need powers to oversee and direct administrations on citizens' behalf.

While there is no set of political institutions which can guarantee – or thwart – popular sovereignty, the design of institutions is not irrelevant to the quest for broader and deeper democracies. The collective action which popular sovereignty requires can be assisted or impeded by institutions. South African democracy can invigorate itself and deepen its reach by developing institutions which make free collective action – and a government response which validates it – as likely as possible. Since institutions need to emerge out of debate and contest, rather than, as much of the literature seems to imply, persons skilled in institutional design, democratisation is most likely where the purpose and function of institutions is subject to vigorous debate – and their role in enhancing collective action to secure a share in popular sovereignty is placed at the centre of the discussion.

RIGHTS AND REDISTRIBUTION

This analysis also has important implications for the pursuit of social justice. It is possible for the poor and marginalised to win greater justice using the instruments of formal democracy – TAC's experience shows that democracy creates opportunities for collective action which can win the weak a say in decisions. While the evidence confirmed only that collective action could win single-issue campaigns, this does not mean that this is all it could ever win. Campaigns to win a fairer distribution of power and resources invariably begin with a particular issue and then grow as the participants discover that they can change the world. Just as there is no limit to the ability of citizens to use democracy to win greater shares in sovereignty, so there is no contradiction between representative democracy and the fight for redistribution. On the contrary, rights to vote, speak, act and organise are essential to effective campaigns to win social equity.

This is so only if poor and marginalised people can act collectively to say what they want and can build the alliances which will enable this to become implementable policy and programmes. The degree of equity in the social order reflects its distribution of collective action: distribution of shares in popular sovereignty and allocation of resources are directly linked. Resources are shared more fairly not when an inspired leader or a particularly gifted group of technicians works out a way of getting them to the poor in a manner which does not jeopardise the creation of new

wealth. It occurs when those with an interest in redistribution act to force themselves into the policy debate – and when they can, in a similar manner to TAC's
approach, build alliances and moral agreements which make sustainable redistribution possible. Greater social equity is not a technical but a political process.

The recipe for effective redistribution is not a particular set of policies, since
different policies have achieved greater equity in different circumstances,[33] but the
political context, which determines not only which issues are placed on the agenda
but the concessions economic elites will make.[34] Contrary to the claims of market
fundamentalists and policy technicians, there is no formula which will determine
how much tax elites are willing to pay or the resources they are willing to see spent
on social equity. The limits and possibilities are determined in each society by a
political context which continually reshapes the limits of what appear to be acceptable compromises – whether through formal negotiations or other processes in
which consensuses are made and unmade by the contest between collective actors.
Amartya Sen's finding that famines do not occur in democracies[35] illustrates the
degree to which an entitlement as basic as that to adequate food depends less on
technical capacities than on a political context which forces office holders to be
aware of people and problems which would escape their concern if citizens did not
enjoy the vote and the rights required to engage their attention. This has important
consequences for the search for a fairer world, as well as for one which is more
democratic.

This challenges the claim that the poor and marginalised cannot become active
democratic citizens unless their basic needs are met – a version of 'you cannot eat
democracy'[36] or, as an American politician put it: 'The right to vote does not have
much meaning on an empty stomach'.[37] A further variation is that it is impossible
to vote rationally on an empty stomach.[38] The argument presented here means that
people without food are unlikely to enjoy fuller stomachs unless they vote – if by this
we also mean engaging in the collective action which the vote and democratic rights
enable. It is easier for people with fuller stomachs to act to influence power. But there
is a great difference between insisting that poverty makes collective action more difficult and the claim that political rights are meaningless to the poor. Rights empower
the poor – if people can use them to act collectively to gain a share in popular sovereignty. Reductions in poverty and inequality happen when people exercise political
rights: they are not necessary conditions before people can do this.

The most obvious consequence is to insist that equity, like democratic governance
more generally, is not a technical but a political challenge. Democratic collective
action is a precondition not only for effective governance, but for action against poverty and inequality too. The success of government action against inequity depends

not on technical policy design, but on enabling the poor to engage effectively with public and private power-holders. South Africa's attempts to address severe inequities bequeathed by apartheid were hampered not by inadequate funds or capacities as much as by a failure of representation. Political deficits – the lack of a clear voice for the poor and a means of ensuring that elites hear that voice – obstruct effective anti-poverty policy far more than technical weaknesses do, partly because poor people are better at identifying what they want and need than technical specialists are.

An obvious objection to this argument is that effective anti-poverty programmes have been implemented in societies which are not democracies, most recently in the East Asian 'tigers'. But the claim made here is not an iron law of society – it applies to formal democracies. It was noted earlier that power-holders in democracies, even of the most minimal sort, face constraints authoritarian regimes do not. Non-democratic elites can use coercion to impose their will on society, silencing discordant voices. They are not forced to listen to the voices of lobbies, nor do they need to persuade citizens to co-operate with their anti-poverty plans. Democracies, on the other hand, need a political response which persuades both special interests and citizens. It is also, of course, very difficult to persuade authoritarian regimes to address the needs of poor people if they have no compelling strategic reason to do this. And, if they make mistakes which are costly to the poor, the people affected cannot act to correct them.

In Africa, it was argued some years ago that state-building, not democracy, was the continent's priority, and that a new breed of leader had emerged who, while not democratic, was committed to effective state-building[39] – which was presumably meant to ensure better living standards for citizens. But the promised undemocratic route has failed to yield the promised effectiveness. And even where it has seemed to yield some benefits in economic growth, there are no marked redistributive effects. The reasons are clearly political. The most prominent of these leaders, Museveni, negated his government's attempts to achieve greater tax effectiveness when he bowed to the demands of better-off and better-connected interests who found the tax regime too onerous.[40] This pattern, in which non-democratic elites sheltered from popular pressures listen only to the voices of the well-heeled, are the norm in societies which are not democracies. Whatever their impact on state-building, they offer few opportunities for redistribution. Democracies are more likely to redistribute than their alternatives – but they cannot do this sustainably and effectively unless groups with an interest in social justice can use collective action to ensure favourable outcomes.

The importance of this point for attitudes to governance cannot be over-emphasised. Academic critiques of technocratic decision-making in development, as well as in governance, are plentiful and influential.[41] They have also influenced the approaches of international financial institutions such as the World Bank, which recognises, at least in principle, the crucial role of citizen voice in the attempt to secure better services for the poor.[42] But mainstream approaches to governance – in South Africa as well as other countries – still routinely see governing, and the fight for greater equity, as a technical question, a matter of finding the right people to come up with the right policies and implement them in the right way. That these approaches have failed repeatedly to produce greater equity – while democratic politics, accompanied by effective collective action, has won gains for the poor and weak where the required collective action is employed[43] – is a point which fights to be heard in a debate dominated by an obsession with government as a machine, rather than an institution embedded in the political realities of the society which it governs. An alternative in which progress is seen as a consequence less of technique than of effective use of collective action is often shunted to the sidelines.

How the poor and the weak begin to acquire the collective agency to influence governance in a way which yields greater equity is an unanswered question. It was noted earlier that the 'golden age' of redistributive democratic politics was centred on the labour movement: it grew out of a period in which the poor were concentrated in mass-production workplaces where they could organise more easily and enjoyed greater bargaining power. In many new democracies, those circumstances have never existed because these societies have never experienced levels of industrialisation which would make them possible. In others, like South Africa, they once existed but have now eroded as work becomes more casual, dispersed and informal. While, as noted above, it is possible in these circumstances for people to combine to achieve greater equity, we are still far from knowing how people who do not work in formal workplaces can press successfully for social and economic change.

The shape and form of an egalitarian democratic politics is emerging only hazily. It will take on different forms to those of Northern social democracy. Although precisely what these forms may be remains unclear, it is essential that they do emerge if democracy is to produce a fairer society, as well as one in which more people share in decisions.

Socio-economic Rights and Agency: Towards an Empowering Jurisprudence

If effective redistribution cannot be achieved through the enlightened plans of technicians in government, then neither can it be achieved purely by legally trained minds from the lofty heights of a judicial bench: if government technical experts cannot 'deliver' equity, neither can judges or courts hand it down in their rulings.

This point is often forgotten in South Africa, where courts are routinely seen as solutions to all political and social conflicts. An enlightened constitution, containing a generous set of social and economic rights, is considered a crucial means to equity.[44] The argument for reliance on these rights and the judicial rulings which enforce them is that they are said to offer a more generous understanding of democracy than that available in the liberal democracies because they understand the need for it to translate into concrete material changes in people's lives: it offers, according to a noted jurist and advocate of this view, 'bread' and 'freedom'.[45] The effect in reality may be rather different.

Giving a court the power to adjudicate social and economic rights can turn unelected jurists into legislators. This is justified by the principle that the minority's right to participate needs protection if all are to share in popular sovereignty. Since this can only be enforced by the courts, democracy does require that judges enjoy the power to override the decisions of elected politicians to protect popular sovereignty. The boundaries between acting to protect rights and usurping the function of elected legislators are, it was noted, very porous, and so some judicial law-making is intrinsic to a functioning democracy. But there are significant differences between a context in which judges intervene to protect the right to participate and one in which they seek to impose a policy outcome. In the first case, judicial law-making is not inevitable; in the second, it is, if we expect judges and courts to decide the level of social and economic provision which would realise social and economic rights. In a much-reported case, a judge ruled that the government policy of granting each household 6 kilolitres (kl) of free water a month was an insufficient realisation of the right to water and that 12 kl would realise the right.[46] It is difficult to understand how legal training could equip anyone to decide how much free water a month a household ought to receive to ensure that equity is achieved. It is equally difficult to understand why the opinion of a learned judge that 12 kl is appropriate should be superior to that of a steel worker who favours 15 kl or a stockbroker who opts for 9 kl. These are matters of opinion, and legal training offers no guarantee of a superior insight into the question: it is a core democratic principle that matters of opinion are settled by the cut and thrust of politics, not judicial decree. The more power is given to the judiciary to impose social outcomes, the more the principle of popular sovereignty is compromised. It also undervalues or discourages action by the poor by making their hopes dependent on enlightened lawyers.

This does not mean that the courts have no role in the quest for greater equity. In the TAC case discussed in the previous chapter, the courts did support the campaign for change – they have also assisted inner-city residents fighting eviction.[47] In both cases, they were supporting collective action by grassroots citizens rather than imposing decisions on them. If we acknowledge that the poor and weak can win and protect their rights only through collective action, the role of the courts is to support people's right and ability to act in defence of their own social goals, not to decide what those goals are.

The South African Constitutional Court has, in recent years, acknowledged this – much to the frustration of legal scholars who would like it to impose solutions on citizens. In disputes such as that on water mentioned above, it has refused to decide how much free water people should receive and has instead ordered the parties to negotiate a solution and report back to the court. The scholars, who, like all devotees of technical expertise, want courts to decide the minimum goods and services people should receive, see this as a betrayal of the poor. It is, in reality, the opposite because it forces authorities to listen to what poor people want rather than deciding this for them. Courts could do more to boost citizens' power to act – they could also insist that the negotiations occur in ways which redress power imbalances by ensuring that poor people really are heard.[48] But, by supporting people's right to act and decide rather than telling them what they need, the Constitutional Court has signalled support for deeper popular sovereignty.

BEYOND MINORITY RULE

This principle does not apply to judges and lawyers alone. It is discussed here not only because recourse to the courts plays a key role in South Africa, but because it underlines the theme of this book: equity, like other social outcomes, can be defined only by the choices of adult citizens, and that these can emerge only through a process of contentious engagement between all collective voices. The social good is what members of a political community, speaking through open political engagement protected by guaranteed rights to participate, say it is – and it can be realised only through free engagement, not by the privileged deliberation of those considered more learned and skilled.

The topic is an appropriate one on which to end because it highlights the core argument of this book: democracy is about the right of people to govern themselves, and to take the action necessary to do this, not simply about the right to choose which people will decide what is good for them. The point is particularly poignant in South Africa, where people have fought for the principle that everyone is entitled to a say in decisions. While that goal was achieved formally in 1994, it remains elusive not only because many are excluded from a say by their poverty, but because the right of minorities to decide for majorities is still deeply embedded in mainstream ways of thinking. It is expressed in different ways. For some, living in the suburbs entitles some to decide for others; for others, it is whether you own a business or are a qualified professional; for still others, it is your political connections. And just about everyone who is taken seriously in the mainstream insists that governments should be run, and their key decisions taken, by people with professional training in the law or economics or the social sciences. Minority rule survives – defined now not by race but by claimed access to expertise or a particular attitude to the world.

This book has sought to challenge this view by holding out the vision of a South Africa – and a world – in which everyone decides, and in which each adult human being enjoys at least in principle an equal right to decide. It is underpinned by a recognition that this will never be achieved, but that, if we work towards the goal, we will ensure not only a fairer society which makes far more people feel that they belong, but also one in which government serves the people better and the basic material needs of all are more likely to be addressed. A core reality of the period before 1994 has not disappeared: South Africa will progress only if it progresses away from minority rule. The nature of the ruling minority may have changed, but the task has not. The arguments presented here are a modest attempt to contribute to it.

In an always imperfect world, the vision of a society in which all can decide – because all have access, in a manner which does not require them to pay an excessive price, to the collective action which alone can shape decisions – remains always beyond us. But, while ever elusive, it is a goal we must hold always in mind if we want a society in which more and more people, particularly those who have been silenced and excluded, acquire more and more of a say in more and more of the decisions which shape their lives.

While the journey is never completed, we need constantly to be moving towards a society in which democracy's rich promise may, through collective agency, become a reality to an ever-expanding spectrum of this society. It is to this goal – of expanding the possibility for increasing numbers of citizens to act collectively to ensure that elected government does what they want, rather than forcing them to do what it wants – that South Africa's democracy must dedicate itself if it wants to move closer to the promise of a society in which the majority really do acquire a share in the power they were denied before 1994.

NOTES

INTRODUCTION

1   Nancy Bermeo *Ordinary People in Extraordinary Times: The Citizenry and the Breakdown of Democracy* Princeton and Oxford, Princeton University Press, 2003

2   For example, Guillermo O'Donnell *Modernization and Bureaucratic-Authoritarianism: Studies in South American Politics* Berkeley, Institute for International Studies, 1979; Juan J Linz and Alfred Stepan (Eds) *The Breakdown of Democratic Regimes: Latin America* Baltimore, Johns Hopkins University Press, 1978

3   The process was described and analysed in a seminal study: Guillermo O'Donnell and Philippe C Schmitter *Transitions from Authoritarian Rule: Tentative Conclusions about Uncertain Democracies* Baltimore, Johns Hopkins University Press, 1986

4   Francis Fukuyama *The End of History and the Last Man* New York, Free Press, 1992

5   Michael Ignatieff 'Are the Authoritarians Winning?' *New York Review of Books* 10 July 2014

6   Simon Tormey 'The Contemporary Crisis of Representative Democracy' *Democratic Theory* Vol. 1, No. 2, 2014, p. 104 (Emphasis in original)

7   Robert H Bates, Ghada Fayad and Anke Hoeffler 'The State of Democracy in Sub-Saharan Africa' *Iinternational Area Studies Review* Vol. 15, No. 4, 2012, pp. 323–338

8   Wendy Brown *Undoing the Demos: Neoliberalism's Stealth Revolution* New York, Zone Books, 2015

9   Christopher Hobson 'Democracy: Trap, Tragedy or Crisis?' *Political Studies Review* Vol. 16, No. 1, 2016, pp. 38–45

10 John Dunn *Breaking Democracy's Spell* New Haven, Yale University Press, 2013, p. 5

11 For example, Tim Cohen 'Bongo Beats Pointless Drum over Book' *Business Day* 6 November 2017

12 For example, Luyolo Mkentane 'PPF Calls for SA to Ditch Constitution' *Cape Times* 24 January 2017

13 Ian Shapiro *The State of Democratic Theory* Princeton and Oxford, Princeton University Press, 2003, p. 1

14 Richard Joseph 'Growth, Security, and Democracy in Africa' *Journal of Democracy* Vol. 25, No. 4, October 2014, p. 64. His Afrobarometer survey data are drawn from Carolyn Logan and Michael Bratton 'Claiming Democracy: Are Voters Becoming Citizens in Africa?' *AfricaPlus* 14 May 2013 http://africaplus.wordpress.com/2013/05/14/claiming-democracy-are-voters-becoming-citizens-in-africa (accessed on 1 August 2018)

15   Joseph 'Growth, Security, and Democracy in Africa' p. 69
16   Edward Webster 'The Promise and the Possibility: South Africa's Contested Industrial Relations Path' *Transformation* No. 81/82, 2013, pp. 208–235
17   Steven Friedman 'Gaining Comprehensive AIDS Treatment in South Africa: The Extraordinary "Ordinary"' in John Gaventa and Rosemary McGee (Eds) *Citizen Action and National Policy Reform* London and New York, Zed Books, 2010, pp. 44–68
18   Terri Lynn Karl and Phillipe C Schmitter 'What Democracy is … and is Not' *Journal of Democracy* Vol. 2, No. 3, Summer 1991, pp. 75–88
19   Michael Bratton and Nicolas van de Walle *Democratic Experiments in Africa* Cambridge, Cambridge University Press, 1997

CHAPTER 1

1   Lukhona Mnguni 'South Africa is Not a Vibrant Democracy' *eNCA.com* 8 November 2016 https://www.enca.com/opinion/south-africa-is-not-a-vibrant-democracy (accessed on 1 August 2018); Ayanda Kota 'SA, We Cannot Say We are Free' *Mail and Guardian* 6 May 2011 https://mg.co.za/article/2011-05-06-sa-we-cannot-say-are-free (accessed on 1 August 2018)
2   Tom Lodge *Consolidating Democracy: South Africa's Second Popular Election* Johannesburg, Wits University Press, 1999; Hennie Kotze and Reinet Loubser 'South Africa's Democratic Consolidation in Perspective: Mapping Socio-political Changes' *Taiwan Journal of Democracy* Vol. 13, No. 1, 2017, pp. 35–58; Itumeleng Mekoa 'Consolidating Democracy in South Africa: Prospects and Challenges' *Politeia* Vol. 35, No. 2, 2016, pp. 1–20; Roger Southall 'South Africa 1999: The ANC and Democratic Consolidation' *Issue: A Journal of Opinion* Vol. 27, No. 2, The South African Elections, 1999, pp. 9–16
3   Perhaps the best-known critique of electoral democracies is Guillermo O'Donnell, 'Delegative Democracy' *Journal of Democracy* Vol. 5, No. 1, January 1994, pp. 55–69. For other writings challenging the democratic status of new electoral 'democracies', see, for example, Steven Levitzky and Lucan Way 'The Rise of Competitive Authoritarianism' *Journal of Democracy* Vol. 13, No. 2, April 2002, pp. 51–65; Andreas Schedler 'The Menu of Manipulation' *Journal of Democracy* Vol. 13, No. 2, April 2002, pp. 36–50. For a challenge addressed specifically at new African democracies, see Richard Joseph, 'Africa, 1990–1997: From *Abertura* to Closure' *Journal of Democracy* Vol. 9, No. 2, April 1998, pp. 3–17
4   Andreas Schedler 'What is Democratic Consolidation?' *Journal of Democracy* Vol. 9, No. 2, April 1998, p. 93
5   O'Donnell and Schmitter *Transitions from Authoritarian Rule*
6   Schedler 'What is Democratic Consolidation?' p. 91
7   Schedler 'What is Democratic Consolidation?' p. 94
8   Schedler 'What is Democratic Consolidation?' p. 92
9   Schedler 'What is Democratic Consolidation?' p. 92
10 Christian Welzel *Freedom Rising: Human Empowerment and the Quest for Emancipation* New York, Cambridge University Press, 2013; Pippa Norris *Democratic Deficit: Critical Citizens Revisited* New York, Cambridge University Press, 2011; Ronald F Inglehart 'How Much Should We Worry?' *Journal of Democracy* Vol. 27, No. 3, July 2016, pp. 18–23

11 Roberto Stefan Foa and Yascha Mounk 'The Danger of Deconsolidation: The Demo-cratic Discontent' *Journal of Democracy* Vol. 27, No. 3, July 2016, pp. 5–17; Paul Howe 'Eroding Norms and Democratic Deconsolidation' *Journal of Democracy* Vol. 28, No. 4, October 2017, pp. 15–29

12 Foa and Mounk 'The Danger of Democratisation' p. 10

13 Philippe C Schmitter 'The Future of Democracy is Not What It Used to Be' *Zeitschrift für Vergleichende Politikwissenschaft/Comparative Governance and Politics* Vol. 11, No. 4, December 2017, pp. 1–25

14 Schmitter 'The Future of Democracy' p. 1

15 Schmitter 'The Future of Democracy' p. 4

16 Schmitter 'The Future of Democracy' p. 4

17 Schmitter 'The Future of Democracy' p. 2

18 Schmitter 'The Future of Democracy' p. 7

19 Schmitter 'The Future of Democracy' p. 7

20 Juan J Linz and Alfred Stepan *Problems of Democratic Transition and Consolidation: Southern Europe, South America and Post-communist Europe* Baltimore and London, Johns Hopkins University Press, 1996, p. 5. See also Juan J Linz 'Transitions to Democracy' *Washington Quarterly* Vol. 13, No. 3, 1990, pp. 143–164

21 Adam Przeworski *Democracy and the Market: Political and Economic Reforms in Eastern Europe and Latin America* Cambridge, Cambridge University Press, 1991, p. 26

22 See, for example, Scott Mainwaring, Guillermo O'Donnell and J Samuel Valenzuela (Eds) *Issues in Democratic Consolidation: The New South American Democracies in Comparative Perspective* Notre Dame, University of Notre Dame Press, 1992

23 Guillermo O'Donnell 'Illusions about Consolidation' *Journal of Democracy* Vol. 7, No. 2, April 1996, pp. 34–51

24 See, for example, Michael Bratton and Robert Mattes 'Support for Democracy in Africa: Intrinsic or Instrumental?' Paper presented to panel 'What Have We Learned about Consolidation?' at the annual meeting of the American Political Science Association, Atlanta, 1–4 September 1999

25 For a discussion and critique, see Leonardo Avritzer *Democracy and the Public Space in Latin America* Princeton and Oxford, Princeton University Press, 2002, in particu-lar chapters 1 and 2, pp. 11–54

26 Dankwart A Rustow, 'Transitions to Democracy: Towards a Dynamic Model' *Com-parative Politics* Vol. 2, No. 3, April 1970, pp. 337–363

27 Richard Gunther, Nikiforos Diamondouros and Hans-Jürgen Puhle (Eds) *The Politics of Democratic Consolidation: Southern Europe in Comparative Perspective* Baltimore, Johns Hopkins University Press, 1995, pp. 12–13, cited in O'Donnell 'Illusions about Consolidation' p. 42

28 These are, of course, all 'dominant party' democratic systems which are regarded as stable democracies. See TJ Pempel (Ed.) *Uncommon Democracies: The One-Party Dominant Regimes* Ithaca and London, Cornell University Press, 1990

29 Bermeo *Ordinary People in Extraordinary Times*

30 Jennifer L McCoy and William C Smith 'Democratic Disequilibrium in Venezuela' *Journal of Interamerican Studies and World Affairs* Vol. 37, No. 2, Summer 1995, pp. 113–179

31 Chantal Mouffe *The Return of the Political* London and New York, Verso, 1993, p. 6

32 Samuel P Huntington *The Third Wave: Democratization in the Late Twentieth Century* Norman, University of Oklahoma Press, 1991, p. 267

33   O'Donnell 'Illusions about Consolidation' p. 37

34   Schedler 'What is Democratic Consolidation?' p. 95

35   Philippe Schmitter with Terry Karl 'The Conceptual Travels of Transitologists and Consolidologists: How Far to the East Should They Attempt to Go?' *Slavic Review* Vol. 53, No. 1, Spring 1994, pp. 173–185

36   Cohen 'Bongo Beats Pointless Drum'

37   Kim Willsher 'French Media Warned Not to Publish Emmanuel Macron Leaks' *The Observer* 6 May 2017. See also a report by Article 19, which campaigns for freedom of expression, stating that journalists are freer in South Africa than in the UK: Graham Ruddick 'Global Press Freedom Plunges to Worst Level this Century' *The Guardian* 30 November 2017

38   William E Leuchtenberg *Franklin Delano Roosevelt and the New Deal, 1932–40* New York, Harper and Row, 1963

39   Schedler notes a tendency to compare Southern democracies with 'a more or less rosy picture of established Western democracies': 'What is Democratic Consolidation?' p. 100

40   Francis Fukuyama 'Why is Democracy Performing so Poorly?' *Journal of Democracy* Vol. 26, No. 1, January 2015, pp. 11–20

41   For discussions of corporatism, see Philippe C Schmitter *The Political Economy of Corporatism* London, Macmillan, 1985; Alan Cawson *Corporatism and Political Theory*, Oxford, Basil Blackwell, 1986

42   Arend Lijphart *Democracy in Plural Societies* New Haven, Yale University Press, 1977

43   Philippe C Schmitter 'The Quality of Democracy: The Ambiguous Virtues of Account-ability' Paper presented at the conference 'The Quality of Democracy: Improvement or Subversion?' Stanford, Stanford University, 10–11 October 2003

44   Stewart said he could not define pornography but 'I know it when I see it'. Peter Lattman 'The Origins of Justice Stewart's "I Know It When I See It"' *Wall Street Journal* Law Blog 27 September 2007 https://blogs.wsj.com/law/2007/09/27/the-origins-of-justice-stewarts-i-know-it-when-i-see-it/ (accessed on 1 August 2018)

45   O'Donnell 'Illusions about Consolidation' pp. 46–47

46   O'Donnell 'Illusions about Consolidation' p. 40

47   Robert Putnam *Making Democracy Work: Civic Traditions in Modern Italy* Princeton, Princeton University Press, 1994

48   David G Green *Power and Party in an English City: An Account of Single-Party Rule* London, Allen and Unwin, 1981

49   To name but one example, Sami al-Haj, a Sudanese cameraman working for the Al Jazeera television channel, was released from the Guantanamo Bay detention camp in May 2008 after being detained without charge for six years. 'Al-Jazeera Camera-man Home from Guantanamo' *Sydney Morning Herald* 2 May 2008 http://www.smh.com.au/news/world/aljazeera-cameraman-home-from-guantanamo/2008/05/02/1209235136671.html (accessed on 1 August 2018)

50   See, for example, Michael Waldman 'Between Voting Rights and Voting Wrongs' *New York Times* 1 May 2012 http://campaignstops.blogs.nytimes.com/2012/05/01/between-voting-rights-and-voting-wrongs/?nl=opinion&emc=edit_ty_20120501 (accessed on 1 August 2018)

51   Jeffrey Toobin 'The Real Voting Scandal of 2016' *The New Yorker* 12 December 2016

52   Alan Travis 'UK Terror Detention Limit is Longest of Any Democracy' *The Guardian* 12 November 2007 http://www.guardian.co.uk/uk/2007/nov/12/humanrights.terrorism (accessed on 1 August 2018). As the title indicates, the report claims that

British law allows for longer periods of detention than American law, a strange claim, given the fact that Guantanamo Bay detainees have been held without charge for years

53   See, for example, Benjamin R Barber *A Passion for Democracy: American Essays* Princeton, Princeton University Press, 1998; Michael Sandel *Democracy's Discontent: America in Search of a Public Philosophy* Cambridge, Mass. and London, the Belknap Press at Harvard University Press, 1998

54   Norris *Democratic Deficit*

55   Robert A Dahl *Polyarchy: Government and Opposition* New Haven, Yale University Press, 1971

56   Schedler 'What is Democratic Consolidation?' p. 105

57   Schmitter 'The Quality of Democracy' p. 15

58   Adriano Nuvunga 'Mozambique's 2014 Elections: A Repeat of Misconduct, Political Tension and Frelimo Dominance' *Journal of African Elections* Vol. 16, No. 2, 2017, pp. 71–94

59   'Where partisan bodies are able to draw electoral districts to their own advantage (as in the US, where this gerrymandering is performed every decade by state legislatures ...), they are likely to do so in ways that will promote partisan and incumbency advantage.' Larry Diamond and Leonardo Morlino *The Quality of Democracy* CDDR Working Paper No. 20, Stanford, Center on Democracy, Development, and the Rule of Law, Stanford Institute on International Studies, Stanford University, September 2004, p. 13

60   Ashutosh Varshney *Battles Half Won: India's Improbable Democracy* New Delhi, Penguin Viking, 2013, p. 84

CHAPTER 2

1   Street Law *Democracy for All* Durban, University of KwaZulu-Natal, 1995

2   David Estlund 'Beyond Fairness and Deliberation: The Epistemic Dimension of Democratic Authority' in James Bohman and William Rehg (Eds) *Deliberative Democracy: Essays in Reason and Politics* Cambridge, Mass. and London, MIT Press, 1999, p. 183

3   Robert Dahl *After the Revolution? Authority in a Good Society* New Haven, Yale University Press, 1970, pp. 45–79

4   Robert Dahl *Democracy and Its Critics* New Haven, Yale University Press, 1989, p. 209

5   Ivor Jennings *The Approach to Self-Government* Cambridge, Cambridge University Press, 1956, p. 56

6   Armendariz M Abdullahi 'Article 39 of the Ethiopian Constitution on Secession and Self-Determination: A Panacea to the Nationality Question in Africa?' *Verfassung und Recht in Übersee/Law and Politics in Africa, Asia and Latin America* Vol. 31, No. 4, 4. Quartal, 1998, pp. 440–455

7   For a discussion of the boundary problem and some of its contemporary implications, see Cristóbal Rovira Kaltwasser 'The Responses of Populism to Dahl's Democratic Dilemmas' *Political Studies* Vol. 62, No. 3, 2014, pp. 470–487

8   Kay Shriner 'The Competence Line in American Suffrage Law: A Political Analysis' *Disability Studies Quarterly* Vol. 22, No. 2, Spring 2002, pp. 61–72

9   Alex Folkes 'The Case for Votes at 16' *Representation* Vol. 41, No. 1, 2004, pp. 52–56; Philip Cowley and David Denver 'Votes at 16? The Case Against' *Representation* Vol. 41, No. 1, 2004, pp. 57–62

10   Ron Hayduk 'Noncitizens Have the Obligations of Citizens – So Why Not the Right to Vote?' *History News Network* 24 February 2004 http://hnn.us/articles/24290.html (accessed on 1 August 2018); see also Ron Hayduk *Democracy for All: Restoring Immigrant Voting Rights in the United States* New York, Routledge, 2006

11   World Bank *The State in a Changing World: World Development Report 1997* New York, Oxford University Press, 1997, p. 161

12   World Bank *The State in a Changing World*

13   Seyla Benhabib 'Citizens, Residents and Aliens in a Changing World: Political Membership in the Global Era' *Social Research* Vol. 66, No. 3, Fall 1999, pp. 709–744

14   John Keane *The Life and Death of Democracy* London, Sydney, New York and Toronto, Pocket Books, 2009, pp. 26–27

15   John Keane *Democracy and Civil Society* London, Verso, 1988

16   With the obvious proviso, pointed out above, that who is an 'adult' will always be contested

17   Steven Friedman 'The Forgotten Sovereign: Citizens, States and Foreign Policy in the South' in Justin Robertson and Maurice A East (Eds) *Diplomacy and Developing Nations: Post-Cold War Foreign Policy-Making Structures and Processes* Abingdon, Routledge, 2005, pp. 225–252

18   Chantal Mouffe *The Democratic Paradox* London and New York, Verso, 2000, p. 4

19   Pierre Rosanvallon *Democratic Legitimacy: Impartiality, Reflexivity, Proximity* Princeton, Princeton University Press, 2011, p. 1

20   Guillermo O'Donnell 'On the State, Democratization and Some Conceptual Problems: A Latin American View with Glances at Some Post-communist Countries' *World Development* Vol. 21, No. 3, 1993, pp. 1355–1369

21   William Riker and Peter Ordeshook 'A Theory of the Calculus of Voting' *American Political Science Review* Vol. 62, No. 1, 1968, pp. 25–42. Riker's work vigorously challenges the notion of democracy as popular sovereignty, making him an odd recruit to the argument advanced here. But his critique of the notion that a vote signifies a specific instruction to a representative can be mobilised in support of deeper notions of popular sovereignty; it need not be the monopoly of those who challenge the ability of political communities to govern themselves

22   Karl and Schmitter 'What Democracy Is' pp. 75–89

23   See, for example, Joshua Cohen 'Deliberation and Democratic Legitimacy' in Bohman and Rehg (Eds) *Deliberative Democracy* pp. 67–92

24   For a discussion of government authority as a key ingredient of democratic quality, see Diamond and Morlino *The Quality of Democracy* pp. 7ff

25   Friedman 'The Forgotten Sovereign'

26   O'Donnell 'On the State, Democratization and Some Conceptual Problems'

27   Steven Friedman 'Archipelagos of Dominance: Party Fiefdoms and South African Democracy' *Zeitschrift für Vergleichende Politikwissenschaft/Journal of Comparative Politics* Vol. 9, No. 3, 2015, pp. 139–159

28   See, for example, Soma Pillay 'Corruption – the Challenge to Good Governance: A South African Perspective' *International Journal of Public Sector Management* Vol. 17, No. 7, 2004, pp. 586–605

29   Office of the United Nations High Commissioner for Human Rights 'Good Governance and Human Rights' nd https://www.ohchr.org/en/issues/development/good governance/pages/goodgovernanceindex.aspx (accessed on 1 August 2018)

30   International Monetary Fund *Good Governance: The IMF's Role* Washington DC, International Monetary Fund, 1997, p. 3

31   Office of the United Nations High Commissioner for Human Rights 'Good Governance'

32   Varshney *Battles Half Won* pp. 259–277

33   Adam Przeworski 'Democracy as a Contingent Outcome of Conflicts' in Jon Elster and Rune Slagstad (Eds) *Constitutionalism and Democracy* Cambridge, Cambridge University Press, 1993, pp. 59–80

34   Claude Lefort *Democracy and Political Theory* Oxford, Basil Blackwell, 1988, p. 19

35   Claude Lefort *The Political Forms of Modern Society* Oxford, Polity Press, 1986, p. 305

36   Mouffe *The Return of the Political* p. 2

37   Mouffe *The Democratic Paradox* p. 105

38   Mouffe *The Democratic Paradox* p. 103

39   Peter Hudson 'Taking the Democratic Subject Seriously' Paper presented at a seminar at the University of South Africa School for Graduate Studies, Pretoria, 24 May 2007, p. 8

40   René Vollgraaff 'WEF: "Africa Can't Eat Democracy"' *fin24* 7 May 2010 https://www .fin24.com/economy/wef-africa-cant-eat-democracy-20100507?cpid=2 (accessed on 1 August 2018)

41   Giovanni Sartori *The Theory of Democracy Revisited* Chatham, Chatham House, 1987

42   Jean-Jacques Rousseau *The Social Contract* (Translated by Maurice Cranston) Harmondsworth, Penguin, 1968, p. 72

43   Rosanvallon *Democratic Legitimacy* p. 9

44   Miguel Abensour '"Savage Democracy" and "Principle of Anarchy"' *Philosophy and Social Criticism* Vol. 28, No. 6, 2002, p. 704

45   Sofia Nasstrom 'Representative Democracy as Tautology: Ankersmit and Lefort on Representation' *European Journal of Political Theory* Vol. 5, No. 3, 2006, p. 322

46   This assumption clearly underpins the argument in Mouffe *The Democratic Paradox*

47   Robert H Phinny 'South Africa's Minorities Have Rights' *New York Times* 24 June 1992

48   Mouffe *The Democratic Paradox* p. 4

49   CB McPherson *The Political Theory of Possessive Individualism* Oxford, Clarendon Press, 1962

50   Chandran Nair 'The West Can't Fix the Climate Crisis. Asia Will Have to Do It.' *The Guardian* 5 December 2017

51   Mouffe *The Democratic Paradox* p. 85

52   Jürgen Habermas *Between Facts and Norms: Contributions to a Discourse Theory of Law and Democracy* Cambridge, Mass., MIT Press, 1996, p. 127

53   TH Marshall *Citizenship and Social Class* London, Pluto, 1992

54   Cited in Institute for Democracy in South Africa (Idasa) *Reflections on Democracy* Pretoria, Idasa, 1997; see also Claude Ake *Democracy and Development in Africa* Washington DC, Brookings Institution, 1996

55   Benjamin Barber *Strong Democracy: Participatory Politics for a New Age* Berkeley, University of California Press, 1984

56   Karl and Schmitter 'What Democracy Is'

57   Dahl *Democracy and Its Critics*

58   Avritzer *Democracy and the Public Space* p. 11

59   Avritzer *Democracy and the Public Space* p. 14

60   Fikile Moya 'How Mbeki Shows South Africa's Need for a True Leadership' *Independent Online* 15 July 2017 https://www.iol.co.za/news/opinion/how-mbeki

-shows-south-africas-need-for-a-true-leadership-10302211 (accessed on 1 August 2018); Amanda Khoza 'Nene: SA Needs Strong Leadership for these Turbulent Times' *News 24* 31 May 2017 https://www.fin24.com/Economy/nene-sa-needs-strong-leadership-for-these-turbulent-times-20170531 (accessed on 1 August 2018)

61 Steven Friedman 'Seeing Ourselves as Others See Us: Racism, Technique and the Mbeki Administration' in Daryl Glaser (Ed.) *Mbeki and After: Reflections on the Legacy of Thabo Mbeki* Johannesburg, Wits University Press, 2010, pp. 163–186

62 Fukuyama 'Why is Democracy Performing So Poorly?' p. 12

63 Shapiro *The State of Democratic Theory* p. 3

64 Charles Tilly *Democracy* New York, Cambridge University Press, 2007, pp. 13–14

65 Tilly *Democracy* pp. 7–15

66 Stephen Schlesinger and Steven Kinzer *Bitter Fruit: The Story of the American Coup in Guatemala* Cambridge, Mass., Harvard University Press, 1999

67 Mandy Turner 'Building Democracy in Palestine: Liberal Peace Theory and the Election of Hamas' *Democratization* Vol. 13, No. 5, 2006, pp. 739–755

68 Sholto Byrnes 'Interview: Samantha Power' *New Statesman* 6 March 2008 https://www.newstatesman.com/world-affairs/2008/03/barack-obama-interview-power (accessed on 1 August 2018)

69 Larry Diamond, Kenta Tsuda and Barron YoungSmith 'Authoritarian Learning: Lessons from the Colored Revolutions' *Brown Journal of World Affairs* Vol. 12, No. 2, Winter/Spring 2006, p. 222

70 'Abbas Continues Rejecting "Jewish State" Notion' *Jerusalem Post* 1 December 2007 https://www.jpost.com/Middle-East/Abbas-continues-rejecting-Jewish-state-notion (accessed on 1 August 2018)

71 David Chandler *Faking Democracy after Dayton* London and Sterling, Pluto Press, 1999, p. 155

72 Chandler *Faking Democracy* p. 24

73 Chandler *Faking Democracy* p. 3

74 Mouffe *The Democratic Paradox* p. 16

75 Leonardo Morlino *Democracy between Consolidation and Crisis: Parties, Groups and Citizens in Southern Europe* Oxford, Oxford University Press, 1998

76 Robert Dahl, *Dilemmas of Pluralist Democracy* New Haven, Yale University Press, 1982

77 Diamond and Morlino *The Quality of Democracy*

78 Marc Buhrmann, Wolfgang Merkel, and Bernhard Wessels *The Quality of Democracy: Democracy Barometer for Established Democracies* NCCR Democracy Working Paper No. 10, Zürich, University of Zürich, 2007

79 Daniel H Levine and Jose E Molina *The Quality of Democracy in Latin America* Boulder, Lynne Rienner, 2011; Andrew Roberts *The Quality of Democracy in Eastern Europe: Public Preferences and Policy Reforms* Cambridge, Cambridge University Press, 2009

80 For example, Arch Puddington and Tyler Roylance 'Anxious Dictators, Wavering Democrats' *Journal of Democracy* Vol. 27, No. 2, April 2016, pp. 86–100, which discusses the 2015 rankings

81 *The Polity Project* Center for Systemic Peace nd http://www.systemicpeace.org/polity project (accessed on 1 August 2018)

82 V-Dem *Varieties of Democracy: Global Standards, Local Knowledge* nd https://www.v-dem.net (accessed on 1 August 2018)

83 For the method, see Freedom House *Methodology: Freedom in the World 2016* nd https://freedomhouse.org/report/freedom-world-2016/methodology (accessed on 1 August 2018)

84 See, for example, Tilly *Democracy*; Larry Diamond *Developing Democracy: Toward Consolidation* Baltimore, Johns Hopkins University Press, 1999; Adrian Karatnycky 'The Decline of Illiberal Democracy' *Journal of Democracy* Vol. 10, No. 1, January 1999, pp. 112–125; Stephen Knack 'Does Foreign Aid Promote Democracy?' *International Studies Quarterly* Vol. 48, No. 1, March 2004, pp. 251–266

85 Freedom House *Methodology*

86 Freedom House *Methodology*

87 Puddington and Roylance 'Anxious Dictators' p. 86

88 Frances Hagopian 'The (Too-Low but) Rising Quality of Democracy in Brazil and Chile?' Paper presented at the conference 'The Quality of Democracy: Improvement or Subversion?' Stanford, Stanford University, 10–11 October 2003

89 See Afrobarometer http://www.afrobarometer.org/ (accessed on 1 August 2018); Latino-barometro www.latinobarometro.org (accessed on 1 August 2018); Asian Barometer www.asianbarometer.org/ (accessed on 1 August 2018); Eurobarometer http://ec.europa.eu/commfrontoffice/publicopinion/index.cfm (accessed on 1 August 2018)

CHAPTER 3

1 Seymour Martin Lipset 'Some Social Requisites of Democracy: Economic Development and Political Legitimacy' *American Political Science Review* Vol. 53, No. 1, March 1959, p. 72

2 Lipset 'Some Social Requisites of Democracy' p. 75

3 Lipset 'Some Social Requisites of Democracy' p. 103

4 Lipset 'Some Social Requisites of Democracy' p. 73

5 Seymour Martin Lipset *Political Man: The Social Basis of Politics* New York, Doubleday, 1960

6 Lipset 'Some Social Requisites of Democracy' p. 97

7 Adam Przeworski, Michael Alvarez, Jose Antonio Cheibub and Fernando Limongi 'What Makes Democracies Endure?' *Journal of Democracy* Vol. 7, No. 1, 1996, p. 39

8 Przeworski et al. 'What Makes Democracies Endure?' p. 41. The rather precise cut-off seems to have been chosen because it was Argentina's national per capita income in the mid-1970s and was clearly insufficient to sustain democracy in that country. This figure is, therefore, the highest at which a democracy has reverted to authoritarianism

9 According to World Bank data, India's gross per capita national income in 2005 was $730, placing it in the category of democracies which should have collapsed after eight and a half years. World Bank Group *GNI per Capita 2005, Atlas Method and PPP* 2007 http://siteresources.worldbank.org/DATASTATISTICS/Resources/GNIPC05.pdf (accessed on 1 August 2018)

10 Przeworski et al. 'What Makes Democracies Endure?' p. 42

11 Paul Collier, Oxford University, speaking at a seminar at which the author was present

12 Seymour Martin Lipset 'The Social Requisites of Democracy Revisited: 1993' Presidential Address *American Sociological Review* Vol. 59, No. 1, February 1994, p. 6

13 Lipset 'The Social Requisites Revisited' p. 7

14 Lipset 'Some Social Requisites of Democracy' p. 70

15 Evidence that the Economist Intelligence Unit shares Lipset's prejudices (and, indeed, those of the 'consolidation' paradigm) is that it distinguishes between 'full' and 'flawed' democracies. The only Western European or North American country which does not make it into the 'full' category is Italy. Criteria include clearly subjective elements such as 'functioning of government' and 'political culture'. Since the index is so clearly a vehicle of the sort of biases about culture and industrialisation which inform Lipset's formulation, the fact that it refutes his empirical claim is made all the more salient. See Lasa Kekıc *The Economist Intelligence Unit's Index of Democracy* 2007 www.economist.com/media/pdf/DEMOCRACY_INDEX_2007_v3.pdf (accessed on 1 August 2018)

16 Lipset 'The Social Requisites Revisited' p. 16

17 Lipset 'Some Social Requisites of Democracy' p. 98

18 Lipset 'The Social Requisites Revisited' p. 16

19 Lipset 'The Social Requisites Revisited' p. 17

20 Lipset seems to be insisting that the resemblance is purely structural, not cultural, and that he was making no claim as to the superiority of European culture. But, read in context, he does seem to be suggesting that Asian societies (he sees no prospect of African success) attain the preconditions for democracy only when they acquire some of the attitudes as well as the social and economic indicators of Western Europe. Lipset 'Some Social Requisites of Democracy' p. 101

21 Putnam *Making Democracy Work*

22 Mark Robinson and Steven Friedman *Civil Society, Democratisation and Foreign Aid in Africa* IDS Discussion Paper No. 383, Brighton, Institute for Development Studies, University of Sussex, 2005

23 For an analysis which locates the genesis of sustainable democracy in Mauritius not in civic tradition but in the fiscal relationship between state and society, see Deborah Bräutigam 'Contingent Consent: Export Taxation and State Building in Mauritius' Paper presented at the annual meeting of the American Political Science Association, Philadelphia, 31 August 2006

24 Alexis de Tocqueville *Democracy in America* New York, Mentor, 1956, p. 208

25 De Tocqueville *Democracy in America* p. 208

26 De Tocqueville *Democracy in America* p. 202

27 Robinson and Friedman *Civil Society, Democratisation and Foreign Aid*

28 De Tocqueville *Democracy in America* p. 198

29 De Tocqueville *Democracy in America* p. 201

30 E Spencer Wellhofer 'Democracy, Fascism and Civil Society' in Sigrid Rossteutscher (Ed.) *Democracy and the Role of Associations: Political, Organizational and Social Contexts* London and New York, Routledge, 2005, p. 25

31 For example, Cohen 'Deliberation and Democratic Legitimacy'

32 Giovanni Sartori *Parties and Party Systems: A Framework for Analysis* New York, Cambridge University Press, 1976

33 Bermeo *Ordinary People in Extraordinary Times*

34 Afrobarometer *Do Africans Still Want Democracy? Afrobarometer Findings Warn of Democratic Recession, Point to Long-Term Gains* Accra, 26 November 2016 http://afrobarometer.org/sites/default/files/press-release/round-6-releases/ab_r6_pr15_Do_Africans_want_democracy_EN.pdf (accessed on 1 August 2018)

35 World Values Survey 'Online Data Analysis' 2014 http://www.worldvaluessurvey.org/WVSOnline.jsp (accessed on 1 August 2018)

36 Pew Research Center 'Globally, Broad Support for Representative and Direct Democracy' 16 October 2017 http://www.pewglobal.org/2017/10/16/globally-broad-support-for-representative-and-direct-democracy/ (accessed on 1 August 2018)

37 Richard Wike, Katie Simmons, Bruce Stokes and Janell Fetterolf 'Globally, Broad Support for Representative and Direct Democracy: But Many Endorse Non-democratic Alternatives' *Pew Research Center* 16 October 2017 http://assets.pewresearch.org/wp-content/uploads/sites/2/2017/10/17102729/Pew-Research-Center_Democracy-Report_2017.10.16.pdf (accessed on 1 August 2018)

38 Evelyne Huber, Dietrich Rueschemeyer and John D Stephens 'The Impact of Economic Development on Democracy' *Journal of Economic Perspectives* Vol. 7, No. 3, Summer 1993, pp. 73–74

39 Huber, Rueschemeyer and Stephens 'The Impact of Economic Development on Democracy' p. 76. See also Ira Katznelson and Aristide Zolberg (Eds) *Working-Class Formation: Nineteeth-Century Patterns in Western Europe and the United States* Princeton, Princeton University Press, 1986

40 John Stephens 'Capitalist Development and Democracy: Empirical Research on the Origins of Democracy' in David Copp, Jean Hampton and John Roemer (Eds) *The Idea of Democracy* Cambridge, Cambridge University Press, 1993, p. 438

41 Adam Przeworski *Capitalism and Social Democracy* Cambridge, Cambridge University Press, 1985

42 Michael Bratton and Nicolas van de Walle *Democratic Experiments in Africa* p. 101

43 Lipset 'The Social Requisites Revisited' p. 2

44 Barrington Moore Jr *The Social Origins of Dictatorship and Democracy: Lord and Peasant in the Making of the Modern World* Boston, Beacon Press, 1966

45 Barrington Moore *Social Origins* p. 418

46 Barrington Moore *Social Origins* p. 417

47 Glenn Adler and Edward Webster (Eds) *Trade Unions and Democratization in South Africa 1985–1997* New York, St Martin's Press, 2000

48 Barrington Moore *Social Origins* p. 414

49 Seymour Martin Lipset, Martin Trow and James Coleman *Union Democracy: The Inside Politics of the International Typographical Union* New York, Free Press, 1956, p. 15

50 Lipset 'The Social Requisites Revisited' p. 13

51 Lipset 'The Social Requisites Revisited' p. 4

52 O'Donnell and Schmitter in *Transitions from Authoritarian Rule* note that, during transitions, 'there are insufficient structural or behavioural parameters to guide and predict the outcome', p. 3

53 Owen Crankshaw *Race, Class and the Changing Division of Labour under Apartheid* London and New York, Routledge, 1997

54 This section adapts arguments developed in Steven Friedman 'Democracy, Inequality and the Reconstitution of Politics' in Joseph S Tulchin with Amelia Brown (Ed.) *Democratic Governance and Social Inequality* Boulder, Lynne Rienner, 2002, pp. 13–40; Steven Friedman *Equity in the Age of Informality: Labour Markets and Redistributive Politics in South Africa* IDS Working Paper No. 160, Brighton, Institute for Development Studies, University of Sussex, July 2002; Steven Friedman 'South Africa: Globalization and the Politics of Redistribution' in Joseph S Tulchin and Gary Bland (Eds) *Getting Globalization Right: The Dilemmas of Inequality* Boulder and London, Lynne Rienner, 2005, pp. 11–49

55 See, for example, Council for Europe *Poverty and Inequality in Societies of Human Rights: The Paradox of Democracies* https://www.coe.int/en/web/portal/-/pauvrete-et-inegalite-dans-les-societes-de-droits-humains-le-paradoxe-des-democraties (accessed on 1 August 2018)

56 For a citation of various sources, see Seymour Martin Lipset, 'Introduction' to TH Marshall *Class, Citizenship and Social Development* Westport, Greenwood Press, 1964, pp. 3–23

57 Karl Marx, letter to the *New York Tribune*, 25 August 1852, cited by Lipset 'Introduction'

58 Przeworski *Capitalism and Social Democracy*

59 Marshall *Citizenship and Social Class*

60 Marshall *Citizenship and Social Class*

61 Przeworski *Capitalism and Social Democracy*

62 World Economic Forum *3 Charts that Explain Global Inequality* 20 January 2016 https://www.weforum.org/agenda/2016/01/3-charts-that-explain-global-inequality/ (accessed on 1 August 2018); Oxfam International *5 Shocking Facts about Extreme Global Inequality and How to Even It Up* 16 January 2017 https://www.oxfam.org/en/even-it/5-shocking-facts-about-extreme-global-inequality-and-how-even-it-davos (accessed on 1 August 2018)

63 For new democracies' response to economic policy challenges, see Stephan Haggard and Robert Kaufman *The Political Economy of Democratic Transitions* Princeton, Princeton University Press, 1995; and Luiz Carlos Bresser Pereira, Jose Maria Maravall and Adam Przeworski *Economic Reform in New Democracies: A Social Democratic Approach* Cambridge, Cambridge University Press, 1993

64 Friedman *Equity in the Age of Informality*

65 Steven Friedman and Sharon Groenmeyer 'A Nightmare on the Brain of the Living? The Endurance and Limits of the Collective Bargaining Regime' *Transformation* Vol. 91, 2016, pp. 163–183

66 Steven Friedman *Free but Unequal: Democracy, Inequality and the State in Latin America and Africa* Johannesburg, Centre for Policy Studies, 2001

67 Philippe C Schmitter 'The Future of Democracy: Could It be a Matter of Scale?' *Social Research* Vol. 66, No. 3, Fall 1999, p. 973

68 Schmitter 'The Future of Democracy'

69 Dani Rodrik *Has Globalisation Gone too Far?* Washington DC, Institute for International Economics, 1997

70 Paul Krugman *Pop Internationalism* Cambridge, Mass. and London, MIT Press, 1998

71 Krugman *Pop Internationalism* pp. 62–63

72 Robert A Dahl 'The Shifting Boundaries of Democratic Governments' *Social Research* Vol. 66, No. 3, Fall 1999, p. 927

73 Michael Keating and David MacCrone *The Crisis of Social Democracy in Europe* Edinburgh, Edinburgh University Press, 2013

74 JP Landman 'Is the Washington Consensus Dead?' Seminar convened by Centre for Policy Studies, Johannesburg, June 1999

75 Rodrik *Has Globalisation Gone too Far?*

76 World Bank *Poverty Reduction and the World Bank: Progress and Challenges in the 1990s* Washington DC, World Bank, 1996; World Bank *Poverty Reduction and the World Bank: Progress in Fiscal 1996 and 1997* Washington DC, World Bank, 1997

77 Raj M Desai 'Rethinking the Universalism versus Targeting Debate' Brookings Blog 31 May 2017 https://www.brookings.edu/blog/future-development/2017/05/31/rethinking-the-universalism-versus-targeting-debate/ (accessed on 1 August 2018)

78 Bernhard Leubolt *Social Policies and Redistribution in South Africa* ILO Working Paper, Geneva, International Labour Office, 25 May 2014

79 Abram de Swaan *In Care of the State* Cambridge, Cambridge University Press, 1988

80 Theda Skocpol and Ira Katznelson *Social Policy in the US: Future Possibilities in Historical Perspective* Princeton, Princeton University Press, 1996

81 Gøsta Esping-Andersen *The Three Worlds of Welfare Capitalism* Princeton, Princeton University Press, 1990; Przeworski *Capitalism and Social Democracy*

82 Steven Friedman 'Beyond the Fringe? South African Social Movements and the Politics of Redistribution' *Review of African Political Economy* Vol. 39, No. 131, 2012, pp. 85–100

83 Christopher Jencks *Rethinking Social Policy* Cambridge, Mass., Harvard University Press, 1992. For examples of the attack on welfare in the US, see Charles Murray *Losing Ground: American Social Policy 1950–1980* New York, Basic Books, 1984 or Michael Tanner *The End of Welfare: Fighting Poverty in the Civil Society* Washington DC, Cato Institute, 1996

CHAPTER 4

1 Thomas Carothers notes 'the long-standing Cold War mindset that most countries in the developing world were "not ready for democracy" '. Thomas Carothers 'The End of the Transition Paradigm' *Journal of Democracy* Vol. 13, No. 1, January 2002, pp. 5–21

2 'The C.I.A. played a direct role in influencing Kasavubu's decision to depose Lumumba on 5 September, 1960 ...' Rene Lamarchand 'The CIA in Africa: How Central? How Intelligent?' *Journal of Modern African Studies* Vol. 13, No. 3, September 1976, p. 413

3 As but one example, former Zimbabwean president Mugabe told an election rally: 'This country shall not again come under the rule and control of the white man, direct or indirect. We are masters of our destiny'. Chris McGreal 'Zimbabwe's Voters Told: Choose Mugabe or You Face a Bullet' *The Guardian* 18 June 2008 http://www.guardian.co.uk/world/2008/jun/18/zimbabwe (accessed on 1 August 2018)

4 John L Comaroff and Jean Comaroff 'Postcolonial Politics and Discourses of Democracy in Southern Africa: An Anthropological Reflection on African Political Modernities' *Journal of Anthropological Research* Vol. 53, No. 2, Summer 1997, pp. 123–146

5 Comaroff and Comaroff 'Postcolonial Politics' pp. 124, 125

6 Comaroff and Comaroff' 'Postcolonial Politics' p. 127 (Emphasis in original)

7 Comaroff and Comaroff' 'Postcolonial Politics' p. 128

8 Comaroff and Comaroff' 'Postcolonial Politics' p. 138

9 Comaroff and Comaroff' 'Postcolonial Politics' p. 138

10 Comaroff and Comaroff' 'Postcolonial Politics' p. 141

11 Percentage polls reported in African Elections Database 'Elections in Botswana' 2008 http://africanelections.tripod.com/bw.html (accessed on 1 August 2018)

12 Pippa Norris *Electoral Engineering: Voting Rules and Political Behavior* Cambridge, Cambridge University Press, 2004, pp. 230–248

13 See Jean Comaroff and John L Comaroff *Theory from the South: Or, How Euro-America is Evolving Toward Africa* Oxford, Routledge, 2016, chapter 5 'Figuring Democracy: An Anthropological Take on African Political Modernities', pp. 109–132. It is rare

for renowned scholars to take criticism as seriously as the Comaroffs took mine. This speaks to a commitment to academic enquiry which should serve as an example to all academics

14   Comaroff and Comaroff 'Figuring Democracy' p. 123
15   Comaroff and Comaroff 'Postcolonial Politics' p. 131
16   Comaroff and Comaroff 'Postcolonial Politics' p. 133 (Emphasis in original)
17   Comaroff and Comaroff 'Figuring Democracy' p. 113
18   Comaroff and Comaroff 'Figuring Democracy' p. 122 (Emphasis in original)
19   Comaroff and Comaroff 'Figuring Democracy' p. 146
20   Comaroff and Comaroff 'Figuring Democracy' note 25 p. 132
21   Comaroff and Comaroff 'Figuring Democracy' p. 126 (Emphasis in original)
22   Comaroff and Comaroff 'Figuring Democracy' p. 126
23   Comaroff and Comaroff 'Figuring Democracy' p. 127
24   Comaroff and Comaroff 'Figuring Democracy' p. 126
25   Comaroff and Comaroff 'Figuring Democracy' p. 125
26   Tony Wright 'The Decline of the Political Party: What Comes After?' London School of Economics and Political Science, British Politics and Policy 29 July 2013 http://blogs.lse.ac.uk/politicsandpolicy/after-the-party/ (accessed on 1 August 2018)
27   Comaroff and Comaroff 'Figuring Democracy' p. 113
28   Varshney *Battles Half Won* p. 39
29   Comaroff and Comaroff 'Figuring Democracy' p. 123
30   Comaroff and Comaroff 'Figuring Democracy' p. 127 (Emphasis added)
31   Comaroff and Comaroff 'Figuring Democracy' p. 127
32   Mikael Karlstrom 'Imagining Democracy: Political Culture and Democratisation in Buganda' *Africa: Journal of the International African Institute* Vol. 66, No. 4, 1996, pp. 485–505
33   Karlstrom 'Imagining Democracy' p. 485
34   Karlstrom 'Imagining Democracy' p. 487
35   Karlstrom 'Imagining Democracy' p. 488 (Emphasis in original)
36   Karlstrom 'Imagining Democracy' p. 489
37   Karlstrom 'Imagining Democracy' p. 494
38   For a description, see Karlstrom 'Imagining Democracy' pp. 496ff
39   Karlstrom 'Imagining Democracy' p. 500
40   Human Rights Watch *In Hope and Fear: Uganda's Presidential and Parliamentary Polls* 2006 http://hrw.org/backgrounder/africa/uganda0206/ (accessed on 1 August 2018)
41   Karlstrom 'Imagining Democracy' p. 487
42   Karlstrom 'Imagining Democracy' p. 489 (Emphasis in original)
43   Karlstrom 'Imagining Democracy' p. 490
44   Kwame Anthony Appiah *In My Father's House: Africa in the Philosophy of Culture* New York, Oxford University Press, 1992, p. 26
45   Jacques-Mariel Nzouankeu 'The African Attitude to Democracy' *International Social Science Journal* Vol. 43, No. 2, 1991, p. 377
46   Maurice Godelier 'Is the West the Model for Humankind? The Baruya of New Guinea between Change and Decay' *International Social Science Journal* Vol. 43, No. 2, 1991, p. 387
47   Appiah *In My Father's House* p. 58
48   Brooke Grundfest Schoepf 'Gender Relations and Development: Political Economy and Cultures' in Ann Seidman and Frederich Anang (Eds) *Twenty-First-Century*

Africa: Towards a New Vision of Self-Sustainable Development, Trenton, Africa World Press, 1992, p. 209

49 Belgian colonisers took the existing identity difference between Hutu and Tutsi and turned the Tutsi into a dominating racial group which cooperated with the coloniser to control and subjugate the Hutu. Mahmood Mamdani *When Victims Become Killers: Colonialism, Nativism and Genocide in Rwanda* Princeton, Princeton University Press, 2000

50 Partha Chatterjee *The Politics of the Governed: Reflections on Popular Politics in Most of the World* New York, Columbia University Press, 2004, p. 37

51 Mahmood Mamdani *Citizen and Subject: Contemporary Africa and the Politics of Late Colonialism* Kampala, Fountain, 1995

52 Claude Ake 'Rethinking African Democracy' *Journal of Democracy* Vol. 2, No. 1, January 1991, p. 34

53 Célestin Monga *The Anthropology of Anger: Civil Society and Democracy in Africa* Boulder, Lynne Rienner, 1996

54 Monga *The Anthropology of Anger* p. 116

55 Monga *The Anthropology of Anger* p. 10

56 Nzouankeu 'The African Attitude' p. 375

57 Nzouankeu 'The African Attitude' p. 374

58 Claude Ake 'The Unique Case of African Democracy' *International Affairs* Vol. 69, No. 2, April 1993, p. 240

59 Chatterjee *The Politics of the Governed* pp. 53–78

60 Chatterjee *The Politics of the Governed* p. 40

61 Bettina von Lieres 'Review Article: New Perspectives on Citizenship in Africa' *Journal of Southern African Studies* Vol. 25, No. 1, March 1999, p. 139

62 Richard Youngs *The Puzzle of Non-Western Democracy* Washington DC, Carnegie Endowment for International Peace, 2015

63 Von Lieres 'New Perspectives' p. 140

64 Von Lieres 'New Perspectives' p. 143

65 Von Lieres 'New Perspectives' p. 143

66 Claude Ake 'The African Context of Human Rights' *Africa Today* Vol. 34, No. 1–2, 1987, p. 6

67 Ake 'The Unique Case' p. 241

68 Julius Ihonvbere 'Underdevelopment and Human Rights Violations in Africa' in George W Shepherd and Mark OC Anikpo (Eds) *Emerging Human Rights* New York, Greenwood Press, 1990, p. 64

69 Issa G Shivji *The Concept of Human Rights in Africa* London, Council for the Development of Social Science Research in Africa (CODESRIA), 1989

70 Giles Mohan and Jeremy Holland 'Human Rights and Development in Africa: Moral Intrusion or Empowering Opportunity?' *Review of African Political Economy* Vol. 28, No. 88, June 2001, p. 178

71 Arjun Appadurai 'Deep Democracy: Urban Governmentality and the Horizon of Politics' *Public Culture* Vol. 14, No. 1, 2002, p. 25

72 Shivji *The Concept of Human Rights* p. 71

73 David R Penna and Patricia J Campbell 'Human Rights and Culture: Beyond Universality and Relativism' *Third World Quarterly* Vol. 19, No. 1, 1988, p. 22

74 The distinction is that of Marshall in *Citizenship and Social Class*

75 Mamdani *Citizen and Subject*

76   D Fred Ellenberger *History of the Basuto Ancient and Modern* New York, Negro Universities Press, 1969, p. 298, cited in Penna and Campbell 'Human Rights and Culture' p. 10

77   Penna and Campbell 'Human Rights and Culture' p. 10

78   Penna and Campbell 'Human Rights and Culture' p. 8

79   Ake 'The Unique Case' pp. 242–243

80   Bonny Ibhawoh 'Human Rights and National Liberation: The Anticolonial Politics of Nnamdi Azikiwe' in Baba G Jallow (Ed.) *Leadership in Colonial Africa: Disruption of Traditional Frameworks and Patterns* New York, Palgrave Macmillan, 2014, pp. 55–68

81   See, for example, Gail Gerhart and Thomas Karis (Eds) *From Protest to Challenge: A Documentary History of African Politics in South Africa: 1882–1990* Pretoria, Unisa Press, 1997

82   Deborah J Yashar 'Contesting Citizenship: Indigenous Movements and Democracy in Latin America' *Comparative Politics* Vol. 31, No. 1, October 1998, p. 23

83   Yashar 'Contesting Citizenship' p. 31

84   Kwasi Wiredu 'Democracy and Consensus in African Traditional Politics: A Plea for a Non-party Polity' in Emmanuel Chukwudi Eze (Ed.) *Postcolonial African Philosophy: A Critical Reader* Oxford, Blackwell, 1997, pp. 303–304

85   Edward Wamala 'Government by Consensus: An Analysis of a Traditional Form of Democracy' in Kwasi Wiredu (Ed.) *A Companion to African Philosophy* Malden, Blackwell, 2004, p. 437

86   Wiredu 'Democracy and Consensus' p. 310

87   Wiredu 'Democracy and Consensus' p. 307

88   Wiredu 'Democracy and Consensus' p. 308

89   Kwasi Wiredu 'Democracy by Consensus: Some Conceptual Considerations' *Philosophical Papers* Vol. 30, No. 3, 2001, p. 239

90   Wiredu 'Democracy by Consensus' p. 237

91   Emmanuel Chukwudi Eze 'Democracy or Consensus: A Response to Wiredu' in Eze (Ed.) *Postcolonial African Philosophy* pp. 313–323

92   Paulin Hountondji *The Struggle for Meaning: Reflections on Philosophy, Culture, and Democracy in Africa* Athens, Ohio, University Center for International Studies, 2002. See also Paulin Hountondji 'Knowledge of Africa, Knowledge by Africans: Two Perspectives on African Studies' *RCCS Annual Review*, No. 1, September 2009, p. 6

93   Wiredu 'Democracy and Consensus' p. 309

94   Emmanuel Ifeanyi Ani 'Africa and the Prospects of Deliberative Democracy' *South African Journal of Philosophy* Vol. 32, No. 3, 2013, p. 208

95   Ademola Kazeem Fayemi 'A Critique of Consensual Democracy and Human Rights in Kwasi Wiredu's Philosophy' *Lumina* Vol. 21, No. 1, March 2010, pp. 7–8

96   See, for example, Steve Biko *I Write What I Like* Oxford, Heinemann, 1987

97   Lani Guinier *The Tyranny of the Majority: Fundamental Fairness in Representative Democracy* New York, Free Press, 1994; Jane Mansbridge 'Should Blacks Represent Blacks, and Women Represent Women? A Contingent "Yes"' *Journal of Politics* Vol. 61, No. 3, 1999, pp. 628–657

98   Aubrey Matshiqi 'Why Manuel is Right and Wrong about Manyi's "Racism"' *Business Day* 8 March 2011

99   This analysis paraphrases the argument developed in Steven Friedman 'Who We Are: Voter Participation, Rationality and the 1999 Election' *Politikon* Vol. 26, No. 2, November 1999, pp. 213–224

100 See analysis in, for example, http://www.nytimes.com/pages/politics/index.html (accessed on 1 August 2018) or http://edition.cnn.com/POLITICS/ (accessed on 1 August 2018)

101 Monga *The Anthropology of Anger* p. 32

102 Alberto Melucci *Challenging Codes: Collective Action in the Information Age* Cambridge, Cambridge University Press, 1996; Alain Touraine *Return of the Actor: Social Theory in Postindustrial Society* Minneapolis, University of Minnesota Press, 1988

103 Melucci *Challenging Codes* p. 73

104 Varshney *Battles Half Won* p. 264

105 Giovanni Capoccia and Daniel Ziblatt 'The Historical Turn in Democratization Studies: A New Agenda for Europe and Beyond' *Comparative Political Studies* Vol. 43, No. 8–9, 2010, pp. 931–968

106 Yashar 'Contesting Citizenship' p. 31

107 Deborah Bräutigam 'Institutions, Economic Reform, and Democratic Consolidation in Mauritius' *Comparative Politics* Vol. 30, No. 1, October 1997, pp. 45–62

108 Ake 'The Unique Case' p. 244

109 Penna and Campbell 'Human Rights and Culture' p. 22

110 Penna and Campbell 'Human Rights and Culture' p. 22

111 Youngs *The Puzzle of Non-Western Democracy*

CHAPTER 5

1   Nic Cheeseman *Democracy in Africa: Successes, Failures, and the Struggle for Political Reform* New York, Cambridge University Press, 2015

2   Ken Ochieng' Opalo 'Foresight Africa Viewpoint: Democracy in Africa in 2017' Brookings Blog 10 January 2017 https://www.brookings.edu/blog/africa-in-focus/2017/01/10/foresight-africa-viewpoint-democracy-in-africa-in-2017/ (accessed on 1 August 2018)

3   The French school of African studies is particularly prone to this approach. See, for example, Patrick Chabal and Jean-Pascal Daloz *Africa Works: Disorder as Political Instrument* Bloomington, Indiana University Press, 1999; Jean-Francois Bayart *The State in Africa: The Politics of the Belly* London, Longman, 1993

4   Sam Adeyemi 'Africa Doesn't Need Charity, It Needs Good Leadership' *World Economic Forum* 4 May 2017 https://www.weforum.org/agenda/2017/05/africa-doesn-t-need-charity-it-needs-good-leadership (accessed on 1 August 2018)

5   Robert Rotberg 'Good Leadership is Africa's Missing Ingredient' *Globe and Mail* 4 March 2013

6   Salim Ahmed Salim 'Why We Haven't Given Africa's Most Prestigious Leadership Award this Year' *Quartz Africa* 23 June 2016 https://qz.com/714618/why-we-havent-given-africas-most-prestigious-leadership-award-for-two-years/ (accessed on 1 August 2018)

7   United Nations Economic Commission for Africa *AIDS: Africa's Greatest Leadership Challenge – Roles and Approaches for an Effective Response* nd https://www.uneca.org/adf2/pages/aids-africas-greatest-leadership-challenge-roles-and-approaches-effective-response (accessed on 1 August 2018)

8   E Gyimah-Boadi 'Africa's Waning Democratic Commitment' *Journal of Democracy* Vol. 26, No. 1, January 2015, pp. 101–113

9   Joseph 'Growth, Security and Democracy' p. 73

10 Afrobarometer *Merged Round 5 Data (34 Countries) (2011–2013) (Last Update: July 2015)* 2015 http://afrobarometer.org/data/merged-round-5-data-34-countries-2011-2013-last -update-july-2015 (accessed on 1 August 2018)

11 Afrobarometer *Round 5*

12 Eric Little and Caroline Logan *The Quality of Democracy and Governance in Africa: New Results from Afrobarometer Round 4*: *A Compendium of Public Opinion Findings from 19 African Countries* Afrobarometer Working Paper No. 108, 2008, p. 9

13 For further discussion of African citizens' attitudes, see Renske Doorenspleet 'Critical Citizens, Democratic Support and Satisfaction in African Democracies' *International Political Science Review* Vol. 33, No. 3, 2012, pp. 279–300

14 The distinction between negative and positive freedom was proposed by Isaiah Berlin 'Two Concepts of Liberty' in Isaiah Berlin *Four Essays on Liberty* London, Oxford University Press, 1969. Berlin preferred the negative variety; the approach here sees both as essential ingredients of a democratic society

15 Steven Friedman and Omano Edigheji *Eternal (and Internal) Tensions? Conceptualising Public Accountability in South African Higher Education* CHE HEIAAF Research Report No. 2, Pretoria, Council on Higher Education, December 2006

16 Friedman and Edigheji *Eternal Tensions* p. 27

17 Makubetse Sekhonyane and Antoinette Louw *Violent Justice, Vigilantism and the State's Response* ISS Monograph No. 72, Pretoria, Institute for Security Studies, 1 April 2002; Bill Dixon and Lisa-Marie Johns *Gangs, Pagad and the State: Vigilantism and Revenge Violence in the Western Cape* CSRV Violence and Transition Series, Vol. 2, Johannesburg, Centre for the Study of Violence and Reconciliation, May 2001; Anthony Minnaar *The New Vigilantism in Post-April 1994 South Africa* Johannesburg, Institute for Human Rights and Criminal Justice Studies, Technikon SA, 2001

18 Masa Kekana 'Moseneke Warns SA Courts Risk Becoming Overly Politicised' *EyeWitness News* 17 November 2016 http://ewn.co.za/2016/11/17/moseneke-warns -sa-courts-risk-becoming-overly-politicised (accessed on 1 August 2018)

19 Gyimah-Boadi 'Africa's Waning Democratic Commitment' p. 108

20 Funmi Olonisakin 'Conflict Management in Africa: The Role of the OAU and Sub-regional Organisations' in Jakkie Cilliers and Annika Hilding-Norberg (Eds) *Building Stability in Africa: Challenges for the New Millennium* ISS Monograph No. 46, Pretoria, Institute for Security Studies, February 2000

21 'Constitutive Act of the African Union' Article 4h

22 New Partnership for Africa's Development *Declaration on Democracy, Political, Economic and Corporate Governance* 2003, Section 7

23 African Union '38th Ordinary Session of the Assembly of Heads of State and Government of the AU' *African Peer Review Mechanism* Durban, 8 July 2002

24 For example: 'On the political situation, the Summit expressed satisfaction that the SADC region generally continues to enjoy political stability and to deepen the culture of democracy, good governance and respect for human rights. This is reflected, among others, in the holding of general elections…'. South African Development Community 'Communiqué: Namibia – Windhoek 6–7 August 2000' in *SADC Head of State and Government Summit Communiques 1980–2006* nd pp. 113–119 https://www .sadc.int/files/3913/5292/8384/SADC_SUMMIT_COMMUNIQUES_1980-2006.pdf (accessed on 1 August 2018)

25 Afrobarometer *Round 5*

26 See Amnesty International *Annual Report: The State of the World's Human Rights* 2013 http://www.amnesty.org/en/annual-report/2013/africa (accessed on 1 August 2018); Human Rights Watch *Africa* nd http://www.hrw.org/africa (accessed on 1 August 2018)

27 See, for example, Amnesty International *Report* 2006 https://www.amnesty.org/en/documents/pol10/003/2006/en/ (accessed on 1 August 2018)

28 Gyimah-Boadi 'Africa's Waning Democratic Commitment'

29 Adam Clymer 'The House Bank: Trying to Halt a Scandal, Speaker Declares House Bank Case Closed but Political Reality Promises to Intrude' *New York Times* 17 April 1992

30 Republic of South Africa Protection of State Information Bill (B6B-2010)

31 Reporters without Borders 'President Refuses to Sign Draconian Bill into Law' 12 September 2013, updated on 20 January 2016 https://rsf.org/en/news/president-refuses-sign-draconian-bill-law (accessed on 1 August 2018)

32 Robinson and Friedman *Civil Society, Democratisation and Foreign Aid*

33 Centre for Policy Studies *Analytical Overview of the Political Economy of the Civil Society Sector in Southern Africa with Regard to the Poverty Reduction Agenda* Johannesburg, Centre for Policy Studies, 2002

34 Centre for Policy Studies *Analytical Overview* p. 39

35 Centre for Policy Studies *Analytical Overview* p. 15

36 Göran Hydén *No Shortcuts to Progress: African Development Management in Perspective* London, Heinemann, 1983, p. 7

37 John Hall *Power and Liberties: The Causes and Consequences of the Rise of the West* London, Penguin Books, 1998, cited in Staffan I Lindberg 'Forms of States, Governance and Regimes: Reconceptualizing the Prospects for Democratic Consolidation in Africa' *International Political Science Review* Vol. 22, No. 2, 2000, p. 182

38 Thandika Mkandawire and Charles Soludo *Our Continent, Our Future* Council for the Development of Social Science Research in Africa, Africa World Press, Asmara and IDRC, Ottawa, 1999, p. 133

39 Mary Tomlinson *Mortgage Bondage? Financial Institutions and Low-Cost Housing Delivery* Johannesburg, Centre for Policy Studies, 1997

40 Mary Tomlinson *From Rejection to Resignation: Beneficiaries' Views on the Government's Housing Subsidy Scheme* Johannesburg, Centre for Policy Studies, 1996

41 Lucie Cluver, Mark Boyes, Mark Orkin, Marija Pantelic, Thembela Molwena and Lorraine Sherr 'Child-Focused State Cash Transfers and Adolescent Risk of HIV Infection in South Africa: A Propensity-Score-Matched Case-Control Study' *The Lancet* Vol. 1, No. 6, December 2013, e362–e370,

42 See, for example, Zola Skweyiya 'Social Cluster Media Briefing by Dr Zola Skweyiya, Minister of Social Development' Union Buildings, Pretoria, 20 November 2006 http://www.info.gov.za/speeches/2006/06112015451003.htm (accessed on 1 August 2018)

43 Monde Makiwane and Eric Udjo *Is the Child Support Grant Associated with an Increase in Teenage Fertility in South Africa? Evidence from National Surveys and Administrative Data* Final Report, Pretoria, Human Sciences Research Council, December 2006

44 Victoria Graham, Yolanda Sadie and Leila Patel 'Social Grants, Food Parcels and Voting Behaviour: A Case Study of Three South African Communities' *Transformation* Vol. 91, 2016, pp. 106–135

45 Steven Friedman 'Sending Them a Message: Culture, Tax Collection and Governance in South Africa' *Policy: Issues and Actors*, Vol. 16, No. 3, 2003

46 Steven Friedman *Participatory Governance and Citizen Action in Post-apartheid South Africa* IILS Discussion Paper 164/2006, Geneva, International Institute of Labour Studies, 2006

47 Adam Branch and Zachariah Cherian Mampilly *Africa Uprising: Popular Protest and Political Change* London, Zed Books, 2015

48 Festus Owete '20 Times African Opposition Leaders Shockingly Defeated Incumbents' *Premium Times,* Abuja 10 December 2016

49 Mamdani *Citizen and Subject*

CHAPTER 6

1   Ted Robert Gurr *Why Men Rebel* Princeton, Princeton University Press, 1970

2   Sidney Tarrow 'National Politics and Collective Action: Recent Theory and Research in Western Europe and the United States' *Annual Review of Sociology* Vol. 14, August 1988, p. 425

3   Barrington Moore Jr *Injustice: The Social Bases of Obedience and Revolt* White Plains, Sharpe, 1978

4   Pippa Norris, Stefaan Walgrave and Peter van Aelst 'Who Demonstrates? Disaffected Rebels, Conventional Participants or Everyone?' Unpublished manuscript, Cambridge, Mass., Kennedy School of Government, Harvard University, 2000, p. 22

5   Steven Friedman and Maxine Reitzes *Democratic Selections? Civil Society and Development in Post-apartheid South Africa* Midrand, Development Bank of Southern Africa, 1995

6   Sidney Tarrow *Power in Movement: Social Movements and Contentious Politics* Cambridge, Cambridge University Press, 1998

7   Melucci *Challenging Codes*; Touraine *Return of the Actor.* Tarrow has distinguished between the 'resource mobilisation' school, which looks at 'individual attitudes, at the groups that organized mass protest, and at the forms of action they employed', and the 'new social movement' approach, which looked at 'larger structural and/or cultural issues'. He notes that the former was found predominantly in the US, the latter mainly in Western Europe, although the geographic fit was not exact. Tarrow 'National Politics and Collective Action' p. 423. Touraine's and Melucci's work is firmly within the social movement school

8   Doug McAdam, Sidney Tarrow and Charles Tilly *Dynamics of Contention* Cambridge, Cambridge University Press, 2001

9   Bresser Pereira, Maravall, and Przeworski *Economic Reforms* p. 4

10 Ralph Miliband *Parliamentary Socialism: A Study in the Politics of Labour* London, Merlin, 1975, pp. 6, 9, cited in Bresser Pereira, Maravall and Przeworski *Economic Reforms* p. 5

11 Sartori *The Theory of Democracy*

12 Bermeo *Ordinary People*

13 Tarrow 'National Politics and Collective Action' p. 422

14 Grzegorz Ekiert and Jan Kubik 'Contentious Politics in New Democracies: East Germany, Hungary, Poland, and Slovakia, 1989–93' *World Politics* Vol. 50, No. 4, 1998, p. 581

15 Ekiert and Kubik 'Contentious Politics' p. 579

16 Tarrow 'National Politics and Collective Action' p. 421

17   For a review of the history of this form of collective action, see Charles Tilly *Social Movements 1768–2004* Boulder and London, Paradigm Publishers, 2004

18   McAdam, Tarrow and Tilly *Dynamics of Contention* p. 5

19   Charles Tilly *Popular Contention in Great Britain 1758–1834* Cambridge, Mass., Harvard University Press, 1995, p. 41

20   David Snyder and Charles Tilly 'Hardship and Collective Violence in France, 1830 to 1960' *American Sociological Review* Vol. 37, No. 5, October 1972, p. 526

21   Norris, Walgrave and Van Aelst 'Who Demonstrates?' p. 26

22   Neil J Smelser *Theory of Collective Behavior* New York, The Free Press of Glencoe, 1963, p. 21

23   Elisabeth Jean Wood *Insurgent Collective Action and Civil War in El Salvador* Cambridge, Cambridge University Press, 2003

24   First National Bank wanted citizens to write to President Thabo Mbeki urging him to make the fight against crime his priority. It commissioned 2.8 million pamphlets with a message about crime: on each was an envelope addressed to the president with postage paid. It abandoned the campaign in the face of hostile reaction from the president and parts of organised business. *SA History Online* 'FNB Cancels Its R20m Anti-crime Initiative Designed to Encourage President Thabo Mbeki to Make Crime His Priority' 2 February 2007 http://www.sahistory.org.za/dated-event/fnb-cancels-its-r20-million -anti-crime-initiative-designed-encourage-president-thabo-mbe (accessed on 1 August 2018)

25   Cawson *Corporatism*

26   Mancur Olson *The Logic of Collective Action: Public Goods and the Theory of Groups* Cambridge, Mass., Harvard University Press, 1971

27   Yolanda Sadie 'Regerings-elite se persepsies oor die rol van belangegroepe in openbare beleids-formulering in Suid-Afrika' *Politikon* Vol. 17, No. 2, December 1990, pp. 82–98

28   Olson *The Logic of Collective Action* p. 3

29   See, for example, the discussion of local government consultation processes in Friedman *Participatory Governance*

30   Charles E Lindblom *Politics and Markets: The World's Political-Economic Systems* New York, Basic Books, 1978

31   Cawson *Corporatism*

32   The business–government engagement which Lindblom describes in *Politics and Markets* is but one example. The range of academic literature produced on lobbying and interest group influence in Northern democracies is far too extensive to be listed here

33   Lindblom *Politics and Markets*

34   Kay Lehman Schoolman 'What Accent the Heavenly Chorus? Political Equality and the American Pressure System' *Journal of Politics* Vol. 46, No. 4, November 1984, p. 1006

35   EE Schattschneider *The Semisovereign People* New York, Holt, Rinehart and Winston, 1960, p. 35

36   In Switzerland, smaller cantons elect judges; in Japan, appointed Supreme Court justices sometimes face retention elections, but these are reportedly a formality. Adam Liptak 'Rendering Justice, with One Eye on Re-election' *New York Times* 25 May 2008 http://www.nytimes.com/2008/05/25/us/25exception.html?ex=1212379200&en= 3d121eb04acf50c8&ei=5070&emc=eta1 (accessed on 1 August 2018)

37 Thomas E Patterson *The Vanishing Voter* New York, Knopf, 2002

38 International Institute for Democracy and Electoral Assistance (International IDEA) *Voter Turnout since 1945: A Global Report* Stockholm, International IDEA, 2002, pp. 117–169

39 Kristen Hubby 'How Many Americans Actually Vote?' *The Daily Dot* 19 December 2016 https://www.dailydot.com/layer8/voter-turnout-2016/ (accessed on 1 August 2018)

40 Vanessa Williamson 'Voter Suppression, Not Fraud, Looms Large in US Elections' Brookings Blog 8 November 2016 https://www.brookings.edu/blog/fixgov/2016/11/08/voter-suppression-in-u-s-elections/ (accessed on 1 August 2018)

41 Mansbridge 'Should Blacks Represent Blacks'

42 Shapiro *The State of Democratic Theory* p. 10

43 Varshney *Battles Half Won* p. 39

44 Karl Marx and Friedrich Engels *The Communist Manifesto* London, Signet, 1998

45 Frances Fox Piven and Richard Cloward *Poor People's Movements: Why They Succeed, How They Fail* New York, Vintage Books, 1979

46 Piven and Cloward *Poor People's Movements* p. xi

47 Piven and Cloward *Poor People's Movements* p. xxi

48 Piven and Cloward *Poor People's Movements* p. xxi

49 Piven and Cloward *Poor People's Movements* p. 36

50 Piven and Cloward *Poor People's Movements* p. 36

51 Przeworski *Capitalism and Social Democracy*

52 Jeremy Baskin *Striking Back: A History of Cosatu* London and New York, Verso, 1991

53 Richard L Wood *Faith in Action: Religion, Race and Democratic Organizing in America* Chicago and London, Chicago University Press, 2002

54 Wood *Faith in Action* p. 44

55 Wood *Faith in Action* p. 51

56 Andrea Cornwall *Making Spaces, Changing Places: Situating Participation in Development* IDS Working Paper No. 170, Brighton, Institute for Development Studies, University of Sussex, October 2002; Andrea Cornwall 'Locating Citizen Participation' *IDS Bulletin* Vol. 33, No. 2, 2002, pp. 49–58. For 'invented' spaces, see Faranak Miraftab 'Invited and Invented Spaces of Participation: Neoliberal Citizenship and Feminists' Expanded Notion of Politics' *Wagadu* Vol. 1, Spring 2004, pp. 1–7

57 Friedman *Participatory Governance*

58 Wood *Faith in Action* p. 90

59 Wood *Faith in Action* p. 63

60 Wood *Faith in Action* p. 46

61 Wood *Faith in Action* p. 49

62 Cyprian deVold, pastor of an African-American Catholic parish in New Orleans, quoted in Wood *Faith in Action* p. 45

63 DeVold, quoted in Wood *Faith in Action* p. 45

64 Wood *Faith in Action* p. 46

65 Priti Patnaik 'Social Audits in India – a Slow but Sure Way to Fight Corruption' *The Guardian* 13 January 2012

66 This account is drawn from Vivek Ramkumar and Sowmya Kidamb *Social Audits as a Budget Monitoring Tool* Washington DC, International Budget Partnership, October 2012, pp. 4–5

67 Social Justice Coalition 'Social Audits' nd http://www.sjc.org.za/social_audits (accessed on 1 August 2018)

68 Sandra Liebenberg 'Social Audits and the Right to Sanitation' *GroundUp* 22 October 2014 https://www.groundup.org.za/article/social-audits-and-right-sanitation_2372/ (accessed on 1 August 2018); Ernest Sonnenberg 'Liebenberg's Argument is a Straw Man' *GroundUp* 23 October 2014 https://www.groundup.org.za/article/liebenbergs-argument-straw-man_2377/ (accessed on 1 August 2018)

69 Chatterjee *The Politics of the Governed* pp. 38–39

70 Chatterjee *The Politics of the Governed* p. 38

71 Chatterjee *The Politics of the Governed* p. 40

72 United Nations Habitat *Slum Almanac 2015–2016* Nairobi, United Nations Habitat, 2016

73 Stuart Wilson 'Litigating Housing Rights in Johannesburg's Inner City: 2004–2008' *South African Journal of Human Rights* Vol. 27, No. 1, 2011, pp. 127–151

74 Mamdani *Citizen and Subject*

75 Hernando de Soto *The Other Path: The Invisible Revolution in the Third World* New York, Harper and Row, 1989

76 See, for example, School of Public and Development Management, University of the Witwatersrand *Are Hernando de Soto's Views Appropriate to South Africa?* P&DM Occasional Paper Series No. 1, Johannesburg, School of Public and Development Management, University of the Witwatersrand, 2006

77 For descriptions of some of this interaction, see Chatterjee *The Politics of the Governed* pp. 54–78

78 Chatterjee *The Politics of the Governed* p. 56

79 Chatterjee *The Politics of the Governed* p. 60

80 Peter M Haas 'Introduction: Epistemic Communities and International Policy Coordination' *International Organization* Vol. 46, No. 1, Knowledge, Power, and International Policy Coordination, Winter 1992, p. 1

81 For discussion of the relationship between corporatism and concrete governance problems in the North, see Cawson *Corporatism*

82 Chatterjee *The Politics of the Governed* p. 49

83 Chatterjee *The Politics of the Governed* p. 47

84 Chatterjee *The Politics of the Governed* p. 41

85 Chatterjee *The Politics of the Governed* p. 41

86 Lipset 'The Social Requisites Revisited' p. 13

87 Gaventa and McGee *Citizen Action*

88 Piven and Cloward *Poor People's Movements* pp. 213ff

89 Neera Chandhoke 'Revisiting the Crisis of Representation Thesis: The Indian Context' *Democratization* Vol. 12, No. 3, June 2005, p. 309

90 Karl von Holdt, Malose Langa, Sepetla Molapo, Nomfundo Mogapi, Kindi Ngubeni, Jacob Dlamini and Adele Kirsten *The Smoke that Calls: Insurgent Citizenship, Collective Violence and the Search for a Place in the New South Africa* Johannesburg, Centre for the Study of Violence and Reconciliation, Society, Work and Development Institute, 2011

91 Friedman 'Archipelagos of Dominance'

92 Chandhoke 'Revisiting the Crisis' p. 322

93 Chandhoke 'Revisiting the Crisis' p. 324

94 Chandhoke 'Revisiting the Crisis' p. 326

95 Zeynep Tufekci and Christopher Wilson 'Social Media and the Decision to Participate in Political Protest' *Journal of Communication* Vol. 62, No. 6, 2012, pp. 363–379

96   Brian D Loader and Dan Mercea 'Networking Democracy? Social Media Innovations in Participatory Politics' *Information, Communication and Society* Vol. 14, No. 6, 2011, p. 757

97   The literature on social media and democracy is far too voluminous to cite here. Loader and Mercea 'Networking Democracy' offer a useful summary of the debate

98   Mehran Kamrava (Ed.) *Beyond the Arab Spring: The Evolving Ruling Bargain in the Middle East* Oxford and New York, Oxford University Press, 2014

99   Imraan Buccus 'Social Media Shift Power Balance' *Sunday Independent* 17 May 2015

100 Business Tech 'How Many People Use Facebook, Twitter and Instagram in South Africa' 18 September 2017 https://businesstech.co.za/news/internet/199318/how-many-people -use-facebook-twitter-and-instagram-in-south-africa/ (accessed on 1 August 2018)

101 Buccus 'Social Media'

102 Republic of South Africa Preventing and Combating of Hate Crimes and Hate Speech Bill (B9-2018)

103 See also World Bank *The State in a Changing World*

104 For an elaboration of this argument using evidence gathered from South African urban negotiation processes, see Steven Friedman *The Elusive 'Community': The Dynamics of Negotiated Urban Development* Johannesburg, Centre for Policy Studies, 1993

105 The World Bank's understanding of civil society includes 'community-based organizations, NGOs, indigenous people's organizations, labor unions, faith-based groups, and foundations'. World Bank *The World Bank and Civil Society Engagement* nd http://web.worldbank.org/WBSITE/EXTERNAL/TOPICS/CSO/0,,contentMDK:20 092185~menuPK:220422~pagePK:220503~piPK:220476~theSitePK:228717,00.html (accessed on 1 August 2018)

106 Chatterjee *The Politics of the Governed*

107 Jane Mansbridge *Beyond Adversary Democracy* Chicago and London, University of Chicago Press, 1983

108 Mamdani *Citizen and Subject*

CHAPTER 7

1   Olson *Logic of Collective Action*

2   Pamela E Oliver and Gerald Markwell 'The Paradox of Group Size in Collective Action: A Theory of the Critical Mass' *American Sociological Review* Vol. 53, No. 1, February 1988, pp. 1–8.

3   Pamela E Oliver 'Formal Models of Collective Action' *Annual Review of Sociology* Vol. 19, 1993, p. 274

4   Wood *Insurgent Collective Action*

5   Olson *Logic of Collective Action* p. 78

6   Olson *Logic of Collective Action* pp. 7ff

7   Robert Dahl *Who Governs? Democracy and Power in an American City* New Haven, Yale University Press, 1961, p. 93

8   Dahl *Who Governs?* p. 114

9   AJ Polan *Lenin and the End of Politics* Methuen, London, 1984

10   Tarrow 'National Politics and Collective Action' p. 423; see also Keane *Democracy and Civil Society*

11   Tarrow 'National Politics and Collective Action' p. 426

12   John D McCarthy and Mayer N Zald 'Resource Mobilization and Social Movements: A Partial Theory' *American Journal of Sociology* Vol. 82, No. 6, May 1977, p. 1215

13   John Gaventa *Power and Powerlessness: Quiescence and Rebellion in an Appalachian Valley* Urbana and Chicago, University of Illinois Press, 1982, p. 8

14   Shapiro *The State of Democratic Theory* p. 4

15   McCarthy and Zald 'Resource Mobilization' p. 1213

16   McCarthy and Zald 'Resource Mobilization' p. 1216

17   McCarthy and Zald 'Resource Mobilization' p. 1225

18   Tarrow *Power in Movement* p. 77 (Emphasis in original)

19   Tarrow *Power in Movement* p. 20

20   Tarrow *Power in Movement* p. 72

21   Tarrow *Power in Movement* p. 71

22   Tarrow *Power in Movement* pp. 73ff

23   Gaventa *Power and Powerlessness*

24   Gaventa *Power and Powerlessness* p. 38

25   Steven Lukes *Power: A Radical View* London, Macmillan, 1974, p. 23, cited in Gaventa *Power and Powerlessness* p. 12

26   Gaventa *Power and Powerlessness* p. 15

27   Peter Bachrach and Morton S Baratz *Power and Poverty: Theory and Practice* New York, Oxford University Press, 1970, p. 43, cited in Gaventa *Power and Powerlessness* p. 14

28   Gaventa *Power and Powerlessness* p. 115

29   Gaventa *Power and Powerlessness* pp. 15–16

30   Gaventa *Power and Powerlessness* p. 20

31   Gaventa *Power and Powerlessness* p. 94

32   Gaventa *Power and Powerlessness* pp. 106ff

33   Greg Philo 'An Unseen World: How the Media Portrays the Poor' *UNESCO Courier* November 2001 https://www.questia.com/magazine/1G1-80865237/an-unseen-world-how-the-media-portrays-the-poor (accessed on 1 August 2018)

34   Gaventa *Power and Powerlessness* p. 104

35   Karl and Schmitter 'What Democracy Is'

36   Tarrow 'National Politics and Collective Action' p. 422

37   Malaika wa Azania 'Why the Poor Vote for the ANC and Will Do So for a Long Time' Thought Leader *Mail and Guardian* 9 August 2013 http://thoughtleader.co.za/malaikawaazania/2013/09/09/why-the-poor-vote-for-the-anc-and-will-do-so-for-a-long-time/ (accessed on 1 August 2018)

38   Harry Blair 'Jump-starting Democracy: Adult Civic Education and Democratic Participation in Three Countries' *Democratization* Vol. 10, No. 1, Spring 2003, pp. 53–54. The author proudly proclaims that these virtues 'have been a fundamental part of the systemic fabric for so long in the West', but also acknowledges declining electoral participation in the US. Clearly, being part of a superior cultural milieu has not disposed Americans to show a greater sense of political efficacy than citizens of many less richly blessed societies

39   Friedman 'Who We Are'; Steven Friedman and Louise Stack 'The Magic Moment' in Steven Friedman and Doreen Atkinson (Eds) *The Small Miracle: South Africa's Negotiated Settlement* Johannesburg, Ravan, 1995, pp. 301–325

40   Gaventa *Power and Powerlessness* pp. 29–30

41   Gaventa *Power and Powerlessness* p. 11

42   Gaventa *Power and Powerlessness* p. 193

43 Michael K Honey *Going Down Jericho Road: The Memphis Strike, Martin Luther King's Last Campaign* New York and London, WW Norton, 2007
44 Gaventa *Power and Powerlessness* p. 92
45 Gaventa *Power and Powerlessness* p. 145
46 Gaventa *Power and Powerlessness* p. 206
47 Gaventa *Power and Powerlessness* p. 211
48 For an argument that the violation of long-held understandings of the limits of power prompted peasant revolts in Burma and Vietnam, see James C Scott *The Moral Economy of the Peasant: Subsistence and Rebellion in Southeast Asia* New Haven, Yale University Press, 1976
49 James C Scott *Weapons of the Weak: Everyday Forms of Peasant Resistance* New Haven, Yale University Press, 1985
50 Scott *Weapons of the Weak* pp. 40–41
51 James C Scott *Domination and the Arts of Resistance: Hidden Transcripts* New Haven, Yale University Press, 1992
52 Scott *Weapons of the Weak* p. 287
53 Scott *Weapons of the Weak* p. 317
54 Scott *Weapons of the Weak* p. 40
55 Scott *Weapons of the Weak* pp. 322, 331
56 Scott *Weapons of the Weak* p. xvi
57 Scott *Weapons of the Weak* p. 265
58 Scott *Weapons of the Weak* p. 34
59 Scott *Weapons of the Weak* p. 31
60 Moore *Injustice* p. 125
61 Piven and Cloward *Poor People's Movements* pp. 4, 5
62 Scott *Weapons of the Weak* p. 297
63 Scott *Weapons of the Weak* pp. 242ff
64 Scott *Weapons of the Weak* p. xv
65 Göran Hydén *Beyond Ujamaa in Tanzania* London, Heinemann, 1980, p. 231
66 Scott *Weapons of the Weak* pp. 242ff. This is also consistent with the argument in Scott's *Moral Economy*
67 Biko *I Write What I Like*
68 Lester M Salomon and Stephen van Evera 'Fear, Apathy and Discrimination: A Test of Three Explanations of Political Participation' *American Political Science Review* Vol. 67, No. 4, December 1973, p. 1288
69 Salomon and van Evera 'Fear, Apathy and Discrimination' p. 1294
70 Salomon and van Evera 'Fear, Apathy and Discrimination' p. 1296
71 Salomon and van Evera 'Fear, Apathy and Discrimination' p. 1289
72 Salomon and van Evera 'Fear, Apathy and Discrimination' p. 1298
73 Mansbridge *Beyond Adversary Democracy*
74 Mansbridge *Beyond Adversary Democracy* p. 59
75 Mansbridge *Beyond Adversary Democracy* p. 65
76 Mansbridge *Beyond Adversary Democracy* p. 87
77 Mansbridge *Beyond Adversary Democracy* p. 61
78 Mansbridge *Beyond Adversary Democracy* pp. 70, 71
79 Mansbridge *Beyond Adversary Democracy* p. 75
80 Mansbridge *Beyond Adversary Democracy* p. 87
81 Mansbridge *Beyond Adversary Democracy* p. 125

82 Monga *The Anthropology of Anger* p. 116
83 Monga *The Anthropology of Anger* pp. 110–111
84 Monga *The Anthropology of Anger* p. 7
85 Monga *The Anthropology of Anger* p. 11
86 Achille Mbembe 'Provisional Notes on the Postcolony' *Africa* Vol. 62, No. 1, 1992, pp. 3–37
87 Mbembe 'The Postcolony' p. 4
88 Mbembe 'The Postcolony' p. 29
89 Mbembe 'The Postcolony' p. 5
90 Mbembe 'The Postcolony' pp. 9, 10
91 Comi Toulabar *Togo sous Eyadema* Paris, Karthala, 1986, cited in Mbembe 'The Postcolony' p. 5
92 Mbembe 'The Postcolony' p. 5
93 See, for example, Mikhail Bakhtin *Rabelais and His World* (Translated by Helene Sinofsky) Bloomington, Indiana University Press, 1984, pp. 303ff
94 Mbembe 'The Postcolony' pp. 5–6
95 Martin Moore and Gordon Ramsay *UK Media Coverage of the 2016 EU Referendum Campaign* London, Centre for the Study of Media, Communication and Power, King's College, 2017
96 Aditya Chakrabortty 'Immigration Has Been Good for Britain. It is Time to Bust the Myths' *The Guardian* 17 May 2018
97 This distinction is proposed in my analysis of the shifting opportunities which opened for collective action against apartheid. Steven Friedman *Understanding Reform* Johannesburg, South African Institute of Race Relations, 1986
98 Tarrow *Power in Movement* p. 75
99 Tarrow *Power in Movement* p. 79
100 Tarrow *Power in Movement* p. 77
101 Piven and Cloward *Poor People's Movements* p. 208
102 Steven Friedman *Building Tomorrow Today: African Workers in Trade Unions 1970–1984*, Johannesburg, Ravan Press, 1985
103 Tarrow *Power in Movement* pp. 72–73
104 Piven and Cloward *Poor People's Movements* pp. 203ff
105 Tarrow *Power in Movement* p. 74
106 Andrea Cornwall and Vera Schutte Coelho (Eds) *Spaces for Change? The Politics of Citizen Participation in New Democratic Arenas* London, Zed Books, 2007

CHAPTER 8

1 This chapter draws on information reported on and analysed in Steven Friedman and Shauna Mottiar 'A Rewarding Engagement? The Treatment Action Campaign and the Politics of HIV/AIDS' *Politics and Society* Vol. 33, No. 4, 2005, pp. 511–565, and Steven Friedman 'Gaining Comprehensive AIDS Treatment'. Interviews on which many of the claims in this chapter are made are cited there
2 Treatment Action Campaign 'An Explanation of the Medicines Act and the Implications of the Court Victory' TAC Statement on the Court Case, 24 April 2001
3 Treatment Action Campaign 'TAC Welcomes Cabinet Statement Committing to Antiretroviral Treatment Rollout' *TAC News Service* (moderator@tac.org.za) 8 August 2003

4   Treatment Action Campaign 'TAC Responds to American Friends Service Committee Nobel Peace Prize Nomination' TAC *News Service* (moderator@tac.org.za) 2 December 2003

5   Treatment Action Campaign 'TAC Welcomes Cabinet Statement'

6   UNAIDS 'South Africa' nd http://www.unaids.org/en/regionscountries/countries/south africa (accessed on 1 August 2018)

7   Treatment Action Campaign 'About TAC' nd www.tac.org.za (accessed on 1 August 2018)

8   Interview, Mark Heywood, cited in Friedman and Mottiar 'A Rewarding Engagement?'

9   Treatment Action Campaign *TAC Political Report 2003/05* Prepared for the Third TAC National Congress, Cape Town, 23–25 September 2005

10   Interview, Nathan Geffen, cited in Friedman and Mottiar 'A Rewarding Engagement?'

11   Interview, Sipho Mthathi, cited in Friedman and Mottiar 'A Rewarding Engagement?'

12   Interviews, Ashwin Desai, Dale McKinley, cited in Friedman and Mottiar 'A Rewarding Engagement?'

13   Interview, Achmat, cited in Friedman and Mottiar 'A Rewarding Engagement?'

14   See discussion of the experience of Gordon Mthembu in Friedman 'Extraordinary "Ordinary"' pp. 51ff

15   Interview, Achmat, cited in Friedman and Mottiar 'A Rewarding Engagement?'

16   Department of Health *National HIV and Syphilis Sero-prevalence Survey of Women Attending Public Antenatal Clinics in South Africa – 2001, Summary Report* Nelson Mandela/HSRC Study of HIV/AIDS, South African National HIV Prevalence, Behavioural Risks and Mass Media Household Survey, 2002

17   Interviews, Thembeka Majali, Zakhele Xaba, Sfiso Nkala, Kathleen Pithouse, Xolani Kunene, cited in Friedman and Mottiar 'A Rewarding Engagement?'

18   Interview, Xaba, cited in Friedman and Mottiar 'A Rewarding Engagement?'

19   Robinson and Friedman *Civil Society, Democratisation and Foreign Aid*

20   Interview, Heywood, cited in Friedman and Mottiar 'A Rewarding Engagement?'

21   Craig Charney *Voices of a New Democracy: African Expectations in the New South Africa* Johannesburg, Centre for Policy Studies, 1995

22   Mandisa Mbali 'Mbeki's Denialism and the Ghosts of Apartheid and Colonialism for Post-apartheid AIDS Policy-Making' Paper presented at a workshop at the School of Development Studies, Durban, University of KwaZulu-Natal, 15 April 2002 http://ccs.ukzn.ac.za/files/mbeki.pdf (accessed on 1 August 2018)

23   'Manto's Garlic Won't Stop AIDS' *Mail and Guardian* 10 November 2003 https://mg.co.za/article/2003-11-10-mantos-garlic-wont-stop-aids (accessed on 1 August 2018)

24   'Mbeki "Glossed over Issues"' *News24* 14 February 2003 https://www.news24.com/SouthAfrica/News/Mbeki-glossed-over-issues-20030214 (accessed on 1 August 2018)

25   Interview, Heywood, cited in Friedman and Mottiar 'A Rewarding Engagement?'

26   See, for example, Treatment Action Campaign 'GlaxoSmithKline Grants License to Cipla in Accordance with Competition Commission Settlement' *TAC Electronic Newsletter* 14 December 2004

27   'Furious activists chanted and booed at the Minister of Health, Dr Manto Tshabalala-Msimang, this week after she became involved in a slanging match with delegates to the country's foremost HIV /AIDS gathering.' Ranjeni Munusamy 'Delegates Boo Minister' *Sunday Times* 12 March 2000

28   Constitutional Court *Minister of Health and Others v Treatment Action Campaign and Others* 2002 Constitutional Court – CCT8/02 2002 (5) SA 721 (CC); 2002 (10) BCLR 1033 (CC) http://www.saflii.org/za/cases/ZACC/2002/15.html (accessed on 1 August 2018)

29   Treatment Action Campaign 'TAC Welcomes Cabinet Statement'

30   Interview, Nozizwe Madlala-Routledge, cited in Friedman 'Extraordinary "Ordinary"'

31   Friedman and Mottiar 'A Rewarding Engagement?' pp. 534ff

32   Interview, Geffen, cited in Friedman and Mottiar 'A Rewarding Engagement?'

33   Interview, Desai, cited in Friedman and Mottiar 'A Rewarding Engagement?'

34   Interviews Mthathi, Heywood, cited in Friedman and Mottiar 'A Rewarding Engage-
      ment?'

35   Interview, Achmat, cited in Friedman and Mottiar 'A Rewarding Engagement?'. For a
      critique of failure to grasp this point, see Kerry Chance and Mandisa Mbali 'Chance/
      Mbali on Limits to Invoking "False Consciousness"' 2 July 2004 CCS-l@lists.nu.ac.za

36   Interview, Achmat, cited in Friedman and Mottiar 'A Rewarding Engagement?'

37   Interview, Achmat, cited in Friedman and Mottiar 'A Rewarding Engagement?'

38   Interview, Achmat, cited in Friedman and Mottiar 'A Rewarding Engagement?'

39   Interview, Desai, cited in Friedman and Mottiar 'A Rewarding Engagement?'

40   Several TAC members have been murdered by people enraged at their HIV-
      positive status. TAC campaigned for the successful prosecution of their attackers:
      in December 2005, the killers of TAC member Lorna Mlofana were convicted. See
      Treatment Action Campaign '21 December 2005 – Another TAC Member Raped
      and Murdered in Khayelitsha. Demonstration against Violence against Women on
      Friday 23 December' TAC Newsletter 21 December 2005; 'Lorna Mlofana's Accused
      are Found Guilty' TAC Newsletter 8 December 2005

41   Interview, Achmat, cited in Friedman and Mottiar 'A Rewarding Engagement?'

42   Interview, Geffen, cited in Friedman and Mottiar 'A Rewarding Engagement?'

43   Personal communication, Geffen, cited in Friedman and Mottiar 'A Rewarding
      Engagement?'

44   Interview, Achmat, cited in Friedman and Mottiar 'A Rewarding Engagement?'

45   Friedman 'Equity in the Age of Informality'

46   Interview, Kevin McKenna, cited in Friedman and Mottiar 'A Rewarding Engagement?'

47   Interview, Njogu Morgan, cited in Friedman and Mottiar 'A Rewarding Engagement?'

48   Interview, Achmat, Geffen, cited in Friedman and Mottiar 'A Rewarding Engagement?'

49   Interview, government official, cited in Friedman and Mottiar 'A Rewarding Engagement?'

50   Interview, Nonkosi Khumalo, cited in Friedman and Mottiar 'A Rewarding Engagement?'

51   Interviews, TAC activists, cited in Friedman and Mottiar 'A Rewarding Engagement?'

52   Renée Bonorchis 'Achmat's Year-Long Walk to Triumph' Business Day 8 December
      2006

53   Interview, Achmat, cited in Friedman and Mottiar 'A Rewarding Engagement?'

54   Interview, Khumalo, cited in Friedman and Mottiar 'A Rewarding Engagement?'

55   Interview, Madlala-Routledge, cited in Friedman Extraordinary "Ordinary"

56   Interview, Achmat, cited in Friedman and Mottiar 'A Rewarding Engagement?'

57   Kerry Cullinan 'Africa: Deputies Bring New Energy to HIV/AIDS' Health-E News
      Service 6 November 2006 https://www.health-e.org.za/2006/11/06/deputies-bring-
      new-energy-to-hivaids/ (accessed on 1 August 2018)

58   Cullinan 'Africa: Deputies Bring New Energy'

59   Moses Mdewu Mackay 'Cosatu Keeps an Eye on AIDS Plan' Daily News 6 March 2007

60   Steven Friedman 'Spring of Hope, Winter of Worry for South African Democracy'
      Business Day 6 August 2006

61   Linda Daniels 'Zuma Takes New Stance on AIDS' Pretoria News 19 September 2006.
      Zuma's stance was particularly noteworthy since, early in the year, he had attracted

negative comment for testifying at his trial on rape charges that he had unprotected sex with an HIV-positive woman

62 Interview, Heywood, cited in Friedman and Mottiar 'A Rewarding Engagement?'
63 Interview, Heywood, cited in Friedman and Mottiar 'A Rewarding Engagement?'
64 Interview, government official, cited in Friedman and Mottiar 'A Rewarding Engagement?'
65 Interview, Geffen, cited in Friedman and Mottiar 'A Rewarding Engagement?'
66 Interviews, Mthathi, Heywood, cited in Friedman and Mottiar 'A Rewarding Engagement?'
67 Interview, Heywood, cited in Friedman and Mottiar 'A Rewarding Engagement?'
68 Interview, Heywood, cited in Friedman and Mottiar 'A Rewarding Engagement?'
69 Interview, Achmat, cited in Friedman and Mottiar 'A Rewarding Engagement?'
70 Interview, Achmat, cited in Friedman and Mottiar 'A Rewarding Engagement?'
71 Interview, Western Cape health official, cited in Friedman and Mottiar 'A Rewarding Engagement?'
72 The province referred to here is Gauteng. Interview, Heywood, cited in Friedman and Mottiar 'A Rewarding Engagement?'
73 'The system does stress the role of the committees and we can gain from using them.' Interview, Heywood, cited in Friedman and Mottiar 'A Rewarding Engagement?'
74 Interview, Heywood, cited in Friedman and Mottiar 'A Rewarding Engagement?'
75 Interview, Heywood, cited in Friedman and Mottiar 'A Rewarding Engagement?'
76 Interview, Geffen, cited in Friedman and Mottiar 'A Rewarding Engagement?'
77 For a discussion of this literature, see Friedman and Mottiar 'A Rewarding Engagement?'

CHAPTER 9

1 O'Donnell and Schmitter *Transitions from Authoritarian Rule* p. 12
2 Friedman 'Archipelagos of Dominance'
3 Steven Friedman 'The Janus Face of the Past: Preserving and Resisting South African Path Dependence' in Xolela Mangcu (Ed.) *The Colour of Our Future: Does Race Matter in Post-apartheid South Africa?* Johannesburg, Wits University Press, 2015, pp. 45–63
4 Cornwall *Making Spaces* p. 1
5 Cornwall *Making Spaces* p. 4
6 Cornwall *Making Spaces* p. 4. See also Anne-Marie Goetz and John Gaventa *Bringing Citizen Voice and Client Focus into Service Delivery* IDS Working Paper No. 138, Brighton, Institute for Development Studies, University of Sussex, 2001
7 Cornwall *Making Spaces* p. 15
8 Cornwall *Making Spaces* p. 16
9 Avritzer *Democracy and the Public Space* p. 52
10 Avritzer *Democracy and the Public Space* pp. 138ff
11 Cornwall *Making Spaces* p. 20
12 For details of low participation, see Anna Clark 'Is Participatory Budgeting Real Democracy? Politics, People's Choice Style in Chicago' *Next City* nd https://nextcity.org/features/view/is-participatory-budgeting-real-democracy-chicago (accessed on 1 August 2018)
13 The experience of participating in trade unions is, therefore, often an important democratic training ground in which participants learn both of their own power to

act as citizens, and of the constraints which this inevitably entails. For an account of this process in the apartheid period, see Steven Friedman *Building Tomorrow Today*

14 For example, case studies in Gaventa and McGee *Citizen Action*

15 See discussion in Friedman 'Beyond the Fringe?'

16 Paul Thulare 'Trading Democracy? Johannesburg Informal Traders and Citizenship' *Policy: Issues and Actors* Vol. 17, No. 1, February 2004

17 Centre for Policy Studies *Analytical Overview*

18 Monty Narsoo 'Civil Society: A Contested Terrain' *Work in Progress* No. 76, 1991, pp. 24–27

19 Youth clubs in South Africa interviewed in the 1990s were aware of a National Youth Development Forum but added that it 'is not meant for people like us'. Gardner Khumalo, Sivuyile Bam and Owen Crankshaw 'Youth Dynamics in Gauteng' Unpublished commissioned study for Gauteng legislature petitions and public participation committee, Johannesburg, Centre for Policy Studies, 1996

20 Centre for Policy Studies *Analytical Overview*

21 Jeremy Cronin *The People Shall Govern – Class Struggles and the Post-1994 State in South Africa. Part 1 – the Freedom Charter and the Post-1994 State* Internal ANC document 2005 http://ccs.ukzn.ac.za/files/Cronin,%20The%20People%20Shall%20 Govern,%20Transformation%20&%20State.pdf (accessed on 1 August 2018)

22 This section relies heavily on Steven Friedman, Kenny Hlela and Paul Thulare 'A Question of Voice: Informality and Pro-poor Policy in Johannesburg, South Africa' in Nabeel Hamdi (Ed.) *Urban Futures: Economic Growth and Poverty Reduction* Rugby, ITDG, 2005, pp. 51–68

23 Republic of South Africa Municipal Systems Act, No. 32 of 2000, Chapter 4, Clause 21

24 For example, Abdou Maliq Simone 'Urban Societies in Africa' in Richard Humphries and Maxine Reitzes (Eds) *Civil Society after Apartheid* Johannesburg, Centre for Policy Studies/Friedrich Ebert Foundation, 1995; Graeme Gotz 'The Limits of Community: The Dynamics of Rural Water Provision' Unpublished report for Rand Water, Johannesburg, Centre for Policy Studies, 1997

25 Thulare 'Trading Democracy?'

26 Jürgen Habermas 'Hannah Arendt's Communications Concept of Power' in Lewis P Hinchman and Sandra K Hinchman (Eds) *Hannah Arendt: Critical Essays* Albany, State University of New York Press, 1994, p. 211

27 Max Weber 'Politics as a Vocation' in HH Gerth and C Wright Mills (Translated and edited) *From Max Weber: Essays in Sociology* New York, Oxford University Press, 1946, pp. 77–128

28 Friedman 'Sending Them a Message'

29 Mafedi Yvonne Mphahlele 'Knowledge Management Practices in the South African Public Sector 2002–2008' Thesis presented in fulfilment of the requirements for the degree of Master of Philosophy (Information and Knowledge Management) Stellenbosch University 2010 file:///C:/Users/Steven/Downloads/mphahlele_knowledge _2010.pdf (accessed on 1 August 2018)

30 James Scott *Seeing Like a State: How Certain Schemes to Improve the Human Condition Have Failed* New Haven, Yale University Press, 1998

31 For example, Steven Robins, Andrea Cornwall and Bettina von Lieres 'Rethinking "Citizenship" in the Postcolony' *Third World Quarterly* Vol. 29, No. 6, 2008, pp. 1069–1086

32 Keane *Democracy and Civil Society*

33 Esping-Andersen *Three Worlds of Welfare Capitalism*

34   Przeworski *Capitalism and Social Democracy*

35   Amartya Sen *Poverty and Famines: An Essay on Entitlement and Deprivation* Oxford, Clarendon Press, 1981

36   Barry Gills and Joel Rocamora 'Low Intensity Democracy' *Third World Quarterly* Vol. 13, No. 3, 1992, pp. 501–523. See, for example, in the Zimbabwean context, Mabasa Sasa 'People Don't Eat Democracy' *Sunday Mail* 18 December 2016 http://www .sundaymail.co.zw/people-dont-eat-democracy/ (accessed on 1 August 2018)

37   Cited in Dale Carpenter 'Bumping the Status Quo: Actual Relief for Actual Victims under Title VII' *University of Chicago Law Review* Vol. 58, No. 2, Spring 1991, pp. 703–732

38   Douglas A Chalmers 'The Demystification of Development' *Proceedings of the Academy of Political Science* Vol. 30, No. 4, August 1972, pp. 109–122

39   Marina Ottaway *Africa's New Leaders: Democracy or State Reconstruction?* Washington DC, Carnegie Endowment for International Peace, 1999

40   Jonathan di John *The Political Economy of Taxation and Tax Reform in Developing Countries* UNU-WIDER Research Paper No. 2006/74, Helsinki, United Nations University World Institute for Development Economics Research, 2006, p. 6. See also Ole Therkildsen 'Uganda Revenue Authority: The Limits of Autonomy' Paper presented at the annual conference of the research programme 'Taxation, Aid and Democracy', Windhoek, 4–5 April 2002

41   For example, Scott *Seeing Like A State*

42   World Bank *World Development Report 2004: Making Services Work for Poor People* Washington DC, World Bank, Oxford University Press, 2004

43   Przeworski *Capitalism and Social Democracy*

44   Mandla Seloane *Socio-economic Rights in the South African Constitution: Theory and Practice* Cape Town, HSRC Press, 2001

45   Albie Sachs 'Social and Economic Rights: Can They be Justiciable?' *Southern Methodist University Law Review* Vol. 53, No. 4, 2000, p. 1389

46   Thembilihle Tshabalala 'Jo'burg Water Meters under Spotlight after Court Ruling' *Mail and Guardian Online* 10 May 2008 http://www.mg.co.za/article/2008-05-10-joburg -water-meters-under-spotlight-after-court-ruling (accessed on 1 August 2018)

47   Wilson 'Litigating Housing Rights'

48   Brian Ray 'Proceduralisation's Triumph and Engagement's Promise in Socio-economic Rights Litigation' *South African Journal on Human Rights* Vol. 27, No. 1, 2011, pp. 107–126; Steven Friedman 'Enabling Agency: The Constitutional Court and Social Policy' *Transformation* Vol. 91, 2016, pp. 19–39

REFERENCES

Abdullahi, Armendariz M 1998 'Article 39 of the Ethiopian Constitution on Secession and Self-Determination: A Panacea to the Nationality Question in Africa?' *Verfassung und Recht in Übersee/Law and Politics in Africa, Asia and Latin America* Vol. 31, No. 4, 4. Quartal, pp. 440–455

Abensour, Miguel 2002 '"Savage Democracy" and "Principle of Anarchy"' *Philosophy and Social Criticism* Vol. 28, No. 6, pp. 703–726

Adler, Glenn and Edward Webster (Eds) 2000 *Trade Unions and Democratization in South Africa 1985–1997* New York, St Martin's Press

Ake, Claude 1987 'The African Context of Human Rights' *Africa Today* Vol. 34, No. 1–2, pp. 5–12

Ake, Claude 1991 'Rethinking African Democracy' *Journal of Democracy* Vol. 2, No. 1, January, pp. 32–44

Ake, Claude 1993 'The Unique Case of African Democracy' *International Affairs* Vol. 69, No. 2, April, pp. 239–244

Ake, Claude 1996 *Democracy and Development in Africa* Washington DC, Brookings Institution

Ani, Emmanuel Ifeanyi 2013 'Africa and the Prospects of Deliberative Democracy' *South African Journal of Philosophy* Vol. 32, No. 3, pp. 207–219

Appadurai, Arjun 2002 'Deep Democracy: Urban Governmentality and the Horizon of Politics' *Public Culture* Vol. 14, No. 1, pp. 21–47

Appiah, Kwame Anthony 1992 *In My Father's House: Africa in the Philosophy of Culture* New York, Oxford University Press

Avritzer, Leonardo 2002 *Democracy and the Public Space in Latin America* Princeton and Oxford, Princeton University Press

Bachrach, Peter and Morton S Baratz 1970 *Power and Poverty: Theory and Practice* New York, Oxford University Press

Bakhtin, Mikhail 1984 *Rabelais and His World* (Translated by Helene Sinofsky) Bloomington, Indiana University Press

Barber, Benjamin 1984 *Strong Democracy: Participatory Politics for a New Age* Berkeley, University of California Press

Barber, Benjamin R 1998 *A Passion for Democracy: American Essays* Princeton, Princeton University Press

Baskin, Jeremy 1991 *Striking Back: A History of Cosatu* London and New York, Verso

Bates, Robert H, Ghada Fayad and Anke Hoeffler 2012 'The State of Democracy in Sub-Saharan Africa' *International Area Studies Review* Vol. 15, No. 4, pp. 323–338

Bayart, Jean-Francois 1993 *The State in Africa: The Politics of the Belly* London, Longman

Benhabib, Seyla 1999 'Citizens, Residents and Aliens in a Changing World: Political Membership in the Global Era' *Social Research* Vol. 66, No. 3, Fall, pp. 709–744

Berlin, Isaiah 1969 *Four Essays on Liberty* London, Oxford University Press

Bermeo, Nancy 2003 *Ordinary People in Extraordinary Times: The Citizenry and the Breakdown of Democracy* Princeton and Oxford, Princeton University Press

Biko, Steve 1987 *I Write What I Like* Oxford, Heinemann

Blair, Harry 2003 'Jump-starting Democracy: Adult Civic Education and Democratic Participation in Three Countries' *Democratization* Vol. 10, No. 1, Spring, pp. 53–76

Bohman, James and William Rehg (Eds) 1999 *Deliberative Democracy: Essays in Reason and Politics* Cambridge, Mass. and London, MIT Press

Branch, Adam and Zachariah Cherian Mampilly 2015 *Africa Uprising: Popular Protest and Political Change* London, Zed Books

Bratton, Michael and Robert Mattes 1999 'Support for Democracy in Africa: Intrinsic or Instrumental?' Paper presented to panel 'What Have We Learned about Consolidation?' at the annual meeting of the American Political Science Association, Atlanta, 1–4 September

Bratton, Michael and Nicolas van de Walle 1997 *Democratic Experiments in Africa* Cambridge, Cambridge University Press

Bräutigam, Deborah 1997 'Institutions, Economic Reform, and Democratic Consolidation in Mauritius' *Comparative Politics* Vol. 30, No. 1, October, pp. 45–62

Bräutigam, Deborah 2006 'Contingent Consent: Export Taxation and State Building in Mauritius' Paper presented at the annual meeting of the American Political Science Association, Philadelphia, 31 August

Bresser Pereira, Luiz Carlos, Jose Maria Maravall and Adam Przeworski 1993 *Economic Reforms in New Democracies: A Social Democratic Approach* Cambridge, Cambridge University Press

Brown, Wendy 2015 *Undoing the Demos: Neoliberalism's Stealth Revolution* New York, Zone Books

Buhrmann, Marc, Wolfgang Merkel and Bernhard Wessels 2007 *The Quality of Democracy: Democracy Barometer for Established Democracies* NCCR Democracy Working Paper No. 10, Zürich, University of Zürich

Capoccia, Giovanni and Daniel Ziblatt 2010 'The Historical Turn in Democratization Studies: A New Agenda for Europe and Beyond' *Comparative Political Studies* Vol. 43, No. 8–9, pp. 931–968

Carothers, Thomas 2002 'The End of the Transition Paradigm' *Journal of Democracy* Vol. 13, No. 1, January, pp. 5–21

Carpenter, Dale 1991 'Bumping the Status Quo: Actual Relief for Actual Victims under Title VII' *University of Chicago Law Review* Vol. 58, No. 2, Spring, pp. 703–732

Cawson, Alan 1986 *Corporatism and Political Theory* Oxford, Basil Blackwell

Chabal, Patrick and Jean-Pascal Daloz 1999 *Africa Works: Disorder as Political Instrument* Bloomington, Indiana University Press

Chalmers, Douglas A 1972 'The Demystification of Development' *Proceedings of the Academy of Political Science* Vol. 30, No. 4, August, pp. 109–122

Chandhoke, Neera 2005 'Revisiting the Crisis of Representation Thesis: The Indian Context' *Democratization* Vol. 12, No. 3, June, pp. 308–330

Chandler, David 1999 *Faking Democracy after Dayton* London and Sterling, Pluto Press

Charney, Craig 1995 *Voices of a New Democracy: African Expectations in the New South Africa* Johannesburg, Centre for Policy Studies

Chatterjee, Partha 2004 *The Politics of the Governed: Reflections on Popular Politics in Most of the World* New York, Columbia University Press

Cheeseman, Nic 2015 *Democracy in Africa: Successes, Failures, and the Struggle for Political Reform* New York, Cambridge University Press

Cluver, Lucie, Mark Boyes, Mark Orkin, Marija Pantelic, Thembela Molwena and Lorraine Sherr 2013 'Child-Focused State Cash Transfers and Adolescent Risk of HIV Infection in South Africa: A Propensity-Score-Matched Case-Control Study' *The Lancet* Vol. 1, No. 6, December, e362–e370

Cohen, Joshua 1999 'Deliberation and Democratic Legitimacy' in James Bohman and William Rehg (Eds) *Deliberative Democracy: Essays in Reason and Politics* Cambridge, Mass. and London, MIT Press, pp. 67–92

Comaroff, Jean and John L Comaroff 2016 'Figuring Democracy: An Anthropological Take on African Political Modernities' in Jean Comaroff and John L Comaroff *Theory from the South: Or, How Euro-America is Evolving Toward Africa* Oxford, Routledge, pp. 109–132

Comaroff, John L and Jean Comaroff 1997 'Postcolonial Politics and Discourses of Democracy in Southern Africa: An Anthropological Reflection on African Political Modernities' *Journal of Anthropological Research* Vol. 53, No. 2, Summer, pp. 123–146

Cornwall, Andrea 2002 'Locating Citizen Participation' *IDS Bulletin* Vol. 33, No. 2, pp. 49–58

Cornwall, Andrea 2002 *Making Spaces, Changing Places: Situating Participation in Development* IDS Working Paper No. 170, Brighton, Institute for Development Studies, University of Sussex, October

Cornwall, Andrea and Vera Schutte Coelho (Eds) 2007 *Spaces for Change? The Politics of Citizen Participation in New Democratic Arenas* London, Zed Books

Cowley, Philip and David Denver 2004 'Votes at 16? The Case Against' *Representation* Vol. 41, No. 1, pp. 57–62

Crankshaw, Owen 1997 *Race, Class and the Changing Division of Labour under Apartheid* London and New York, Routledge

Dahl, Robert 1961 *Who Governs? Democracy and Power in an American City* New Haven, Yale University Press

Dahl, Robert 1970 *After the Revolution? Authority in a Good Society* New Haven, Yale University Press

Dahl, Robert A 1971 *Polyarchy: Government and Opposition* New Haven, Yale University Press

Dahl, Robert 1982 *Dilemmas of Pluralist Democracy* New Haven, Yale University Press

Dahl, Robert 1989 *Democracy and Its Critics* New Haven, Yale University Press

Dahl, Robert A 1999 'The Shifting Boundaries of Democratic Governments' *Social Research* Vol. 66, No. 3, Fall, pp. 915–931

De Soto, Hernando 1989 *The Other Path: The Invisible Revolution in the Third World* New York, Harper and Row

De Swaan, Abram 1988 *In Care of the State* Cambridge, Cambridge University Press

De Tocqueville, Alexis 1956 *Democracy in America* (Abridged and edited by Richard D Heffner) New York, Mentor

Diamond, Larry 1999 *Developing Democracy: Toward Consolidation* Baltimore, Johns Hopkins University Press

Diamond, Larry and Leonardo Morlino 2004 *The Quality of Democracy* CDDR Working Paper No. 20, Stanford, Center on Democracy, Development, and the Rule of Law, Stanford Institute on International Studies, Stanford University, September

Diamond, Larry, Kenta Tsuda and Barron YoungSmith 2006 'Authoritarian Learning: Lessons from the Colored Revolutions' *Brown Journal of World Affairs* Vol. 12, No. 2, Winter/Spring, pp. 215–222

Di John, Jonathan 2006 *The Political Economy of Taxation and Tax Reform in Developing Countries* UNU-WIDER Research Paper No. 2006/74, Helsinki, United Nations University World Institute for Development Economics Research

Dixon, Bill and Lisa-Marie Johns 2001 *Gangs, Pagad and the State: Vigilantism and Revenge Violence in the Western Cape* CSVR Violence and Transition Series, Vol. 2, Johannesburg, Centre for the Study of Violence and Reconciliation, May

Doorenspleet, Renske 2012 'Critical Citizens, Democratic Support and Satisfaction in African Democracies' *International Political Science Review* Vol. 33, No. 3, pp. 279–300

Dunn, John 2013 *Breaking Democracy's Spell* New Haven, Yale University Press

Ekiert, Grzegorz and Jan Kubik 1998 'Contentious Politics in New Democracies: East Germany, Hungary, Poland, and Slovakia, 1989–93' *World Politics* Vol. 50, No. 4, pp. 547–581

Esping-Andersen, Gøsta 1990 *The Three Worlds of Welfare Capitalism* Princeton, Princeton University Press

Estlund, David 1999 'Beyond Fairness and Deliberation: The Epistemic Dimension of Democratic Authority' in James Bohman and William Rehg (Eds) *Deliberative Democracy: Essays in Reason and Politics* Cambridge, Mass. and London, MIT Press, pp. 173–204

Eze, Emmanuel Chukwudi 1997 'Democracy or Consensus: A Response to Wiredu' in Emmanuel Chukwudi Eze (Ed.) *Postcolonial African Philosophy: A Critical Reader* Oxford, Blackwell, pp. 313–323

Fayemi, Ademola Kazeem 2010 'A Critique of Consensual Democracy and Human Rights in Kwasi Wiredu's Philosophy' *Lumina* Vol. 21, No. 1, March, pp. 1–13

Foa, Roberto Stefan and Yascha Mounk 2016 'The Danger of Deconsolidation: The Democratic Discontent' *Journal of Democracy* Vol. 27, No. 3, July, pp. 5–17

Folkes, Alex 2004 'The Case for Votes at 16' *Representation* Vol. 41, No. 1, pp. 52–56

Friedman, Steven 1985 *Building Tomorrow Today: African Workers in Trade Unions 1970–1984* Johannesburg, Ravan Press

Friedman, Steven 1986 *Understanding Reform* Johannesburg, South African Institute of Race Relations

Friedman, Steven 1993 *The Elusive 'Community': The Dynamics of Negotiated Urban Development* Johannesburg, Centre for Policy Studies

Friedman, Steven 1999 'Who We Are: Voter Participation, Rationality and the 1999 Election' *Politikon* Vol. 26, No. 2, November, pp. 213–224

Friedman, Steven 2001 *Free but Unequal: Democracy, Inequality and the State in Latin America and Africa* Johannesburg, Centre for Policy Studies

Friedman, Steven 2002 'Democracy, Inequality and the Reconstitution of Politics' in Joseph S Tulchin with Amelia Brown (Ed.) *Democratic Governance and Social Inequality* Boulder, Lynne Rienner, pp. 13–40

Friedman, Steven 2002 *Equity in the Age of Informality: Labour Markets and Redistributive Politics in South Africa* IDS Working Paper No. 160, Brighton, Institute for Development Studies, University of Sussex, July

Friedman, Steven 2003 'Sending Them a Message: Culture, Tax Collection and Governance in South Africa' *Policy: Issues and Actors* Vol. 16, No. 3

Friedman, Steven 2005 'The Forgotten Sovereign: Citizens, States and Foreign Policy in the South' in Justin Robertson and Maurice A East (Eds) *Diplomacy and Developing Nations:*

Post-Cold War Foreign Policy-Making Structures and Processes Abingdon, Routledge pp. 225–252

Friedman, Steven 2005 'South Africa: Globalization and the Politics of Redistribution' in Joseph S Tulchin and Gary Bland (Eds) *Getting Globalization Right: The Dilemmas of Inequality* Boulder and London, Lynne Rienner, pp. 11–49

Friedman, Steven 2006 *Participatory Governance and Citizen Action in Post-apartheid South Africa* IILS Discussion Paper 164/2006, Geneva, International Institute of Labour Studies

Friedman, Steven 2010 'Gaining Comprehensive AIDS Treatment in South Africa: The Extraordinary "Ordinary"' in John Gaventa and Rosemary McGee (Eds) *Citizen Action and National Policy Reform* London and New York, Zed Books, pp. 44–68

Friedman, Steven 2010 'Seeing Ourselves as Others See Us: Racism, Technique and the Mbeki Administration' in Daryl Glaser (Ed.) *Mbeki and After: Reflections on the Legacy of Thabo Mbeki* Johannesburg, Wits University Press, pp. 163–186

Friedman, Steven 2012 'Beyond the Fringe? South African Social Movements and the Politics of Redistribution' *Review of African Political Economy* Vol. 39, No. 131, pp. 85–100

Friedman, Steven 2015 'Archipelagos of Dominance: Party Fiefdoms and South African Democracy' *Zeitschrift für Vergleichende Politikwissenschaft/Journal of Comparative Politics* Vol. 9, No. 3, pp. 139–159

Friedman, Steven 2015 'The Janus Face of the Past: Preserving and Resisting South African Path Dependence' in Xolela Mangcu (Ed.) *The Colour of Our Future: Does Race Matter in Post-apartheid South Africa?* Johannesburg, Wits University Press, pp. 45–63

Friedman, Steven 2016 'Enabling agency: The Constitutional Court and Social Policy' *Transformation* Vol. 91, pp. 19–39

Friedman, Steven and Omano Edigheji 2006 *Eternal (and Internal) Tensions? Conceptualising Public Accountability in South African Higher Education* CHE HEIAAF Research Report No. 2, Pretoria, Council on Higher Education December

Friedman, Steven and Sharon Groenmeyer 2016 'A Nightmare on the Brain of the Living? The Endurance and Limits of the Collective Bargaining Regime' *Transformation* Vol. 91, pp. 163–183

Friedman, Steven, Kenny Hlela and Paul Thulare 2005 'A Question of Voice: Informality and Pro-poor Policy in Johannesburg, South Africa' in Nabeel Hamdi (Ed.) *Urban Futures: Economic Growth and Poverty Reduction* Rugby, ITDG, pp. 51–68

Friedman, Steven and Shauna Mottiar 2005 'A Rewarding Engagement? The Treatment Action Campaign and the Politics of HIV/AIDS' *Politics and Society* Vol. 33, No. 4, pp. 511–565

Friedman, Steven and Maxine Reitzes 1995 *Democratic Selections? Civil Society and Development in Post-apartheid South Africa* Midrand, Development Bank of Southern Africa

Friedman, Steven and Louise Stack 1995 'The Magic Moment' in Steven Friedman and Doreen Atkinson (Eds) *The Small Miracle: South Africa's Negotiated Settlement* Johannesburg, Ravan Press, pp. 301–325

Fukuyama, Francis 1992 *The End of History and the Last Man* New York, Free Press

Fukuyama, Francis 2015 'Why is Democracy Performing So Poorly?' *Journal of Democracy* Vol. 26, No. 1, January, pp. 11–20

Gaventa, John 1982 *Power and Powerlessness: Quiescence and Rebellion in an Appalachian Valley* Urbana and Chicago, University of Illinois Press

Gaventa, John and Rosemary McGee (Eds) 2010 *Citizen Action and National Policy Reform* London and New York, Zed Books

Gerhart, Gail and Thomas Karis T (Eds) 1997 *From Protest to Challenge: A Documentary History of African Politics in South Africa: 1882–1990* Pretoria, Unisa Press

Gills, Barry and Joel Rocamora 1992 'Low Intensity Democracy' *Third World Quarterly* Vol. 13, No. 3, pp. 501–523

Godelier, Maurice 1991 'Is the West the Model for Humankind? The Baruya of New Guinea between Change and Decay' *International Social Science Journal* Vol. 43, No. 2, pp. 387–399

Goetz, Anne-Marie and John Gaventa 2001 *Bringing Citizen Voice and Client Focus into Service Delivery* IDS Working Paper No. 138, Brighton, Institute for Development Studies, University of Sussex

Graham, Victoria, Yolanda Sadie and Leila Patel 2016 'Social Grants, Food Parcels and Voting Behaviour: A Case Study of Three South African Communities' *Transformation* Vol. 91, pp. 106–135

Green, David G 1981 *Power and Party in an English City: An Account of Single-Party Rule* London, Allen and Unwin

Guinier, Lani 1994 *The Tyranny of the Majority: Fundamental Fairness in Representative Democracy* New York, Free Press

Gunther, Richard, Nikiforos Diamondouros and Hans-Jürgen Puhle (Eds) 1995 *The Politics of Democratic Consolidation: Southern Europe in Comparative Perspective* Baltimore, Johns Hopkins University Press

Gurr, Ted Robert 1970 *Why Men Rebel* Princeton, Princeton University Press

Gyimah-Boadi, E 2015 'Africa's Waning Democratic Commitment' *Journal of Democracy* Vol. 26, No. 1, January, pp. 101–113

Haas, Peter M 1992 'Introduction: Epistemic Communities and International Policy Coordination' *International Organization* Vol. 46, No. 1, Knowledge, Power, and International Policy Coordination, Winter, pp. 1–35

Habermas, Jürgen 1994 'Hannah Arendt's Communications Concept of Power' in Lewis P Hinchman and Sandra K Hinchman (Eds) *Hannah Arendt: Critical Essays* Albany, State University of New York Press, pp. 211–230

Habermas, Jürgen 1996 *Between Facts and Norms: Contributions to a Discourse Theory of Law and Democracy* Cambridge, Mass., MIT Press

Haggard, Stephan and Robert Kaufman 1995 *The Political Economy of Democratic Transitions* Princeton, Princeton University Press

Hagopian, Frances 2003 'The (Too-Low but) Rising Quality of Democracy in Brazil and Chile?' Paper presented at the conference 'The Quality of Democracy: Improvement or Subversion?' Stanford, Stanford University, 10–11 October

Hayduk, Ron 2006 *Democracy for All: Restoring Immigrant Voting Rights in the United States* New York, Routledge

Hobson, Christopher 2016 'Democracy: Trap, Tragedy or Crisis?' *Political Studies Review* Vol. 16, No. 1, pp. 38–45

Honey, Michael K 2007 *Going Down Jericho Road: The Memphis Strike, Martin Luther King's Last Campaign* New York and London, WW Norton

Hountondji, Paulin 2002 *The Struggle for Meaning: Reflections on Philosophy, Culture, and Democracy in Africa* Athens, Ohio, University Center for International Studies

Hountondji, Paulin 2009 'Knowledge of Africa, Knowledge by Africans: Two Perspectives on African Studies' *RCCS Annual Review*, No. 1, September, pp. 1–11

Howe, Paul 2017 'Eroding Norms and Democratic Deconsolidation' *Journal of Democracy* Vol. 28, No. 4, October, pp. 15–29

Huber, Evelyne, Dietrich Rueschemeyer and John D Stephens 1993 'The Impact of Economic Development on Democracy' *Journal of Economic Perspectives* Vol. 7, No. 3, Summer, pp. 71–86

Hudson, Peter 2007 'Taking the Democratic Subject Seriously' Paper presented at a seminar at the University of South Africa School for Graduate Studies, Pretoria, 24 May

Huntington, Samuel P 1991 *The Third Wave: Democratization in the Late Twentieth Century* Norman, University of Oklahoma Press

Hydén, Göran 1980 *Beyond Ujamaa in Tanzania* London, Heinemann

Hydén, Göran 1983 *No Shortcuts to Progress: African Development Management in Perspective* London, Heinemann

Ibhawoh, Bonny 2014 'Human Rights and National Liberation: The Anticolonial Politics of Nnamdi Azikiwe' in Baba G Jallow (Ed.) *Leadership in Colonial Africa: Disruption of Traditional Frameworks and Patterns* New York, Palgrave Macmillan, pp. 55–68

Ihonvbere, Julius 1990 'Underdevelopment and Human Rights Violations in Africa' in George W Shepherd and Mark OC Anikpo (Eds) *Emerging Human Rights* New York, Greenwood Press, pp. 55–68

Inglehart, Ronald F 2016 'How Much Should We Worry?' *Journal of Democracy* Vol. 27, No. 3, July, pp. 18–23

Jencks, Christopher 1992 *Rethinking Social Policy* Cambridge, Mass., Harvard University Press

Jennings, Ivor 1956 *The Approach to Self-Government* Cambridge, Cambridge University Press

Joseph, Richard 1998 'Africa, 1990–1997: From *Abertura* to Closure' *Journal of Democracy* Vol. 9, No. 2, April, pp. 3–17

Joseph, Richard 2014 'Growth, Security, and Democracy in Africa' *Journal of Democracy* Vol. 25, No. 4, October, pp. 61–75

Kaltwasser, Cristóbal Rovira 2014 'The Responses of Populism to Dahl's Democratic Dilemmas' *Political Studies* Vol. 62, No. 3, pp. 470–487

Kamrava, Mehran (Ed.) 2014 *Beyond the Arab Spring: The Evolving Ruling Bargain in the Middle East* Oxford and New York, Oxford University Press

Karatnycky, Adrian 1999 'The Decline of Illiberal Democracy' *Journal of Democracy* Vol. 10, No. 1, January, pp. 112–125

Karl, Terri Lynn and Phillipe C Schmitter 1991 'What Democracy is … and is Not' *Journal of Democracy* Vol. 2, No. 3, Summer, pp. 75–88

Karlstrom, Mikael 1996 'Imagining Democracy: Political Culture and Democratisation in Buganda' *Africa: Journal of the International African Institute* Vol. 66, No. 4, pp. 485–505

Katznelson, Ira and Aristide Zolberg (Eds) 1986 *Working-Class Formation: Nineteenth-Century Patterns in Western Europe and the United States* Princeton, Princeton University Press

Keane, John 1988 *Democracy and Civil Society* London, Verso

Keane, John 2009 *The Life and Death of Democracy* London, Sydney, New York and Toronto, Pocket Books

Keating, Michael and David MacCrone 2013 *The Crisis of Social Democracy in Europe* Edinburgh, Edinburgh University Press

Knack, Stephen 2004 'Does Foreign Aid Promote Democracy?' *International Studies Quarterly* Vol. 48, No. 1, March, pp. 251–266

Kotze, Hennie and Reinet Loubser 2017 'South Africa's Democratic Consolidation in Perspective: Mapping Socio-political Changes' *Taiwan Journal of Democracy* Vol. 13, No. 1, pp. 35–58

Krugman, Paul 1998 *Pop Internationalism* Cambridge, Mass. and London, MIT Press

Lamarchand, Rene 1976 'The CIA in Africa: How Central? How Intelligent?' *Journal of Modern African Studies* Vol. 13, No. 3, September, pp. 401–426

Landman, JP 1999 'Is the Washington Consensus Dead?' Seminar convened by Centre for Policy Studies, Johannesburg, June

Lefort, Claude 1986 *The Political Forms of Modern Society* Oxford, Polity Press

Lefort, Claude 1988 *Democracy and Political Theory* Oxford, Basil Blackwell

Leubolt, Bernhard 2014 *Social Policies and Redistribution in South Africa* ILO Working Paper, Geneva, International Labour Office, 25 May

Leuchtenberg, William E 1963 *Franklin Delano Roosevelt and the New Deal, 1932–40* New York, Harper and Row

Levine, Daniel H and Jose E Molina 2011 *The Quality of Democracy in Latin America* Boulder, Lynne Rienner

Levitzky, Steven and Lucan Way 2002 'The Rise of Competitive Authoritarianism' *Journal of Democracy* Vol. 13, No. 2, April, pp. 51–65

Lijphart, Arend 1977 *Democracy in Plural Societies* New Haven, Yale University Press

Lindberg, Staffan I 2001 'Forms of States, Governance and Regimes: Reconceptualizing the Prospects for Democratic Consolidation in Africa' *International Political Science Review* Vol. 22, No. 2, pp. 173–199

Lindblom, Charles E 1978 *Politics and Markets: The World's Political-Economic Systems* New York, Basic Books

Linz, Juan J 1990 'Transitions to Democracy' *Washington Quarterly* Vol. 13, No. 3, pp. 143–164

Linz, Juan J and Alfred Stepan (Eds) 1978 The *Breakdown of Democratic Regimes: Latin America* Baltimore, Johns Hopkins University Press

Linz, Juan J and Alfred Stepan 1996 *Problems of Democratic Transition and Consolidation: Southern Europe, South America and Post-communist Europe* Baltimore and London, Johns Hopkins Press

Lipset, Seymour Martin 1959 'Some Social Requisites of Democracy: Economic Development and Political Legitimacy' *American Political Science Review* Vol. 53, No. 1, March, pp. 69–105

Lipset, Seymour Martin 1960 *Political Man: The Social Basis of Politics* New York, Doubleday

Lipset, Seymour Martin 1964 'Introduction' to TH Marshall *Class, Citizenship and Social Development* Westport, Greenwood Press, pp. 3–23

Lipset, Seymour Martin 1994 'The Social Requisites of Democracy Revisited: 1993' Presidential Address *American Sociological Review* Vol. 59, No. 1, February, pp. 1–22

Lipset, Seymour Martin, Martin Trow and James Coleman 1956 *Union Democracy: The Inside Politics of the International Typographical Union* New York, Free Press

Little, Eric and Caroline Logan 2008 *The Quality of Democracy and Governance in Africa: New Results from Afrobarometer Round 4: A Compendium of Public Opinion Findings from 19 African Countries* Afrobarometer Working Paper No. 108 http://afrobarometer.org/publications/wp108-quality-democracy-and-governance-africa-new-results-afrobarometer-round-4 (accessed on 1 August 2018)

Loader, Brian D and Dan Mercea 2011 'Networking Democracy? Social Media Innovations in Participatory Politics' *Information, Communication and Society* Vol. 14, No. 6, pp. 757–769

Lodge, Tom 1999 *Consolidating Democracy: South Africa's Second Popular Election* Johannesburg, Wits University Press

Lukes, Steven 1974 *Power: A Radical View* London, Macmillan

McAdam, Doug, Sidney Tarrow and Charles Tilly 2001 *Dynamics of Contention* Cambridge, Cambridge University Press

McCarthy, John D and Mayer N Zald 1977 'Resource Mobilization and Social Movements: A Partial Theory' *American Journal of Sociology* Vol. 82, No. 6, May, pp. 1212–1241

McCoy, Jennifer L and William C Smith 1995 'Democratic Disequilibrium in Venezuela' *Journal of Interamerican Studies and World Affairs* Vol. 37, No. 2, Summer, pp. 113–179

McPherson, CB 1962 *The Political Theory of Possessive Individualism* Oxford, Clarendon Press

Mainwaring, Scott, Guillermo O'Donnell and J Samuel Valenzuela (Eds) 1992 *Issues in Democratic Consolidation: The New South American Democracies in Comparative Perspective* Notre Dame, University of Notre Dame Press

Mamdani, Mahmood 1995 *Citizen and Subject: Contemporary Africa and the Politics of Late Colonialism* Kampala, Fountain

Mamdani, Mahmood 2000 *When Victims Become Killers: Colonialism, Nativism and Genocide in Rwanda* Princeton, Princeton University Press

Mansbridge, Jane 1983 *Beyond Adversary Democracy* Chicago and London, University of Chicago Press

Mansbridge, Jane 1999 'Should Blacks Represent Blacks, and Women Represent Women? A Contingent "Yes"' *Journal of Politics* Vol. 61, No. 3, pp. 628–657

Marshall, TH 1964 *Class, Citizenship and Social Development* Westport, Greenwood Press

Marshall, TH 1992 *Citizenship and Social Class* London, Pluto

Marx, Karl and Friedrich Engels 1998 *The Communist Manifesto* London, Signet

Mbali, Mandisa 2002 'Mbeki's Denialism and the Ghosts of Apartheid and Colonialism for Post-apartheid AIDS Policy-Making' Paper presented at a workshop at the School of Development Studies, Durban, University of KwaZulu-Natal, 15 April http://ccs.ukzn.ac.za/files/mbeki.pdf (accessed on 1 August 2018)

Mbembe, Achille 1992 'Provisional Notes on the Postcolony' *Africa* Vol. 62, No. 1, pp. 3–37

Mekoa, Itumeleng 2016 'Consolidating Democracy in South Africa: Prospects and Challenges' *Politeia* Vol. 35, No. 2, pp. 1–20

Melucci, Alberto 1996 *Challenging Codes: Collective Action in the Information Age* Cambridge, Cambridge University Press

Miliband, Ralph 1975 *Parliamentary Socialism: A Study in the Politics of Labour* London, Merlin

Minnaar, Anthony 2001 *The New Vigilantism in Post-April 1994 South Africa* Johannesburg, Institute for Human Rights and Criminal Justice Studies, Technikon South Africa

Miraftab, Faranak 2004 'Invited and Invented Spaces of Participation: Neoliberal Citizenship and Feminists' Expanded Notion of Politics' *Wagadu* Vol. 1, Spring, pp. 1–7

Mkandawire, Thandika and Charles Soludo 1999 *Our Continent, Our Future* Council for the Development of Social Science Research in Africa, Africa World Press, Asmara and IDRC, Ottawa

Mohan, Giles and Jeremy Holland 2001 'Human Rights and Development in Africa: Moral Intrusion or Empowering Opportunity?' *Review of African Political Economy* Vol. 28, No. 88, June, pp. 177–196

Monga, Célestin 1996 *The Anthropology of Anger: Civil Society and Democracy in Africa* Boulder, Lynne Rienner

Moore, Barrington, Jr 1966 *The Social Origins of Dictatorship and Democracy: Lord and Peasant in the Making of the Modern World* Boston, Beacon Press

Moore, Barrington, Jr 1978 *Injustice: The Social Bases of Obedience and Revolt* White Plains, Sharpe

Moore, Martin and Gordon Ramsay 2017 *UK Media Coverage of the 2016 EU Referendum Campaign* London, Centre for the Study of Media, Communication and Power, King's College

Morlino, Leonardo 1998 *Democracy between Consolidation and Crisis: Parties, Groups and Citizens in Southern Europe* Oxford, Oxford University Press

Mouffe, Chantal 1993 *The Return of the Political* London and New York, Verso

Mouffe, Chantal 2000 *The Democratic Paradox* London and New York, Verso

Murray, Charles 1984 *Losing Ground: American Social Policy 1950–1980* New York, Basic Books

Narsoo, Monty 1991 'Civil Society: A Contested Terrain' *Work in Progress* No. 76, pp. 24–27

Nasstrom, Sofia 2006 'Representative Democracy as Tautology: Ankersmit and Lefort on Representation' *European Journal of Political Theory* Vol. 5, No. 3, pp. 321–342

Norris, Pippa 2004 *Electoral Engineering: Voting Rules and Political Behavior* Cambridge, Cambridge University Press

Norris, Pippa 2011 *Democratic Deficit: Critical Citizens Revisited* New York, Cambridge University Press

Norris, Pippa, Stefaan Walgrave and Peter van Aelst 2000 'Who Demonstrates? Disaffected Rebels, Conventional Participants or Everyone?' Unpublished manuscript, Cambridge, Mass., Kennedy School of Government, Harvard University

Nuvunga, Adriano 2017 'Mozambique's 2014 Elections: A Repeat of Misconduct, Political Tension and Frelimo Dominance' *Journal of African Elections* Vol. 16, No. 2, pp. 71–94

Nzouankeu, Jacques-Mariel 1991 'The African Attitude to Democracy' *International Social Science Journal* Vol. 43, No. 2, pp. 373–385

O'Donnell, Guillermo 1979 *Modernization and Bureaucratic-Authoritarianism: Studies in South American Politics* Berkeley, Institute for International Studies

O'Donnell, Guillermo 1993 'On the State, Democratization and Some Conceptual Problems: A Latin American View with Glances at Some Post-communist Countries' *World Development* Vol. 21, No. 8, pp. 1355–1369

O'Donnell, Guillermo 1994 'Delegative Democracy' *Journal of Democracy* Vol. 5, No. 1, January, pp. 55–69

O'Donnell, Guillermo 1996 'Illusions about Consolidation' *Journal of Democracy* Vol. 7, No. 2, April, pp. 34–51

O'Donnell, Guillermo and Philippe C Schmitter 1986 *Transitions from Authoritarian Rule: Tentative Conclusions about Uncertain Democracies* Baltimore, Johns Hopkins University Press

Oliver, Pamela E 1993 'Formal Models of Collective Action' *Annual Review of Sociology* Vol. 19, pp. 271–300

Oliver, Pamela E and Gerald Markwell 1988 'The Paradox of Group Size in Collective Action: A Theory of the Critical Mass' *American Sociological Review* Vol. 53, No. 1, February, pp. 1–8

Olonisakin, Funmi 2000 'Conflict Management in Africa: The Role of the OAU and Sub-regional Organisations' in Jakkie Cilliers and Annika Hilding-Norberg (Eds) *Building Stability in Africa: Challenges for the New Millennium* ISS Monograph No. 46, Pretoria, Institute for Security Studies, February, pp. 50–57

Olson, Mancur 1971 *The Logic of Collective Action: Public Goods and the Theory of Groups* Cambridge, Mass., Harvard University Press

Ottaway, Marina 1999 *Africa's New Leaders: Democracy or State Reconstruction?* Washington DC, Carnegie Endowment for International Peace

Patterson, Thomas E 2002 *The Vanishing Voter* New York, Knopf

Pempel, TJ (Ed.) 1990 *Uncommon Democracies: The One-Party Dominant Regimes* Ithaca and London, Cornell University Press

Penna, David R and Patricia J Campbell 1998 'Human Rights and Culture: Beyond Universality and Relativism' *Third World Quarterly* Vol. 19, No. 1, pp. 7–27

Pillay, Soma 2004 'Corruption – the Challenge to Good Governance: A South African Perspective' *International Journal of Public Sector Management* Vol. 17, No. 7, pp. 586–605

Piven, Frances Fox and Richard Cloward 1979 *Poor People's Movements: Why They Succeed, How They Fail* New York, Vintage Books

Polan, AJ 1984 *Lenin and the End of Politics* Methuen, London

Przeworski, Adam 1985 *Capitalism and Social Democracy* Cambridge, Cambridge University Press

Przeworski, Adam 1991 *Democracy and the Market: Political and Economic Reforms in Eastern Europe and Latin America* Cambridge, Cambridge University Press

Przeworski, Adam 1993 'Democracy as a Contingent Outcome of Conflicts' in Jon Elster and Rune Slagstadt (Eds) *Constitutionalism and Democracy* Cambridge, Cambridge University Press, pp. 59–80

Przeworski, Adam, Michael Alvarez, Jose Antonio Cheibub and Fernando Limongi 1996 'What Makes Democracies Endure?' *Journal of Democracy* Vol. 7, No. 1, pp. 39–55

Puddington, Arch and Tyler Roylance 2016 'Anxious Dictators, Wavering Democrats' *Journal of Democracy* Vol. 27, No. 2, pp. 86–100

Putnam, Robert 1994 *Making Democracy Work: Civic Traditions in Modern Italy* Princeton, Princeton University Press

Ray, Brian 2011 'Proceduralisation's Triumph and Engagement's Promise in Socio-economic Rights Litigation' *South African Journal on Human Rights* Vol. 27, No. 1, pp. 107–126

Riker, William and Peter Ordeshook 1968 'A Theory of the Calculus of Voting' *American Political Science Review* Vol. 62, No. 1, pp. 25–42

Roberts, Andrew 2009 *The Quality of Democracy in Eastern Europe: Public Preferences and Policy Reforms* Cambridge, Cambridge University Press

Robins, Steven, Andrea Cornwall and Bettina von Lieres 2008 'Rethinking "Citizenship" in the Postcolony' *Third World Quarterly* Vol. 29, No. 6, pp. 1069–1086

Robinson, Mark and Steven Friedman 2005 *Civil Society, Democratisation and Foreign Aid in Africa* IDS Discussion Paper No. 383, Brighton, Institute for Development Studies, University of Sussex

Rodrik, Dani 1997 *Has Globalisation Gone too Far?* Washington DC, Institute for International Economics

Rosanvallon, Pierre 2011 *Democratic Legitimacy: Impartiality, Reflexivity, Proximity* Princeton, Princeton University Press

Rousseau, Jean-Jacques 1968 *The Social Contract* (Translated by Maurice Cranston) Harmondsworth, Penguin

Rustow, Dankwart A 1970 'Transitions to Democracy: Towards a Dynamic Model' *Comparative Politics*, Vol. 2, No. 3, April, pp. 337–363

Sachs, Albie 2000 'Social and Economic Rights: Can They be Justiciable?' *Southern Methodist University Law Review* Vol. 53, No. 4, pp. 1381–1391

Sadie, Yolanda 1990 'Regerings-elite se persepsies oor die rol van belangegroepe in openbare beleids-formulering in Suid-Afrika' *Politikon* Vol. 17, No. 2, December, pp. 82–98

Salomon, Lester M and Stephen van Evera 1973 'Fear, Apathy and Discrimination: A Test of Three Explanations of Political Participation' *American Political Science Review* Vol. 67, No. 4, December, pp. 1288–1306

Sandel, Michael 1998 *Democracy's Discontent: America in Search of a Public Philosophy* Cambridge, Mass. and London, Belknap Press at Harvard University Press

Sartori, Giovanni 1976 *Parties and Party Systems: A Framework for Analysis* New York, Cambridge University Press

Sartori, Giovanni 1987 *The Theory of Democracy Revisited* Chatham, Chatham House

Schattschneider, EE 1960 *The Semisovereign People* New York, Holt, Rinehart and Winston

Schedler, Andreas 1998 'What is Democratic Consolidation?' *Journal of Democracy* Vol. 9, No. 2, pp. 91–107

Schedler, Andreas 2002 'The Menu of Manipulation' *Journal of Democracy* Vol. 13, No. 2, April, pp. 36–50

Schlesinger, Stephen and Steven Kinzer 1999 *Bitter Fruit: The Story of the American Coup in Guatemala* Cambridge, Mass., Harvard University Press

Schmitter, Philippe C 1985 *The Political Economy of Corporatism* London, Macmillan

Schmitter, Philippe C 1999 'The Future of Democracy: Could It be a Matter of Scale?' *Social Research* Vol. 66, No. 3, Fall, pp. 933–958

Schmitter, Philippe C 2003 'The Quality of Democracy: The Ambiguous Virtues of Accountability' Paper presented at the conference 'The Quality of Democracy: Improvement or Subversion?' Stanford, Stanford University, 10–11 October

Schmitter, Philippe C 2017 'The Future of Democracy is Not What It Used to Be' *Zeitschrift für Vergleichende Politikwissenschaft/Comparative Governance and Politics* Vol. 11, No. 4, December, pp. 1–25

Schmitter, Philippe with Terry Karl 1994 'The Conceptual Travels of Transitologists and Consolidologists: How Far to the East Should They Attempt to Go?' *Slavic Review* Vol. 53, No. 1, Spring, pp. 173–185

Schoepf, Brooke Grundfest 1992 'Gender Relations and Development: Political Economy and Cultures' in Ann Seidman and Frederick Anang (Eds) *Twenty-First-Century Africa: Towards a New Vision of Self-Sustainable Development* Trenton, Africa World Press, pp. 203–241

Schoolman, Kay Lehman 1984 'What Accent the Heavenly Chorus? Political Equality and the American Pressure System' *Journal of Politics* Vol. 46, No. 4, November, pp. 1006–1032

School of Public and Development Management, University of the Witwatersrand 2006 *Are Hernando de Soto's Views Appropriate to South Africa?* P&DM Occasional Paper Series No. 1, Johannesburg, School of Public and Development Management, University of the Witwatersrand

Scott, James C 1976 *The Moral Economy of the Peasant: Subsistence and Rebellion in Southeast Asia* New Haven, Yale University Press

Scott, James C 1985 *Weapons of the Weak: Everyday Forms of Peasant Resistance* New Haven, Yale University Press

Scott, James C 1992 *Domination and the Arts of Resistance: Hidden Transcripts* New Haven, Yale University Press

Scott, James C 1998 *Seeing Like a State: How Certain Schemes to Improve the Human Condition Have Failed* New Haven, Yale University Press

Sekhonyane, Makubetse and Antoinette Louw 2002 *Violent Justice, Vigilantism and the State's Response* ISS Monograph No. 72, Pretoria, Institute for Security Studies, 1 April

Seloane, Mandla 2001 *Socio-economic Rights in the South African Constitution: Theory and Practice* Cape Town, HSRC Press

Sen, Amartya 1981 *Poverty and Famines: An Essay on Entitlement and Deprivation* Oxford, Clarendon Press

Shapiro, Ian 2003 *The State of Democratic Theory* Princeton and Oxford, Princeton University Press

Shivji, Issa G 1989 *The Concept of Human Rights in Africa* London, Council for the Development of Social Science Research in Africa (CODESRIA)

Shriner, Kay 2002 'The Competence Line in American Suffrage Law: A Political Analysis' *Disability Studies Quarterly* Vol. 22, No. 2, Spring, pp. 61–72

Simone, Abdou Maliq 1995 'Urban Societies in Africa' in Richard Humphries and Maxine Reitzes (Eds) *Civil Society after Apartheid* Johannesburg, Centre for Policy Studies/ Friedrich Ebert Foundation

Skocpol, Theda and Ira Katznelson 1996 *Social Policy in the US: Future Possibilities in Historical Perspective* Princeton, Princeton University Press

Smelser, Neil J 1963 *Theory of Collective Behavior* New York, The Free Press of Glencoe

Snyder, David and Charles Tilly 1972 'Hardship and Collective Violence in France, 1830 to 1960' *American Sociological Review* Vol. 37, No. 5, October, pp. 520–532

Southall, Roger 1999 'South Africa 1999: The ANC and Democratic Consolidation' *Issue: A Journal of Opinion* Vol. 27, No. 2, The South African Elections, pp. 9–16

Stephens, John 1993 'Capitalist Development and Democracy: Empirical Research on the Origins of Democracy' in David Copp, Jean Hampton and John Roemer (Eds) *The Idea of Democracy* Cambridge, Cambridge University Press, pp. 409–447

Tanner, Michael 1996 *The End of Welfare: Fighting Poverty in the Civil Society* Washington DC, Cato Institute

Tarrow, Sidney 1988 'National Politics and Collective Action: Recent Theory and Research in Western Europe and the United States' *Annual Review of Sociology* Vol. 14, August, pp. 421–440

Tarrow, Sidney 1998 *Power in Movement: Social Movements and Contentious Politics* Cambridge, Cambridge University Press

Therkildsen, Ole 2002 'Uganda Revenue Authority: The Limits of Autonomy' Paper presented at the annual conference of the research programme 'Taxation, Aid and Democracy', Windhoek, 4–5 April

Thulare, Paul 2004 'Trading Democracy? Johannesburg Informal Traders and Citizenship' *Policy: Issues and Actors* Vol. 17, No. 1, February

Tilly, Charles 1995 *Popular Contention in Great Britain 1758–1834* Cambridge, Mass., Harvard University Press

Tilly, Charles 2004 *Social Movements 1768–2004* Boulder and London, Paradigm Publishers

Tilly, Charles 2007 *Democracy* New York, Cambridge University Press

Tomlinson, Mary 1996 *From Rejection to Resignation: Beneficiaries' Views on the Government's Housing Subsidy Scheme* Johannesburg, Centre for Policy Studies

Tomlinson, Mary 1997 *Mortgage Bondage? Financial Institutions and Low-Cost Housing Delivery* Johannesburg, Centre for Policy Studies

Tormey, Simon 2014 'The Contemporary Crisis of Representative Democracy' *Democratic Theory* Vol. 1, No. 2, pp. 104–112

Touraine, Alain 1988 *Return of the Actor: Social Theory in Postindustrial Society* Minneapolis, University of Minnesota Press

Tufekci, Zeynep and Christopher Wilson 2012 'Social Media and the Decision to Participate in Political Protest' *Journal of Communication* Vol. 62, No. 6, pp. 363–379

Turner, Mandy 2006 'Building Democracy in Palestine: Liberal Peace Theory and the Election of Hamas' *Democratization* Vol. 13, No. 5, pp. 739–755

Varshney, Ashutosh 2013 *Battles Half Won: India's Improbable Democracy* New Delhi, Penguin Viking

Von Holdt, Karl, Malose Langa, Sepetla Molapo, Nomfundo Mogapi, Kindi Ngubeni, Jacob Dlamini and Adele Kirsten 2011 *The Smoke that Calls: Insurgent Citizenship, Collective Violence and the Search for a Place in the New South Africa* Johannesburg, Centre for the Study of Violence and Reconciliation, Society, Work and Development Institute

Von Lieres, Bettina 1999 'Review Article: New Perspectives on Citizenship in Africa' *Journal of Southern African Studies* Vol. 25, No. 1, March, pp. 139–148

Wamala, Edward 2004 'Government by Consensus: An Analysis of a Traditional Form of Democracy' in Kwasi Wiredu (Ed.) *A Companion to African Philosophy* Malden, Blackwell, pp. 435–442

Weber, Max 1946 'Politics as a Vocation' in HH Gerth and C Wright Mills (Translated and edited) *From Max Weber: Essays in Sociology* New York, Oxford University Press, pp. 77–128

Webster, Edward 2013 'The Promise and the Possibility: South Africa's Contested Industrial Relations Path' *Transformation* No. 81/82, pp. 208–235

Wellhofer, E Spencer 2005 'Democracy, Fascism and Civil Society' in Sigrid Rossteutscher (Ed.) *Democracy and the Role of Associations: Political, Organizational and Social Contexts* London and New York, Routledge, pp. 17–40

Welzel, Christian 2013 *Freedom Rising: Human Empowerment and the Quest for Emancipation* New York, Cambridge University Press

Wilson, Stuart 2011 'Litigating Housing Rights in Johannesburg's Inner City: 2004–2008' *South African Journal on Human Rights* Vol. 27, No. 1, pp. 127–151

Wiredu, Kwasi 1997 'Democracy and Consensus in African Traditional Politics: A Plea for a Non-party Polity' in Emmanuel Chukwudi Eze (Ed.) *Postcolonial African Philosophy: A Critical Reader* Oxford, Blackwell, pp. 303–304

Wiredu, Kwasi 2001 'Democracy by Consensus: Some Conceptual Considerations' *Philosophical Papers* Vol. 30, No. 3, pp. 227–244

Wood, Elisabeth Jean 2003 *Insurgent Collective Action and Civil War in El Salvador* Cambridge, Cambridge University Press

Wood, Richard L 2002 *Faith in Action: Religion, Race and Democratic Organizing in America* Chicago and London, Chicago University Press

Yashar, Deborah J 1998 'Contesting Citizenship: Indigenous Movements and Democracy in Latin America' *Comparative Politics* Vol. 31, No. 1, October, pp. 23–42

Youngs, Richard 2015 *The Puzzle of Non-Western Democracy* Washington DC, Carnegie Endowment for International Peace

MEDIA ARTICLES

'Abbas Continues Rejecting "Jewish State" Notion' *Jerusalem Post* 1 December 2007 https://www.jpost.com/Middle-East/Abbas-continues-rejecting-Jewish-state-notion (accessed on 1 August 2018)

Adeyemi, Sam 2017 'Africa Doesn't Need Charity, It Needs Good Leadership' *World Economic Forum* 4 May https://www.weforum.org/agenda/2017/05/africa-doesn-t-need-charity -it-needs-good-leadership (accessed on 1 August 2018)

'Al-Jazeera Cameraman Home from Guantanamo' *Sydney Morning Herald* 2 May 2008 http://www.smh.com.au/news/world/aljazeera-cameraman-home-from-guantanamo /2008/05/02/1209235136671.html (accessed on 1 August 2018)

Bonorchis, Renée 2006 'Achmat's Year-Long Walk to Triumph' *Business Day* 8 December

Buccus, Imraan 2015 'Social Media Shift Power Balance' *Sunday Independent* 17 May

Business Tech 2017 'How Many People Use Facebook, Twitter and Instagram in South Africa' 18 September https://businesstech.co.za/news/internet/199318/how-many-people-use -facebook-twitter-and-instagram-in-south-africa/ (accessed on 1 August 2018)

Byrnes, Sholto 2008 'Interview: Samantha Power' *New Statesman* 6 March https://www .newstatesman.com/world-affairs/2008/03/barack-obama-interview-power (accessed on 1 August 2018)

Chakrabortty, Aditya 2018 'Immigration Has Been Good for Britain. It is Time to Bust the Myths' *The Guardian* 17 May

Chance, Kerry and Mandisa Mbali 2004 'Chance/Mbali on Limits to Invoking "False Consciousness"' 2 July CCS-l@lists.nu.ac.za

Clymer, Adam 1992 'The House Bank: Trying to Halt a Scandal, Speaker Declares House Bank Case Closed but Political Reality Promises to Intrude' *New York Times* 17 April

Cohen, Tim 2017 'Bongo Beats Pointless Drum over Book' *Business Day* 6 November

Cullinan, Kerry 2006 'Africa: Deputies Bring New Energy to HIV/AIDS' *Health-E News Service* 6 November https://www.health-e.org.za/2006/11/06/deputies-bring-new-energy -to-hivaids/ (accessed on 1 August 2018)

Daniels, Linda 2006 'Zuma Takes New Stance on AIDS' *Pretoria News* 19 September

Desai, Raj M 2017 'Rethinking the Universalism versus Targeting Debate' Brookings Blog 31 May https://www.brookings.edu/blog/future-development/2017/05/31/rethinking-the -universalism-versus-targeting-debate/ (accessed on 1 August 2018)

Friedman, Steven 2006 'Spring of Hope, Winter of Worry for South African Democracy' *Business Day* 6 August

Hayduk, Ron 2004 'Noncitizens Have the Obligations of Citizens – So Why Not the Right to Vote?' *History News Network* 24 February http://hnn.us/articles/24290.html (accessed on 1 August 2018)

Hubby, Kristen 2016 'How Many Americans Actually Vote?' *The Daily Dot* 19 December https://www.dailydot.com/layer8/voter-turnout-2016/ (accessed on 1 August 2018)

Ignatieff, Michael 2014 'Are the Authoritarians Winning?' *New York Review of Books* 10 July

Kekana, Masa 2016 'Moseneke Warns SA Courts Risk Becoming Overly Politicised' *EyeWitness News* 17 November http://ewn.co.za/2016/11/17/moseneke-warns-sa-courts -risk-becoming-overly-politicised (accessed on 1 August 2018)

Kekic, Lasa 2007 *The Economist Intelligence Unit's Index of Democracy* www.economist .com/media/pdf/DEMOCRACY_INDEX_2007_v3.pdf (accessed on 1 August 2018)

Khoza, Amanda 2017 'Nene: SA Needs Strong Leadership for These Turbulent Times' *News 24* 31 May https://www.fin24.com/Economy/nene-sa-needs-strong-leadership-for-these -turbulent-times-20170531 (accessed on 1 August 2018)

Kota, Ayanda 2011 'SA, We Cannot Say We are Free' *Mail and Guardian* 6 May https://mg.co .za/article/2011-05-06-sa-we-cannot-say-are-free (accessed on 1 August 2018)

Lattman, Peter 2007 'The Origins of Justice Stewart's "I Know It When I See It"' *Wall Street Journal* Law Blog 27 September https://blogs.wsj.com/law/2007/09/27/the-origins-of-justice-stewarts-i-know-it-when-i-see-it/ (accessed on 1 August 2018)

Liebenberg, Sandra 2014 'Social Audits and the Right to Sanitation' *GroundUp* 22 October https://www.groundup.org.za/article/social-audits-and-right-sanitation_2372/ (accessed on 1 August 2018)

Liptak, Adam 2008 'Rendering Justice, with One Eye on Re-election' *New York Times* 25 May http://www.nytimes.com/2008/05/25/us/25exception.html?ex=1212379200&en=3d121eb04acf50c8&ei=5070&emc=eta1 (accessed on 1 August 2018)

Logan, Carolyn and Michael Bratton 2013 'Claiming Democracy: Are Voters Becoming Citizens in Africa?' *AfricaPlus* 14 May http://africaplus.wordpress.com/2013/05/14/claiming-democracy-are-voters-becoming-citizens-in-africa (accessed on 1 August 2018)

McGreal, Chris 2008 'Zimbabwe's Voters Told: Choose Mugabe or You Face a Bullet' *The Guardian* 18 June http://www.guardian.co.uk/world/2008/jun/18/zimbabwe (accessed on 1 August 2018)

Mackay, Moses Mdewu 2007 'Cosatu Keeps an Eye on AIDS Plan' *Daily News* 6 March

'Manto's Garlic Won't Stop AIDS' *Mail and Guardian* 10 November 2003 https://mg.co.za/article/2003-11-10-mantos-garlic-wont-stop-aids (accessed on 1 August 2018)

Matshiqi, Aubrey 2010 'Why Manuel is Right and Wrong about Manyi's "Racism"' *Business Day* 8 March

'Mbeki "Glossed over Issues"' *News24* 14 February 2003 https://www.news24.com/SouthAfrica/News/Mbeki-glossed-over-issues-20030214 (accessed on 1 August 2018)

Mkentane, Luyolo 2017 'PPF Calls for SA to Ditch Constitution' *Cape Times* 24 January

Mnguni, Lukhona 2016 'South Africa is Not a Vibrant Democracy' *eNCA.com* 8 November https://www.enca.com/opinion/south-africa-is-not-a-vibrant-democracy (accessed on 1 August 2018)

Moya, Fikile 2017 'How Mbeki Shows South Africa's Need for a True Leadership' *Independent Online* 15 July https://www.iol.co.za/news/opinion/how-mbeki-shows-south-africas-need-for-a-true-leadership-10302211 (accessed on 1 August 2018)

Munusamy, Ranjeni 2000 'Delegates Boo Minister' *Sunday Times* 12 March

Nair, Chandran 2017 'The West Can't Fix the Climate Crisis. Asia Will Have to Do It' *The Guardian* 5 December

Ochieng' Opalo, Ken 2017 'Foresight Africa Viewpoint: Democracy in Africa in 2017' Brookings Blog 10 January https://www.brookings.edu/blog/africa-in-focus/2017/01/10/foresight-africa-viewpoint-democracy-in-africa-in-2017/ (accessed on 1 August 2018)

Owete, Festus 2016 '20 Times African Opposition Leaders Shockingly Defeated Incumbents' *Premium Times*, Abuja, 10 December

Patnaik, Priti 2012 'Social Audits in India – a Slow but Sure Way to Fight Corruption' *The Guardian* 13 January

Philo, Greg 2001 'An Unseen World: How the Media Portrays the Poor' *UNESCO Courier* November https://www.questia.com/magazine/1G1-80865237/an-unseen-world-how-the-media-portrays-the-poor (accessed on 1 August 2018)

Phinny, Robert H 1992 'South Africa's Minorities Have Rights' *New York Times* 24 June

Rotberg, Robert 2013 'Good Leadership is Africa's Missing Ingredient' *Globe and Mail* 4 March

Ruddick, Graham 2017 'Global Press Freedom Plunges to Worst Level this Century' *The Guardian* 30 November

SA History Online 2007 'FNB Cancels Its R20m Anti-crime Initiative Designed to Encourage President Thabo Mbeki to Make Crime His Priority' 2 February http://www.sahistory .org.za/dated-event/fnb-cancels-its-r20-million-anti-crime-initiative-designed -encourage-president-thabo-mbe (accessed on 1 August 2018)

Salim, Salim Ahmed 2016 'Why We Haven't Given Africa's Most Prestigious Leadership Award this Year' *Quartz Africa* 23 June https://qz.com/714618/why-we-havent-given -africas-most-prestigious-leadership-award-for-two-years/ (accessed on 1 August 2018)

Sasa, Mabasa 2016 'People Don't Eat Democracy' *Sunday Mail* 18 December http://www .sundaymail.co.zw/people-dont-eat-democracy/ (accessed on 1 August 2018)

Sonnenberg, Ernest 2014 'Liebenberg's Argument is a Straw Man' *GroundUp* 23 October https://www.groundup.org.za/article/liebenbergs-argument-straw-man_2377/ (accessed on 1 August 2018)

Toobin, Jeffrey 2016 'The Real Voting Scandal of 2016' *The New Yorker* 12 December

Travis, Alan 2007 'UK Terror Detention Limit is Longest of Any Democracy' *The Guardian* 12 November http://www.guardian.co.uk/uk/2007/nov/12/humanrights.terrorism (accessed on 1 August 2018)

Tshabalala, Thembilihle 2008 'Jo'burg Water Meters under Spotlight after Court Ruling' *Mail and Guardian Online* 10 May http://www.mg.co.za/article/2008-05-10-joburg-water -meters-under-spotlight-after-court-ruling (accessed on 1 August 2018)

Vollgraaff, René 2010 'WEF: "Africa Can't Eat Democracy"' *fin24* 7 May https://www.fin24 .com/economy/wef-africa-cant-eat-democracy-20100507?cpid=2 (accessed on 1 August 2018)

Wa Azania, Malaika 2013 'Why the Poor Vote for the ANC and Will Do So for a Long Time' Thought Leader *Mail and Guardian* 9 August http://thoughtleader.co.za/malaikawaazania/ 2013/09/09/why-the-poor-vote-for-the-anc-and-will-do-so-for-a-long-time/ (accessed on 1 August 2018)

Waldman, Michael 2012 'Between Voting Rights and Voting Wrongs' *New York Times* 1 May http://campaignstops.blogs.nytimes.com/2012/05/01/between-voting-rights-and -voting-wrongs/?nl=opinion&emc=edit_ty_20120501 (accessed on 1 August 2018)

Williamson, Vanessa 2016 'Voter Suppression, Not Fraud, Looms Large in US elections' Brookings Blog 8 November https://www.brookings.edu/blog/fixgov/2016/11/08/ voter-suppression-in-u-s-elections/ (accessed on 1 August 2018)

Willsher, Kim 2017 'French Media Warned Not to Publish Emmanuel Macron Leaks' *The Observer* 6 May

Wright, Tony 2013 'The Decline of the Political Party: What Comes After?' London School of Economics and Political Science, British Politics and Policy, 29 July http://blogs.lse .ac.uk/politicsandpolicy/after-the-party/ (accessed on 1 August 2018)

REPORTS AND DOCUMENTS

African Elections Database 2008 'Elections in Botswana' http://africanelections.tripod.com/ bw.html (accessed on 1 August 2018)

African Union 2002 '38th Ordinary Session of the Assembly of Heads of State and Government of the AU' *African Peer Review Mechanism* Durban, 8 July

Afrobarometer 2015 *Merged Round 5 Data (34 Countries) (2011–2013) (Last Update: July 2015)* http://afrobarometer.org/data/merged-round-5-data-34-countries-2011-2013-last -update-july-2015 (accessed on 1 August 2018)

Afrobarometer 2016 *Do Africans Still Want Democracy? Afrobarometer Findings Warn of Democratic Recession, Point to Long-Term Gains* Accra, 26 November http://afrobarometer .org/sites/default/files/press-release/round-6-releases/ab_r6_pr15_Do_Africans_want _democracy_EN.pdf (accessed on 1 August 2018)

Amnesty International 2006 *Report* https://www.amnesty.org/en/documents/pol10/003/ 2006/en/ (accessed on 1 August 2018)

Amnesty International 2013 *Annual Report: The State of the World's Human Rights* http:// www.amnesty.org/en/annual-report/2013/africa (accessed on 1 August 2018)

Asian Barometer www.asianbarometer.org/ (accessed on 1 August 2018)

Center for Systemic Peace nd *The Polity Project* http://www.systemicpeace.org/polity project (accessed on 1 August 2018)

Centre for Policy Studies 2002 *Analytical Overview of the Political Economy of the Civil Society Sector in Southern Africa with Regard to the Poverty Reduction Agenda* Johannesburg, Centre for Policy Studies

Clark, Anna nd 'Is Participatory Budgeting Real Democracy? Politics, People's Choice Style in Chicago' *Next City* https://nextcity.org/features/view/is-participatory-budgeting-real -democracy-chicago (accessed on 1 August 2018)

Constitutional Court 2002 *Minister of Health and Others v Treatment Action Campaign and Others* Constitutional Court – CCT8/02 2002 (5) SA 721 (CC); 2002 (10) BCLR 1033 (CC) http://www.saflii.org/za/cases/ZACC/2002/15.html (accessed on 1 August 2018)

Council for Europe 2013 *Poverty and Inequality in Societies of Human Rights: The Paradox of Democracies* https://www.coe.int/en/web/portal/-/pauvrete-et-inegalite-dans-les- societes-de-droits-humains-le-paradoxe-des-democraties (accessed on 1 August 2018)

Cronin, Jeremy 2005 *The People Shall Govern – Class Struggles and the Post-1994 State in South Africa. Part 1 – the Freedom Charter and the Post-1994 State* Internal ANC document http://ccs.ukzn.ac.za/files/Cronin,%20The%20People%20Shall%20Govern,%20 Transformation%20&%20State.pdf (accessed on 1 August 2018)

Department of Health 2002 *National HIV and Syphilis Sero-prevalence Survey of Women Attending Public Antenatal Clinics in South Africa – 2001, Summary Report* Nelson Mandela/HSRC Study of HIV/AIDS, South African National HIV Prevalence, Behavioural Risks and Mass Media Household Survey

Eurobarometer http://ec.europa.eu/commfrontoffice/publicopinion/index.cfm (accessed on 1 August 2018)

Freedom House nd *Methodology: Freedom in the World 2016* https://freedomhouse.org/ report/freedom-world-2016/methodology (accessed on 1 August 2018)

Gotz, Graeme 1997 'The Limits of Community: The Dynamics of Rural Water Provision' Unpublished report for Rand Water, Johannesburg, Centre for Policy Studies

Human Rights Watch 2006 *In Hope and Fear: Uganda's Presidential and Parliamentary Polls* http://www.hrw.org/backgrounder/africa/uganda2006/ (accessed on 1 August 2018)

Human Rights Watch nd *Africa* http://www.hrw.org/africa (accessed on 1 August 2018)

Institute for Democracy in South Africa (Idasa) 1997 *Reflections on Democracy* Pretoria, Idasa

International Institute for Democracy and Electoral Assistance (International IDEA) 2002 *Voter Turnout since 1945: A Global Report* Stockholm, International IDEA

International Monetary Fund 1997 *Good Governance: The IMF's Role* Washington DC, International Monetary Fund

Khumalo, Gardner, Sivuyile Bam and Owen Crankshaw 1996 'Youth Dynamics in Gauteng' Unpublished commissioned study for Gauteng legislature petitions and public participation committee, Johannesburg, Centre for Policy Studies

Latinobarometro www.latinobarometro.org (accessed on 1 August 2018)

Makiwane, Monde and Eric Udjo 2006 *Is the Child Support Grant Associated with an Increase in Teenage Fertility in South Africa? Evidence from National Surveys and Administrative Data* Final Report, Pretoria, Human Sciences Research Council, December

Mphahlele, Mafedi Yvonne 2010 'Knowledge Management Practices in the South African Public Sector 2002–2008' Thesis presented in fulfilment of the requirements for the degree of Master of Philosophy (Information and Knowledge Management) Stellenbosch University file:///C:/Users/Steven/Downloads/mphahlele_knowledge_2010.pdf (accessed on 1 August 2018)

New Partnership for Africa's Development 2003 *Declaration on Democracy, Political, Economic and Corporate Governance*

Office of the United Nations High Commissioner for Human Rights nd 'Good Governance and Human Rights' https://www.ohchr.org/en/issues/development/goodgovernance/pages/goodgovernanceindex.aspx (accessed on 1 August 2018)

Oxfam International 2017 *5 Shocking Facts about Extreme Global Inequality and How to Even It Up* 16 January https://www.oxfam.org/en/even-it/5-shocking-facts-about-extreme-global-inequality-and-how-even-it-davos (accessed on 1 August 2018)

Pew Research Center 2017 'Globally, Broad Support for Representative and Direct Democracy' 16 October http://www.pewglobal.org/2017/10/16/globally-broad-support-for-representative-and-direct-democracy/ (accessed on 1 August 2018)

Ramkumar, Vivek and Sowmya Kidamb 2012 *Social Audits as a Budget Monitoring Tool* October, Washington DC, International Budget Partnership

Reporters without Borders 2016 'President Refuses to Sign Draconian Bill into Law' 12 September 2013, updated on 20 January 2016 https://rsf.org/en/news/president-refuses-sign-draconian-bill-law (accessed on 1 August 2018)

Republic of South Africa 2000 Municipal Systems Act, No. 32 of 2000

Republic of South Africa 2010 Protection of State Information Bill (B6B-2010)

Republic of South Africa 2018 Preventing and Combating of Hate Crimes and Hate Speech Bill (B9-2018)

Skweyiya, Zola 2006 'Social Cluster Media Briefing by Dr Zola Skweyiya, Minister of Social Development' Union Buildings, Pretoria, 20 November http://www.info.gov.za/speeches/2006/06112015451003.htm (accessed on 1 August 2018)

Social Justice Coalition nd 'Social Audits' http://www.sjc.org.za/social_audits (accessed on 1 August 2018)

Southern African Development Community 2000 nd 'Communiqué: Namibia – Windhoek 6–7 August 2000' in *SADC Head of State and Government Summit Communiques 1980–2006* pp. 113–119 https://www.sadc.int/files/3913/5292/8384/SADC_SUMMIT_COMMUNIQUES_1980-2006.pdf (accessed on 1 August 2018)

Street Law 1995 *Democracy for All* Durban, University of KwaZulu-Natal, 1995

Treatment Action Campaign 2001 'An Explanation of the Medicines Act and the Implications of the Court Victory' TAC Statement on the Court Case, 24 April

Treatment Action Campaign 2003 'TAC Responds to American Friends Service Committee Nobel Peace Prize Nomination' *TAC News Service* (moderator@tac.org.za) 2 December

Treatment Action Campaign 2003 'TAC Welcomes Cabinet Statement Committing to Antiretroviral Treatment Rollout' TAC News Service (moderator@tac.org.za) 8 August

Treatment Action Campaign 2004 'GlaxoSmithKline Grants License to Cipla in Accordance with Competition Commission Settlement' *TAC Electronic Newsletter* 14 December http://www.tac.org.za (accessed on 1 August 2018)

Treatment Action Campaign 2005 'Lorna Mlofana's Accused are Found Guilty' *TAC Newsletter* 8 December http://www.tac.org.za (accessed on 1 August 2018)

Treatment Action Campaign 2005 *TAC Political Report 2003/05* Prepared for the Third TAC National Congress, Cape Town, 23–25 September

Treatment Action Campaign 2005 '21 December 2005 – Another TAC Member Raped and Murdered in Khayelitsha. Demonstration against Violence against Women on Friday 23 December' *TAC Newsletter* 21 December http://www.tac.org.za (accessed on 1 August 2018)

Treatment Action Campaign nd 'About TAC' www.tac.org.za (accessed on 1 August 2018)

UNAIDS nd 'South Africa' http://www.unaids.org/en/regionscountries/countries/southafrica (accessed on 1 August 2018)

United Nations Economic Commission for Africa nd *AIDS: Africa's Greatest Leadership Challenge – Roles and Approaches for an Effective Response* https://www.uneca.org/adf2/pages/aids-africas-greatest-leadership-challenge-roles-and-approaches-effective-response (accessed on 1 August 2018)

United Nations Habitat 2016 *Slum Almanac 2015–2016* Nairobi, United Nations Habitat

V-Dem nd *Varieties of Democracy: Global Standards, Local Knowledge* https://www.v-dem.net (accessed on 1 August 2018)

Wike, Richard, Katie Simmons, Bruce Stokes and Janell Fetterolf 2017 'Globally, Broad Support for Representative and Direct Democracy: But Many Endorse Non-democratic Alternatives' Pew Research Center 16 October http://assets.pewresearch.org/wp-content/uploads/sites/2/2017/10/17102729/Pew-Research-Center_Democracy-Report_2017.10.16.pdf (accessed on 1 August 2018)

World Bank 1996 *Poverty Reduction and the World Bank: Progress and Challenges in the 1990s* Washington DC, World Bank

World Bank 1997 *Poverty Reduction and the World Bank: Progress in Fiscal 1996 and 1997* Washington DC, World Bank

World Bank 1997 *The State in a Changing World: World Development Report 1997* New York, Oxford University Press

World Bank 2004 *World Development Report 2004: Making Services Work for Poor People* Washington DC, World Bank, Oxford University Press

World Bank nd *The World Bank and Civil Society Engagement* http://web.worldbank.org/WBSITE/EXTERNAL/TOPICS/CSO/0,,contentMDK:20092185~menuPK:220422~pagePK:220503~piPK:220476~theSitePK:228717,00.html (accessed on 1 August 2018)

World Bank Group 2007 *GNI per Capita 2005, Atlas Method and PPP* http://siteresources.worldbank.org/DATASTATISTICS/Resources/GNIPC05.pdf (accessed on 1 August 2018)

World Economic Forum 2016 *3 Charts that Explain Global Inequality* 20 January https://www.weforum.org/agenda/2016/01/3-charts-that-explain-global-inequality/ (accessed on 1 August 2018)

World Values Survey 2014 'Online Data Analysis' http://www.worldvaluessurvey.org/WVSOnline.jsp (accessed on 1 August 2018)

INDEX

Printed and bound by CPI Group (UK) Ltd, Croydon, CR0 4YY

09/06/2025

14685795-0002

.